ISBN: 978129035126

Published by:
HardPress Publishing
8345 NW 66TH ST #2561
MIAMI FL 33166-2626

Email: info@hardpress.net
Web: http://www.hardpress.net

```
BL 1010 .S3  v.35
Milindapa nh a.
The questions of King
 Milinda
```

THE

SACRED BOOKS OF THE EAST

London

HENRY FROWDE

OXFORD UNIVERSITY PRESS WAREHOUSE

AMEN CORNER, E.C.

THE
SACRED BOOKS OF THE EAST

TRANSLATED

BY VARIOUS ORIENTAL SCHOLARS

AND EDITED BY

F. MAX MÜLLER

VOL. XXXV

Oxford
AT THE CLARENDON PRESS
1890

[*All rights reserved*]

Oxford
PRINTED AT THE CLARENDON PRESS
BY HORACE HART, PRINTER TO THE UNIVERSITY

THE QUESTIONS

OF

KING MILINDA

TRANSLATED FROM THE PÁLI

BY

T. W. RHYS DAVIDS

Oxford

AT THE CLARENDON PRESS

1890

[*All rights reserved*]

CONTENTS.

	PAGE
INTRODUCTION	xi
The Si*m*halese version of the Milinda . . .	xii
Buddhaghosa's four references to it	xiv
MSS. and edition of the text	xvi
King Milinda the same as Menander . . .	xviii
Notices of him in classical writers	xix
His coins	xx
His birthplace, Kalasi, probably = Karisi . . .	xxiii
The author not the same as Nâgâr*g*u*n*a . . .	xxv
Passages in the Pi*t*akas referred to silently . .	xxvii
Pâli books, &c., referred to by name . . .	xxix
Pi*t*aka passages quoted	xxxi
Length of the Pi*t*akas	xxxvi
Results of these comparisons	xxxviii
Differences between our author and the Pi*t*akas .	xl
Proper names outside the Pi*t*akas	xliii
Differences of language between our author and the Pi*t*akas	xlv
The Milinda as a work of art	xlviii
TRANSLATION OF THE TEXT.	
Book I. The Secular Narrative	1
Description of Sâgala	2
Previous births of Milinda and Nâgasena . . .	4
Milinda's greatness and wisdom and love of disputation	6
Birth story of Nâgasena	10
His admission as a novice into the Order . . .	20
His conversion	25
His attainment of Arahatship	29
Milinda confutes Âyupâla	30
Nâgasena arrives; his character	34
Milinda goes to him	36

	PAGE
Book II. The Distinguishing Characteristics of Ethical Qualities	40
Individuality and name	41
The chariot simile	43
The riddle of seniority	45
(Interlude) How kings and scholars respectively discuss	46
No soul in the breath	48
Aim of Buddhist renunciation	49
Re-incarnation	50
Wisdom and reasoning distinguished	51
'Virtue's the base'	53
Faith	54
Perseverance	57
Mindfulness	58
Meditation	60
Continued identity and re-individualisation	63–77
Wisdom and intelligence distinguished	66
Time	77
Origin and development of qualities	82
Is there a soul?	86
Thought and sight	89
Contact, sensation, and idea	92
Book III. The Removal of Difficulties	100
Rich and poor	100
Renunciation again	101
Nirvâna and Karma	106
Difficulties of various kinds as to transmigration, individuality, and the Buddha	120
Book IV. The Solving of Dilemmas	137
Milinda finds dilemmas in the Holy Writ	137
And takes the Buddhist vows	138
Third meeting between him and Nâgasena	140
1st Dilemma. If the Buddha has really quite passed away, what is the good of paying honour to his relics?	144
2nd Dilemma. How can the Buddha be omniscient, when it is said that he reflects?	154
3rd Dilemma. Why did he admit Devadatta to the Order, if he knew of the schism he would create?	162

CONTENTS.

	PAGE
4th Dilemma. Vessantara's earthquake	170
5th Dilemma. King Sivi	179
7th Dilemma. Difference in prophecies as to the duration of the faith	185
8th Dilemma. The Buddha's sinlessness and his sufferings	190
9th Dilemma. Why should the Buddha have meditated?	196
10th Dilemma. Why did the Buddha boast?	198
11th Dilemma. How could the Buddha revoke regulations he had made?	202
12th Dilemma. Why did the Buddha refuse to answer certain questions?	204
13th Dilemma. Contradictory statements by the Buddha as to fear	206
14th Dilemma. How can Pirit cure disease?	213
15th Dilemma. How could the evil one turn people against the Buddha?	219
16th Dilemma. Contradiction as to conscious crime	224
17th Dilemma. Contradiction as to the Buddha's wish to be the chief	225
18th Dilemma. How could a schism have arisen in the Buddha's life?	227
19th Dilemma. Why do members of the Order accept reverence?	232
20th Dilemma. The evil results of preaching	234
22nd Dilemma. Was not the Buddha once angry with Sudinna?	237
23rd Dilemma. The tree talking	241
24th Dilemma. The Buddha's last meal	242
25th Dilemma. Adoration of relics	246
26th Dilemma. The splinter of rock	248
27th Dilemma. Contradictory description of the Samaṇa	251
28th Dilemma. Buddha's boasting	253
29th Dilemma. How can the kind punish others?	254
30th Dilemma. Was not the Buddha angry at Kātumâ?	257
31st Dilemma. How could Moggallâna have had miraculous powers seeing that he was murdered?	261
32nd Dilemma. Why should the rules of the Order be kept secret?	264
33rd Dilemma. Contradictions about falsehood	268

	PAGE
34th Dilemma. Did not the Omniscient One once doubt?	270
35th Dilemma. Suicide	273
36th Dilemma. Love to all beings	279
37th Dilemma. Wickedness and prosperity	283
38th Dilemma. Women's wiles	294
39th Dilemma. Did not the Arahats once show fear?	297
40th Dilemma. Did not the Omniscient One once change his mind?	301
Appendix. Devadatta in the *G*âtakas	303
Addenda et Corrigenda	305
Index of Proper Names	307
Index of Subjects	311
Transliteration of Oriental Alphabets adopted for the Translations of the Sacred Books of the East	317

INTRODUCTION.

THE work of which a translation is here, for the first time, presented to the English reading public, has had a strange and interesting history. Written in Northern India, at or a little after the beginning of the Christian era, and either in Sanskrit itself or in some North Indian Prakrit, it has been entirely lost in the land of its origin, and (so far as is at present known) is not extant in any of the homes of the various sects and schools of the Buddhists, except only in Ceylon, and in those countries which have derived their Buddhism from Ceylon. It is true that General Cunningham says [1] that the name of Milinda 'is still famous in all Buddhist countries.' But he is here drawing a very wide conclusion from an isolated fact. For in his note he refers only to Hardy, who is good evidence for Ceylon, but who does not even say that the 'Milinda' was known elsewhere.

Preserved there, and translated at a very early date into Pâli, it has become, in its southern home, a book of standard authority, is put into the hands of those who have begun to doubt the cardinal points of Buddhist doctrine, has been long a popular work in its Pâli form, has been translated into Si*m*halese, and occupies a unique position, second only to the Pâli Pi*t*akas (and perhaps also to the celebrated work of Buddhaghosa, the 'Path of Purity'). From Ceylon it has been transferred, in its Pâli form, to both Burma and Siam, and in those countries also it enjoys so high a repute, that it has been commented on (if not translated). It is not merely the only work composed among the Northern Buddhists which is regarded with reverence by the orthodox Buddhists of the southern

---

[1] In his 'Ancient Geography of India,' p. 186.

schools; it is the only one which has survived at all amongst them. And it is the only prose work composed in ancient India which would be considered, from the modern point of view, as a successful work of art.

The external evidence for these statements is, at present, both very slight and, for the most part, late. There appeared at Colombo in the year of Buddha 2420 (1877 A.D.) a volume of 650 pages, large 8vo.—the most considerable in point of size as yet issued from the Si*m*halese press—entitled MILINDA PRA*S*NAYA. It was published at the expense of five Buddhist gentlemen whose names deserve to be here recorded. They are Karolis Piris, Âbraham Liwerâ, Luis Mendis, Nandis Mendis Amara-sekara, and Chârlis Arnolis Mendis Wijaya-ratna Amara-sekara. It is stated in the preface that the account of the celebrated discussion held between Milinda and Nâgasena, about 500 years after the death of the Buddha, was translated into the Mâgadhî language by 'teachers of old' (purwâ*k*ârin wisin);—that that Pâli version was translated into Si*m*halese, at the instance and under the patronage of King Kîrtti *S*rî Râ*g*a-si*m*ha, who came to the throne of Ceylon in the year of Buddha 2290 (1747 A.D.), by a member of the Buddhist Order named Hîna*t*i-kumburê Suma*n*gala, a lineal successor, in the line of teacher and pupil (anu*s*ishya), of the celebrated Woeli-wi*t*a Sara*n*a*n*kara, who had been appointed Sa*m*gha-râ*g*a, or chief of the Order—that 'this priceless book, unsurpassable as a means either for learning the Buddhist doctrine, or for growth in the knowledge of it, or for the suppression of erroneous opinions,' had become corrupt by frequent copying—that, at the instigation of the well-known scholar Moho*tt*i-watte Gunânanda, these five had had the texts corrected and restored by several learned Bhikkhus (kîpa namak lawâ), and had had indices and a glossary added, and now published the thus revised and improved edition.

The Si*m*halese translation, thus introduced to us, follows the Pâli throughout, except that it here and there adds, in the way of gloss, extracts from one or other of the numerous Pi*t*aka texts referred to, and also that it starts with a prophecy, put into the mouth of the Buddha when on his death-bed, that this discussion would take place about 500 years after his death, and that it inserts further, at the point indicated in my note on p. 3 of the present version, an account of how the Si*m*halese translator came to write his version. His own account of the matter adds to the details given above that he wrote the work at the Uposatha Ârâma of the Mahâ Wihâra near Srî-wardhana-pura, 'a place famous for the possession of a temple containing the celebrated Tooth Relic, and a monastery which had been the residence of Wœliwi*t*a Sara*n*aṅkara, the Sa*m*gha-râga, and of the famous scholars and commentators Darami*t*i-pola Dhamma-rakkhita and Madhurasato*t*a Dhammakkhandha.'

As Kîrtti Srî Râga-si*m*ha reigned till 1781[1], this would only prove that our Pâli work was extant in Ceylon in its present form, and there regarded as of great antiquity and high authority, towards the close of the last century. And no other mention of the work has, as yet, been discovered in any older Si*m*halese author. But in the present deplorable state of our ignorance of the varied and ancient literature of Ceylon, the argument ex silentio would be simply of no value. Now that the Ceylon Government have introduced into the Legislative Council a bill for the utilisation, in the interests of education, of the endowments of the Buddhist monasteries, it may be hoped that the value of the books written in those monasteries will not be forgotten, and that a sufficient yearly sum will be put aside for the editing and publication of a literature of such great historical value[2]. At present we can only deplore the impossibility of tracing the history of the 'Questions of Milinda' in other works written by the scholarly natives of its southern home.

That it will be mentioned in those works there can be

---

[1] See Turnour's Mahavansa, p. lxviii.
[2] I believe that none of the many vernacular literatures of India can compare for a moment with the Si*m*halese, whether judged from the point of view of literary excellence, variety of contents, age, or historical value. And yet a few hundreds a year for ten years would probably suffice, on the system followed by the Pâli Text Society, for the editing and publication of the whole.

but little doubt. For the great Indian writer, who long ago found in that beautiful and peaceful island the best scope for his industrious scholarship, is already known to have mentioned the book no less than four times in his commentaries; and that in such a manner that we may fairly hope to find other references to it when his writings shall have been more completely published. In his commentary on the Book of the Great Decease, VI, 3, Buddhaghosa refers to the quotation of that passage made in the conversation between Milinda and Nâgasena, translated below, at IV, 2, 1[1]. And again, in his commentary on the Amba*tth*a Sutta (D. III, 2, 12) he quotes the words of a conversation between Milinda and Nâgasena on the subject he is there discussing. The actual words he uses (they will be found at pp. 275, 276 of the edition of the Sumaṅgala Vilâsinî, edited for the Pâli Text Society by Professor Carpenter and myself) are not the same as those of our author at the corresponding passage of Mr. Trenckner's text (pp. 168, 169; IV, 3, 11), but they are the same in substance.

The above two references in Buddhaghosa to our author were pointed out by myself. Dr. Morris has pointed out two others, and in each of those also Buddhaghosa is found to quote words differing from Mr. Trenckner's text. The former of these two was mentioned in a letter to the 'Academy' of the 12th November, 1881. In the Manoratha Pûra*n*î, his commentary on the Aṅguttara, on the passage marked in Dr. Morris's edition as I, 5, 8, Buddhaghosa says:—

'Imasmi*m* pan' atthe Milinda-râ*g*â dhammakathika-Nâgasenattehra*m* pu*kkh*i: "Bhante Nâgasena, ekasmim a*kkh*arakkha*n*e pavattita-*k*itta-sa*m*khârâ sa*k*e rûpino assa kîva mahâ-râsi bhaveyyâti?"'

And he then gives the answer:—'Vâhasatâna*m* kho mahâ-râ*g*a vihîna*m* a*ddh*a-*k*ûla*ñ k*a vâhâ vîhi sattammanâni dve *k*a tumbâ eka*kkh*arakkha*n*e

---

[1] This was already pointed out in a note to my translation of the text commented on ('Buddhist Suttas,' vol. xi of the Sacred Books of the East, p. 112).

pavattitassa *k*ittassa saṅkham pi na upenti kalam pi na upenti kala-bhâgam pi na upentîti.'

This passage of the Milinda, referred to by Buddhaghosa, will be found on p. 102 of Mr. Trenckner's edition, translated below at IV, 1, 19. But the question is not found there at all, and the answer, though much the same in the published text, still differs in the concluding words. Mr. Trenckner marks the passage in his text as corrupt, and it may well be that Buddhaghosa has preserved for us an older and better reading.

The other passage quoted by Dr. Morris (in the 'Academy' of the 11th January, 1881) is from the Papañ*k*a Sûdanî, Buddhaghosa's still unedited Commentary on the Ma*ggh*ima Nikâya. It is in the comment on the Brahmâyu Suttanta, and as it is not accessible elsewhere I give this passage also in full here. With reference, oddly enough, to the same passage referred to above (pp. 168, 169 of the text, translated below at IV, 3, 11) Buddhaghosa there says:—

'Vutta*m* eta*m* Nâgasenattherena Milindarañ ñâ pu*tth*ena: "Na mahârâ*g*a Bhagavâ guyha*m* dasseti *kh*âya*m* Bhagavâ dassetîti."'

In this case, as in the other quotation of the same passage, the words quoted are not quite the same as those given in the published text, and on the other hand they agree with, though they are much shorter than, the words as given in the Sumaṅgala Vilâsinî.

It would be premature to attempt to arrive at the reason of this difference between Buddhaghosa's citations and Mr. Trenckner's edition of the text. It may be that Buddhaghosa is consciously summarising, or that he is quoting roughly from memory, or that he is himself translating or summarising from the original work, or that he is quoting from another Pâli version, or that he is quoting from another recension of the text of the existing Pâli version. We must have the full text of all his references to the 'Questions of Milinda' before us, before we try to choose between these, and possibly other, alternative explanations. What is at present certain is that when

Buddhaghosa wrote his great works, that is about 430 A.D., he had before him a book giving the conversations between Milinda and Nâgasena. And more than that. He introduces his comment above referred to on the Amba*ttha* Sutta by saying, after simply quoting the words of the text he is explaining: 'What would be the use of any one else saying anything on this? For Nâgasena, the Elder, himself said as follows in reply to Milinda, the king [1]'— and he then quotes Nâgasena, and adds not a word of his own. It follows that the greatest of all Buddhist writers known to us by name regarded the 'Questions of Milinda' as a work of so great authority that an opinion put by its author into the mouth of Nâgasena should be taken as decisive. And this is not only the only book, outside the Pâli Pi*t*akas, which Buddhaghosa defers to in this way, it is the only book, except the previous commentaries, which he is known even to refer to at all. But, on the other hand, he says nothing in these passages to throw any further light on the date, or any light on the authorship, of the work to which he assigns so distinguished, even so unique, a position.

So far as to what is known about our 'Questions of Milinda' in Ceylon. The work also exists, certainly in Pâli, and probably in translations into the local dialects, in Burma and Siam. For Mr. Trenckner mentions (Introduction, p. iv) a copy in the Burmese character of the Pâli text sent to him by Dr. Rost, there is another copy in that character in the Colombo Museum[2], and Mr. J. G. Scott, of the Burmese Civil Service, has sent to England a Burmese Nissaya of the Milinda (a kind of translation, giving the Pâli text, word for word, followed by the interpretation of those words in Burmese[3]). A manuscript of the Pâli text, brought from Siam, is referred to in the Si*m*halese MSS. in the marginal note quoted by Mr. Trenckner at p. vi of the

---

[1] Kim ettha aññena vattabba*m*? Vuttam eta*m* Nâgasenattheren' eva Milinda-raññâ pu*tth*ena.... (Suma*n*gala Vilâsinî, loc. cit.).

[2] See p. 51 of the 'Journal of the Pâli Text Society' for 1882.

[3] This Nissaya is now in the possession of his brother, the Bursar of St. John's College, Cambridge.

Introduction to his edition. And there exists in the library of Trinity College, Cambridge, a complete MS., in excellent condition, in the Siamese-Pâli character [1], while there are numerous fragments in the Paris Bibliothèque Nationale of one or more MSS. of the text, in the same Kambojan character used in Siam for the writing of Pâli texts [2].

It may be noticed here that there are seven MSS. of the text written in the Ceylon character known to exist in Europe. Two of them (one a very ancient one) are in the Copenhagen University Library, two in the Bibliothèque Nationale [2], one in the Cambridge University Library [3], and two in the India Office Library [4]. Three only of these seven have been used by Mr. Trenckner for his very able and accurate edition of the text, published in 1880.

That is all the external evidence at present available. What can be inferred from the book itself is about as follows. It consists of the discussion of a number of points of Buddhist doctrine treated in the form of conversations between King Milinda and Nâgasena the Elder (Thera). It must be plain to every reader of the following pages that these are not real conversations. What we have before us is really an historical romance, though the didactic aim overshadows the story. Men of straw, often very skilfully put together, are set up for the purpose, not so much of knocking them down again, as of elucidating some points of ethical or psychological belief while doing so. The king himself plays a very subordinate part. The questions raised, or dilemmas stated, are put into his mouth. But the solutions, to give opportunity for which the questions or dilemmas are invented, are the really important part of the work, and these are put into the mouth of Nâgasena. The dialogues are introduced by a carefully constructed

---

[1] By the kindness of the Master and Fellows of the College I have been allowed to collate this MS. in London.
[2] See 'Journal of the Pâli Text Society' for 1882, p. 35.
[3] See 'Journal of the Pâli Text Society' for 1883, p. 146.
[4] See 'Journal of the Pâli Text Society' for 1882, p. 119.

preliminary story, in which the reader's interest in them is aroused by anticipation. And the ability of this part of the work is very great. For in spite of the facts that all the praise lavished therein upon both Milinda and Nâgasena is in reality only praise of the book itself, and that the reader knows this very well, yet he will find it almost impossible to escape from the influence of the eloquent words in which importance and dignity are lent to the occasion of their meeting; and of the charm and skill with which the whole fiction is maintained.

The question then arises whether the personages were any more real than the conversations. Milinda is supposed to be the Menander, who appears in the list of the Greek kings of Baktria, since he is described in the book as being a king of the Yonakas reigning at Sâgala (the Euthydemia of the Greeks), and there is no other name in the list which comes so near to Milinda. This identification of the two names is certainly correct. For whether it was our author who deliberately made the change in adapting the Greek name to the Indian dialect in which he wrote, or whether the change is due to a natural phonetic decay, the same causes will have been of influence. Indra or Inda is a not uncommon termination of Indian names, and meaning king is so appropriate to a king, that a foreign king's name ending in -ander would almost inevitably come to end in -inda. Then the sequence of the liquids of m-n-n would tend in an Indian dialect to be altered in some way by dissimilation, and Mr. Trenckner adduces seven instances in Pâli of l taking the place of n, or n of l, in similar circumstances[1].

There remains only the change of the first E in Menander to I. Now in the Indian part of the inscription, on undoubted coins of Menander, the oldest authorities read Minanda as the king's name[2], and though that interpretation has now, on the authority of better specimens, been given up, there is no doubt that Milinda runs more easily

---

[1] 'Pâli Miscellany,' part i, p. 55.
[2] For instance, Wilson in his 'Ariana Antiqua,' p. 283.

from the tongue than Melinda, and Mil may well have seemed as appropriate a commencement for a Milakkha's name as -inda is for the ending of a king's name. So Men-ander became Mil-inda.

It may be added here that other Greek names are mentioned by our author—Devamantiya at I, 42, and the same officer, together with Anantakâya, Mankura, and Sabbadinna, at II, 3. There is a similar effort in these other Pâli forms of Greek words to make them give some approach to a meaning in the Indian dialect: but in each case the new forms remain as really unintelligible to an Indian as Mil-inda would be. Thus Deva-mantiya, which may be formed on Demetrios, looks, at first sight, Indian enough. But if it meant anything, it could only mean 'counsellor of the gods.' And so also both Ananta and Kâya are Indian words. But the compound Ananta-kâya would mean 'having an infinite body,' which is absurd as the name of a courtier. It may possibly be made up to represent Antiochos. What Mankura and Sabbadinna (called simply Dinna at p. 87) may be supposed to be intended for it is difficult to say[1]. But the identification of Milinda with Menander is as certain as that of *K*andagutta with Sandrokottos.

Very little is told us, in the Greek or Roman writers, about any of the Greek kings of Baktria. It is a significant fact that it is precisely of Menander-Milinda that they tell us most, though this most is unfortunately not much.

Strabo, in his Geography[2], mentions Menander as one of the two Baktrian kings who were instrumental in spreading the Greek dominion furthest to the East into India. He crossed the Hypanis (that is the Sutlej) and penetrated as far as the Isamos (probably the Jumna).

Then in the title of the lost forty-first book of Justin's work, Menander and Apollodotus are mentioned as 'Indian kings.'

Finally, Plutarch[3] tells us an anecdote of Menander.

---

[1] Compare Mr. Trenckner's note at p. 70 of the 'Pâli Miscellany.'
[2] Edit. Müller, xi, 11, 1. [3] De Repub. Ger., p. 821.

He was, he says, as a ruler noted for justice, and enjoyed such popularity with his subjects, that upon his death, which took place in camp, diverse cities contended for the possession of his ashes. The dispute was only adjusted by the representatives of the cities agreeing that the relics should be divided amongst them, and that they should severally erect monuments (μνημεῖα, no doubt dâgabas or sthûpas) to his memory.

This last statement is very curious as being precisely analogous to the statement in the 'Book of the Great Decease [1],' as to what occurred after the death of the Buddha himself. But it would be very hazardous to draw any conclusion from this coincidence.

The only remaining ancient evidence about Menander-Milinda (apart from what is said by our author himself), is that of coins. And, as is usually the case, the evidence of the coins will be found to confirm, but to add very little to, what is otherwise known.

As many as twenty-two [2] different coins have been discovered, some of them in very considerable numbers, bearing the name, and eight of them the effigy, of Menander. They have been found over a very wide extent of country, as far west as Kâbul, as far east as Mathurâ, and one of them as far north as Kashmîr. Curiously enough we find a confirmation of this wide currency of Menander-Milinda's coins in the work of the anonymous author of the 'Periplus Maris Erythræi.' He says [3] that Menander's coins, together with those of Apollodotos, were current, many years after his death, at Barygaza, the modern Baroach, on the coast of Gujarat.

The portrait on the coins is very characteristic, with a long face and an intelligent expression, and is sometimes that of a young man, and at other times that of a very old man. It may be inferred therefore that his reign

---

[1] Mahâparinibbâna Suttanta VI, 58-62, translated in my 'Buddhist Suttas' (vol. xi of the Sacred Books of the East), pp. 133-135.

[2] This number would be greatly increased if the differences of the monograms were allowed for.

[3] Chapter 47 of Müller's edition.

INTRODUCTION.   xxi

was as long as his power was extensive. All the coins have a legend in Greek letters on one side, and a corresponding legend in Ariano-pâli letters on the other side. On twenty-one out of the twenty-two, the inscriptions, according to the latest interpretations from a comparison of the best examples, are respectively,

BASILEÔS SÔTÊROS MENANDROU
and
MAHARAGASA TRADATASA MENANDRASA [1].

Wilson read [2] the last word Minadasa. But when he wrote, in 1840, the alphabet was neither so well known as it is now, nor had such good examples come to hand. So that though the Mi- is plain enough on several coins, it is almost certainly a mere mistake for Me, from which it only differs by the centre vowel stroke being slightly prolonged.

Fifteen of the coins have a figure of Pallas either on one side or the other. A 'victory,' a horse jumping, a dolphin, a head (perhaps of a god), a two-humped camel, an elephant goad, a boar, a wheel, and a palm branch are each found on one side or the other of one of the coins; and an elephant, an owl, and a bull's head each occur twice. These are all the emblems or figures on the coins. None of them are distinctively Buddhist, though the wheel might be claimed as the Buddhist wheel, and the palm branch and the elephant would be quite in place on Buddhist coins. It may be said, therefore, that the bulk of the coins are clearly pagan, and not Buddhist; and that though two or three are doubtful, even they are probably not Buddhist.

One coin, however, a very rare one, differs, as to its inscription, from all the rest that have the legend. It has on one side

BASILEÔS DIKAIOU MENANDROU,
and on the other,
MAHARAGASA DHARMIKASA [3] MENANDRASA.

---

[1] See Alfred Von Sallet, 'Die Nachfolger Alexander's des Grossen in Baktrien und Indien,' Berlin, 1879; and Professor Percy Gardiner's 'Catalogue of the Coins of the Greek and Scythic Kings of Baktria and India,' London, 1886.

[2] In his 'Ariana Antiqua,' p. 283, London, 1841.

[3] The r is a little doubtful and is written, if at all, after the dh, though intended to be pronounced before the m.

Is any reference intended here to the Buddhist Dharma as distinct from the ordinary righteousness of kings? I think not. The coin is one of those with the figure of Pallas on the side which bears the Greek legend, and five others of the Baktrian Greek kings use a similar legend on their coins. These are Agathocles, Heliokles, Archebios, Strato, and Zoilos. There is also another coin in the series with a legend into which the word Dharma enters, but which has not yet been deciphered with certainty—that bearing in the Greek legend the name of Sy-Hermaios, and supposed to have been struck by Kadphises I. If there is anything Buddhist in this coin of Menander's, then the others also must be Buddhist. But it is much simpler to take the word dharmikasa in the sense of the word used in the corresponding Greek legend, and to translate it simply 'the Righteous,' or, better still, 'the Just.' Only when we call to mind how frequent in the Pâli texts is the description of the ideal king (whether Buddhist or not) as dhammiko dhamma-râga, we cannot refuse to see the connection between this phrase and the legend of the coins, and to note how at least six of the Greek kings, one of whom is Menander, are sufficiently desirous to meet the views of their Buddhist subjects to fix upon 'Righteousness' or 'Justice' as the characteristic by which they wish to be known. The use of this epithet is very probably the foundation of the tradition preserved by Plutarch, that Menander was, as a ruler, noted for justice; and it is certainly evidence of the Buddhist influences by which he was surrounded. But it is no evidence at all that he actually became a Buddhist.

To sum up.—Menander-Milinda was one of those Greek kings who carried on in Baktria the Greek dominion founded by Alexander the Great. He was certainly one of the most important, probably the most important, of those kings. He carried the Greek arms further into India than any of his predecessors had done, and everything confirms the view given by our author at I, 9 of his justice and his power, of his ability and his wealth. He must have reigned for a considerable time in the latter part of the second century B.C., probably from about 140 to about 115, or even 110 B.C.[1] His fame extended, as did that of no other Baktrian king, to the West, and he is the only Baktrian Greek king who has been remembered in India. Our author makes him say, incidentally[2], that he was born at Kalasi in Alasanda (= Alexandria), a name given to an island presumably in the Indus. And, as was referred to above, Plutarch has preserved the tradition that he died in camp, in a campaign against the Indians in the valley of the Ganges.

[It is interesting to point out, in this connection, that the town (gâma) of Kalasi has not been found mentioned elsewhere. Now among the very numerous coins of the Baktrian kings there is one, and only one, giving in the legend, not the name of a king, but the name of a city, the city of Karisi. As this coin was struck about 180 B.C. by Eukratides, who was probably the first of these kings to obtain a settlement on the banks of the Indus, it is possible that the two names, one in the Pâli form (or more probably in the form of the dialect used by our author), the other in the local form, are identical; and that the coin was struck in commemoration of the fact of the Greeks having reached the Indus. If that be so, then that they gave the name Alasanda (Alexandria) to the island on which the town was built, and not to the town itself, seems to show that the town was not founded by them, but was already an important place when they took it.]

Beyond this all is conjecture. When our author says that Milinda was converted to Buddhism[3], he may be either relating an actual tradition, or he may be inventing for his own purposes. There is nothing inherently impossible, or even improbable, in the story. We know that all the Baktrians, kings and people alike, eventually became

---

[1] See the chronological table in the Introduction to Professor Gardner's work, quoted below.
[2] See the translation below of III, 7, 5.
[3] See p. 420 of the Pâli text.

Buddhist. But the passage occurs in a part of the book which is open to much doubt. We have to place against it the negative evidence that none of Menander's coins show any decisive signs of his conversion. And the passage in question goes much further. It says that he afterwards gave up the kingdom to his son, and having entered the Buddhist Order, attained to Arahatship. The Siṃhalese MSS. add a marginal note to the effect that the whole of this passage with its context was derived from a MS. brought from Siam. Mr. Trenckner is therefore of opinion [1] that it belongs to a spurious supplement. That may be so, in spite of the fact that it is quite in our author's style, and forms an appropriate close to the book. But it is incredible that an author of the literary skill so evident throughout the work should have closed his book deliberately in the middle of a paragraph, without any closing words to round it off. The Siamese MS. may after all have preserved the reading of older and better MSS. than those in Ceylon, and the last leaf of the book may have been lost there. There must have been some conclusion, if not in the manner of the paragraph under discussion, then in some other words which we may not be able to trace. But even if our author actually wrote that Menander did become a Bhikkhu and an Arahat, that is very poor evidence of the fact, unless he not only intended what he states to be taken quite literally, but also wrote soon after the events he thus deliberately records.

Now the opinion has been expressed above that we have to deal with a book of didactic ethics and religious controversy cast into the form of historical romance. If this is correct no one would be more astonished than the author himself at the inconsistency of modern critics if they took his historical statements au grand sérieux, while they made light of his ethical arguments. It is true that he would scarcely have been guilty of anything that seemed grossly improbable, at the time when he wrote, to the readers whom he addressed. But if, as is most probable, he wrote in North-

---

[1] 'Introduction,' pp. v, vi.

Western India when the memory of the actual facts of Menander's reign was fading away—that is, some generations after his death—he may well have converted him to Buddhism, as the most fitting close to the discussion he records, without intending at all to convey thereby any real historical event.

This brings us to the next point of our argument.

We have seen that the work must have been written some considerable time before Buddhaghosa, and after the death of Menander. Can its date be determined with greater accuracy than this? The story of Nâgasena introduces to us his father So*n*uttara, his teachers Roha*n*a, Assagutta of the Vattaniya hermitage, and Dhammarakkhita of the Asoka Ârâma near Pâ*t*aliputta, and there is also mention of a teacher named Âyupâla dwelling at the Sankheyya hermitage near Sâgala. None of these persons and none of these places are read of elsewhere in any Buddhist text, whether Sanskrit or Pâli. For the A*s*vagupta referred to in passing at p. 351 of the Divyâvadâna has nothing in common (except the name) with our Assagutta, the Roha*n*a of Anguttara, III, 66, is quite distinct from our Roha*n*a, and there is not the slightest reason for supposing Nâgasena to be another form of the name Nâgâr*gu*na, found in both the Chinese and Tibetan Buddhist literatures[1], and in the Jain lists[2]. The famous Buddhist scholar so called was the reputed founder of the Mahâyâna school of Buddhism. Our Nâgasena represents throughout the older teaching. If there is any connection at all between the two names, Nâgasena must have been invented as a contrast to Nâgâr*gu*na, and not with the least idea of identifying two men whose doctrines are so radically opposed. Even were there any reason to believe this to be the case, it would not help us much, for the date

---

[1] See the passages quoted by Dr. Wenzel in the 'Journal of the Pâli Text Society' for 1886, pp. 1–4.
[2] See Professor Weber in the 'Handschriftenverzeichniss der königlichen Bibliothek in Berlin,' vol. v, part 2, p. 365.

of Nâgârguna is quite as much open to dispute as that of the author of the 'Questions of Milinda[1].'

I ought to mention here that an opinion of a Nâgasena is, according to Burnouf[2], discussed at length in the Abhidharma Kosa Vyâkhyâ; and that Schiefner[3] quotes from a Tibetan work, the Bu-ston, the statement that a schism took place under a Thera Nâgasena 137 years after the Buddha's death. It would be very interesting if the former were our Nâgasena. And if Schiefner's restoration of the name found in his Tibetan authority be correct, and the authority itself be trustworthy, it is possibly the fading memory of that Nâgasena which induced our author to adopt the name as that of the principal interlocutor in his 'Questions of Milinda.'

Finally, Professor Kern, of Leiden—who believes that Buddha is the sun, and most of his principal disciples stars—believes also not only that our Nâgasena is an historical person, but also that there never was a Buddhist cleric of that name; and that Nâgasena is simply Patañgali, the author of the Yoga philosophy, under another name. If this is not a joke, it is a strange piece of credulity.

The only reason alleged in support of it is that Patañgali has the epithets of Nâgesa and of Phanin. That he was a Hindu who believed in the soul-theory of the current animistic creed, while all the opinions put into Nâgasena's mouth are those of a thorough-going Buddhist and non-individualist, is to count as nothing against this chance similarity, not of names, but of the name on one side with an epithet on the other. To identify John Stuart Mill with Dean Milman would be sober sense compared with this proposal.

---

[1] Compare on this point Dr. Wenzel, loc. cit., with Dr. Burgess in the 'Archaeological Reports for Southern India,' vol. i, pp. 5–9. Dr. Burgess thinks the most probable date of his death is about 200 A.D.

The identification of Nâgârguna and Nâgasena was made independently by Major Bird in the 'Journal of the Bombay Branch of the Royal Asiatic Society' for October, 1844 (who was followed by the Rev. R. Spence Hardy at p. 517 of his 'Manual of Buddhism,' published in 1860), and by Benfey in his article 'Indien' in Ersch and Gruber's Encyclopedia (who was followed by Burnouf at p. 570 of his 'Introduction,' &c., published in 1844).

[2] Loc. cit. [3] Note to his translation of Târanâtha, p. 298.

But it is deliberately put forward to support an accusation against the Buddhists of having falsely appropriated to themselves every famous man in India[1]. Any mud, it would seem, is good enough to pelt the Buddhists with. Yet who is it, after all, who really makes the 'appropriation,' the Buddhists or Professor Kern himself?

It would seem, therefore, that most of our author's person and place names are probably inventions of his own[2].

But it is quite different with the books quoted by our author. In several passages he has evidently in his mind certain Pâli texts which deal with similar matters. So far as yet ascertained the texts thus silently referred to, either in the present volume or in the subsequent untranslated portion of the book, are as follows:

Page of this volume.

8	Dîgha Nikâya II, 1, 2.
10	,, ,, II, 20.
10	,, ,, II, 1.
38	,, ,, II, 10.
38	,, ,, II, 11.
40	Kathâ Vatthu I, 1.
41	Anguttara I, 15, 4–7.
41	Dîgha Nikâya II, 17.
41	,, ,, II, 23.
42	,, ,, II, 26.
59	,, ,, XVII.
80	Mahâvagga I, 1, 1.
129	Various (see my note).
132	Kullavagga IX, 1, 4.
163	Kullavagga VII, 1, 27.
170	Vessantara Gâtaka.
179	Sivi Gâtaka.
204	Magghima Nikâya LXIII.

[1] Kern's 'Buddhismus' (the German translation), vol. ii, p. 443.

[2] As these pages were passing through the press I have found Assagutta of the Vattaniya hermitage, mentioned in the last chapter of the Saddhamma Samgaha, which is passing through the press for the Pâli Text Society. But this is taken no doubt from the Milinda, and is not an independent reference to any such teacher as an historical person. (The Saddhamma Samgaha was written by Dhamma-kitti in Ceylon, probably in the twelfth century.)

Page of this volume.	
212 . .	Gâtaka (No. 69).
256 . .	Sutta Vibhaṅga (Pâr. 4).
257 . .	Kâtuma Sutta (No. 67).
259 . .	Kullavagga IX, 1, 3.
264 . .	Mahâvagga II, 16, 8.
275 . .	Dhamma-kakka-pavattana Sutta.
277 . .	Aṅguttara II, 1, 1.
283 . .	The 540th Gâtaka.
285 . .	Amba Gâtaka (No. 474).
285 . .	Dummedha Gâtaka (No. 122).
286 . .	Tittira Gâtaka (No. 438).
286 . .	Khantivâda Gâtaka (No. 313).
287 . .	Kûla-Nandiya Gâtaka (No. 222).
287 . .	Takkha-sûkara Gâtaka (No. 492).
288 . .	Kariyâ-pitaka II, 6.
288 . .	Sîlava-nâga Gâtaka (No. 72).
288 . .	Sabba-dâtha Gâtaka (No. 241).
289 . .	Apannaka Gâtaka (No. 1).
289 . .	Nigrodha-miga Gâtaka (No. 12).
290 . .	Nigrodha Gâtaka (No. 445).
290 . .	Mahâ-paduma Gâtaka (No. 472).
290 . .	Mahâ-patâpa Gâtaka (No. 358).
294 . .	Ummagga Gâtaka (No. 546).
298 . .	Kullavagga VII, 3, 11.
302 . .	Aṅguttara IV, 13.
Page of the Pâli Text.	
220 . .	Gâtaka, No. 310 (vol. iii, p. 32).
231 . .	Sutta Nipâta I, 4.
236 . .	Gâtaka (vol. i, p. 56).
256 . .	„ (vol. iv, p. 232, line 20).
277 . .	Vessantara Gâtaka.
289 . .	Gâtaka (vol. i, p. 57).
291 . .	Gâtaka (Nos. 258, 541, 494, and 243).
313 . .	Magghima Nikâya, No. 75 (p. 502).

In several other passages he refers to a Pâli book, or a chapter in a Pâli book, by name. This is much more valuable for our purposes than the silent, and sometimes doubtful, references in the last list. So far as is yet ascertained, these references are as follows:

INTRODUCTION. xxix

Page of this volume.	
1, 2	Vinaya, Sutta, Abhidhamma.
21	The Suttantas.
21	The Abhidhamma.
21	Dhamma Sa*m*ga*n*i.
21	Vibhaṅga.
21	Dhâtu Kathâ.
21	Puggala Pa*ññ*atti.
21	Kathâ Vatthu.
22	Yamaka.
22	Pa*tth*âna.
22	The Abhidhamma Pi*t*aka.
25	The Abhidhamma.
27	The Abhidhamma.
28	The three Pi*t*akas.
31	Mahâ Samaya Suttanta (No. 20 in the Dîgha).
31	Mahâ Maṅgala Suttanta (Sutta Nipâta II, 4).
32	Sama-kitta-pariyâya Suttanta (unknown).
32	Râhulovâda Suttanta (No. 147 in the Ma*ggh*ima).
32	Parâbhava Suttanta (Sutta Nipâta I, 6).
34	The three Pi*t*akas.
56	Sa*m*yutta Nikâya (the words quoted are in the Sutta Nipâta).
71, 88	The Abhidhamma.
137	The ninefold Scriptures.
195	Moliya Sîvaka chapter of the Sa*m*yutta.
213	Ratana Sutta (in the Sutta Nipâta II, 1).
213	Khandha Parittâ (not traced).
213	Mora Parittâ (*G*âtaka, Nos. 159, 491).
213	Dha*g*agga Parittâ (in the *G*âtaka Book).
213	Â*t*ânâ*t*iya Parittâ (in the Dîgha Nikâya).
213	Aṅgulimâla Parittâ (not traced).
232	The Pâtimokkha.
4–267	Pâtimokkha, Vinaya Pi*t*aka.

Page of the Pâli Text.	
241	Dhamma-dâyâda Sutta of the Ma*ggh*ima Nikâya (vol. i, p. 13).
242	Sa*m*yutta Nikâya (vol. i, p. 67).
258	Dakkhi*n*â Vibhaṅga of the Ma*ggh*ima Nikâya (No. 142).
281	*K*ariyâ Pi*t*aka G. 53.

Page of the Pâli Text.		
341	. .	Navaṅgam Buddha-vakanam.
341	. .	The Gâtaka Book.
341	. .	The Dîgha Nikâya.
341	. .	The Maggḥima Nikâya.
342	. .	The Samyutta Nikâya.
342	. .	The Khuddaka Nikâya.
348	. .	The three Piṭakas.
349	. .	Mahâ Râhulovâda (in the Maggḥima, No. 147).
349	. .	Mahâ Maṅgala Suttanta (in the Sutta Nipâta II, 4).
349	. .	Sama-kitta Pariyâya (not traced).
349	. .	Parâbhava Suttanta (in the Sutta Nipâta I, 6).
349	. .	Purâbheda Suttanta (Sutta Nipâta IV, 10).
349	. .	Kalaha-vivâda Suttanta (Sutta Nipâta IV, 11).
349	. .	Kûla Vyûha Suttanta (Sutta Nipâta IV, 12).
349	. .	Mahâ Vyûha Suttanta (Sutta Nipâta IV, 13).
349	. .	Tuvataka Suttanta (Sutta Nipâta IV, 14).
349	. .	Sâriputta Suttanta (Sutta Nipâta IV, 16).
350	. .	Mahâ-samaya Suttanta (in the Dîgha, No. 20).
350	. .	Sakkha-paṅha Suttanta (Dîgha, No. 21).
350	. .	Tirokudda Suttanta (in the Khuddaka Pâṭha, No. 7).
350	. .	Ratana Suttanta (in the Sutta Nipâta II, 1).
350	. .	The Abhidhamma.
362	. .	Ekuttara Nikâya (=Aṅguttara I, 13, 7).
369	. .	Dhaniya-sutta of the Sutta Nipâta (I, 2).
371	. .	Kummûpama Suttanta of the Samyutta Nikâya (not yet printed).
372	. .	Vidhura Puṇṇaka Gâtaka.
377	. .	Sakka Samyutta of the Samyutta Nikâya (not yet printed).
378	. .	Dhammapada (verse 327).
379	. .	Samyutta (55, 7).
381	. .	Sutasoma Gâtaka (No. 537).
384	. .	Kaṇha Gâtaka (No. 440, vol. iv, p. 10).
385	. .	Sutta Nipâta (I, 12, 1).
389	. .	Samyutta Nikâya.
392	. .	Ekuttara Nikâya (=Aṅguttara X, 5, 8).
396	. .	Lomahamsana Pariyâya.
399	. .	Samyutta Nikâya (III, 5, 6, vol. i, p. 73).
401	. .	,, ,, (XVI, 1, 3, vol. ii, p. 194).
402	. .	Kakkavâka Gâtaka (No. 451, vol. iv, p. 71).
403	. .	Kulla Nârada Gâtaka (not traced).

INTRODUCTION. xxxi

Page of the Pâli Text.		
403	. .	Saṃyutta Nikâya (not traced).
405	. .	Lakkhaṇa Suttanta of the Dîgha Nikâya (No. 30).
406	. .	Bhallâṭiya Gâtaka (No. 504, vol. iv, p. 439).
408	. .	Parinibbâna-suttanta of the Dîgha Nikâya (D. XVI, 5, 24).
408	. .	Dhammapada (verse 32).
409	. .	Saṃyutta Nikâya (XIV, 16, vol. ii, p. 158).
411	. .	Sutta Nipâta (II, 6, 10).
414	. .	„ „ (III, 11, 43).

Lastly, our author quotes a large number of passages from the Piṭaka texts, which he introduces (without naming any book) by the formulas: 'It was said by the Blessed One;' or, 'It is said by you' (you in the plural, you members of the Order); or, 'It was said by so and so' (naming some particular member of the Order). A great many of these quotations have already been traced, either by Mr. Trenckner or myself. Occasionally words thus attributed, by our author, to the Buddha, are, in the Piṭakas, attributed to some one else. Such passages are distinguished in the following list by an asterisk added to the letter B, which marks those of them attributed by our author to the Buddha. The women quoted are distinguished by the title 'Sister.'

II, 1, 1, p. 45.	Sister Vagirâ.	Saṃyutta Nikâya V, 10, 6.
II, 1, 9, p. 53.	B*.	„ „ VII, 1, 6.
II, 1, 9, p. 54.	B.	Not traced.
II, 1, 11, p. 57.	B.	„ „
II, 1, 13, p. 61.	B.	Saṃyutta Nikâya XXI, 5.
II, 2, 4, p. 69.	B.	Not traced.
II, 3, 1, p. 79.	B.	Maggḥima Nikâya XXI.
II, 3, 2, p. 80.	B.	„ „ XVIII.
III, 4, 3, p. 101.	B*.	Saṃyutta Nikâya II, 3, 2.
III, 4, 4, p. 104.	B.	Aṅguttara III, 35, 4.
III, 6, 1, p. 114.	B.	Not traced.
IV, 1, 10, p. 145.	Sâriputta.	„ „
IV, 1, 13, p. 150.	B.	Dîgha Nikâya XIV, 6, 1.
IV, 1, 35, p. 170.	B.	„ „ XIV, 3, 13.
IV, 1, 42, p. 179.	In the Sutta.	Not traced.
IV, 1, 53, p. 185.	B.	Kullavagga X, 1, 6.
IV, 1, 55, p. 186.	B.	Dîgha Nikâya XIV, 5, 62.

THE QUESTIONS OF KING MILINDA.

IV, 1, 67, p. 196.	You.	Not traced.
IV, 1, 67, p. 196.	You.	,, ,,
IV, 1, 71, p. 199.	B.	Dîgha Nikâya XIV, 3, 60.
IV, 1, 71, p. 199.	B.	,, ,, XIV, 3, 63.
IV, 2, 1, p. 202.	B.	Not traced.
IV, 2, 1, p. 202.	B.	Dîgha Nikâya XIV, 6, 3.
IV, 2, 4, p. 204.	B.	,, ,, XIV, 2, 32.
IV, 2, 6, p. 206.	B.	Dhammapada 129.
IV, 2, 6, p. 206.	B.	Not traced.
IV, 2, 15, p. 213.	B.	Dhammapada 127, 8.
IV, 2, 20, p. 214.	You.	Not traced.
IV, 2, 20, p. 214.	You.	,, ,,
IV, 2, 27, p. 224.	You.	,, ,,
IV, 2, 29, p. 225.	B.	Dîgha Nikâya XIV, 2, 32.
IV, 2, 29, p. 225.	B.	Not traced.
IV, 2, 31, p. 227.	You.	,, ,,
IV, 2, 31, p. 227.	You.	,, ,,
IV, 3, 1, p. 229.	B.	Various (see note).
IV, 3, 1, p. 229.	You.	Aggañña Sutta (Dîgha).
IV, 3, 5, p. 234.	You.	Not traced.
IV, 3, 5, p. 234.	You.	,, ,,
IV, 3, 15, p. 238.	Sâriputta.	,, ,,
IV, 3, 15, p. 238.	B.	Parâgika I, 5, 11.
IV, 3, 19, p. 241.	B*.	Gâtaka III, 24.
IV, 3, 19, p. 241.	B.	Gâtaka IV, 210.
IV, 3, 21, p. 242.	The Theras.	Dîgha Nikâya XIV, 4, 23.
IV, 3, 21, p. 243.	B.	,, ,, XIV, 4, 57.
IV, 3, 24, p. 246.	B.	Not traced.
IV, 3, 24, p. 246.	B.	Mahâ-parinibbâna Sutta (D. XVI, 5, 24).
IV, 3, 27, p. 248.	You.	Not traced.
IV, 3, 27, p. 248.	You.	Kullavagga VII, 3, 9.
IV, 3, 31, p. 251.	B.	Not traced.
IV, 3, 31, p. 251.	B.	,, ,,
IV, 3, 33, p. 253.	B.	Brahmagala Sutta (D. I, 1, 5).
IV, 3, 33, p. 253.	B.	Sela Sutta (SN. III, 7, 7).
IV, 3, 35, p. 254.	B*.	The 521st Gâtaka.
IV, 3, 38, p. 257.	B.	Dhaniya Sutta (SN. I, 2, 2).
IV, 4, 1, p. 261.	B.	Anguttara I, 14, 1.
IV, 4, 4, p. 264.	B.	Anguttara III, 124.
IV, 4, 9, p. 268.	B.	Pâtimokkha (Pâk. 1).
IV, 4, 11, p. 270.	B.	Not traced.
IV, 4, 11, p. 271.	B.	,, ,,

INTRODUCTION. xxxiii

IV, 4, 13, p. 273.	B.	Sutta Vibhaṅga (Pâr. 3, 5, 13).
IV, 4, 13, p. 273.	B.	Not traced.
IV, 4, 16, p. 279.	B.	Aṅguttara XI, 2, 5, and the 169th *G*âtaka.
IV, 4, 16, p. 280.	You.	The 540th *G*âtaka.
IV, 4, 17, p. 283.	You.	Not traced.
IV, 4, 42, p. 294.	B*.	The 536th *G*âtaka.
IV, 4, 44, p. 297.	B.	Not traced.
IV, 4, 46, p. 301.	You.	,, ,,
The Pâli Text.		
P. 211, l. 6.	B.	Muni Sutta (SN. I, 12, 3).
211, l. 8.	B.	*K*ulkavagga VI, 1, 5.
213, l. 6.	B.	Dhammapada 168.
213, l. 7.	B.	Ma*ggh*ima Nikâya 77.
215, l. 10.	B.	Not traced.
215, l. 12.	B.	Aṅguttara I, 14, 4.
217, l. 9.	B.	Sa*m*yutta Nikâya XXI.
217, l. 11.	B.	Not traced.
219, l. 14.	B.	,, ,,
219, l. 15.	It is said.	*G*âtaka (No. 433).
221, l. 20.	B.	*Kh*addanta *G*âtaka (vol. v, p. 49).
221, l. 24.	It is said.	Not traced.
223, l. 16.	B.	Ma*gghi*ma Nikâya (No. 87).
223, l. 18.	It is said.	,, ,, ,,
225, l. 2.	B.	Sela Sutta (SN. III, 7, 33).
228, l. 2.	B.	Sutta Nipâta I, 4, 6 = III, 4, 26.
230, l. 13.	B*.	Kapi *G*âtaka (vol. iii, p. 354).
232, l. 7.	You.	Not traced.
232, l. 10.	You.	,, ,,
235, l. 2.	B.	Ma*ggh*ima I, p. 177 = Vinaya I, p. 8.
235, l. 4.	B.	Ma*ggh*ima (No. 86).
236, l. 27.	B.	Aṅguttara I, 15, 10.
240, l. 3.	B.	Ma*ggh*ima Nikâya (No. 142).
242, l. 17.	Sâriputta.	Not traced.
242, l. 26.	B.	Sa*m*yutta Nikâya 44.
245, l. 1.	B.	Sa*m*yutta 6, 14 (vol. i, p. 157) = Thera-gâthâ 256, 7 = Divyâvadâna, p. 300.
253, l. 1.	You.	Not traced.
255, l. 8.	You.	,, ,,
262.	B.	,, ,,
323.	You.	,, ,,

The Pâli Text.		
P. 333.	B.	Dhammapada 54–56 (taken in part from Aṅguttara III, 79).
366, l. 6.	B.	Saṃyutta XX, 8, 5.
366, l. 10.	Sâriputta.	Thera-gâthâ 985.
367, l. 8.	B.	Not traced (see S. XII, 63, 8).
367, l. 19.	Mahâ Kakkâyana.	Thera-gâthâ 501.
368, l. 2.	B.	Saṃyutta 46, 7.
368, l. 6.	Sâriputta.	Not traced.
368, l. 20.	Kulla Panthaka.	,, ,,
369, l. 5.	B.	Sutta Nipâta I, 2, 12.
369, l. 22.	The Theras who held the Synod (at Râgagaha).	Not traced.
370, l. 11.	Sâriputta.	Not traced.
371, l. 14.	Upasena.	Thera-gâthâ 577.
371, l. 28.	B.	Saṃyutta I, 17, 2 (vol. i, p. 7).
372, l. 12.	Râhula.	Not traced.
372, l. 23.	B.	Gâtaka (No. 545).
373, l. 13.	Sâriputta.	Not traced.
374, l. 5.	Sâriputta.	,, ,,
374, l. 16.	Sâriputta.	,, ,,
375, l. 15.	B.	Magghima (vol. i, p. 33).
376, l. 3.	Anuruddha.	Not traced.
376, l. 17.	Râhula.	,, ,,
377, l. 14.	B.	Saṃyutta 55, 7.
378, l. 5.	Sâriputta.	Not traced.
378, l. 17.	B.	Mahâ-parinibbâna Sutta (D. XVI, 2, 12).
379, l. 1.	B.	Dhammapada 327.
379, l. 14.	B.	Saṃyutta 55, 7.
380, l. 1.	Sâriputta.	Not traced.
381, l. 15.	B.	Sutasoma Gâtaka (No. 537).
383, l. 3.	Sister Subhaddâ.	Not traced.
384, l. 4.	B.	Kaṇha Gâtaka (vol. iv, p. 10).
385, l. 1.	B.	(?) Magghima Nikâya (No. 62).
385, l. 28.	B.	Sutta Nipâta I, 12, 1.
386, l. 12.	B.	Dhammapada 81.
386, l. 19.	B.	Dhammapada 404 (from SN. III, 9, 35).
386, l. 26.	Subhûti.	Not traced.
387, l. 8.	B.	Dhammapada 28.
387, l. 16.	Sister Subhaddâ.	Not traced.
388, l. 14.	B.	Magghima Nikâya (vol. i, p. 424).

INTRODUCTION. XXXV

The Pāli Text.		
p. 389, l. 9.	B.	Saṃyutta Nikāya XVI, 3.
390, l. 17.	Vaṅgîsa.	Not traced.
391, l. 6.	Subhûti.	,, ,,
391, l. 21.	B.	Dhammapada 350.
392, l. 3.	B.	Aṅguttara X, 5, 8.
392, l. 10.	B.	Not traced.
393, l. 3.	Vaṅgîsa.	,, ,,
393, l. 25.	B.	,, ,,
394, l. 6.	Upasena.	,, ,,
394, l. 16.	Upasena.	,, ,,
394, l. 28.	Sâriputta.	,, ,,
395, l. 9.	Mahâ Kassapa.	,, ,,
395, l. 22.	Upasena.	Thera-gâthâ 580.
396, l. 3.	B.	Magghima Nikâya (vol. i, p. 74).
396, l. 20.	Sâriputta.	Not traced.
397, l. 15.	Sâriputta.	,, ,,
398, l. 5.	Pindola.	,, ,,
399, l. 16.	B.	Saṃyutta Nikâya III, 5, 6 (vol. i, p. 73).
401, l. 10.	B.	Saṃyutta Nikâya XVI, 1, 3 (vol. ii, p. 194).
402, l. 8.	B.	Kakkavâka Gâtaka (vol. iv, p. 71; not in III, 520).
402, l. 26.	Brahmâ.	Saṃyutta Nikâya VI, 2, 4 (vol. i, p. 154 = Thera-gâthâ 142).
403, l. 13.	B.	Kulla-nârada Gâtaka (vol. iv, p. 223).
403, l. 27.	B.	Saṃyutta Nikâya (vol. iii, p. 125).
404, l. 12.	Pindola.	Not traced.
405, l. 3.	B.	Digha Nikâya XXX.
405, l. 22.	Anuruddha.	Not traced.
407, l. 1.	Sâriputta.	Thera-gâthâ 982, 3.
407, l. 20.	Anuruddha.	Not traced.
408, l. 8.	B.	Digha Nikâya XVI, 5, 24.
408, l. 22.	B.	Dhammapada 32.
409, l. 17.	B.	Saṃyutta Nikâya XIV, 16 (= Thera-gâthâ 148, 266).
410, l. 8.	Sâriputta.	Not traced [1].
411, l. 9.	Sâriputta.	,, ,,
411, l. 29.	B.	Sutta Nipâta II, 6, 10.

[1] That is, not in the Piṭakas. The stanza is found in the commentary on the Dhammapada Fausböll, p. 147, and also in Buddhaghosa's Papañca Sûdanî (see Trenckner's note)—each time with a variation at the close of the verse.

The Pâli Text.		
P. 412, l. 21.	Megharâga.	Not traced.
413, l. 6.	Rahula.	,, ,,
414, l. 1.	B.	Sutta Nipâta (not traced [1]).
414, l. 18.	B.	,, ,, III, 11, 43.
415, l. 14.	B.	Not traced.
416, l. 4.	Sâriputta.	,, ,,
416, l. 29.	Upâli.	,, ,,
417, l. 12.	B.	,, ,,
418, l. 1.	Moggallâna.	,, ,,
419, l. 11.	Sâriputta.	,, ,,

Now the Pâli Pi/akas consist of the following twenty-nine books:

Title.	No. of printed pages 8vo.	
1. The Sutta Vibhaṅga	617*	
2. The Khandhakas	668*	THE VINAYA PI/AKA.
a. Mahâvagga . 360		
b. K'ullavagga . 308		
3. The Parivâra	226*	
Total	1511*	
4. The Dîgha Nikâya	750	THE SUTTA PI/AKA. (The four great Nikâyas.)
5. The Magg/ima Nikâya	1000	
6. The Sa//yutta Nikâya	1250	
7. The Aṅguttara Nikâya	1500	
Total	4500	
8. The Khuddaka Pâ/ha	10*	THE KHUDDAKA NIKÂYA. (The repeaters of the Dîgha add these to the Sutta Pi/aka. The repeaters of the Magg/ima add them to the Abhidhamma Pi/aka.)
9. The Dhammapadas	40*	
10. The Udânas	80*	
11. The Iti-vuttakas	100*	
12. The Sutta Nipâta	200*	
13. The Vimâna Vatthu	85*	
14. The Peta Vatthu	90*	
15. The Thera-Gâthâ	100*	
16. The Therî-Gâthâ	35*	
17. The Gâtakas	70	
18. The Niddesa	300	
19. The Pa/isambhidâ	400	
20. The Apadânas	400	
21. The Buddha Vaṅsa	60*	
22. The K'ariyâ Pi/aka	30*	
Total	2000	

---

[1] Mr. Trenckner gives no reference, and I have searched through the Sutta Nipâta, which has no index, in vain.

23. The Dhamma Saṅgaṇi . .	260
24. The Vibhaṅga	325
25. The Kathâ Vatthu . . .	440
26. The Puggala Paññatti . .	75*
27. The Dhâtu Kathâ . . .	100
28. The Yamakas	400
29. The Paṭṭhâna	600
Total Abhidhamma . ——	2200
	10,211

} THE ABHIDHAMMA PIṬAKA.

This shows the total extent of the three Piṭakas to be about 10,000 pages 8vo. as printed, or to be printed, by the Pâli Text Society[1]. If our English Bible, in the older authorised version, were to be printed in the same manner and type and on the same size of page, it would occupy about 5,000 pages. So that the Buddhist Bible without its repetitions (some of which are very frequent, and others very long), would only occupy about double the space of the English Bible. This would not have been a literature too large to be familiarly known to our author. What is the conclusion which can fairly be drawn, from a comparison of the last list with those preceding it, as to his knowledge of those books now held, by living Buddhists, to be canonical?

The answer to this question will be of some importance for another reason beyond the help it will afford towards settling the date of the original 'Questions of Milinda.' As is well known, Asoka, in the only one of his edicts, addressed specially to the members of the Buddhist Order of mendicants, selects seven portions of the Buddhist Scriptures, which he mentions by name, and expresses his desire that not only the brethren and sisters of the Order, but also the laity, should constantly learn by heart and reflect upon those seven. Now not one of the seven titles which occur in the edict is identical with any of the twenty-nine in the last list. Whereupon certain Indianists have rejoiced at being able to score a point, as they think, against these

---

[1] This estimate excludes the space occupied by notes. The books marked with an asterisk in the foregoing list have already been printed.

unbrahmanical Buddhists, and have jumped to the conclusion that the Buddhist canon must be late and spurious; and that the Buddhism of Asoka's time must have been very different from the Buddhism of the Pâli Piṭakas. That would be much the same as if a Japanese scholar, at a time when he knew little or nothing of Christianity, except the names of the books in the Bible, were to have found an open letter of Constantine's in which he urges both the clergy and laity to look upon the Word of God as their only authority, and to constantly repeat and earnestly meditate upon the Psalm of the Shepherd, the words of Lemuel, the Prophecy of the Servant of the Lord, the Sermon on the Mount, the Exaltation of Charity, the Question of Nicodemus, and the story of the Prodigal Son—and that our Oriental critic should jump to the conclusion that the canonical books of the Christians could not have been known in the time of Constantine, and that the Christianity of Constantine was really quite different from, and much more simple than the Christianity of the Bible. As a matter of fact the existence of such a letter would prove very little, either way, as to the date of the books in the Bible as we now have them. If our Japanese scholar were to discover afterwards a Christian work, even much later than the time of Constantine, in which the canonical books of the Christians were both quoted and referred to, he would have much surer ground for a sounder historical criticism. And he would possibly come to see that the seven portions selected for special honour and commendation were not intended as an exhaustive list even of remarkable passages, much less for an exhaustive list of canonical books, but that the number seven was merely chosen in deference to the sacred character attaching to that number in the sacred literature.

Such a book is our Milinda. It is, as we have seen, later than the canonical books of the Pâli Piṭakas, and on the other hand, not only older than the great commentaries, but the only book, outside the canon, regarded in them as an authority which may be implicitly followed. And I venture to think that the most simple working hypothesis by which to explain the numerous and varied references and quotations it makes, as shown in the preceding lists, from the Pi/akas as a whole, and from the various books contained in them, is that the Pâli Pi/akas were known, in their entirety, and very nearly, if not quite, as we now have them, to our author. For out of the twenty-nine books of the Pi/akas, we find in the lists of works referred to by him the three Pi/akas as a whole, the Vinaya Pi/aka as a whole, and all of its component books except the Parivâra (which was composed in Ceylon), the Sutta Pi/aka and each of the four great Nikâyas, the Abhidhamma Pi/aka and each of its seven component books, and the Khuddaka Nikâya as a whole and several of its separate books. And when we further recollect the very large number of quotations appearing in my lists as not yet traced in the Pi/akas, we see the necessity of being very chary in drawing any argument ex silentio with respect to those books not occurring in the lists.

To sum up.—It may be said generally that while the Sutta Vibhaṅga and the Khandhakas, the four great Nikâyas, and the Abhidhamma were certainly known to our author, he very likely had no knowledge of the Parivâra; and it remains to be seen how far his knowledge of the Khuddaka Nikâya, which he happens to mention once [1] as a whole by name, did actually extend. At present it is only clear that he knew the Khuddaka Pâ/#a, the Dhammapada collection of sacred verses, the Sutta Nipâta, the Thera and Theri-gâthâ, the *G*âtakas, and the Kariyâ Pi/aka. I hope to return to this question in the Introduction to my second volume, only pointing out here that the doubtful books (those concerning which our author is apparently silent) would occupy about two thousand pages octavo, out of the ten thousand of which the three Pi/akas would, if printed, consist: and that those two thousand pages belong, for the most part, precisely to that part of the Pi/akas which have not yet been edited, so that there they may very likely, after all, be quoted in one or other

---

[1] Page 342 of the printed text.

of the numerous quotations entered as 'not traced' in my lists[1].

Such being the extent, so far as can at present be shown, of our author's knowledge of the three Piṭakas, the question arises as to the degree and accuracy of his knowledge. In the great majority of cases his quotations or references entirely agree with the readings shown by our texts. But there are a few exceptions. And as these are both interesting and instructive, it will be advisable to point them out in detail.

The reference to the Aviki Hell as being outside the earth, if not at variance with, is at least an addition to the teaching of the Piṭakas as to cosmogony[2]. But there is some reason to believe that the passage may be an interpolation, and the difference itself is not only doubtful but also of no particular importance.

The description of the contents of the Puggala Paññatti given in I, 26, does not really agree with the text. The book, in its first section, sets out six different sorts of discrimination or distinction. One paragraph only is devoted to each of the first five discriminations, and the author or authors then proceed, in the rest of the book, to deal with the details of the last of the six. Our author gives the six as the divisions of the book itself.

But I think it is clear that so far as the description is inaccurate, the error is due, not to any difference between the text as he had it and that which we now possess, but simply to our author laying too great a stress upon the opening paragraphs of the book.

In the reference to the Buddha's first sermon, the Foundation of the Kingdom of Righteousness (in I, 38), our author says that 'eighteen koṭis of Brahma gods, and an innumerable company of other gods, attained to compre-

---

[1] About half of the canonical books, besides a considerable number of the uncanonical works, have already been edited in the last few years, chiefly owing to the Pâli Text Society's labours.
[2] See the passages quoted in my note at p. 9.

hension of the truth.' There is no statement of the kind in the Pi*t*aka account of this event (see my translation in 'Buddhist Suttas,' pp. 146–155). But it is not inconsistent with the Pâli, and is doubtless added from some edifying commentary.

There is a difference of reading between the lines put into Sâriputta's mouth, at II, 2, 4, and those ascribed to Sâriputta in the Thera Gâthâ (1002, 1003). If the Milinda reading is not found in some hitherto unpublished passage, we have here a real case of divergence.

Perhaps the most important apparent variation between our author and the Pi*t*aka texts is the statement put by him, in IV, 4, 9, into the mouth of the Buddha, that a deliberate lie is one of the offences called Pârâ*g*ika, that is, involving exclusion from the Order. Now in the old Canon Law there are only four Pârâ*g*ika offences—breach of chastity, theft, murder, and a false claim to extraordinary spiritual powers (see my translation in vol. i, pp. 1–5 of the 'Vinaya Texts'); and falsehood is placed quite distinctly under another category, that of the Pâ*k*ittiyas, offences requiring repentance (see p. 32 of the same translation). If our author was a member of the Order, as he almost certainly was, it would seem almost incredible that he should make an error in a matter of such common knowledge, and of such vital importance, as the number and nature of the Pârâ*g*ikas. And indeed, in the immediate context, he refers to the Pâ*k*ittiya rule, though not in the exact words used in the text of the Pâtimokkha. I think that he must have known very well what he was talking about. And that a passage, not yet traced, will be found in the unpublished parts of the Pi*t*akas, in which the Buddha is made to say that falsehood is a Pârâ*g*ika—just as a Christian might maintain that falsehood is forbidden in the Ten Commandments, and yet be perfectly aware of the exact phraseology of the Ten Words.

In IV, 4, 26, our author identifies the learned pig in the Ta*kkh*a-sûkara *G*âtaka with the Bodisat. He differs here from the *G*âtaka Commentary, in which the Bodisat is identified with the tree-god, who acts as a kind of Greek chorus in the story. And the summaries in IV, 4, 28 of

Ruru *G*âtaka, and in IV, 4, 30 of the Sabba-dâ*th*a *G*âtaka, do not exactly agree with Professor Fausböll's text[1]. But the commentary is not the text; and it is well known that there are numerous such light variations in the different expansions of the verses, which latter alone form the actual text.

In IV, 4, 44 we find our author giving a version of a well-known incident in the Buddhist Gospel story different from the oldest version of it in the Pi*t*aka texts. This is another instance of an expansion of the original adopted from some unknown commentator, and does not argue an ignorance of the text as we have it.

I have noticed in the untranslated portion of our author, four or five cases of readings apparently different from the Pi*t*aka texts he refers to. These I hope to deal with in my next volume. But I may notice here that two stanzas, given on p. 414 of the text, and said on p. 413 to be 'in the Sutta Nipâta,' are not found in Professor Fausböll's edition of that work; and we have there, in all probability, another case of real divergence. But the reading in the Milinda may possibly be found to be incorrect.

The general result of this comparison, when we remember the very large number of passages quoted, will be held, I trust, to confirm the conclusion reached above, that our author knew the Pi*t*akas practically as we now have them, that is as they have been handed down in Ceylon.

Outside the Pi*t*akas there are unfortunately no references to actual books. But there are several references to countries and persons which are of importance, in as much as they show a knowledge in our author of places or occurrences not mentioned in the sacred books. It will be most convenient to arrange these passages first in an alphabetical list, and then to make a few remarks on the conclusions the list suggests. They are as follows:—

Name.	Page of the Pâli Text.
Anantakâya (Yonako)	29, 30.
Alasando (dîpo)	82, 327, 331, 359.
Asoka (dhamma-râ*g*â)	121.

[1] See my notes to the passages quoted.

INTRODUCTION. xliii

Name.	Page of the Páli Text.
Asokârâma (near Patna)	16, 17.
Assagutta (âyasmâ)	6, 7, 14.
Âyupâla (âyasmâ)	19.
Ûhâ (nadî)	70.
Kalasi (gâmo)	83.
Kasmîra (raṭṭhaṃ)	82, 327, 331.
Kola-paṭṭana (seaport)	359.
Gandhâra (raṭṭhaṃ)	327, 331.
Kandagutto (râgâ)	292.
Kîna (? China)	121, 327, 331, 359.
Takkola (? = Karkoṭa)	359.
Tissatthera (lekhâkariyo)	71.
Devamantiya (Yonako)	22–24, 29, 30.
Dhamma-rakkhita (âyasmâ)	16, 18.
Nikumba (raṭṭhaṃ)	327.
Bindumatî (gaṇikâ)	121.
Bhaddasâla (senâpati-putto)	292.
Bharukakkha (men of)	331.
Maṅkura (Yonako)	29, 30.
Madhura (nigamo)	331.
Yonakâ (the tribe)	1, 4, 20, 68.
Rakkhita-tala (in the Himâlayas)	6, 7, 12, 16.
Rohaṇa (âyasmâ)	7, 10.
Vaṅga (Bengal)	359.
Vattaniya (senâsanaṃ)	10, 12, 14–16.
Vigamba-vatthu (senâsanaṃ)	12.
Vilâta (raṭṭhaṃ)	327, 331.
Saka-yavana (the countries of)	327, 331.
Saṅkheyya (parivenaṃ)	19, 22.
Sabbadinna or Dinna (Yonako)	29, 56.
Sâgala (nagaraṃ)	1, 3, 5, 14, 22.
Suraṭṭha (nigamo)	359, men of, 331.
Suvaṇṇa-bhûmi (? Burma)	359.
Somuttara (brâhmaṇo)	9.

It will be noticed that the only names of persons, besides those occurring in the story itself, are, in one passage, Asoka and Bindumatî the courtesan, and in another Kandragupta and Bhaddasâla who fought against him. Of places, besides those in the story, we have a considerable number of names referring to the Panjâb, and adjacent countries: and besides these the names only of a few places or countries on the sea coast. The island Alasanda in the Indus, and the town of Kalasi situated in that island, have been discussed above. The country of the Sakas and Yavanas, Gandhâra, Kashmîr, Bharuka*kkh*a, Surat, and Madhura, explain themselves. Nikumba and Vilâta were probably in the same neighbourhood, but these names have not been met with elsewhere, and I can suggest no identification of them. The places on the sea coast, to which a merchant ship could sail, mentioned on p. 359, are mostly well known. Kolapattana must, I think, be some place on the Koromandel coast, and Suva*nn*a-bhûmi be meant for the seaboard of Burma and Siam. The author mentions no places in the interior south of the Ganges.

At four places he gives lists of famous rivers. In three out of the four he simply repeats the list of five—Gaṅgâ, Yamunâ, A*k*iravatî, Sarabhû, and Mahî—so often enumerated together in the Pi*t*akas[1]. In the fourth passage (p. 114) he adds five others—the Sindhu, the Sarassatî, the Vetravatî, the Vita*ms*â, and the *K*andabhâgâ. Of these the first two are well known. Professor Eduard Müller suggests[2] that the Vita*ms*â is the same as the Vitastâ (the Hydaspes of the Greeks and the modern Bihat). The Vetravatî is one of the principal affluents of the Jumna; and the *K*andrabhâgâ rises in the North-West Himâlayas, and is not unfrequently referred to as the Asiknî of the Vedas, the Akesines of the Greek geographers, the modern Kinâb[3].

The list is meagre enough. An ethical treatise is scarcely the place to look for much geographical or historical matter. But unless our author deliberately concealed his knowledge, and made all the remarks he put into the mouth of Nâgasena correspond with what that teacher might fairly be expected to have known, the whole list points to the definite conclusion that the writer of the 'Questions of Milinda' resided in the far North-West of

---

[1] See pp. 70, 87, 380 of the Pâli text.
[2] 'Journal of the Pâli Text Society,' 1888, p. 87.
[3] See Lassen, 'Indische Alterthumskunde,' vol. i, p. 43 (first edition, p. 55 of the second edition), and the passages there quoted.

India, or in the Panjâb itself. And this is confirmed by the great improbability of any memory of Menander having survived elsewhere, and more especially in Ceylon, where we should naturally look for our author's residence if he did not live in the region thus suggested.

As my space is here limited, I postpone to the next volume the discussion as to how far the knowledge displayed by our author, the conditions of society with which he shows himself acquainted, and the religious beliefs he gives utterance to, afford evidence of his date. I will only say here that on all these points his work shows clear signs of being later than the Pi/aka texts. And in the present state of our knowledge, or rather of our ignorance, of Pâli, there is very little to be drawn from the language used by our author. In the first place we do not know for certain whether we have the original before us, or a translation from the Sanskrit or from some Northern dialect. And if, as is probably the case, we have a translation, it would be very difficult to say whether any peculiarity we may find in it is really due to the translator, or to the original author. No doubt a translator, finding in his original a word not existing in Pâli, but formed according to rules of derivation obtaining in Pâli, would coin the corresponding Pâli form. And in doing so he might very likely be led into mistake, if his original were Prakrit, by misunderstanding the derivation of the Prakrit word before him. Childers in comparing Buddhist Sanskrit with Pâli, has pointed out several cases where such mistakes have occurred, and has supposed that in every case the Sanskrit translator misunderstood a Pâli word before him[1]. As I have suggested elsewhere it is, to say the least, quite as likely that the Sanskrit Buddhist texts are often founded on older works, not in Pâli, but in some other Prakrit[2]. And it may be possible hereafter to form some opinion as to what that dialect was which the Sanskrit writers must have had be-

---

[1] See the articles in his 'Pâli Dictionary,' referred to under note 3, p. xi of the Introduction.
[2] See the note on pp. 178, 179 of my 'Buddhist Suttas.'

fore them, to lead them into the particular blunders they have made. In the same way an argument may be drawn from the words found exclusively in Milinda as to the dialect which he spoke, and in which he probably wrote. A list of the words our author uses, and not found in the Pitakas, can only be tentative, as we have not as yet the whole of the Pitaka texts in print. But it will be useful, even now, to give the following imperfect list of such as I have noted in my copy of Childers' 'Dictionary.'

Word.	Page of the Pâli Text.	Note.
Âlaka	418	See 'Journal,' 1886, p. 158.
Anekamsikatâ	93	,, ,, ,, p. 123.
Ânâpako	147	Peon, officer.
Anîkattha	234	Sentinel.
Anughâyati	343	Trace by smell.
Anuparivattati	204, 253, 307	Turn towards.
Antobhaviko	95	'Journal,' 1886, p. 124.
Âvapana	279	,, ,, p. 157.
Asipâsâ	191	A caste so called.
Anupeseti	31, 36	Send after.
Âsâdaniyam	205	Injury.
Atonâ [1]	191	Professional beggars.
Âyûhito	181	Busy.
Âyûhako	207	Busy.
Bhaddiputtâ [2]	191	} A caste so called.
Bhattiputtâ	133	
Bhavatîha	92, 93, 342	Introducing verses.
Kandakanta	118	A kind of gem.
Kavaka	156, 200	Wretch.
Dhamadhamâyati	117	To blow.
Ekâniko	402	On the one true path.
Ghanikâ	191	Musicians.
Gilânako	74	A sick man, a patient.
Hiriyati	171	Is made afraid of sin.
Issatthako	419	Archer.
Galûpikâ	407	Leech.
Kali-devatâ	191	Worshippers of Kali.
Katumika	78, 79	Reminding.
Kummiga	346	Animal.

[1] Hînati-kumburê (p. 252) reads anânayo.
[2] The Simhalese has bhaddiputrayo.

INTRODUCTION. xlvii

Name.	Page of the Pâli Text.	Note.
anaka	377	Anchor.
ka	137, 242, 256, 362	Epithet of the Nikâyas.
ghako	34, 191, 331	Tumbler.
haniyo	172	Sharp (of medicine).
nkata	384	Done by me.
thayati	173	Churn.
ibhaddâ	191	A caste so called.
hâyiko	201	(?) Farmer.
âka	105	The weapon so called.
vâmaka	194, 376	Pilot.
ssa	210	Rudely.
batâ	191	A caste so called.
khanno	144, 390	Lost, fallen.
maggakâ	343	Touchers of.
mutti	112	Release.
rañgita	75	Marked over.
sanha	198	Subtle.
yoga[1]	118	Cauldron.
sallîyati	139	To be secluded.
sîsaka	90	Chignon.
âhikâ	402	A bird so called.
ka	18, &c.	See my note to p. 28.
sati	43	Compound (a medicine).
ani[2]	85	Cubit.
kika	226	True.
âyiko	22	Learned in doctrine.
âna	147	Dog.
nyathâ	1	See Trenckner's 'Pâli Miscellany,' p. 55.
ila	62	Gong.
chako	90	Who knows the Pitakas.
hadeti	241 (see 315)	Perfume the body.
ana	32	Synthesis.
alati	143	Revoke.
arama	41, 44	Cessation.
gâdharo	153, 200	Magician.
âvakaro	43, 400 and foll.	See my note on p. 68.
gin	2, 400 foll.	Ascetic.

[1] This word has been found in the Pitakas (e.g. Maggḥima I, 480) in the e of 'practice.'
[2] The Pitaka form is ratana.

This list might be considerably extended if words were included which differ from those used in the Pi*t*akas only by the addition of well-known suffixes or prefixes—such, for instance, as viparivattati, at p. 117, only found as yet elsewhere in the Tela Ka*t*âha Gâthâ, verse 37. But such words are really only a further utilisation of the existing resources of the language, and would afford little or no ground for argument as to the time and place at which our author wrote. I have thought it best, therefore, to omit them, at least at present.

If we turn from isolated words to the evidence of style it will be acknowledged by every reader that the Milinda has a marked style of its own, different alike from the formal exactness of most of the Pi*t*aka texts, and from the later manner of any other Pâli or Sanskrit-Buddhist authors as yet published. It is no doubt the charm of its style which has been one of the principal reasons for the great popularity of the book. Even a reader who takes no interest in the points that are raised, or in the method in which the questions are discussed, will be able, I trust, to see, even through the dark veil of a lame and wooden translation, what the merits of the original must be. And to a devout Buddhist, in whose eyes the book he was reading offered a correct solution of the most serious difficulties in religion, of the deepest problems of life,—to whose whole intellectual training and sympathies the way in which the puzzles are put, and solved, so exactly appealed,—to such a reader both the easy grace of the opening dialogue, as of a ship sailing in calm waters, and the real eloquence of occasional passages, more especially of the perorations by which the solutions are sometimes closed, must have been a continual feast. I venture to think that the 'Questions of Milinda' is undoubtedly the master-piece of Indian prose; and indeed is the best book of its class, from a literary point of view, that had then been produced in any country. Limits of space prevent the discussion of this last proposition, however interesting: and it would be, no doubt, difficult to prove that anything from India was better than the corresponding thing produced by our noble selves, or by those whose Karma we inherit. But in ancient Indian literature there are only two or three works which can at all compare with it. It ought not to seem odd that these also are Buddhist and Pâli; that is, that they come from the same school. And while the Dîgha Nikâya may be held to excel it in stately dignity, the Visuddhi Magga in sustained power, and the *G*âtaka book in varied humour, the palm will probably be eventually given to the 'Questions of Milinda' as a work of art.

I am aware that this conclusion is entirely at variance with the often repeated depreciation of Buddhist literature. But the fact is that this depreciation rests upon ignorance, and is supported by prejudice. As a critical judgment it will not survive the publication and translation of those great Buddhist works which it overlooks or ignores. Some Sanskrit scholars, familiar with the Brahmin estimate of matters Indian, and filled with a very rational and proper admiration for the many fine qualities which the old Brahmins possessed, may find it hard to recognise the merits of sectarian works written in dialects which violate their most cherished laws of speech. But the historical student of the evolution of thought, and of the rise of literature in India, will more and more look upon the question as a whole, and will estimate at its right value all Indian work, irrespective of dialect or creed.

T. W. RHYS DAVIDS.

Temple,
    August, 1889.

THE QUESTIONS

OF

KING MILINDA.

THE QUESTIONS
OF
KING MILINDA.

Reverence be to the Blessed One, the
Arahat, the Sammâ-sambuddha.

BOOK I.

THE SECULAR NARRATIVE [1].

1. King Milinda, at Sâgala the famous town of yore,
To Nâgasena, the world famous sage, repaired.
(So the deep Ganges to the deeper ocean flows.)
To him, the eloquent, the bearer of the torch
Of Truth, dispeller of the darkness of men's minds,
Subtle and knotty questions did he put, many,
Turning on many points. Then were solutions given
Profound in meaning, gaining access to the heart,
Sweet to the ear, and passing wonderful and strange.
For Nâgasena's talk plunged to the hidden depths
Of Vinaya and of Abhidhamma (Law and Thought)

---

[1] Bâhira-kathâ, literally 'outside talk;' so called in contradistinction to the religious character of the subjects treated of in the remaining books.

Unravelling all the meshes of the Suttas' net,
Glittering the while with metaphors and reasoning high.
Come then! Apply your minds, and let your hearts rejoice,
And hearken to these subtle questionings, all grounds
Of doubt well fitted to resolve.

---

2. Thus hath it been handed down by tradition—There is in the country of the Yonakas [1] a great centre of trade [2], a city that is called Sâgala, situate in a delightful country well watered and hilly, abounding in parks and gardens and groves and lakes and tanks, a paradise of rivers and mountains and woods. Wise architects have laid it out [3], and its people know of no oppression, since all their enemies and adversaries have been put down. Brave is its defence, with many and various strong towers and ramparts, with superb gates and entrance archways; and with the royal citadel in its midst, white walled and deeply moated. Well laid out are its streets, squares, cross roads, and market places [4]. Well displayed are the innumerable sorts of costly merchandise [2] with which its shops are filled. It is richly adorned with hundreds of alms-

---

[1] That is Ionians, the Pâli word for Baktrian Greeks.

[2] Nânâ-pu/a-bhedana*m*, literally 'the distributing place of parcels of merchandise of many kinds.' Trenckner renders it 'surrounded with a number of dependent towns,' but surely entrepôt is the idea suggested.

[3] Sutavanta-nimmitam; which Trenckner renders 'pious are its people.' But I prefer the Si*m*halese interpretation.

[4] This list recurs at pp. 34, 330 of the text. See below, p. 53.

halls of various kinds ; and splendid with hundreds of thousands of magnificent mansions, which rise aloft like the mountain peaks of the Himâlayas. Its streets are filled with elephants, horses, carriages, and foot-passengers, frequented by groups of handsome men and beautiful women, and crowded by men of all sorts and conditions, Brahmans, nobles, artificers, and servants. They resound with cries of welcome to the teachers of every creed, and the city is the resort of the leading men of each of the differing sects. Shops are there for the sale of Benares muslin, of Ko/umbara stuffs [1], and of other cloths of various kinds ; and sweet odours are exhaled from the bazaars, where all sorts of flowers and perfumes are tastefully set out. Jewels are there in plenty, such as men's hearts desire, and guilds of traders in all sorts of finery display their goods in the bazaars that face all quarters of the sky. So full is the city of money, and of gold and silver ware, of copper and stone ware, that it is a very mine of dazzling treasures. And there is laid up there much store of property and corn and things of value in warehouses—foods and drinks of every sort, syrups and sweetmeats of every kind. In wealth it rivals Uttara-kuru, and in glory it is as Â/akamandâ, the city of the gods [2].

3. Having said thus much we must now relate the previous birth history of these two persons (Milinda

---

[1] It is worth noting, as there is a doubt about the spelling, that Hîna/i-kumburê reads Ko/umbara, not Kodumbara.

[2] Here follow in Hîna/i-kumburê's version two pages of introductory matter, explaining how he came to undertake his translation.

and Nâgasena) and the various sorts of puzzles[1]. This we shall do under six heads:—
1. Their previous history (Pubba-yoga).
2. The Milinda problems.
3. Questions as to distinguishing characteristics.
4. Puzzles arising out of contradictory statements.
5. Puzzles arising out of ambiguity.
6. Discussions turning on metaphor.

And of these the Milinda problems are in two divisions—questions as to distinctive characteristics, and questions aiming at the dispelling of doubt; and the puzzles arising out of contradictory statements are in two divisions—the long chapter, and the problems in the life of the recluse.

THEIR PREVIOUS HISTORY (PUBBA-YOGA).

4. By Pubba-yoga is meant their past Karma (their doings in this or previous lives). Long ago, they say, when Kassapa the Buddha was promulgating the faith, there dwelt in one community near the Ganges a great company of members of the Order. There the brethren, true to established rules and duties, rose early in the morning, and taking the long-handled brooms, would sweep out the courtyard and collect the rubbish into a heap, meditating the while on the virtues of the Buddha.

5. One day a brother told a novice to remove the heap of dust. But he, as if he heard not, went about his business; and on being called a second time, and a third, still went his way as if he had not heard. Then the brother, angry with so intractable a novice, dealt him a blow with the broom stick.

---

[1] These six words are added from Hînaṭi-kumburê.

[3] This time, not daring to refuse, he set about the task crying; and as he did so he muttered to himself this first aspiration: 'May I, by reason of this meritorious act of throwing out the rubbish, in each successive condition in which I may be born up to the time when I attain Nirvâna, be powerful and glorious as the midday sun!'

6. When he had finished his work he went to the river side to bathe, and on beholding the mighty billows of the Ganges seething and surging, he uttered this second aspiration: 'May I, in each successive condition in which I may be born till I attain Nirvâna, possess the power of saying the right thing, and saying it instantly, under any circumstance that may arise, carrying all before me like this mighty surge!'

7. Now that brother, after he had put the broom away in the broom closet, had likewise wandered down to the river side to bathe, and as he walked he happened to overhear what the novice had said. Then thinking: 'If this fellow, on the ground of such an act of merit, which after all was instigated by me, can harbour hopes like this, what may not I attain to?' he too made his wish, and it was thus: 'In each successive condition in which I may be born till I attain Nirvâna, may I too be ready in saying the right thing at once, and more especially may I have the power of unravelling and of solving each problem and each puzzling question this young man may put—carrying all before me like this mighty surge!'

8. Then for the whole period between one Buddha and the next these two people wandered from existence to existence among gods and men. And our Buddha saw them too, and just as he did

to the son of Moggalî and to Tissa the Elder, so to them also did he foretell their future fate, saying: 'Five hundred years after I have passed away will these two reappear, and the subtle Law and Doctrine taught by me will they two explain, unravelling and disentangling its difficulties by questions put and metaphors adduced.'

9. Of the two the novice became the king of the city of Sâgala in India, Milinda by name, learned, eloquent, wise, and able; and a faithful observer, and that at the right time, of all the various acts of devotion and ceremony enjoined by his own sacred hymns concerning things past, present, and to come. Many were the arts and sciences he knew— holy tradition and secular law; the Sânkhya, Yoga, Nyâya, and Vai*s*eshika systems of philosophy; arithmetic; music; medicine; the four Vedas, the Purâ*n*as, and the Itihâsas; astronomy, magic, causation[1], and spells; the art of war; poetry; conveyancing[2]— in a word, the whole nineteen[3].

[4] As a disputant he was hard to equal, harder

---

[1] Hetu, literally 'cause.' Trenckner has 'logic (?);' Hina*t*i-kumburê repeats the word.

[2] Muddâ, literally 'seal-ring.' The meaning of the term (which recurs in similar lists at Dîgha I, 1, 25; I, 2, 14; and below, p. 59 of the text) is quite clear, but the exact details of the 'art' are unknown. I follow Buddhaghosa's comment on those passages. Trenckner leaves the word untranslated, and Hîna*t*i-kumburê says, 'Ængillen œl-wîma,' that is, 'adhering with the finger,' which I do not understand, unless it means the sealing of a document. At IV, 3, 25, the context makes it probable that 'law of property' would be the best rendering.

[3] The number of the Sippas (Arts and Sciences) is usually given as eighteen. In the *G*âtaka (p. 58, l. 29, Professor Fausböll's edition) it is twelve.

still to overcome ; the acknowledged superior of all the founders of the various schools of thought. And as in wisdom so in strength of body, swiftness, and valour there was found none equal to Milinda in all India. He was rich too, mighty in wealth and prosperity, and the number of his armed hosts knew no end.

10. Now one day Milinda the king proceeded forth out of the city to pass in review the innumerable host of his mighty army in its fourfold array (of elephants, cavalry, bowmen, and soldiers on foot). And when the numbering of the forces was over, the king, who was fond of wordy disputation, and eager for discussion with casuists, sophists[1], and gentry of that sort, looked at the sun (to ascertain the time), and then said to his ministers: 'The day is yet young. What would be the use of getting back to town so early ? Is there no learned person, whether wandering teacher[2] or Brahman, the head of some school or order, or the master of some band of pupils (even though he profess faith

---

[1] Lokâyatas and Vita*nd*as. Other Pâli passages, where they are mentioned, are *K*ullavagga V, 3, 2 ; Aṅguttara III, 58, 1; Sumaṅgala Vilâsinî, 96, 247 ; and below, § 22 (p. 17). See also Weber, 'Bhagavatî,' II, 246 ; Muir, 'Sanskrit Texts,' III, 95 ; Deussen, 'Das Vedânta-System,' 310.

[2] Sama*n*a. There is no expression in English corresponding to this common word in Pâli texts. It means any ' religious ' (in the technical meaning of that word) who is not a recluse according to the orthodox Brahman rules. It includes therefore many who were not Buddhists, and also even Brahmans if they had joined the Buddhists or *G*ains, or any other of the non-conforming bodies. The Sama*n*as remained in one place during the rains, and for the rest of the year wandered from place to place, promulgating their particular views. They were not necessarily ascetics in any strict use of that term ; though they were usually celibates.

in the Arahat, the Supreme Buddha), who would be able to talk with me, and resolve my doubts?'

11. Thereupon the five hundred Yonakas said to Milinda the king: 'There are the six Masters, O king!—Pûra*n*a Kassapa, Makkhali of the cowshed[1], the Niga*nth*a of the Nâta clan, Sa*ñ*gaya the son of the Bela*tth*a woman, A*g*ita of the garment of hair, and Pakudha Ka*kk*âyana. These are well known as famous founders of schools, followed by bands of disciples and hearers, and highly honoured by the people. Go, great king! put to them your problems, and have your doubts resolved[2].'

12. So king Milinda, attended by the five hundred Yonakas, mounted the royal car with its splendid equipage, and went out to the dwelling-place of Pûra*n*a Kassapa, exchanged with him the compliments of friendly greeting, and took his seat courteously apart. And thus sitting he said to

---

[1] So called because he was said to have been born in a cowshed. See the Sumangala, p. 143. All these six teachers were contemporaries of the Buddha, and lived therefore about five hundred years before Milinda.

[2] All this is a mere echo of the opening paragraphs in the Sâma*ññ*a-phala (D. 2), where A*g*âtasattu is described as visiting these six famous sophists. And the plagiarism is all the more inartistic as the old names are retained, and no explanation is given of their being born twice at an interval of five hundred years. One may indeed ask what is a glaring anachronism to our good Buddhist romancer compared with the advantage of introducing the stock-names when he has to talk of heretics? But the whole book is so full of literary skill, that it is at least strange that its author should have made this blunder; and there are other reasons for thinking the whole episode an interpolation. (See note on §§ 13, 15.) So that probably our § 15 came originally immediately after § 10, and then (after the episode in §§ 15–36) § 37 takes up the narrative interrupted at the end of § 10.

him: 'Who is it, venerable Kassapa, who rules the world?'

'The Earth, great king, rules the world!'

'But, venerable Kassapa, if it be the Earth that rules the world, how comes it that some men go to the Aviki hell[1], thus getting outside the sphere of the Earth?' [5]

When he had thus spoken, neither could Puraṇa Kassapa swallow the puzzle, nor could he bring it up; crestfallen, driven to silence, and moody[2], there he sat.

13. Then Milinda the king said to Makkhali of the cowshed[3]: 'Are there, venerable Gosâla, good and evil acts? Is there such a thing as fruit, ultimate result, of good and evil acts?'

'There are no such acts, O king; and no such fruit, or ultimate result. Those who here in the world are nobles, they, O king, when they go to the

---

[1] Aviki (probably 'the Waveless'). The mention of this particular hell as being outside the earth is noteworthy. One would expect to find the Lokântarika hell so described. Spence Hardy indeed goes so far as to say that the Aviki is seven hundred miles directly under the great Bo Tree at Budh Gâyâ (Manual, p. 26), which would be within the sphere of the earth. But there is nothing in the Pâli texts yet published as to its position. See Kullavagga VII, 4, 8; Anguttara III, 56; Gâtaka I, 71, 96; Pañka Gati Dîpana, 20. There is a list of the hells at Sutta Nipâta III, 10, but the Aviki is not one of them. This blunder, improbable in a writer so learned as our author elsewhere shows himself, is another reason for thinking these sections to be an interpolation.

[2] Pattakkhando pagghâyanto. See my note on Kullavagga IV, 4, 7, and compare Anguttara III, 73, 4.

[3] This, again, is most clumsy, as the rival teachers must have dwelt far apart. And it will be seen that, notwithstanding the parade of the six names at the beginning of this episode, the remaining four are no further mentioned.

other world, will become nobles once more. And those who are Brahmans, or of the middle class, or workpeople, or outcasts here, will in the next world become the same. What then is the use of good or evil acts[1]?'

'If, venerable Gosâla, it be as you say then, by parity of reasoning, those who, here in this world, have a hand cut off, must in the next world become persons with a hand cut off, and in like manner those who have had a foot cut off or an ear or their nose!'

And at this saying Makkhali was silenced.

14. Then thought Milinda the king within himself[2]: 'All India is an empty thing, it is verily like chaff! There is no one, either recluse or Brahman, capable of discussing things with me, and dispelling my doubts.' And he said to his ministers: 'Beautiful is the night and pleasant! Who is the recluse or Brahman we can visit to-night to question him, who will be able to converse with us and dispel our doubts[3]?' And at that saying the counsellors remained silent, and stood there gazing upon the face of the king.

15. Now at that time the city of Sâgala had for twelve years been devoid of learned men, whether Brahmans, Samaṇas, or laymen. But wherever the king heard that such persons dwelt, thither he would

---

[1] This is quite in accord with the opinions attributed to Makkhali Gosâla in the Sâmañña-phala (D. 2, 20), and in the Sumaṅgala Vilâsinî on it (see especially p. 166).

[2] See below, p. 30.

[3] This is an echo of the words in the corresponding passage of the Sâmañña-phala Sutta (D. 2, 1).

go and put his questions to them [1]. [6] But they all alike, being unable to satisfy the king by their solution of his problems, departed hither and thither, or if they did not leave for some other place, were at all events reduced to silence. And the brethren of the Order went, for the most part, to the Himâlaya mountains.

16. Now at that time there dwelt, in the mountain region of the Himâlayas, on the Guarded Slope, an innumerable company of Arahats (brethren who, while yet alive, had attained Nirvâna). And the venerable Assagutta, by means of his divine power of hearing, heard those words of king Milinda. And he convened an assembly of the Order on the summit of the Yugandhara mountain, and asked the brethren: 'Is there any member of the Order able to hold converse with Milinda the king, and resolve his doubts?'

Then were they all silent. And a second and a third time he put the same question to them, and still none of all the number spake. Then he said to the assembled Order: 'There is, reverend Sirs, in the heaven of the Thirty-three [2], and east of the Vegayanta palace, a mansion called Ketumatî, wherein dwells the god Mahâsena. He is able to hold converse with Milinda the king, and to resolve his doubts.' And the innumerable company of

---

[1] This paragraph is so unnecessary after what has been said in the preceding episode, and at the same time so contradictory to the fact of two teachers at least living in or near the city, that it would really seem probable that it (or perhaps § 14) came originally directly after § 10, the rest being an interpolation, and a clumsy one.

[2] These are the principal gods of the Vedic pantheon.

Arahats vanished from the summit of the Yugandhara mountain, and appeared in the heaven of the Thirty-three.

17. And Sakka, the king of the gods, beheld those brethren of the Order as they were coming from afar. And at the sight of them he went up to the venerable Assagutta, and bowed down before him, and stood reverently aside. And so standing he said to him: 'Great, reverend Sir, is the company of the brethren that has come. What is it that they want? I am at the service of the Order. What can I do for you?'

And the venerable Assagutta replied: 'There is, O king, in India, in the city of Sâgala, a king named Milinda. As a disputant he is hard to equal, harder still to overcome, he is the acknowledged superior of all the founders of the various schools of thought. He is in the habit of visiting the members of the Order and harassing them by questions of speculative import.'

Then said Sakka, the king of the gods, to him: 'That same king Milinda, venerable one, left this condition to be born as a man. And there dwells in the mansion Ketumatî a god, Mahâsena by name, who is able to hold converse with him and to resolve his doubts. [7] That god we will beseech to suffer himself to be reborn into the world of men.'

18. So Sakka, the king of the gods, preceded by the Order, entered the Ketumatî mansion; and when he had embraced Mahâsena the god, he said to him: 'The Order of the brethren, Lord, makes this request of you—to be reborn into the world of men.'

'I have no desire, Sir, for the world of men, so overladen with action (Karma). Hard is life as a man. It is here, Sir, in the world of the gods that, being reborn in ever higher and higher spheres, I hope to pass away!'

And a second and a third time did Sakka, the king of the gods, make the same request, and the reply was still the same. Then the venerable Assagutta addressed Mahâsena the god, and said: 'On passing in review, Lord, the worlds of gods and men, there is none but thee that we find able to succour the faith by refuting the heretical views of Milinda the king. The whole Order beseeches thee, Lord, saying: "Condescend, O worthy one, to be reborn among men, in order to lend to the religion of the Blessed One thy powerful aid."'

Then was Mahâsena the god overjoyed and delighted in heart at the thought that he would be able to help the faith by refuting the heresy of Milinda; and he gave them his word, and said: 'Very well then, venerable ones, I consent to be reborn in the world of men.'

19. Then the brethren, having thus accomplished the task they had taken in hand, vanished from the heaven of the Thirty-three, and reappeared on the Guarded Slope in the Himâlaya mountains. And the venerable Assagutta addressed the Order, and said: 'Is there, venerable ones, any brother belonging to this company of the Order, who has not appeared in the assembly?'

Thereupon a certain brother said there was, that Rohana had a week previously gone into the mountains, and become buried in meditation, [8] and suggested that a messenger should be sent to him. And at that very moment the venerable Rohana aroused himself from his meditation, and was aware that the Order was expecting him [1]. And vanishing from the mountain top, he appeared in the presence of the innumerable company of the brethren.

And the venerable Assagutta said to him: 'How now, venerable Rohana! When the religion of the Buddha is in danger of crumbling away, have you no eyes for the work of the Order?'

'It was through inadvertence, Sir,' said he.

'Then, venerable Rohana, atone for it.'

'What, Sir, should I do?'

'There is a Brahman village, venerable Rohana, called Kagangala [2], at the foot of the Himâlaya mountains, and there dwells there a Brahman called Sonuttara. He will have a son called Nâgasena. Go to that house for alms during seven years and ten months. After the lapse of that time thou shalt draw away the boy from a worldly life, and cause him to enter the Order. When he shall have abandoned the world, then shalt thou be free of the atonement for thy fault.'

'Let it be even as thou sayest,' said the venerable Rohana in assent.

20. Now Mahâsena the god passed away from the world of the gods, and was reborn in the womb of the wife of the Brahman Sonuttara. And at the moment of his conception three strange, wonderful things took place:—arms and weapons became all

---

[1] Patimâneti. Childers does not give this meaning to the word. But it is the usual one. Compare Sumangala, vol. i, pp. 276, 280; Vinaya Pitaka IV, 212; Kullavagga VI, 13, 2; Gâtaka II, 423.

[2] This is a famous place in Buddhist story. It is at the extreme limit, to the East, of the Buddhist Holy Land, the 'Middle Country.' See Sumangala Vilâsinî on D. 2, 40 (p. 173); Mahâvagga V, 13, 12; Gâtaka I, 49.

ablaze, the tender grain became ripe in a moment, and there was a great rain (in the time of drought). And the venerable Rohana went to that house for alms for seven years and ten months from the day of Mahâsena's re-incarnation, but never once did he receive so much as a spoonful of boiled rice, or a ladleful of sour gruel, or a greeting, or a stretching forth of the joined hands, or any sort of salutation. Nay rather it was insults and taunts that fell to his share: and there was no one who so much as said, 'Be so good, Sir, as to go on to the next house[1].'

But when all that period had gone by he one day happened to have those very words addressed to him. And on that day the Brahman, on his way back from his work in the fields, [9] saw the Elder as he met him on his return, and said: 'Well, hermit, have you been to our place?'

'Yes, Brahman, I have.'

'But did you get anything there?'

'Yes, Brahman, I did.'

And he was displeased at this, and went on home, and asked them: 'Did you give anything to that hermit?'

'We gave him nothing,' was the reply.

21. Thereupon the Brahman, the next day, seated himself right in the doorway, thinking to himself: 'To-day I'll put that hermit to shame for having told a lie.' And the moment that the Elder in due course came up to the house again, he said: 'Yesterday you said you had got something at my house, having

---

[1] This is the ordinary polite formula used by an Indian peasant when he wishes to express his inability (or his disinclination) to give food to a mendicant friar.

all the while got nothing! Is lying allowed to you fellows?'

And the Elder replied: 'Brahman, for seven years and ten months no one even went so far as to suggest politely that I should pass on. Yesterday this courtesy was extended to me. It was to that that I referred.'

The Brahman thought to himself: 'If these men, at the mere experience of a little courtesy, acknowledge in a public place, and with thanks, that they have received an alms, what will they not do if they really receive a gift!' And he was much struck by this, and had an alms bestowed upon the Elder from the rice and curry prepared for his own use, and added furthermore: 'Every day you shall receive here food of the same kind.' And having watched the Elder as he visited the place from that day onwards, and noticed how subdued was his demeanour, he became more and more pleased with him, and invited him to take there regularly his midday meal. And the Elder gave, by silence, his consent; and daily from that time forth, when he had finished his meal, and was about to depart, he would pronounce some short passage or other from the words of the Buddha[1].

22. Now the Brahman's wife had, after her ten months, brought forth her son; and they called his name Nâgasena. He grew up in due course till he became seven years old, and his father said to the child: 'Do you want, [10] dear Nâgasena, to study the learning traditional in this Brahmanical house of ours?'

---

[1] This custom is a rule with the mendicant friars. It is their way of 'returning thanks,' as we should say. See below, p. 25.

'What is it called, father?' said he.

'The three Vedas are called learning (Sikkhâ), other kinds of knowledge are only arts, my dear.'

'Yes, I should like to learn them, father,' said the boy.

Then So*n*uttara the Brahman gave to a Brahman teacher a thousand pieces as his teaching fee, and had a divan spread for him aside in an inner chamber, and said to him: 'Do thou, Brahman, teach this boy the sacred hymns by heart.'

So the teacher made the boy repeat the hymns, urging him to get them by heart. And young Nâgasena, after one repetition of them, had learnt the three Vedas by heart, could intone them correctly, had understood their meaning, could fix the right place of each particular verse[1], and had grasped the mysteries they contained[2]. All at once there arose in him an intuitive insight into the Vedas, with a knowledge of their lexicography, of their prosody, of their grammar, and of the legends attaching to the characters in them. He became a philologist and grammarian, and skilled alike in casuistry and in the knowledge of the bodily marks that foreshadow the greatness of a man[3].

23. Then young Nâgasena said to his father: 'Is

---

[1] Suvava*tth*âpitâ, or perhaps its use in ceremonies or sacrifices. The phrase only occurs in this passage. It is literally, 'The three Vedas were well fixed by the boy.' Hîna*t*i-kumburê simply repeats the word.

[2] On the exact force of the special terms translated in these clauses, one may further compare the corresponding phrases used of learning the Buddhist texts in *K*ullavagga IV, 14, 17; IX, 5, 1.

[3] The above are the stock phrases for the learning of a scholarly Brahman, and one or two points in the details are uncertain.

there anything more to be learned in this Brahmanical family of ours, or is this all?'

'There is no more, Nâgasena, my dear. This is all,' was the reply.

And young Nâgasena repeated his lesson to his teacher for the last time, and went out of the house, and in obedience to an impulse arising in his heart as the result of previous Karma, sought a place of solitude, where he gave himself up to meditation. And he reviewed what he had learnt throughout from beginning to end, and found no value in it anywhere at all. And he exclaimed in bitterness of soul: 'Empty forsooth are these Vedas, and as chaff. There is in them neither reality, nor worth, nor essential truth!'

That moment the venerable Rohana, seated at his hermitage at Vattaniya, felt in his mind what was passing in the heart of Nâgasena. And he robed himself, and taking his alms-bowl in his hand, he vanished from Vattaniya and appeared near the Brahman village Kagangala. And young Nâgasena, as he stood again in the doorway, saw him coming in the distance. At the sight of him he became happy and glad, and a sweet hope sprang up in his heart that from him he might learn the essential truth. And he went [11] to him, and said: 'Who art thou, Sir, that thou art thus bald-headed, and wearest yellow robes?'

'They call me a recluse, my child' (Pabbagita: literally, 'one who has abandoned;' that is, the worldly life).

'And why do they call thee "one who has abandoned?"'

'Because a recluse is one who has receded from

the world in order to make the stain of sinful things recede. It is for that reason, my child, that they call me a recluse.'

'Why, Sir, dost thou not wear hair as others do?'

'A recluse shaves off his hair and beard on the recognition of the sixteen impediments therein to the higher life. And what are those sixteen [1]? The impediments of ornamenting it, and decking it out, of putting oil upon it, of shampooing it, of placing garlands round it, of using scents and unguents, and myrobalan seeds, and dyes, and ribbons, and combs, of calling in the barber, of unravelling curls, and of the possibility of vermin. When their hair falls off they are grieved and harassed; yea, they lament sometimes, and cry, and beat their breasts, or fall headlong in a swoon—and entangled by these and such impediments men may forget those parts of wisdom or learning which are delicate and subtle.'

'And why, Sir, are not thy garments, too, as those of other men?'

'Beautiful clothes, my boy, such as are worn by worldly men, are inseparable from the five cravings[2]. But whatsoever dangers lurk in dress he who wears the yellow robes knows nothing of. It is for that reason that my dress is not as other men's.'

'Dost thou know, Lord, what is real knowledge?'

'Yes, lad, the real knowledge I know; and what is the best hymn (mantra) in the world, that too I know.'

'Couldst thou teach it, Lord, to me too?'

---

[1] This odd idea of the 'impediments' in the wearing of hair and beard is in accord both with modern habits of shaving, and also with a good deal of early Christian and mediæval ethics.

[2] The lust of the eye, of the ear, &c.

'Yes, I could.'

'Teach me, then.'

'Just now is not the right time for that; we have come down to the village for alms.'

24. Then young Nâgasena took the alms-bowl the venerable Rohana was carrying, and led him into the house, and with his own hand supplied him with food, hard and soft, as much as he required. And when he saw that he had finished his meal, and withdrawn his hand from the bowl, he said to him : ' Now, Sir, will you teach me that hymn ?'

'When thou hast become free from impediments, my lad, by taking upon thee, and with thy parents' consent, the hermit's dress I wear, then I can teach it thee.'

25. So young [12] Nâgasena went to his father and mother, and said : ' This recluse says he knows the best hymn in the world, but that he cannot teach it to any one who has not entered the Order as his pupil. I should like to enter the Order and learn that hymn.'

And his parents gave their consent; for they wished him to learn the hymn, even at the cost of retiring from the world ; and they thought that when he had learned it he would come back again [1].

Then the venerable Rohana took Nâgasena to the Vattaniya hermitage, to the Vigamba Vatthu, and having spent the night there, took him on to the Guarded Slope, and there, in the midst of the innumerable company of the Arahats, young Nâgasena was admitted, as a novice, into the Order.

---

[1] Under the rules of the Buddhist Order any one can leave it as soon as he likes.

26. And then, when he had been admitted to the Order, the venerable Nâgasena said to the venerable Rohana: 'I have adopted your dress; now teach me that hymn.'

Then the venerable Rohana thought thus to himself: 'In what ought I first to instruct him, in the Discourses (Suttanta) or in the deeper things of the faith (Abhidhamma)?' and inasmuch as he saw that Nâgasena was intelligent, and could master the Abhidhamma with ease, he gave him his first lesson in that.

And the venerable Nâgasena, after hearing it repeated but once, knew by heart the whole of the Abhidhamma — that is to say, the Dhamma Sangaṇi, with its great divisions into good, bad, and indifferent qualities, and its subdivisions into couples and triplets[1]— the Vibhanga, with its eighteen chapters, beginning with the book on the constituent elements of beings—the Dhâtu Kathâ, with its fourteen books, beginning with that on compensation and non-compensation—the Puggala Paññatti, with its six divisions into discrimination of the various constituent elements, discrimination of the various senses and of the properties they apprehend, and so on[2]—the Kathâ Vatthu, with its thousand sections, five hundred on as many points

---

[1] Compare, for instance, p. 125 of the edition of this summary of Buddhist ethical psychology, edited for the Pâli Text Society, by Dr. Edward Müller, of Bern (London, 1885).

[2] The six kinds of discrimination (Paññatti) referred to, are those set out in § 1 of the Puggala. The work itself is an ethical tractate dealing only with the last of the six (the discrimination of individuals). See the edition by Dr. Morris, published by the Pâli Text Society (London, 1883).

of our own views, and five hundred on as many points of our opponents' views—the Yamaka, with its ten divisions into complementary propositions as to origins, as to constituent elements, and so on—and the Pa*tth*âna, with its twenty-four chapters on the reason of causes, the reason of ideas, and the rest. And he said [13]: 'That will do, Sir. You need not propound it again. That will suffice for my being able to rehearse it.'

27. Then Nâgasena went to the innumerable company of the Arahats, and said: 'I should like to propound the whole of the Abhidhamma Pi*t*aka, without abridgement, arranging it under the three heads of good, bad, and indifferent qualities.' And they gave him leave. And in seven months the venerable Nâgasena recited the seven books of the Abhidhamma in full. And the earth thundered, the gods shouted their applause, the Brahma gods clapped their hands, and there came down a shower from heaven of sweet-scented sandal-wood dust, and of Mandârava flowers! And the innumerable company of the Arahats, then and there at the Guarded Slope, admitted the venerable Nâgasena, then twenty years of age, to full membership in the higher grade of the Order.

28. Now the next day after he had thus been admitted into full membership in the Order, the venerable Nâgasena robed himself at dawn, and taking his bowl, accompanied his teacher on his round for alms to the village below. And as he went this thought arose within him: 'It was, after all, empty-headed and foolish of my teacher to leave the rest of the Buddha's word aside, and teach me the Abhidhamma first!'

And the venerable Rohana became aware in his own mind of what was passing in the mind of Nâgasena, and he said to him: 'That is an unworthy reflection that thou art making, Nâgasena; it is not worthy of thee so to think.'

'How strange and wonderful,' thought Nâgasena, 'that my teacher should be able to tell in his own mind what I am thinking of! I must ask his pardon.' And he said: 'Forgive me, Sir; I will never make such a reflection again.'

[14] 'I cannot forgive you, Nâgasena, simply on that promise,' was the reply. 'But there is a city called Sâgala, where a king rules whose name is Milinda, and he harasses the brethren by putting puzzles to them of heretical tendency. You will have earned your pardon, Nâgasena, when you shall have gone there, and overcome that king in argument, and brought him to take delight in the truth.'

'Not only let king Milinda, holy one, but let all the kings of India come and propound questions to me, and I will break all those puzzles up and solve them, if only you will pardon me!' exclaimed Nâgasena. But when he found it was of no avail, he said: 'Where, Sir, do you advise me to spend the three months of the rains now coming on[1]?'

29. 'There is a brother named Assagutta dwelling at the Vattaniya hermitage. Go, Nâgasena, to him; and in my name bow down to his feet, and say: "My teacher, holy one, salutes you reverently, and asks whether you are in health and ease, in full vigour and comfort. He has sent me here to pass

---

[1] It would be against the rules to go at once, during the rains, to Sâgala. So he would spend that time in preparation.

the three months of the rains under your charge." When he asks you your teacher's name, tell it him. But when he asks you his own name, say: "My teacher, Sir, knows your name."'

And Nâgasena bowed down before the venerable Rohana, and passing him on his right hand as he left him, took his bowl and robe, and went on from place to place till he came to the Vattaniya hermitage, begging for his food on the way. And on his arrival he saluted the venerable Assagutta, and said exactly what he had been told to say, [15] and to the last reply Assagutta said: 'Very well then, Nâgasena, put by your bowl and robe.' And the next day Nâgasena swept out the teacher's cell, and put the drinking water and tooth-cleansers ready for him to use. The Elder swept out the cell again, threw away the water and the tooth-cleansers, and fetched others, and said not a word of any kind. So it went on for seven days. On the seventh the Elder again asked him the same questions as before. And on Nâgasena again making the same replies, he gave him leave to pass the rainy season there.

30. Now a certain woman, a distinguished follower of the faith, had for thirty years and more administered to the wants of the venerable Assagutta. And at the end of that rainy season she came one day to him, and asked whether there was any other brother staying with him. And when she was told that there was one, named Nâgasena, she invited the Elder, and Nâgasena with him, to take their midday meal the next day at her house. And the Elder signified, by silence, his consent. The next forenoon the Elder robed himself, and taking his bowl in his hand, went down, accompanied by Nâgasena as his

attendant, to the dwelling-place of that disciple, and there they sat down on the seats prepared for them. And she gave to both of them food, hard and soft, as much as they required, waiting upon them with her own hands. When Assagutta had finished his meal, and the hand was withdrawn from the bowl, he said to Nâgasena: 'Do thou, Nâgasena, give the thanks to this distinguished lady.' And, so saying, he rose from his seat, and went away. [16]

31. And the lady said to Nâgasena: 'I am old, friend Nâgasena. Let the thanksgiving be from the deeper things of the faith.'

And Nâgasena, in pronouncing the thanksgiving discourse[1], dwelt on the profounder side of the Abhidhamma, not on matters of mere ordinary morality, but on those relating to Arahatship[2]. And as the lady sat there listening, there arose in her heart the Insight into the Truth[3], clear and stainless, which perceives that whatsoever has beginning, that has the inherent quality of passing away. And Nâgasena also, when he had concluded that thanksgiving discourse, felt the force of the truths he himself had preached, and he too arrived at insight[4]—he too

---

[1] See the note above, p. 15.

[2] Suññatâ, used here in the sense of Nirvâna. Compare Anguttara II, 5, 6; Gâtaka III, 191; Kullavagga XII, 2, 5.

[3] Dhamma-kakkhu. This perception of the impermanency of all things and all beings is called 'the Eye for the Truth,' and is the sign of the entrance upon the path to Arahatship, i. e. Nirvâna. It is the same among Buddhists as conversion is among the Christians. Compare Acts xxvi. 18 ('Open their eyes, and turn them from darkness to light, and from the power of Satan unto God') and other similar passages.

[4] Vipassanâ. Childers says this is an attribute of Arahatship; and Trenckner translates it 'superior intelligence.' But Arahats

entered, as he sat there, upon the stream (that is to say, upon the first stage of the Excellent Way to Arahatship).

32. Then the venerable Assagutta, as he was sitting in his arbour, was aware that they both had attained to insight, and he exclaimed: 'Well done! well done, Nâgasena! by one arrow shot you have hit two noble quarries!' And at the same time thousands of the gods shouted their approval.

Now the venerable Nâgasena arose and returned to Assagutta, and saluting him, took a seat reverently apart. And Assagutta said to him: 'Do thou now go, Nâgasena, to Pâ*t*aliputta. There, in the Asoka Park, dwells the venerable Dhammarakkhita. Under him you should learn the words of the Buddha.'

'How far is it, Sir, from here to Pâ*t*aliputta.'

'A hundred leagues[1], Nâgasena.'

'Great, Sir, is the distance. It will be difficult to get food on the way. How shall I get there?'

'Only go straight on, Nâgasena. You shall get food on the way, rice from which the black grains have been picked out, with curries and gravies of various sorts.'

'Very well, Sir!' said Nâgasena, and bowing

---

only have it, because they have all the powers possessed by those in the previous stages of the path, and it is only superior as being above and beyond the intelligence of the worldly wise, or even of the mere moralist. It is less than the 'Divine Eye,' and Nâgasena was not yet an Arahat. Compare the passages quoted by Childers under Dhamma-*k*akkhu and Dibba-*k*akkhu, and also Mahâvagga I, 6, 33; *G*âtaka I, 140; Sumaṅgala Vilâsinî, 237, 278.

[1] Yo*g*anas: that is, leagues of seven miles each. See my 'Ancient Coins and Measures of Ceylon,' p. 16, in Thomas's 'Numismata Orientalia,' vol. i.

down before his teacher, and passing him on the right side as he went, he took his bowl and his robe and departed for Pâṭaliputta.

33. [17] At that time a merchant of Pâṭaliputta was on his way back to that city with five hundred waggons. And when he saw the venerable Nâgasena coming in the distance, he stopped the waggons, and saluted Nâgasena, and asked him: 'Whither art thou going, father?'

'To Pâṭaliputta, householder.'

'That is well, father. We too are going thither. It will be more convenient for thee to go with us.'

And the merchant, pleased with Nâgasena's manners, provided him with food, hard and soft, as much as he required, waiting upon him with his own hands. And when the meal was over, he took a low seat, and sat down reverently apart. So seated, he said to the venerable Nâgasena: 'What, father, is your name?'

'I am called Nâgasena, householder.'

'Dost thou know, father, what are the words of Buddha?'

'I know the Abhidhamma.'

'We are most fortunate, father; this is indeed an advantage. I am a student of the Abhidhamma, and so art thou. Repeat to me, father, some passages from it.'

Then the venerable Nâgasena preached to him from the Abhidhamma, and by degrees as he did so there arose in Nâgasena's heart the Insight into the Truth, clear and stainless, which perceives that whatsoever has in itself the necessity of beginning, that too has also the inherent quality of passing away.

34. And the Pâṭaliputta merchant sent on his

waggons in advance, and followed himself after them. And at a place where the road divided, not far from Pâṭaliputta, he stopped, and said to Nâgasena: 'This is the turning to the Asoka Park. Now I have here a rare piece of woollen stuff, sixteen cubits by eight. [18] Do me the favour of accepting it.' And Nâgasena did so. And the merchant, pleased and glad, with joyful heart, and full of content and happiness, saluted the venerable Nâgasena, and keeping him on his right hand as he passed round him, went on his way.

35. But Nâgasena went on to the Asoka Park to Dhamma-rakkhita. And after saluting him, and telling him on what errand he had come, he learnt by heart, from the mouth of the venerable Dhamma-rakkhita, the whole of the three baskets [1] of the Buddha's word in three months, and after a single recital, so far as the letter (that is, knowing the words by heart) was concerned. And in three months more he mastered the spirit (that is, the deeper meaning of the sense of the words).

But at the end of that time the venerable Dham-

---

[1] Piṭakas. This expression is not used in the sacred books of the canon itself. When it first came into use is unknown. This is the earliest passage in which it has hitherto been found in the technical sense of a division of the Scriptures. It was in full use at the time of Buddhaghosa (see the Sumaṅgala Vilâsinî, pp. 15, 16, 17, 18, &c., and the Samanta Pâsâdikâ, printed in Oldenberg's 'Vinaya Piṭaka,' vol. iii, p. 293). The tertium quid of the comparison is not the basket or the box as a receptacle for preservation, but as a means of handing on (as Eastern navvies removing earth put it into baskets and pass these latter on from hand to hand). So the expression 'three baskets' means not 'the three collections,' but 'the three bodies of oral tradition as handed down from teacher to teacher.' See Trenckner's decisive argument in his 'Pâli Miscellanies,' pp. 67–69.

ma-rakkhita addressed him, and said : ' Just, Nâgasena, as a herdsman tends the cows, but others enjoy their produce, so thou too carriest in thy head the whole three baskets of the Buddha's word, and still art not yet a partaker of the fruit of Sama*n*aship.'

' Though that be so, holy one, say no more,' was the reply. And on that very day, at night, he attained to Arahatship and with it to the fourfold power of that Wisdom possessed by all Arahats (that is to say: the realisation of the sense, and the appreciation of the deep religious teaching contained in the word, the power of intuitive judgment, and the power of correct and ready exposition)[1]. And at the moment of his penetrating the truth all the gods shouted their approval, and the earth thundered, and the Brahma gods clapped their hands, and there fell from heaven a shower of sweet-scented sandal dust and of Mandârava flowers.

36. Now at that time the innumerable company of the Arahats at the Guarded Slope in the Himâlaya mountains sent a message to him to come, for they were anxious to see him. And when he heard the message the venerable Nâgasena vanished from the Asoka Park and appeared before them. And they said: ' Nâgasena, that king Milinda is in the habit of harassing the brethren by knotty questions and by argumentations this way and that. Do thou, Nâgasena, go and [19] master him.'

' Not only let king Milinda, holy ones, but let all the kings of India, come and propound questions to

---

[1] The four Pa*t*isambhidâs, which form the subject of one of the books of the Sutta Pi*t*aka.

me. I will break all those puzzles up and solve them. You may go fearlessly to Sâgala.'

Then all the Elders went to the city of Sâgala, lighting it up with their yellow robes like lamps, and bringing down upon it the breezes from the heights where the sages dwell [1].

[2] 37. At that time the venerable Âyupâla was living at the Saṅkheyya hermitage. And king Milinda said to his counsellors: 'Beautiful is the night and pleasant! Who is the wandering teacher or Brahman we can visit to night to question him who will be able to converse with us and to resolve our doubts?'

And the five hundred Yonakas replied: 'There is the Elder, Lord, named Âyupâla, versed in the three baskets, and in all the traditional lore. He is living now at the Saṅkheyya hermitage. To him you might go, O king, and put your questions to him.'

'Very well, then. Let the venerable one be informed that we are coming.'

---

[1] Isi-vâta*m* parivâta*m* (nagara*m*) aka*m*su. The meaning of this phrase, which has not been found elsewhere, is doubtful. Trenckner renders 'making it respire the odour of saints.' The literal translation would be 'making it blown round about by *R*ishi-wind.' Perhaps it may be meant to convey the idea of 'scented with the sweet breath of the wise.' But in any case the connotation is intended to be a pleasant one. Calling to mind the analogous phrase vi*g*anavâta*m* ârâma*m*, 'a hermitage with breezes from the desert.' (Mahâvagga I, 22, 17 = *K*ullavagga VI, 4, 8.) I venture to suggest the rendering adopted above. Hîna*t*i-kumburê (p. 24) has *R*ishiwarayaṅge gamanâgamanaye*m* *g*anita wa kîvara wâtaye*m* pratiwâtaya kalâhuya. 'They set its air in commotion produced by the waving of the robes of the coming and going *R*ishis.'

[2] We here take up the original episode of Milinda as interrupted at § 15 (or if there is an interpolation at § 10).

Then the royal astrologer sent a message to Âyupâla to the effect that king Milinda desired to call upon him. And the venerable one said: 'Let him come.'

So Milinda the king, attended by the five hundred Yonakas, mounted his royal chariot and proceeded to the Saṅkheyya hermitage, to the place where Âyupâla dwelt, and exchanged with him the greetings and compliments of friendship and courtesy, and took his seat respectfully apart. And then he said to him:

38. 'Of what use, venerable Âyupâla, is the renunciation of the world carried out by the members of your Order, and in what do you place the summum bonum?'

'Our renunciation, O king,' replied the Elder, 'is for the sake of being able to live in righteousness, and in spiritual calm.'

'Is there, Sir, any layman who lives so?'

'Yes, great king, there are such laymen. At the time when the Blessed One set rolling the royal chariot wheel of the kingdom of righteousness at Benares, at the Deer Park, [20] eighteen koṭis of the Brahma gods, and an innumerable company of other gods, attained to comprehension of the truth [1]. And not one of those beings, all of whom were laymen, had renounced the world. And again when the Blessed One delivered the Mahâ Samaya discourse [2], and the discourse on the 'Greatest Blessing [3],'

---

[1] See my 'Buddhist Suttas,' pp. 153–155. There is nothing about the eighteen koṭis in the Piṭaka text referred to.

[2] No. 20 in the Dîgha Nikâya.

[3] In the Mahâ Maṅgala, translated in my 'Buddhism,' pp. 125–127.

and the Exposition of Quietism[1], and the Exhortation to Râhula[2], the multitude of gods who attained to comprehension of the truth cannot be numbered. And not one of those beings, all of whom were laymen, had renounced the world[3].'

'Then, most venerable Âyupâla, your renunciation is of no use. It must be in consequence of sins committed in some former birth, that the Buddhist Samanas renounce the world, and even subject themselves to the restraints of one or other of the thirteen aids to purity[4]! Those who remain on one seat till they have finished their repast were, forsooth, in some former birth, thieves who robbed other men of their food. It is in consequence of the Karma of having so deprived others of food that they have now only such food as they can get at one sitting; and are not allowed to eat from time to time as they want. It is no virtue on their part, no meritorious abstinence, no righteousness of life. And they who live in the open air were, forsooth, in

---

[1] Sama-kitta-pariyâya Suttanta. It is not certain which Sutta is here referred to. Trenckner identifies it with a short Sutta in the Anguttara (II, 4, 5). It is true that the ten short Suttas in A. II, 4 are (in the Burmese MSS. only) called collectively Sama-kitta Vagga. But the separate Suttas have no separate titles; the title of the Vagga is not found in the Simhalese MSS., and is probably later than the text; and it is not, after all, identical with the title here given.

[2] There are several Suttas of this name in the Pâli Pitakas. The one referred to here (and also, it may be added, in the Asoka Edicts) is probably the shorter one (Kûla Râhulovâda Sutta) found both in the Maggḥima (No. 147) and in the Samyutta (XXXIV, 120). See Trenckner's note on this passage.

[3] This way of looking at gods as laymen, still 'in the world,' is thoroughly Buddhist.

[4] The dhutangas, enumerated by Childers sub voce.

some former birth, dacoits who plundered whole villages. It is in consequence of the Karma of having destroyed other people's homes, that they live now without a home, and are not allowed the use of huts. It is no virtue on their part, no meritorious abstinence, no righteousness of life. And those who never lie down, they, forsooth, in some former birth, were highwaymen who seized travellers, and bound them, and left them sitting there. It is in consequence of the Karma of that habit that they have become Nesa*gg*ikâ in this life (men who always sit) and get no beds to lie on. It is no virtue on their part, no meritorious abstinence, no righteousness of life!'

39. And when he had thus spoken the venerable Âyupâla was silenced, and had not a word to say in reply. Then the five hundred Yonakas said to the king: 'The Elder, O king, is learned, but is also diffident. It is for that reason that he makes no rejoinder. But the king on seeing how silent Âyupâla had become, clapped his hands [21] and cried out: 'All India is an empty thing, it is verily like chaff! There is no one, either Sama*n*a or Brahman, capable of discussing things with me and dispelling my doubts[1]!'

As he looked, however, at the assembly and saw how fearless and self-possessed the Yonakas appeared, he thought within himself: 'For a certainty there must be, methinks, some other learned brother capable of disputing with me, or those Yonakas would not be thus confident.' And he said to them:

---

[1] See above, p. 10, § 14.

'Is there, my good men, any other learned brother to discuss things with me and dispel my doubts?'

40. Now at that time the venerable Nâgasena, after making his alms-tour through the villages, towns, and cities, had in due course arrived at Sâgala, attended by a band of Sama*n*as, as the leader of a company of the Order; the head of a body of disciples; the teacher of a school; famous and renowned, and highly esteemed by the people. And he was learned, clever, wise, sagacious, and able; a skilful expounder, of subdued manners, but full of courage; well versed in tradition, master of the three Baskets (Pi*t*akas), and erudite in Vedic lore [1]. He was in possession of the highest (Buddhist) insight, a master of all that had been handed down in the schools, and of the various discriminations [2] by which the most abstruse points can be explained. He knew by heart the ninefold divisions of the doctrine of the Buddha to perfection [3], and was equally skilled in discerning both the spirit and the letter of the Word. Endowed with instantaneous and varied power of repartee, and wealth of language, and beauty of eloquence, he was difficult to equal, and still more difficult to excel, difficult to answer, to repel, or to refute. He was imperturbable as the depths of the sea, immovable as the king of mountains; victorious in the struggle with evil, a dispeller

---

[1] This is always explained as wise in the Buddhist Vedas, that is, the three Pi*t*akas.

[2] Pa*t*isambhidâs: see above, the note on p. 29.

[3] Pârami-ppatto. This is an unusual use of Pârami, but it occurs again below, p. 36, in a similar connection, and there can be no doubt of its meaning. Trenckner translates it 'better than any one else.'

of darkness and diffuser of light; mighty in eloquence, a confounder of the followers of other masters, and a crusher-out of the adherents of rival doctrines (malleus hereticorum). Honoured and revered by the brethren and sisters of the Order, and its lay adherents of either sex, and by kings and their high officials, he was in the abundant receipt of all the requisites of a member of the Order —robes and bowl and lodging, and whatever is needful for the sick—receiving the highest veneration no less than material gifts. To the wise and discerning who came to him with listening ear he displayed the ninefold jewel of the Conqueror's word, he pointed out to them the path of righteousness, bore aloft for them the torch of truth, set up for them the sacred pillar of the truth[1], and celebrated for their benefit the sacrifice of the truth. For them he waved the banner, raised the standard, blew the trumpet, and beat the drum of truth. And with his mighty lion's voice, [22] like Indra's thunder but sweet the while, he poured out upon them a plenteous shower, heavy with drops of mercy, and brilliant with the coruscations of the lightning flashes of his knowledge, of the nectar waters of the teaching of the Nirvâ*n*a of the truth—thus satisfying to the full a thirsty world.

41. There then, at the Saṅkheyya hermitage, did the venerable Nâgasena, with a numerous company of the brethren, dwell[2]. Therefore is it said:

---

[1] Dhamma-yûpa*m*; with allusion to the sacred sacrificial post, which plays so great a part in Brahman ritual.

[2] Literally 'with eighty thousand:' but this merely means to say, with a large (undefined) number. See the use of the phrase in the Nâ*l*apâna *G*âtaka (Fausböll, No. 20).

'Learned, with varied eloquence, sagacious, bold,
Master of views, in exposition sound,
The brethren—wise themselves in holy writ,
Repeaters of the fivefold sacred word—
Put Nâgasena as their leader and their chief.
Him, Nâgasena of clear mind and wisdom deep,
Who knew which was the right Path, which the false,
And had himself attained Nirvâna's placid heights!

Attended by the wise, by holders to the Truth,
He had gone from town to town, and come to Sâgala;
And now he dwelt there in Sankheyya's grove,
Appearing, among men, like the lion of the hills.'

42. And Devamantiya said to king Milinda: 'Wait a little, great king, wait a little! There is an Elder named Nâgasena, learned, able, and wise, of subdued manners, yet full of courage, versed in the traditions, a master of language, and ready in reply, one who understands alike the spirit and the letter of the law, and can expound its difficulties and refute objections to perfection[1]. He is staying at present at the Sankheyya hermitage. You should go, great king, and put your questions to him. He is able to discuss things with you, and dispel your doubts.'

Then when Milinda the king heard the name Nâgasena, thus suddenly introduced, he was seized with fear, and with anxiety, and the hairs of his body stood on end[2]. But he asked Devamantiya: 'Is that really so?'

---

[1] See above, p. 34, note 3.
[2] The name itself, which means 'Chief of Nâga Snakes,' is

And Devamantiya replied : ' He is capable, Sire, of discussing things with the guardians of the world —with Indra, Yama, Varu*n*a, Kuvera, Pra*g*âpati, Suyâma, [23] and Santushita—and even with the great Brahma himself, the progenitor of mankind, how much more then with a mere human being !'

' Do you then, Devamantiya,' said the king, ' send a messenger to say I am coming.'

And he did so. And Nâgasena sent word back that he might come. And the king, attended by the five hundred Yonakas, mounted his royal chariot, and proceeded with a great retinue to the Sankheyya hermitage, and to the place where Nâgasena dwelt.

43. At that time the venerable Nâgasena was seated with the innumerable company of the brethren of the Order, in the open hall in front of the hermitage[1]. So king Milinda saw the assembly from afar, and he said to Devamantiya : ' Whose, Devamantiya, is this so mighty retinue ?'

' These are they who follow the venerable Nâgasena,' was the reply.

Then at the sight there came over king Milinda

---

terrible enough, especially as the Nâgas were looked upon as supernatural beings. But it is no doubt also intended that the king had heard of his fame.

[1] Ma*n*dala-mâla, that is a hall consisting only of a roof, supported by pillars which are connected by a dwarf wall two or three feet in height. The roof projects beyond the pillars, so that the space within is well shaded. It is a kind of open air drawing-room attached to most hermitages, and may be so small that it can be rightly rendered arbour (see above, p. 25), or sufficiently large to accommodate a considerable number. Usually of wood, sometimes of stone, it is always graceful in appearance and pleasant to use. It is mentioned in the corresponding passage of the Sâma*ññ*a Phala (D. II, 10).

a feeling of fear and of anxiety, and the hairs of his body stood on end[1]. But nevertheless, though he felt like an elephant hemmed in by rhinoceroses, like a serpent surrounded by the Garu*d*as (the snake-eating mythical birds), like a jackal surrounded by boa-constrictors, or a bear by buffaloes, like a frog pursued by a serpent, or a deer by a panther, like a snake in the hands of a snake charmer, or a rat played with by a cat, or a devil charmed by an exorcist, like the moon when it is seized by Râhu, like a snake caught in a basket, or a bird in a cage, or a fish in a net, like a man who has lost his way in a dense forest haunted by wild beasts, like a Yakkha (ogre) who has sinned against Vessavana (the king of ogres and fairies), or like a god whose term of life as a god has reached its end—though confused and terrified, anxious, and beside himself in an agony of fear like that—yet at the thought that he must at least avoid humiliation in the sight of the people, he took courage, and said to Devamantiya: 'You need not [24] trouble to point out to me which is Nâgasena. I shall pick him out unaided.'

'Certainly, Sire, recognise him yourself,' said he[2].

44. Now Nâgasena was junior in seniority (reckoned from the date of his full membership in the

---

[1] This again, like the passage at p. 8, is an echo of the Sâma*ññ*a Phala. (See D. 2, 10 of our forthcoming edition, or p. 116 of Grimblot.)

[2] In the corresponding passage of the Sâma*ññ*a Phala *G*ivaka points out the Buddha to A*g*âtasattu (§ 11, Grimblot, p. 117). This would be in the memory of all his readers, and our author alters the story in this case to show how superior Milinda was to the royal interlocutor in the older dialogue.

Order) to the half of that great company seated in front of him, and senior to the half seated behind him. And as he looked over the whole of the assembly, in front, and down the centre, and behind, king Milinda detected Nâgasena seated in the middle, and, like a shaggy lion who knows no fear or frenzy, entirely devoid of nervous agitation, and free from shyness and trepidation. And as soon as he saw him, he knew by his mien that that was Nâgasena, and he pointed him out to Devamantiya.

'Yes, great king,' said he, 'that is Nâgasena. Well hast thou, Sire, recognised the sage.'

Whereupon the king rejoiced that he had recognised Nâgasena without having had him pointed out to him. But nevertheless, at the sight of him, the king was seized with nervous excitement and trepidation and fear. Therefore is it said:

'At the sight of Nâgasena, wise and pure,
Subdued in all that is the best subjection,
Milinda uttered this foreboding word—
"Many the talkers I have visited,
Many the conversations I have had,
But never yet, till now, to-day, has fear,
So strange, so terrible, o'erpowered my heart.
Verily now defeat must be my lot,
And victory his, so troubled is my mind."'

Here ends the introductory secular narrative (Bâhira-kathâ)[1].

---

[1] See note on p. 1. This book closes in Hînati-kumburê's Simhalese version with the title 'Pûrwa Yoga yayi;' and is of course identical with the Pubba-yoga referred to above, p. 4, as the first division of the work.

BOOK II.

Lakkhana Pañha.

THE DISTINGUISHING CHARACTERISTICS OF ETHICAL QUALITIES.

Chapter 1.

1. [25] Now Milinda the king went up to where the venerable Nâgasena was, and addressed him with the greetings and compliments of friendship and courtesy, and took his seat respectfully apart. And Nâgasena reciprocated his courtesy, so that the heart of the king was propitiated.

And Milinda began by asking, [1] 'How is your Reverence known, and what, Sir, is your name?'

'I am known as Nâgasena, O king, and it is by that name that my brethren in the faith address me. But although parents, O king, give such a name as Nâgasena, or Sûrasena, or Vîrasena, or Sîhasena, yet this, Sire,—Nâgasena and so on—is only a generally understood term, a designation in common use. For there is no permanent individuality (no soul) involved in the matter[2].'

---

[1] There is a free translation of the Simhalese version of the following dialogues (down to the end of our § 4) in Spence Hardy's 'Manual of Buddhism,' pp. 424–429. But it is very unreliable as a reproduction of either the Simhalese or the Pâli, and slurs over the doubtful passages.

[2] Na puggalo upalabbhati. This thesis, that 'there is no individual,' is discussed at the opening of the Kathâ Vatthu (leaf ka of my MS.) Put into modern philosophical phraseology it amounts to saying that there is no permanent subject underlying the temporary phenomena visible in a man's individuality. But

Then Milinda called upon the Yonakas and the brethren to witness: 'This Nâgasena says there is no permanent individuality (no soul) implied in his name. Is it now even possible to approve him in that?' And turning to Nâgasena, he said: 'If, most reverend Nâgasena, there be no permanent individuality (no soul) involved in the matter, who is it, pray, who gives to you members of the Order your robes and food and lodging and necessaries for the sick? Who is it who enjoys such things when given? Who is it who lives a life of righteousness? Who is it who devotes himself to meditation? Who is it who attains to the goal of the Excellent Way, to the Nirvâ*n*a of Arahatship? And who is it who destroys living creatures? who is it who takes what is not his own? who is it who lives an evil life of worldly lusts, who speaks lies, who drinks strong drink, who (in a word) commits any one of the five sins which work out their bitter fruit even in this life[1]? If that be so there is neither merit nor demerit; there is neither doer nor causer of good or evil deeds[2]; there is neither fruit nor result of good or evil Karma[3]. [26]—If, most reverend Nâgasena, we are to think that were a man

---

I doubt whether, even in our author's time, the conception 'subject' was common ground, or that the word puggala had acquired that special connotation.

[1] Pa*ñk*ânantariya-kamma*m* karoti. See my note on *K*ullavagga VII, 3, 9 ('Vinaya Texts,' vol. iii, p. 246, in the Sacred Books of the East).

[2] This is no doubt said in these words with allusion to the opinion ascribed in the Sâma*ññ*a Phala (D. II, 17) to Pûra*n*a Kassapa.

[3] This is the opinion ascribed in identical words in the Sâma*ññ*a Phala (D. II, 23) to A*g*ita of the garment of hair.

to kill you there would be no murder [1], then it follows that there are no real masters or teachers in your Order, and that your ordinations are void.—You tell me that your brethren in the Order are in the habit of addressing you as Nâgasena. Now what is that Nâgasena? Do you mean to say that the hair is Nâgasena?'

'I don't say that, great king.'

'Or the hairs on the body, perhaps?'

'Certainly not.'

'Or is it the nails, the teeth, the skin, the flesh, the nerves, the bones, the marrow, the kidneys, the heart, the liver, the abdomen, the spleen, the lungs, the larger intestines, the lower intestines, the stomach, the fæces, the bile, the phlegm, the pus, the blood, the sweat, the fat, the tears, the serum, the saliva, the mucus, the oil that lubricates the joints, the urine, or the brain, or any or all of these, that is Nâgasena[2]?'

And to each of these he answered no.

'Is it the outward form then (Rûpa) that is Nâgasena, or the sensations (Vedanâ), or the ideas (Saññâ), or the confections (the constituent elements of character, Samkhârâ), or the consciousness (Viññâna), that is Nâgasena[3]?'

And to each of these also he answered no.

---

[1] This is practically the same opinion as is ascribed in the Sâmaññâ Phala (D. II, 26) to Pakudha Ka*kk*âyana.

[2] This list of the thirty-two forms (â*k*âras) of organic matter in the human body occurs already in the Khuddaka Pâ*th*a, § 3. It is the standard list always used in similar connections; and is, no doubt, supposed to be exhaustive. There are sixteen (half as many) â*k*âras of the mind according to Dîpava*m*sa I, 42.

[3] These are the five Skandhas, which include in them the whole bodily and mental constituents of any being. See p. 80.

'Then is it all these Skandhas combined that are Nâgasena?'

'No! great king.'

'But is there anything outside the five Skandhas that is Nâgasena?'

And still he answered no.

'Then thus, ask as I may, I can discover no Nâgasena. Nâgasena is a mere empty sound. Who then is the Nâgasena that we see before us? It is a falsehood that your reverence has spoken, an untruth!'

And the venerable Nâgasena said to Milinda the king: 'You, Sire, have been brought up in great luxury, as beseems your noble birth. If you were to walk this dry weather on the hot and sandy ground, trampling under foot the gritty, gravelly grains of the hard sand, your feet would hurt you. And as your body would be in pain, your mind would be disturbed, and you would experience a sense of bodily suffering. How then did you come, on foot, or in a chariot?'

'I did not come, Sir, on foot [27]. I came in a carriage.'

'Then if you came, Sire, in a carriage, explain to me what that is. Is it the pole that is the chariot?'

'I did not say that.'

'Is it the axle that is the chariot?'

'Certainly not.'

'Is it the wheels, or the framework, or the ropes, or the yoke, or the spokes of the wheels, or the goad, that are the chariot?'

And to all these he still answered no.

'Then is it all these parts of it that are the chariot?'

'No, Sir.'

'But is there anything outside them that is the chariot?'

And still he answered no.

'Then thus, ask as I may, I can discover no chariot. Chariot is a mere empty sound. What then is the chariot you say you came in? It is a falsehood that your Majesty has spoken, an untruth! There is no such thing as a chariot! You are king over all India, a mighty monarch. Of whom then are you afraid that you speak untruth? And he called upon the Yonakas and the brethren to witness, saying: 'Milinda the king here has said that he came by carriage. But when asked in that case to explain what the carriage was, he is unable to establish what he averred. Is it, forsooth, possible to approve him in that?'

When he had thus spoken the five hundred Yonakas shouted their applause, and said to the king: 'Now let your Majesty get out of that if you can?'

And Milinda the king replied to Nâgasena, and said: 'I have spoken no untruth, reverend Sir. It is on account of its having all these things—the pole, and the axle, the wheels, and the framework, the ropes, the yoke, the spokes, and the goad—that it comes under the generally understood term, the designation in common use, of "chariot."'

'Very good! Your Majesty has rightly grasped the meaning of "chariot." And just even so it is on account of all those things you questioned me about —[28] the thirty-two kinds of organic matter in a human body, and the five constituent elements of being—that I come under the generally understood term, the designation in common use, of "Nâgasena."

For it was said, Sire, by our Sister Vagirâ in the presence of the Blessed One:

'"Just as it is by the condition precedent of the co-existence of its various parts that the word 'chariot' is used, just so is it that when the Skandhas are there we talk of a 'being[1].'"'

'Most wonderful, Nâgasena, and most strange. Well has the puzzle put to you, most difficult though it was, been solved. Were the Buddha himself here he would approve your answer. Well done, well done, Nâgasena!'

2. 'How many years seniority have you, Nâgasena?'

'Seven, your Majesty.'

'But how can you say it is your "seven?" Is it you who are "seven," or the number that is "seven?"'

Now that moment the figure of the king, decked in all the finery of his royal ornaments, cast its shadow on the ground, and was reflected in a vessel of water. And Nâgasena asked him: 'Your figure, O king, is now shadowed upon the ground, and reflected in the water, how now, are you the king, or is the reflection the king?'

'I am the king, Nâgasena, but the shadow comes into existence because of me.'

'Just even so, O king, the number of the years is seven, I am not seven. But it is because of me, O king, that the number seven has come into existence; and it is mine in the same sense as the shadow is yours[2].'

---

[1] From the Samyutta Nikâya V, 10, 6.
[2] Hardy (p. 427, § 4 of the first edition) has quite missed the point of this crux.

'Most wonderful again, and strange, Nâgasena. Well has the question put to you, most difficult though it was, been solved!'

---

3. The king said: 'Reverend Sir, will you discuss with me again?'

'If your Majesty will discuss as a scholar (pandit), well; but if you will discuss as a king, no.'

'How is it then that scholars discuss?'

'When scholars talk a matter over one with another then is there a winding up[1], an unravelling; one or other is convicted of error[2], and he then acknowledges his mistake; [29] distinctions are drawn, and contra-distinctions[3]; and yet thereby they are not angered. Thus do scholars, O king, discuss.'

'And how do kings discuss?'

'When a king, your Majesty, discusses a matter, and he advances a point, if any one differ from him on that point, he is apt to fine him, saying: "Inflict such and such a punishment upon that fellow!" Thus, your Majesty, do kings discuss[4].'

'Very well. It is as a scholar, not as a king, that I will discuss. Let your reverence talk unrestrainedly, as you would with a brother, or a novice, or a lay disciple, or even with a servant. Be not afraid!'

---

[1] Âve*th*ana*m*; not in Childers, but see *G*âtaka II, 9; IV, 383, 384; and Morris in the 'Journal of the Pâli Text Society,' 1887.

[2] Niggâho karîyati, as for instance below, p. 142.

[3] Pa*t*iviseso; not in Childers, but see again *G*âtaka II, 9.

[4] Hardy, loc. cit. § 5, puts all this into the mouths of 'the priests.'

'Very good, your Majesty,' said Nâgasena, with thankfulness.

'Nâgasena, I have a question to ask you;' said the king.

'Pray ask it, Sire.'

'I have asked it, your Reverence.'

'That is answered already.'

'What have you answered?'

'To what, then, does your Majesty refer?'

But Milinda the king thought: 'This Bhikkhu is a great scholar. He is quite capable of discussing things with me. And I shall have a number of points on which to question him, and before I can ask them all, the sun will set. It would be better to carry on the discussion at home to-morrow.' And he said to Devamantiya: 'You may let his reverence know that the discussion with the king shall be resumed to-morrow at the palace.' And so saying, he took leave of Nâgasena, and mounted his horse, and went away, muttering as he went, 'Nâgasena, Nâgasena!'

And Devamantiya delivered his message to Nâgasena, who accepted the proposal with gladness. And early the next morning Devamantiya and Anantakâya and Mankura and Sabbadinna went to the king, and said: 'Is his reverence, Nâgasena, to come, [30] Sire, to-day?'

'Yes, he is to come.'

'With how many of the brethren is he to come?'

'With as many as he likes.'

And Sabbadinna said: 'Let him come with ten.' But the king repeated what he had said. And on Sabbadinna reiterating his suggestion, the king rejoined: 'All this preparation has been made, and I say:

"Let him come with as many as he likes," yet Sabbadinna says: "Let him come with ten." Does he suppose we are not capable of feeding so many?' Then Sabbadinna was ashamed.

---

4. And Devamantiya and Anantakâya and Mankura went to Nâgasena and told him what the king had said. And the venerable Nâgasena robed himself in the forenoon, and taking his bowl in his hand, went to Sâgala with the whole company of the brethren. And Anantakâya, as he walked beside Nâgasena, said:

'When, your reverence, I say, "Nâgasena," what is that Nâgasena?'

The Elder replied: 'What do you think Nâgasena is?'

'The soul, the inner breath which comes and goes, that I suppose to be Nâgasena.'

'But if that breath having gone forth should not return, or having returned should not go forth, would the man be alive?'

'Certainly [31] not, Sir.'

'But those trumpeters, when they blow their trumpets, does their breath return again to them?'

'No, Sir, it does not.'

'Or those pipers, when they blow their pipes or horns, does their breath return again to them?'

'No, Sir.'

'Then why don't they die?'

'I am not capable of arguing with such a reasoner. Pray tell me, Sir, how the matter stands.'

'There is no soul in the breath. These inhalations and exhalations are merely constituent powers of the bodily frame,' said the Elder. And he talked to him from the Abhidhamma [1] to such effect that [1] Anantakâya confessed himself as a supporter of the Order.

5. And the venerable Nâgasena went to the king, and sat down on the seat prepared for him. And the king provided Nâgasena and his following with food, both hard and soft, as much as they required: and presented each brother with a suit of garments, and Nâgasena himself with a set of three robes. And then he said to him: 'Be pleased to keep your seat here, and with you ten of the brethren. Let the rest depart.'

And when he saw that Nâgasena had finished his meal, he took a lower seat, and sat beside him, and said: 'What shall we discuss?'

'We want to arrive at truth. Let our discussion be about the truth.'

And the king said: 'What is the object, Sir, of your [2] renunciation, and what the summum bonum at which you aim?'

'Why do you ask? Our renunciation is to the end that this sorrow may perish away, and that no further sorrow may arise; the complete passing away, without cleaving to the world, is our highest aim.'

'How now, Sir! Is it for such high reasons that all members of it have joined the Order?'

[32] 'Certainly not, Sire. Some for those reasons,

[1-1] I venture to think it is incorrect to put a full stop, as Mr. Trenckner has done, after a k â s i.

[2] Plural. 'You members of the Buddhist Order.' The question is further elaborated below, III, 1, 3, and above, 1, 38.

but some have left the world in terror at the tyranny of kings. Some have joined us to be safe from being robbed, some harassed by debt, and some perhaps to gain a livelihood.'

'But for what object, Sir, did you yourself join.'

'I was received into the Order when I was a mere boy, I knew not then the ultimate aim. But I thought: "They are wise scholars, these Buddhist Samaṇas, they will be able to teach me." And by them I have been taught; and now do I both know and understand what is at once the reason for, and the advantage of renunciation.'

'Well put, Nâgasena!'

6. The king said: 'Nâgasena, is there any one who after death is not reindividualised?'

'Some are so, and some not.'

'Who are they?'

'A sinful being is reindividualised, a sinless one is not.'

'Will you be reindividualised?'

'If when I die, I die with craving for existence in my heart, yes; but if not, no [1].'

'Very good, Nâgasena!'

7. The king said: 'Nâgasena, he who escapes reindividualisation is it by reasoning that he escapes it?'

'Both by reasoning [2], your Majesty, and by wisdom [3], and by other good qualities.'

'But are not reasoning and wisdom surely much the same?'

'Certainly not. Reasoning is one thing, wisdom

---

[1] Repeated below, with an illustration, Chap. 2, § 7, p. 76.
[2] Yoniso manasikâra.   [3] Paññâ. See pp. 59, 64, 128.

another. Sheep and goats, oxen and buffaloes, camels and asses have reasoning, but wisdom they have not.'

'Well put, Nâgasena!'

8. The king said: 'What is the characteristic mark of reasoning, and what of wisdom?'

'Reasoning has always comprehension as its mark; but wisdom has cutting off[1].'

'But how is comprehension the characteristic of reasoning, and cutting off of wisdom? Give me an illustration.'

'You remember the barley reapers?'

'Yes, certainly.' [33]

'How do they reap the barley?'

'With the left hand they grasp the barley into a bunch, and taking the sickle into the right hand, they cut it off with that.'

'Just even so, O king, does the recluse by his thinking grasp his mind, and by his wisdom cut off his failings. In this way is it that comprehension is the characteristic of reasoning, but cutting off of wisdom.'

'Well put, Nâgasena!'

9. The king said: 'When you said just now, "And by other good qualities," to which did you refer?'

---

[1] In the long list of the distinguishing characteristics of ethical qualities given by Buddhaghosa in the Sumaṅgala, p. 63, pagânana is the mark of paññindriya, aviggâya akampiyam of paññâ-bala, and tad-uttariyam of paññâ simply. He gives no 'mark' of yoniso manasikâra.

'Good conduct, great king, and faith, and perseverance, and mindfulness, and meditation[1].

'And what is the characteristic mark of good conduct?'

'It has as its characteristic that it is the basis of all good qualities. The five moral powers[2]—faith, perseverance, mindfulness, meditation, and wisdom—; the seven conditions of Arahatship[3]—self-possession, investigation of the Dhamma, perseverance, joy, calm, meditation, and equanimity—; the Path; readiness of memory (unbroken self-possession)[4]; the four kinds of right exertion[5]; the four constituent bases of extraordinary powers[6]; the four stages of ecstasy[7]; the eight forms of spiritual emancipation[8]; the four modes of self-concentration[9]; and the eight states of intense contemplation[10] have each and all of them good conduct (the observance of outward morality) as their basis. And to him who builds upon that foundation, O king, all these good conditions will not decrease[11].'

'Give me an illustration.'

'Just, O king, as all those forms of animal and vegetable life which grow, develope, and mature, do so with the earth as their basis; just so does the recluse, who is devoted in effort, develope in himself the five moral powers, and so on, by means of virtue, on the basis of virtue.'

'Give me a further illustration.'

---

[1] Sila*m*, saddhâ, viriya*m*, sati, samâdhi.
[2] Indriya-balâni. [3] Bo*ggh*a*n*gâ. [4] Satipa*tth*âna.
[5] Sammappadhâna. [6] Iddhipâda. [7] G*h*âna.
[8] Vimokhâ. [9] Samâdhi. [10] Samâpatti.
[11] The above-mentioned meritorious conditions are those the sum of which make Arahatship.

'Just, O king, as all the occupations which involve bodily exertion are carried on in ultimate dependence upon the earth, just so does the recluse develope in himself the five moral powers, and so on, by means of virtue, on the basis of virtue.' [34]

'Give me a still better illustration.'

'Just, O king, as the architect of a city, when he wants to build one, first clears the site of the town, and then proceeds to get rid of all the stumps and thorny brakes, and thus makes it level, and only then does he lay out the streets and squares, and crossroads and market places, and so build the city; just so does the recluse develope in himself the five moral powers, and so on, by means of virtue, on the basis of virtue.'

'Can you give me one more simile?'

'Just, O king, as an acrobat[1], when he wants to exhibit his skill, first digs over the ground, and proceeds to get rid of all the stones and fragments of broken pottery, and thus to make it smooth, and only then, on soft earth, shows his tricks; just even so does the recluse develope in himself the five moral powers, and so on, by means of virtue, on the basis of virtue. For it has been said, Sire, by the Blessed One:

"Virtue's the base on which the man who's wise
Can train his heart, and make his wisdom grow.
Thus shall the strenuous Bhikkhu, undeceived,
Unravel all the tangled skein of life [2].

---

[1] Laṅghako, not in Childers; but compare *Gâtaka* I, 431, and below, pp. 191, 331 of the text.

[2] This verse occurs twice in the Sa*m*yutta (I, 3, 3, and VII, 1, 6).

"This is the base—like the great earth to men—
And this the root of all increase in goodness,
The starting-point of all the Buddhas' teaching,
Virtue, to wit, on which true bliss depends[1]."'
'Well said, Nâgasena!'

10[2]. The king said, 'Venerable Nâgasena, what is the characteristic mark of faith?'

'Tranquillisation, O king, and aspiration[3].'

'And how is tranquillisation the mark of faith?'

'As faith, O king, springs up in the heart it breaks through the five hindrances—lust, malice, mental sloth, spiritual pride, and doubt—and the heart, free from these hindrances, [35] becomes clear, serene, untroubled.'

'Give me an illustration.'

'Just, O king, as a suzerain king, when on the march with his fourfold army, might cross over a small stream, and the water, disturbed by the elephants and cavalry, the chariots and the bowmen, might become fouled, turbid[4], and muddy. And

---

[1] Vara-pâtimokkhiyo, a poetical expression found only in this passage, and of the exact connotation of which I am uncertain. It is not in Childers; and Hîna/i-kumburê gives no assistance. The whole line may mean, 'The scheme of a virtuous life as laid down in the most excellent Pâtimokkha.' See the use of Sa*m*yutta-Nikâya-vare below, p. 36 of the text. On the whole section compare M. P. S. I, 12.

[2] This section is summarised in Hardy's 'Manual of Buddhism,' pp. 411, 412 (1st edition).

[3] Sampasâdana and sampakkhandana. Buddhaghosa, loc. cit., does not give faith in his list, but he gives the power of faith (saddhâ-bala), and as its 'mark' 'that it cannot be shaken by incredulity.'

[4] Lu/ita, not in Childers; but compare Aṅguttara I, 55, and 'Book of the Great Decease,' IV, 26-32.

when he was on the other side the monarch might give command to his attendants, saying: "Bring some water, my good men. I would fain drink." Now suppose the monarch had a water-clearing gem[1], and those men, in obedience to the order, were to throw the jewel into the water; then at once all the mud would precipitate itself, and the sandy atoms of shell and bits of water-plants would disappear, and the water would become clear, transparent, and serene, and they would then bring some of it to the monarch to drink. The water is the heart; the royal servants are the recluse; the mud, the sandy atoms, and the bits of water-plants are evil dispositions; and the water-cleansing gem is faith.'

'And how is aspiration the mark of faith?'

'In as much as the recluse, on perceiving how the hearts of others have been set free, aspires to enter as it were by a leap upon the fruit of the first stage, or of the second, or of the third in the Excellent Way, or to gain Arahatship itself, and thus applies himself to the attainment of what he has not reached, to the experience of what he has not yet felt, to the realisation of what he has not yet realised,—therefore is it that aspiration is the mark of faith.'

'Give me an illustration.'

'Just, O king, as if a mighty storm [36] were to break upon a mountain top and pour out rain, the water would flow down according to the levels, and after filling up the crevices and chasms and gullies

---

[1] Udakappasâdako mani. Doubtless a magic gem is meant: with allusion particularly to the Wondrous Gem (the Mani-ratana) of the mythical King of Glory (see my 'Buddhist Suttas,' p. 256).

of the hill, would empty itself into the brook below, so that the stream would rush along, overflowing both its banks. Now suppose a crowd of people, one after the other, were to come up, and being ignorant of the real breadth or depth of the water, were to stand fearful and hesitating on the brink. And suppose a certain man should arrive, who knowing exactly his own strength and power should gird himself firmly and, with a spring, land himself on the other side. Then the rest of the people, seeing him safe on the other side, would likewise cross. That is the kind of way in which the recluse, by faith [1], aspires to leap, as it were by a bound, into higher things. For this has been said, O king, by the Blessed One in the Sa*m*yutta Nikâya:

"By faith he crosses over the stream,
By earnestness the sea of life;
By steadfastness all grief he stills,
By wisdom is he purified [2]."'

'Well put, Nâgasena!'

---

[1] In the Buddha, in the sufficiency of the Excellent Way he taught, and in the capacity of man to walk along it. It is spoken of slightingly (compared with Arahatship) in Mahâvagga V, 1, 21—in the Mahâparinibbâna Sutta VI, 9 (of Ânanda, who has faith, compared with the brethren, who have entered one or other of the stages of the Excellent Way)—and in Anguttara III, 21 (in comparison with intuitive insight and intellectual perception). For this last comparison see further the Puggala Pa*ññ*atti III, 3. From these passages a fair idea of the Buddhist view of faith could be formed. Although the Buddhist faith and the Christian faith are in things contradictory, the two conditions of heart are strikingly similar both in origin and in consequence.

[2] This verse is not yet reached in the Pâli Text Society's edition of the Sa*m*yutta, but it is found also in the Sutta Nipâta I, 10, 4.

11[1]. The king said: 'What, Nâgasena, is the characteristic mark of perseverance?'

'The rendering of support, O king, is the mark of perseverance[2]. All those good qualities which it supports do not fall away.'

'Give me an illustration.'

'Just as a man, if a house were falling, would make a prop for it of another post, and the house so supported would not fall; just so, O king, is the rendering of support the mark of perseverance, and all those good qualities which it supports do not fall away.'

'Give me a further illustration.'

'Just as when a large army has broken up a small one, then the king of the latter would call to mind every possible ally and reinforce his small army[3], and by that means the small army might in its turn break up the large one; just so, O king, is the rendering of support the mark of perseverance, and all those good qualities which it supports do not fall away [37]. For it has been said by the Blessed One: "The persevering hearer of the noble truth, O Bhikkhus, puts away evil and cultivates goodness, puts away that which is wrong and develops in himself that which is right, and thus does he keep himself pure."'

---

[1] This section is summarised by Hardy, loc. cit. p. 409.

[2] Buddhaghosa, loc. cit., says that paggaha (tension) is the mark of viriyindriya.

[3] Aññamaññam anusâreyya anupeseyya. This is the way in which Hina/i-kumburê understands this doubtful passage. Hardy has bungled the whole simile. Both the words are new, and I am not sure that the first does not after all come from the root sar, to follow.

'Well put, Nâgasena!'

12. The king said: 'What, Nâgasena, is the characteristic mark of mindfulness[1]?'

'Repetition, O king, and keeping up[2].'

'And how is repetition the mark of mindfulness?'

'As mindfulness, O king, springs up in his heart he repeats over the good and evil, right and wrong, slight and important, dark and light qualities, and those that resemble them, saying to himself: "These are the four modes of keeping oneself ready and mindful, these the four modes of spiritual effort, these the four bases of extraordinary powers, these the five organs of the moral sense, these the five mental powers, these the seven bases of Arahatship, these the eight divisions of the Excellent Way, this is serenity and this insight, this is wisdom and this emancipation[3]." Thus does the recluse follow after

---

[1] Sati, summarised in Hardy's 'Manual,' p. 412.

[2] Apilâpana and upagaṇhana, both new words. This definition is in keeping with the etymological meaning of the word sati, which is 'memory.' It is one of the most difficult words (in its secondary, ethical, and more usual meaning) in the whole Buddhist system of ethical psychology to translate. Hardy renders 'conscience,' which is certainly wrong; and Gogerly (see my 'Buddhist Suttas,' p. 144) has 'meditation,' which is equally wide of the mark. I have sometimes rendered it 'self-possession.' It means that activity of mind, constant presence of mind, wakefulness of heart, which is the foe of carelessness, inadvertence, self-forgetfulness. And it is a very constant theme of the Buddhist moralist. Buddhaghosa, loc. cit., makes upaṭṭhâna, 'readiness,' its mark.

[3] These are the various moral qualities and mental habits which together make up Arahatship, and may be said also to make up Buddhism (as the Buddha taught it). It was on these that he laid special stress, in his last address to the members of the Order, just before his death ('Book of the Great Decease,' III, 65, in my 'Buddhist Suttas,' pp. 60-63); and the details of them will be found in the note to that passage.

those qualities that are desirable, and not after those that are not; thus does he cultivate those which ought to be practised, and not those which ought not. That is how repetition is the mark of mindfulness.'

'Give me an illustration.'

'It is like the treasurer of the imperial sovran[1], who reminds his royal master early and late of his glory, saying: "So many are thy war elephants, O king, and so many thy cavalry[2], thy war chariots and thy bowmen, so much the quantity of thy money, and gold, and wealth, may your Majesty keep yourself in mind thereof."'

'And how, Sir, is keeping up a mark of mindfulness?'

'As mindfulness springs up in his heart, O king, he searches out the categories of good qualities and their opposites, saying to himself: "Such and such qualities are good, and such bad; [38] such and such qualities helpful, and such the reverse." Thus does the recluse make what is evil in himself to disappear, and keeps up what is good. That is how keeping up is the mark of mindfulness.'

'Give me an illustration.'

'It is like the confidential adviser of that imperial

---

[1] *Kakkavattissa* bha*nd*âgâriko, no doubt with allusion to the gahapati-ratana*m*, one of the seven treasures of the mythical King of Glory (see my 'Buddhist Suttas,' p. 257). It is particularly interesting to me to find here the use of the word 'treasurer' instead of 'householder;' for it was in that exact sense that I had understood the word gahapati in that connection, at a time when, in the then state of Pâli scholarship, it seemed very bold to do so.

[2] Literally 'horses.' The whole list is again a manifest allusion to the corresponding one in the Sutta of the Great King of Glory.

sovran[1] who instructs him in good and evil, saying: "These things are bad for the king and these good, these helpful and these the reverse." And thus the king makes the evil in himself die out, and keeps up the good.'

'Well put, Nâgasena!'

13[2]. The king said: 'What, Nâgasena, is the characteristic mark of meditation[3]?'

'Being the leader, O king. All good qualities have meditation as their chief, they incline to it, lead up towards it, are as so many slopes up the side of the mountain of meditation.'

'Give me an illustration.'

'As all the rafters of the roof of a house, O king, go up to the apex, slope towards it, are joined on together at it, and the apex is acknowledged to be the top of all; so is the habit of meditation in its relation to other good qualities.'

'Give me a further illustration.'

'It is like a king, your Majesty, when he goes down to battle with his army in its fourfold array. The whole army—elephants, cavalry, war chariots, and bowmen—would have him as their chief, their

---

[1] Parinâyaka, the seventh treasure of the King of Glory. (Compare the 'Buddhist Suttas,' p. 259.) It will be seen that our author is in substantial agreement with the older tradition, and does not, like the Lalita Vistara, understand under this officer a general.

[2] Omitted by Hardy.

[3] Samâdhi. Buddhaghosa, loc. cit. p. 65, gives also 'being the chief' as its mark, but he previously (p. 64) gives avikkhepa, 'serenity,' as the mark of sammâ-samâdhi, and also (p. 63) of samâdhindriya, while 'being unshaken by spiritual pride' is his mark (p. 63) of Samâdhi-bala.

lines would incline towards him, lead up to him, they would be so many mountain slopes, one above another, with him as their summit, round him they would all be ranged. [39] And it has been said, O king, by the Blessed One: "Cultivate in yourself, O Bhikkhus, the habit of meditation. He who is established therein knows things as they really are[1].'"

'Well put, Nâgasena!'

---

14. The king said: 'What, Nâgasena, is the characteristic mark of wisdom[2]?'

'I have already told you, O king, how cutting off, severance, is its mark[3], but enlightenment is also its mark.'

'And how is enlightenment its mark?'

'When wisdom springs up in the heart, O king, it dispels the darkness of ignorance, it causes the radiance of knowledge to arise, it makes the light of intelligence to shine forth[4], and it makes the Noble Truths plain. Thus does the recluse who is devoted to effort perceive with the clearest wisdom the impermanency (of all beings and things), the suffering (that is inherent in individuality), and the absence of any soul.'

'Give me an illustration.'

'It is like a lamp, O king, which a man might introduce into a house in darkness. When the lamp had been brought in it would dispel the darkness,

---

[1] Sa*m*yutta Nikâya XXI, 5.
[2] Paññâ. Hardy in the 'Manual of Buddhism,' pp. 414, 415, gives a jumble of this passage and several others.
[3] See above, p. 51.
[4] Vida*m*seti, not in Childers; but compare Theri Gâthâ, 74; Anguttara III, 103; and *G*âtaka III, 222.

cause radiance to arise, and light to shine forth, and make the objects there plainly visible. Just so would wisdom in a man have such effects as were just now set forth.'

'Well put, Nâgasena!'

---

15. The king said: 'These qualities which are so different[1], Nâgasena, do they bring about one and the same result?'

'They do. The putting an end to evil dispositions.'

'How is that? Give me an illustration.'

'They are like the various parts of an army—elephants, cavalry, war chariots, and archers—who all work to one end, to wit: the conquest in battle of the opposing army.'

'Well put, Nâgasena!'

Here ends the First Chapter.

---

[1] That is, the five referred to above, p. 51, § 9.

Book II. Chapter 2.

1. [40] The king said: 'He who is born, Nâgasena, does he remain the same or become another?'

'Neither the same nor another.'

'Give me an illustration.'

'Now what do you think, O king? You were once a baby, a tender thing, and small in size, lying flat on your back. Was that the same as you who are now grown up?'

'No. That child was one, I am another.'

'If you are not that child, it will follow that you have had neither mother nor father, no! nor teacher. You cannot have been taught either learning, or behaviour, or wisdom. What, great king! is the mother of the embryo in the first stage different from the mother of the embryo in the second stage, or the third, or the fourth [1]? Is the mother of the baby a different person from the mother of the grown-up man? Is the person who goes to school one, and the same when he has finished his schooling another? Is it one who commits a crime, another who is punished by having his hands or feet cut off [2]?'

'Certainly not. But what would you, Sir, say to that?'

The Elder replied: 'I should say that I am the same person, now I am grown up, as I was when I was a tender tiny baby, flat on my back. For all these states are included in one by means of this body.'

'Give me an illustration.'

---

[1] On these four stages see *Gâtaka* IV, 496, and *Samyutta* X, 1, 3.

[2] Hardy makes sad nonsense of all this.

'Suppose a man, O king, were to light a lamp, would it burn the night through?'

'Yes, it might do so.'

'Now, is it the same flame that burns in the first watch of the night, Sir, and in the second?'

'No.'

'Or the same that burns in the second watch and in the third?'

'No.'

'Then is there one lamp in the first watch, and another in the second, and another in the third?'

'No. The light comes from the same lamp all the night through.'

'Just so, O king, is the continuity of a person or thing maintained. One comes into being, another passes away; and the rebirth is, as it were, simultaneous. Thus neither as the same nor as another does a man go on to the last phase of his self-consciousness[1].'

'Give me a further illustration.'

---

[1] Hardy (p. 429) renders this as follows: 'In the same way, great king, one being is conceived, another is born, another dies; when comprehended by the mind, it is like a thing that has no before, and no after; no preceding, no succeeding existence. Thus the being who is born does not continue the same, nor does he become another; the last winyâna, or consciousness, is thus united with the rest.' (!) He confesses himself in doubt as to the last few words, but is quite unconscious of having completely misinterpreted the whole paragraph.

The meaning is really quite plain in both the Pâli and the Siṃhalese. A man, at any one moment, is precisely all that he is then conscious of. The phase of his self-consciousness, the totality of that of which he is conscious, is always changing; and is so different at death from what it was at birth that, in a certain sense, he is not the same at the one time as he was at the other. But there is a continuity in the whole series;—a continuity dependent

'It is like milk, [41] which when once taken from the cow, turns, after a lapse of time, first to curds, and then from curds to butter, and then from butter to ghee. Now would it be right to say that the milk was the same thing as the curds, or the butter, or the ghee?'

'Certainly not; but they are produced out of it.'

'Just so, O king, is the continuity of a person or thing maintained. One comes into being, another passes away; and the rebirth is, as it were, simultaneous. Thus neither as the same nor as another does a man go on to the last phase of his self-consciousness.'

'Well put, Nâgasena!'

2[1]. The king said: 'Is a man, Nâgasena, who will not be reborn, aware of the fact?'

'Yes, O king.'

'And how does he know it?'

'By the cessation of all that is cause, proximate or remote[2], of rebirth.'

'Give me an illustration.'

'Suppose a farmer, great king, had ploughed and sown and filled his granary; and then for a period should neither plough nor sow, but live on the

---

on the whole body. And this fits the simile, in which the lamp is the body, and the flame the changing self-consciousness; whereas it is impossible to make the simile fit the conclusion as rendered by Hardy.

On the phrase apubbam akariyam see Dr. Morris's note at p. 101 of the Pâli Text Society's Journal, 1887, and the passages he there quotes.

[1] Omitted in Hardy. The correlative question is discussed below, III, 5, 8, p. 112.

[2] That is to say, Tanhâ and Upâdâna.

stored-up grain, or dispose of it in barter, or deal with it as he had need. Would the farmer be aware, great king, that his granary was not getting filled?'

'Yes, he ought to know it.'

'But how?'

'He would know that the cause, proximate and remote, of the filling of the granary had ceased.'

'Just so with the man you spoke of. By the cessation of all that leads to rebirth, he would be conscious of having escaped his liability to it.'

'Well explained, Nâgasena!'

---

3 [1]. The king said: 'He who has intelligence, Nâgasena, has he also wisdom [2]?'

'Yes, great king.' [**42**]

'What; are they both the same?'

'Yes.'

'Then would he, with his intelligence—which, you say, is the same as wisdom—be still in bewilderment or not?'

'In regard to some things, yes; in regard to others, no.'

'What would he be in bewilderment about?'

'He would still be in bewilderment as to those parts of learning he had not learnt, as to those countries he had not seen, and as to those names or terms he had not heard.'

'And wherein would he not be in bewilderment?'

'As regards that which has been accomplished by insight—(the perception, that is,) of the imper-

---

[1] Summarised in Hardy's 'Manual,' p. 414.
[2] Ñâna and paññâ.

manence of all beings, of the suffering inherent in individuality, and of the non-existence of any soul [1].'

' Then what would have become of his delusions on those points.'

' When intelligence has once arisen, that moment delusion has died away.'

' Give me an illustration.'

' It is like the lamp, which when a man has brought into a darkened room, then the darkness would vanish away, and light would appear.'

' And what, Nâgasena, on the other hand, has then become of his wisdom ?'

' When the reasoning wisdom has effected that which it has to do, then the reasoning ceases to go on. But that which has been acquired by means of it remains—the knowledge, to wit, of the impermanence of every being, of the suffering inherent in individuality, and of the absence of any soul.'

' Give me an illustration, reverend Sir, of what you have last said.'

' It is as when a man wants, during the night, to send a letter, and after having his clerk called, has a lamp lit, and gets the letter written. Then, when that has been done, he extinguishes the lamp. But though the lamp had been put out the writing would still be there. Thus does reasoning cease, and knowledge remain.'

' Give me a further illustration.'

' In Eastern districts [43] the peasants have a custom of arranging five pots full of water behind

---

[1] That is, he might still be wrong on matters of mere worldly knowledge, but would be clear in his mind as to the fundamental truths of religion. Compare the analogous distinctions often drawn as to the inspiration of Scripture, or the infallibility of the Pope.

each hut with the object of putting out at once any spark of fire that may be kindled. Suppose now the house had caught fire, and they had thrown those five potfulls of water over the hut, and the fire had gone out, would those peasants then think of still going on using the water-pots?'

'No, Sir, the water-pots would be done with. What would be the use of them (on that occasion) any more?'

'The five water-pots are the five organs of moral sense—faith, to wit, and perseverance in effort, and mindfulness, and meditation, and the reasoning wisdom. The peasantry are the recluse, who is devoted in effort[1]; the fire is sinfulness. As the fire is put out by the water in the five pots, so is sinfulness extinguished by the five organs of moral sense, and when once extinguished it does not again arise[2].'

'Give me a further illustration.'

'It is like a physician who goes to the sick man with the five kinds of drugs made from medicinal

---

[1] Yogâvakaro; one of the technical terms in constant use by our author, but not found in the Pâli Pitakas. Hardy renders it, 'who is seeking Nirvâna;' but though this may be suggested by the term, it is not its meaning. Literally it is 'he whose sphere, whose constant resort, is Yoga.' Now yoga is 'diligence, devotion, mental concentration;' and there is nothing to show that our author is using the word as an epithet of Arahatship. It seems to me, therefore, that the whole compound merely means one of those 'religious,' in the technical sense, who were also religious in the higher, more usual sense. It would thus be analogous to the phrase samgâmâvakaro, 'at home in war,' used of a war elephant in the Samgâmâvakara Gâtaka (Fausböll, II, 95), and of a soldier below, Mil. 44.

[2] This must, I think, be understood in a modified sense, for the first of the four Great Exertions (Sammappadhânas) is the effort to prevent sinful conditions arising.

roots[1], and grinding them up, gives him to drink, and thereby his sickness passes away. Would the physician in that case think of making any further use of the medicine?'

'Certainly not, the medicine has done its work. What would be the use of any more?'

'Just so, O king, when sinfulness is destroyed by the five moral powers, then reasoning ceases, but knowledge remains.'

[44] 'Give me a further illustration.'

'It is like a warrior, at home in war, who takes five javelins and goes down to battle to conquer the foe. And when he has cast them the enemy is broken. There is no need for him to go on casting javelins any more.'

'Well put, Nâgasena!'

---

4. The king said: 'He who will not be reborn, Nâgasena, does he still feel any painful sensation?'

The Elder replied: 'Some he feels and some not.'

'Which are they?'

'He may feel bodily pain, O king; but mental pain he would not.'

'How would that be so?'

'Because the causes, proximate or remote, of bodily pain still continue, he would be liable to it. But the causes, proximate or remote, of mental agony having ceased, he could not feel it. For it has been said by the Blessed One: "One kind of pain he suffers, bodily pain: but not mental."'

'Then why, Sir, does he not die?'

'The Arahat, O king, has need neither to curry

---

[1] Pañka mûla bhessaggâni: not the five principal sorts of medicine mentioned by Childers.

favour nor to bear malice. He shakes not down the unripe fruit, but awaits the full time of its maturity. For it has been said, O king, by the Elder, Sâriputta, the Commander of the faith [45]:

"It is not death, it is not life I welcome;
As the hireling his wage, so do I bide my time.
It is not death, it is not life I want;
Mindful and thoughtful do I bide my time[1].'"

'Well put, Nâgasena!'

---

5. The king said: 'Is a pleasant sensation, Nâgasena, good or evil or indifferent?'

'It may be any one of the three.'

'But surely, Sir, if good conditions are not painful, and painful ones not good, then there can arise no good condition that is at the same time painful[2].'

'Now, what do you think, great king? Suppose a man were to hold in one hand a red-hot ball of iron, and in the other a lump of icy snow, would they both hurt him?'

'Yes; they both would.'

'But are they both hot?'

'Certainly not.'

'But are they both cold?'

'No.'

'Then acknowledge yourself put in the wrong! If the heat hurts, and they are not both hot, the pain cannot come from the heat. If the cold hurts,

---

[1] These verses are nearly the same as those put in reverse order into Sâriputta's mouth in the Theri Gâthâ, 1003, 1002. And the first two lines, as Dr. Rost was good enough to point out to me, are identical (except as to a slight grammatical variation) with Manu VI, 45.

[2] And the same, therefore, of pleasant sensations that are evil.

and they are not both cold, the pain cannot come from the cold. How then, O king, can they both hurt you, since they are not both hot, nor both cold, and (as one is hot and the other cold) the pain comes neither from the hot nor from the cold?'

'I am not equal to argument with you. Be so good, Sir, as to explain how the matter stands.'

Then the Elder reasoned with king Milinda, persuading him by talk on the subject drawn from the Abhidhamma, such as: 'There are these six pleasures, O king, connected with life in the world, and these other six with renunciation. There are six griefs connected with life in the world, and six with renunciation. There are six kinds of indifference to pleasure and to grief connected with life in the world, and six with renunciation. [46] Altogether there are thus six series of six, that is to say, thirty-six kinds of sensations in the present, and the like number in the past, and the like in the future. And adding all these up in one total we arrive at one hundred and eight kinds of sensation.'

'Well put, Nâgasena!'

6[1]. The king said: 'What is it, Nâgasena, that is reborn?'

'Name-and-form is reborn.'

'What, is it this same name-and-form that is reborn?'

'No: but by this name-and-form deeds are done, good or evil, and by these deeds (this Karma) another name-and-form is reborn.'

---

[1] This dialogue is in Hardy, p. 429 (No. 7).

'If that be so, Sir, would not the new being be released from its evil Karma[1]?'

The Elder replied: 'Yes, if it were not reborn. But just because it is reborn, O king, it is therefore not released from its evil Karma.'

'Give me an illustration.'

'Suppose, O king, some man were to steal a mango from another man, and the owner of the mango were to seize him and bring him before the king, and charge him with the crime. And the thief were to say: "Your Majesty! I have not taken away this man's mangoes. Those that he put in the ground are different from the ones I took. I do not deserve to be punished." How then? would he be guilty?'

'Certainly, Sir. He would deserve to be punished.'

'But on what ground?'

'Because, in spite of whatever he may say, he would be guilty in respect of the last mango which resulted from the first one (the owner set in the ground).'

'Just so, great king, deeds good or evil are done by this name-and-form and another is reborn. But that other is not thereby released from its deeds (its Karma).'

'Give me a further illustration.'

'It is like rice or sugar so stolen, of which the same might be said as of the mango. [47] Or it is like the fire which a man, in the cold season, might kindle, and when he had warmed himself, leave still burning, and go away. Then if that fire were to set

---

[1] Repeated below, III, 5, 7, p. 112.

another man's field on fire, and the owner of the field were to seize him, and bring him before the king, and charge him with the injury, and he were to say: "Your Majesty! It was not I who set this man's field on fire. The fire I left burning was a different one from that which burnt his field. I am not guilty." Now would the man, O king, be guilty?'

'Certainly, Sir.'

'But why?'

'Because, in spite of whatever he might say, he would be guilty in respect of the subsequent fire that resulted from the previous one.'

'Just so, great king, deeds good or evil are done by this name-and-form and another is reborn. But that other is not thereby released from its deeds (its Karma).'

'Give me a further illustration.'

'Suppose, O king, a man were to take a lamp and go up into the top storey of his house, and there eat his meal. And the lamp blazing up were to set the thatch on fire, and from that the house should catch fire, and that house having caught fire the whole village should be burnt. And they should seize him and ask: "What, you fellow, did you set our village on fire for?" And he should reply: "I've not set your village on fire! The flame of the lamp, by the light of which I was eating, was one thing; the fire which burnt your village was another thing." Now if they, thus disputing, should go to law before you, O king, in whose favour would you decide the case?'

'In the villagers' favour.'

'But why?'

'Because, Sir, in spite of whatever the man might say, the one fire was produced from the other.'

'Just so, great king, it is one name-and-form which has its end in death, and another name-and-form which is reborn. But the second is the result of the first, and is therefore not set free from its evil deeds.'

'Give me a further illustration.'

'Suppose, O king, a man were to choose a young girl in marriage, and give a price[1] for her and go away. [48] And she in due course should grow up to full age, and then another man were to pay a price for her and marry her. And when the first one had come back he should say: "Why, you fellow, have you carried off my wife?" And the other were to reply: "It's not your wife I have carried off! The little girl, the mere child, whom you chose in marriage and paid a price for is one; the girl grown up to full age whom I chose in marriage and paid a price for, is another." Now if they, thus disputing, were to go to law about it before you, O king, in whose favour would you decide the case?'

'In favour of the first.'

'But why?'

'Because, in spite of whatever the second might say, the grown-up girl would have been derived from the other girl.'

'Just so, great king, it is one name-and-form which has its end in death, and another name-and-form

---

[1] Suṅka*m* datvâ. Literally 'paying a tax.' So early were early marriages! Compare Theri Gâthâ, 402. Hînaṭi-kumburê, p. 58, has wœ/up dî, 'having provided her with means of subsistence.' But, of course, the Suṅka must have been a price paid to the parents.

which is reborn. But the second is the result of the first, and is therefore not set free from its evil deeds.'

'Give me a further illustration.'

'Suppose a man, O king, were to buy of a herdsman a vessel of milk, and go away leaving it in his charge, saying: " I will come for it to-morrow;" and the next day it were to become curds. And when the man should come and ask for it, then suppose the other were to offer him the curds, and he should say: " It was not curds I bought of you; give me my vessel of milk." And the other were to reply: " Without any fault of mine[1] your milk has turned to curds." Now if they, thus disputing, were to go to law about it before you, O king, in whose favour would you decide the case?'

'In favour of the herdsman.'

'But why?'

'Because, in spite of whatever the other might say, the curds were derived from the milk.'

'Just so, great king, it is one name-and-form that finds its end in death, and another that is reborn. But that other is the result of the first, and is therefore not thereby released from its evil deeds (its bad Karma).'

'Very good, Nâgasena!'

7[2]. The king said: 'Will you, Nâgasena, be reborn?'

---

[1] Agânato: there is an ambiguity here, as the word may mean 'to me not knowing it,' or 'to you not knowing it.' Hînati-kumburê takes the latter interpretation, and renders: 'O come! Do you not know that your milk has become curds?' (Embala, tâge kiri mawû bawa no dannehi dœyi.)

[2] Not in Hardy.

' Nay, great king, what is the use of asking that question again ? Have I not already told you that if, when I die, [49] I die with craving in my heart, I shall; but if not, not [1] ? '

' Give me an illustration.'

' Suppose, O king, a man were to render service to the king [2] : and the king, pleased with him, were to bestow an office upon him. And then that he, while living through that appointment, in the full possession and enjoyment of all the pleasures of sense, should publicly declare that the king had repaid him naught. Now would that man, O king, be acting rightly ? '

' Most certainly not.'

' Just so, great king, what is the use of asking that question again ? Have I not already told you that if, when I die, I die with craving in my heart, I shall; and if not, not ? '

' You are ready, Nâgasena, in reply.'

---

8. The king said : ' You were talking just now of name-and-form. What does " name " mean in that expression, and what " form " ? '

' Whatever is gross therein, that is " form": whatever is subtle, mental, that is " name." '

' Why is it, Nâgasena, that name is not reborn separately, or form separately ? '

' These conditions, great king, are connected one with the other; and spring into being together.'

' Give me an illustration.'

' As a hen, great king, would not get a yoke or

---

[1] See above, Chapter 1, § 6, p. 50.

[2] This simile, with a different conclusion, recurs below, II, 3, 10 (p. 93).

an egg-shell separately, but both would arise in one, they two being intimately dependent one on the other; just so, if there were no name there would be no form. What is meant by name in that expression being intimately dependent on what is meant by form, they spring up together. And this is, through time immemorial, their nature[1].'

'You are ready, Nâgasena, in reply.'

9. The king said: 'You speak, Nâgasena, of time immemorial. What does this word "time" mean?'

'Past time, O king, and present, and future.'

'But what? is there such a thing as time?'

'There is time which exists, and time which does not.'

'Which then exists, and which not?'

[50] 'There are Confections (constituent potentialities of being)[2], O king, which are past in the sense of having passed away, and ceased to be, or of having been dissolved, or altogether changed. To them time is not. But there are conditions of heart which are now producing their effect, or still have in them the inherent possibility of producing

---

[1] Evam eta*m* dîgham addhâna*m* sa*m*bhâvita*m*: which Hardy, p. 141, renders: 'They accompany each other (as to the species, but not as to the individual) during infinitude.' But even the Si*m*halese text cannot be made to mean this.

[2] Sa*m*khârâ. See the full list in my 'Buddhism,' pp. 91, 92 (a list, indeed, not found as yet in the Pi*t*akas, and probably later, but yet founded on the older divisions, and explanatory of them). They are all those divisions into which existence (or the process of becoming and ceasing to be as Buddhism looks at it) should be divided, and are practically so many sorts of action (Karma). For the older divisions see the note at the passages quoted in 'Vinaya Texts,' I, 76.

effect, or which will otherwise lead to reindividualisation. To them time is. Where there are beings who, when dead, will be reborn, there time is. Where there are beings who, when dead, will not be reborn, there time is not; and where there are beings who are altogether set free (who, having attained Nirvâṇa in their present life, have come to the end of that life), there time is not—because of their having been quite set free[1].'

'You are ready, Nâgasena, in reply.'

Here ends the Second Chapter.

---

[1] Parinibbutattâ. Hardy renders this whole clause (the last lines): 'Nirvâṇa is attained, time is no longer.' But this is one of the endless confusions arising out of not knowing the distinction between Nirvâṇa and Parinirvâṇa. To a man who had 'attained Nirvâṇa' there would still be time as long as he was in the enjoyment of it, that is as long as he continued in his present (and last) existence. The Siṃhalese is perfectly clear.

Book II. Chapter 3.

1. The king said: 'What is the root, Nâgasena, of past time, and what of present, and what of future time?'

'Ignorance. By reason of Ignorance came the Confections, by reason of the Confections consciousness, by reason of consciousness name-and-form, by reason of name-and-form the six organs of sense [1], by reason of them contact, by reason of contact sensation, by reason of sensation thirst, by reason of thirst craving, by reason of craving becoming, by reason of becoming birth, by reason of birth old age and death, grief, lamentation, sorrow, pain, and despair. Thus is it that the ultimate point in the past of all this time is not apparent.'

'You are ready, Nâgasena, in reply.'

---

2. The king said: 'You say that the ultimate point of time is not apparent. Give me an illustration of that.'

'Suppose, O king, a man were to plant in the ground a tiny seed, and that it were to come up as a shoot, and in due course grow, develope, and mature until it produced a fruit. [51] And then the man, taking a seed from that fruit, were again to plant it in the ground, and all should happen as before. Now would there be any end to this series?'

'Certainly not, Sir.'

---

[1] Sa*l*âyatanâni, that is the eye, ear, nose, tongue, body (as the organ of touch), and mind (or, as we should say, brain).

'Just so, O king, the ultimate point in the past of the whole of this time is not apparent.'

'Give me a further illustration.'

'The hen lays an egg. From the egg comes a hen. From the hen an egg. Is there any end to this series?'

'No.'

'Just so, O king, the ultimate point in the past of the whole of this time is not apparent.'

'Give me a further illustration.'

Then the Elder drew a circle on the ground and asked the king: 'Is there any end to this circle?'

'No, it has no end.'

'Well, that is like those circles spoken of by the Blessed One[1]. "By reason of the eye and of forms there arises sight[2], when these three come together there is touch, by reason of touch sensation, by reason of sensation a longing (Tanhâ, thirst), by reason of the longing action (Karma), and from action eye is once more produced[3]." Now is there any end to this series?'

'No.'

---

[1] Hinaṭi-kumburê applies this to the previous words (the circles of the chain of life quoted in § 1 from the Mahâvagga I, 1, 2), and he is followed by Hardy, p. 434. Trenckner makes it apply to the following words, giving the reference to No. 18 in the Maggḥima Nikâya, and I think he is right. Whichever way it is taken, the result is much the same.

[2] Kakkhu-viññâna. It is not clear from the terse phraseology of this passage whether this is supposed to be a subjective stage preliminary to the 'touch' (phasso), or whether it is inclusive of it. (Compare Dhamma Sangani, 589, 599, 620.) I am inclined to think it is the former. But if the latter be meant it might be rendered 'there arises that consciousness (of existence) which is dependent upon the eye.' See below, § 4.

[3] That is, another eye in another birth.

Then setting out a precisely corresponding circle of each of the other organs of sense (of the ear, nose, tongue, body, and mind[1]), he in each case put the same question. And the reply being always the same, he concluded:

'Just so, O king, the ultimate point of time in the past is not apparent.'

'You are ready, Nâgasena, in reply.'

3. The king said: 'When you say that the ultimate point is not apparent, what do you mean by "ultimate point"?'

'Of whatsoever time is past. It is the ultimate point of that, O king, that I speak of.'

'But, if so, when you say that it is not apparent, do you mean to say that of everything? Is the ultimate point of everything unknown?'

'Partly so, and partly not.'

'Then which is so, and which not?'

'Formerly, O king, everything in every form, everything in every mode, was ignorance. It is to us as if it were not. In reference to that the ultimate beginning is unknown. But that, which has not been, becomes; as soon as it has begun to become it dissolves away again. In reference to that the ultimate beginning is known[2].' **[52]**

'But, reverend Sir, if that which was not, becomes, and as soon as it has begun to become passes again

---

[1] In the text the whole sentence is repeated of each.

[2] That is, 'the beginning of each link in the chain—the beginning of each individuality—can be traced, but not the beginning of each chain. Each life is a link in a chain of lives, bound together by cause and effect, different, yet the same. There are an infinite number of such chains; and there is no reference in the discussion to any greater unity, or to any "ultimate point" of all the chains.'

away, then surely, being thus cut off at both ends, it must be entirely destroyed[1]?'

'Nay, surely, O king, if it be thus cut off at both ends, can it not at both ends be made to grow again[2]?'

'Yes, it might. But that is not my question. Could it grow again from the point at which it was cut off?'

'Certainly.'

'Give me an illustration.'

Then the Elder repeated the simile of the tree and the seed, and said that the Skandhas (the constituent elements of all life, organic and inorganic) were so many seeds, and the king confessed himself satisfied.

4. The king said: 'Are there any Confections[3] which are produced?'

'Certainly.'

'Which are they?'

'Where there is an eye, and also forms, there is sight[4], where there is sight there is a contact through the eye, where there is contact through the eye there is a sensation, where there is sensation there is a longing[5], where there is longing there is a grasping[6], where there is grasping there is a becoming,

---

[1] That is, 'each individuality must be separate. The supposed chain does not really exist.'

[2] There is an odd change of gender here. Possibly the word 'ignorance' has been dropped out. Trenckner says the passage is corrupt, and the Siṃhalese is so involved as to be unintelligible.

[3] Saṅkhârâ, potentialities, possible forms, of sentient existence.

[4] Kakkhu-viññâna. See note 2 above, p. 80.

[5] Taṇhâ, thirst.

[6] Upâdâna, a stretching out towards a satisfaction of the longing, and therefore a craving for life, time, in which to satisfy it.

where there is becoming there is birth, and at birth old age and death, grief, lamentation, pain, sorrow, and despair begin to be. Thus is the rise of the whole of this class of pain.—Where there is neither eye nor form there is no sight, where there is not sight there is no contact through the eye, where there is not contact there is no sensation, where there is not sensation there is no longing, where there is not longing there is no grasping, where there is not grasping there is no becoming, where there is not becoming there is no birth, and where there is not birth there is neither old age nor death nor grief, lamentation, pain, sorrow, and despair. Thus is the ending of all this class of pain.'

'Very good, Nâgasena!'

5. The king said: 'Are there any Confections (qualities) which spring into being without a gradual becoming?'

'No. They all have a gradual becoming.'

'Give me an illustration.'

'Now what do you think, great king? Did this house in which you are sitting spring suddenly into being?'

[53] 'Certainly not, Sir. There is nothing here which arose in that way. Each portion of it has had its gradual becoming—these beams had their becoming in the forest, and this clay in the earth, and by the moil and toil of women and of men[1] was this house produced.'

---

[1] It is a small matter, but noteworthy, that the Buddhist texts always put the women first.

'Just so, great king, there is no Confection which has sprung into being without a gradual becoming. It is by a process of evolution that Confections come to be!'

'Give me a further illustration.'

'They are like all kinds of trees and plants which, when set in the ground, grow, develope, and mature, and then yield their fruits and flowers. The trees do not spring into being without a becoming. It is by a process of evolution that they become what they are. Just so, great king, there is no Confection which has sprung into being without a gradual becoming. It is by a process of evolution that Confections come to be!'

'Give me a further illustration.'

'They are like the pots of various kinds which a potter might form when he has dug up the clay out of the earth. The pots do not spring into being without a becoming. It is by a process of evolution that they become what they are. Just so, great king, there is no Confection which has sprung into being without a gradual becoming. It is by a process of evolution that Confections come to be!'

'Give me a further illustration.'

'Suppose, O king, there were no bridge of metal on a mandolin[1], no leather, no hollow space, no frame, no neck, no strings, no bow, and no human effort or exertion, would there be music?'

'Certainly not, Sir.'

'But if all these things were there, would not there be a sound?'

---

[1] Vînâya pattam. I don't know what this is. The Simhalese merely repeats the words.

'Of course there would.'

'Just so, great king, there is no Confection which has sprung into being without a gradual becoming. It is by a process of evolution that Confections come to be!'

'Give me a further illustration.'

'Suppose, O king, there were no fire-stick apparatus[1], no twirling-stick[1], and no cord for the twirling-stick, and no matrix[1], and no burnt rag for tinder, and no human effort and exertion, could there be fire by attrition?'

'Certainly not.'

'But if all these conditions were present, then might not fire appear?'

'Yes, certainly.'

[54] 'Just so, great king, there is no Confection which has sprung into being without a gradual becoming. It is by a process of evolution that Confections come to be!'

'Give me one more illustration.'

'Suppose, O king, there were no burning glass, and no heat of the sun, and no dried cow-dung for tinder, could there be fire?'

'Certainly not.'

'But where these things are present there fire might be struck, might it not?'

'Yes.'

'Just so, great king, there is no Confection which

---

[1] Ara*n*i, ara*n*i-potako, and uttarâra*n*i. The exact differentiation of these parts of the fire-stick apparatus is uncertain. The Si*m*halese throws no real light on them, as it translates them respectively ya/a lîya, 'under wood,' matu lîya, 'upper wood,' and uturu lîya, also 'upper wood.' This method of ignition was probably quite as strange to Hîna/i-kumburê as it is to us.

has sprung into being without a gradual becoming. It is by a process of evolution that Confections come to be!'

'Give me another illustration.'

'Suppose, O king, there were no looking-glass, and no light, and no face in front of it, would there appear an image?'

'No.'

'But given these things, there might be a reflection?'

'Yes, Sir, there might.'

'Just so, great king, there is no Confection which has sprung into being without a gradual becoming. It is by a process of evolution that Confections come to be!'

'Very good, Nâgasena!'

6. The king said: 'Is there, Nâgasena, such a thing as the soul[1]?'

'What is this, O king, the soul (Vedagu)?'

'The living principle within[2] which sees forms through the eye, hears sounds through the ear, experiences tastes through the tongue, smells odours through the nose, feels touch through the body, and discerns things (conditions, "dhammâ") through the mind—just as we, sitting here in the palace, can look out of any window out of which we wish to look, the east window or the west, or the north or the south.'

The Elder replied: 'I will tell you about the five

---

[1] Vedagû, see below, III, 5, 6, p. 111, not found in this meaning in the Pi/akas.

[2] Abbhantare gîvo, also not found in this sense in the Pi/akas. Attâ, rendered just above 'image' or 'reflection,' is the word used in them for soul. Hîna/i-kumburê renders this here by prâ*n*a gîwa, 'breath-soul.' See below, III, 7, 15, p. 132; and above, II, 4, p. 48; and II, 2, 6, p. 71.

doors¹, great king. Listen, and give heed attentively. If the living principle within sees forms through the eye in the manner that you mention, [55] choosing its window as it likes, can it not then see forms not only through the eye, but also through each of the other five organs of sense ? And in like manner can it not then as well hear sounds, and experience taste, and smell odours, and feel touch, and discern conditions through each of the other five organs of sense, besides the one you have in each case specified?'

'No, Sir.'

'Then these powers are not united one to another indiscriminately, the latter sense to the former organ, and so on. Now we, as we are seated here in the palace, with these windows all thrown open, and in full daylight, if we only stretch forth our heads, see all kinds of objects plainly. Can the living principle do the same when the doors of the eyes are thrown open ? When the doors of the ear are thrown open, can it do so ? Can it then not only hear sounds, but see sights, experience tastes, smell odours, feel touch, and discern conditions ? And so with each of its windows ?'

'No, Sir.'

[56] 'Then these powers are not united one to another indiscriminately. Now again, great king, if Dinna here were to go outside and stand in the gateway, would you be aware that he had done so?'

'Yes, I should know it.'

'And if the same Dinna were to come back again, and stand before you, would you be aware of his having done so?'

---

¹ It is odd he does not say six.

'Yes, I should know it.'

'Well, great king, would the living principle within discern, in like manner, if anything possessing flavour were laid upon the tongue, its sourness, or its saltness, or its acidity, or its pungency, or its astringency, or its sweetness [1]?'

'Yes, it would know it.'

'But when the flavour had passed into the stomach would it still discern these things?'

'Certainly not.'

'Then these powers are not united one to the other indiscriminately. Now suppose, O king, a man were to have a hundred vessels of honey brought and poured into one trough, and then, having had another man's mouth closed over and tied up, were to have him cast into the trough full of honey. Would he know whether that into which he had been thrown was sweet or whether it was not?'

'No, Sir.'

'But why not?'

'Because the honey could not get into his mouth.'

'Then, great king, these powers are not united one to another indiscriminately [2].'

'I am not capable of discussing with such a reasoner. Be pleased, Sir, to explain to me how the matter stands.'

Then the Elder convinced Milinda the king with discourse drawn from the Abhidhamma, saying: 'It is by reason, O king, of the eye and of forms that sight arises, and those other conditions—contact,

---

[1] This list recurs below, II, 4, 1.

[2] That is: 'Your "living principle within" cannot make use of whichever of its windows it pleases. And the simile of a man inside a house does not hold good of the soul.' See the end of II, 3, 16.

sensation, idea, thought, abstraction, sense of vitality, and attention [1]—arise each simultaneously with its predecessor. And a similar succession of cause and effect arises when each of the other five organs of sense is brought into play. [57] And so herein there is no such thing as soul (Vedagu) [2].'

7. The king said: 'Does thought-perception [3] arise wherever sight arises [4] ?'

'Yes, O king, where the one is there is the other.'

'And which of the two arises first?'

'First sight, then thought.'

'Then does the sight issue, as it were, a command to thought, saying : " Do you spring up there where I have?" or does thought issue command to sight, saying : " Where you spring up there will I."'

'It is not so, great king. There is no intercourse between the one and the other.'

'Then how is it, Sir, that thought arises wherever sight does ?'

'Because of there being a sloping down, and because of there being a door, and because of there being a habit [5], and because of there being an association.'

'How is that ? Give me an illustration of mind arising where sight arises because of there being a sloping down.'

'Now what do you think, great king ? When it rains [6], where will the water go to ?'

---

[1] The last four are *k*etanâ, ekaggatâ, *g*îvitindriya*m*, and manasikâro; and in the Si*m*halese are simply repeated in their Si*m*halese form.

[2] This conclusion is all wrong in Hardy, pp. 457, 458.

[3] Mano-viññâ*n*a*m*.   [4] *K*akkhu-viññâ*n*a*m*.

[5] *K*i*nn*attâ, which Hîna*t*i-kumburê renders purudu bœwin.

[6] Deve vassante: 'when the god rains.'

'It will follow the slope of the ground.'

'And if it were to rain again, where would the water go to?'

'It would go the same way as the first water had gone.'

'What then? Does the first water issue, as it were, command to the second, saying: "Do you go where I have?" Or does the second issue command to the first, saying: "Whithersoever you go, thither will I"?'

'It is not so, Sir. There is no intercourse between the two. Each goes its way because of the slope of the ground.'

'Just so, great king, [58] is it by reason of the natural slope that where sight has arisen there also does thought arise. And neither does the sight-perception issue command to the mind-perception, saying: "Where I have arisen, there do thou also spring up;" nor does the mind-perception inform the sight-perception, saying: "Where thou hast arisen, there will I also spring up." There is no conversation, as it were, between them. All that happens, happens through natural slope.'

'Now give me an illustration of there being a door.'

'What do you think, great king? Suppose a king had a frontier city, and it was strongly defended with towers and bulwarks, and had only one gateway. If a man wanted to leave the city, how would he go out?'

'By the gate, certainly.'

'And if another man wanted to leave it, how would he go out?'

'The same way as the first.'

'What then? Would the first man tell the second:

"Mind you go out the same way as I do"? Or would the second tell the first: "The way you go out, I shall go out too"?'

'Certainly not, Sir. There would be no communication between them. They would go that way because that was the gate.'

'Just so, great king, with thought and sight.'

'Now give me an illustration of thought arising where sight is because of habit.'

'What do you think, great king? If one cart went ahead, which way would a second cart go?'

'The same as the first.'

'But would the first tell the second to go where it went, [59] or the second tell the first that it would go where it (the first) had gone?'

'No, Sir. There would be no communication between the two. The second would follow the first out of habit.'

'Just so, great king, with sight and thought.'

'Now give me an illustration of how thought arises, where sight has arisen, through association.'

'In the art of calculating by using the joints of the fingers as signs or marks[1], in the art of arithmetic pure and simple[2], in the art of estimating the probable

---

[1] Muddâ. Hîna/i-kumburê is here a little fuller than Buddhaghosa at vol. i, p. 95 of the Sumaṅgala. He says: yam se œṅgili purukhi alwâ gena saññâ ko/a kiyana hasta mudra sâstraya, 'the finger-ring art, so called from seizing on the joints of the fingers, and using them as signs.'

[2] Gaṇanâ. Hîna/i-kumburê says: akkhidra wu gaṇam sâstraya, 'the art of unbroken counting,' which is precisely Buddhaghosa's explanation (confirming the reading we have there adopted), and probably means arithmetic without the aids involved in the last phrase. We have here in that case an interesting peep into the

yield of growing crops¹, and in the art of writing, O king, the beginner is clumsy. But after a certain time with attention and practice he becomes expert. Just so is it that, where sight has arisen, thought too by association springs up.'

And in response to similar questions, the Elder declared that in the same way thought sprang up wherever there was hearing, or taste, or smell, or touch: that in each case it was subsequent to the other, but arose without communication from [60] the natural causes above set out.

8. The king said: 'Where thought (mental perception²) is, Nâgasena, is there always sensation?'

'Yes, where thought arises there is contact, and there is sensation, and there is idea, and there is conceived intention, and there is reflection, and there is investigation³.'

---

9. 'Reverend Sir, what is the distinguishing characteristic of contact (Phassa)?'

'Touch⁴, O king.'

'But give me an illustration.'

'It is as when two rams are butting together, O

---

progress of arithmetical knowledge. When our author wrote, the old way of counting on the fingers was still in vogue, but the modern system was coming into general use.

¹ Saṅkhâ, literally 'calculation,' but which Hardy amplifies into Kshetraya wriksha vilokaya koṭa phala pramânaya kiyannâwû saṃkhyâ sâstraya.

² Mano-viññâṇa as all through the last section. The reader must not forget that mano is here strictly an organ of sense, on an exact level with eye, ear, tongue, &c.

³ Ketanâ, vitakko, and vikâro. See fuller further on, §§ 11, 13, 14.

⁴ Phusana. So also Buddhaghosa at p. 63 of the Sumaṅgala.

king. The eye should be regarded as one of those two, the form (object) as the other, and the contact as the union of the two.'

'Give me a further illustration.'

'It is as when two cymbals [1] are clashed together. The one is as the eye, the other as the object, and the junction of the two is like contact.'

'Very good, Nâgasena!'

---

10. 'Reverend Sir, what is the characteristic mark of sensation (Vedanâ)?'

'The being experienced, great king, and enjoyed [2].'

'Give me an illustration.'

'It is like the case of the man [3] on whom the king, pleased with a service he has rendered him, should bestow an office. He while living, through that appointment, in the full possession and enjoyment of all the pleasures of sense, would think: "Formerly I did the king a service. For that the king, pleased with me, gave me this office. It is on that account that I now experience such sensations."—And it is like the case of the man [61] who having done good deeds is re-born, on the dissolution of the body after death, into some happy conditions of bliss in heaven. He, while living there in the full possession and enjoyment of all the pleasures of sense, would think: "Formerly I must have done good deeds. It is on that account that I now experience such sensations." Thus is it, great king, that the being experienced and enjoyed is the characteristic mark of sensation.'

'Very good, Nâgasena!'

---

[1] Sammâ, compare Theri Gâthâ, 893, 911.
[2] Buddhaghosa, loc. cit., only gives the first of these.
[3] See for a similar illustration above, II, 2, 7. p. 76.

11. 'What is the distinguishing characteristic, Nâgasena, of idea (Saññâ)?'

'Recognition, O king[1]. And what does he recognise?—blueness and yellowness and redness and whiteness and brownness.'

'Give me an illustration.'

'It is like the king's treasurer, O king, who when he sees, on entering the treasure, objects the property of the king of all those colours, recognises (that they have such). Thus it is, great king, that recognition is the mark of idea.'

'Very good, Nâgasena!'

'What is the distinguishing characteristic, Nâgasena, of the conceived purpose (Ketanâ)?'

'The being conceived, O king, and the being prepared[2].'

'Give me an illustration.'

'It is like the case of a man, O king, who should prepare poison, and both drink of it himself, and give of it to others to drink. He himself would suffer pain, and so would they. In the same way some individual, having thought out with intention some evil deed, on the dissolution of the body after death, would be reborn into some unhappy state of woe in purgatory, and so also would those who followed his advice.—And it is like the case of a

---

[1] So also Buddhaghosa, Sumaṅgala, p. 63.

[2] Buddhaghosa, loc. cit., gives no mark of Ketanâ, but he gives both it and 'the being prepared' as the marks of the Confections. It is not clear from the Milinda alone how to render the term Ketanâ, but I follow Aṅguttara III, 77 (where it is placed on a level with aspiration), and Dhamma Saṃgaṇi 5 (where it is said to be born of the contact of mind, perception, and exertion).

man, O king, who should prepare a mixture of ghee, butter, oil, honey and molasses, and should both drink thereof himself and give of it to others to drink. He himself would have pleasure, and so would they. [62] In the same way some individual, having thought out with intention some good deed, will be reborn, on the dissolution of the body after death, into some happy state of bliss in heaven, and so also would those who follow his advice. Thus is it, great king, that the being conceived, and the being prepared, are marks of the conceived purpose.'

'Very good, Nâgasena!'

12. 'What, Nâgasena, is the distinguishing characteristic of perception (Viññâna)?'

'Recognition[1], great king.'

'Give me an illustration.'

'It is like the case of the guardian of a city who, when seated at the cross roads in the middle of the city, could see a man coming from the East, or the South, or the West, or the North. In the same way, O king, he knows an object which he sees with his eye, or a sound which he hears with his ear, or an odour which he smells by his nose, or a taste which he experiences with his tongue, or a touchable thing which he touches with his body, or a quality that he recognises by his mind. Thus is it, great king, that knowing is the mark of perception.'

'Very good, Nâgasena!'

13. 'What is the distinguishing characteristic, Nâgasena, of reflection (Vitakka).

---

[1] Vigânana. So also Buddhaghosa, loc. cit., and below, III, 7, 15, p. 131.

'The effecting of an aim[1].'

'Give me an illustration.'

'It is like the case of a carpenter, great king, who fixes in a joint a well-fashioned piece of wood. Thus is it that the effecting of an aim is the mark of reflection.'

'Very good, Nâgasena!'

14. 'What is the distinguishing characteristic, Nâgasena, of investigation (Vikâra)?'

'Threshing out again and again[2].'

'Give me an illustration.'

'It is like the case of the copper vessel, which, when it is being beaten into shape [63], makes a sound again and again as it gradually gathers shape[3]. The beating into shape is to be regarded as reflection, and the sounding again and again as investigation. Thus is it, great king, that threshing out again and again is the mark of investigation.'

'Very good, Nâgasena!'

Here ends the Third Chapter[4].

---

[1] Appanâ, which Hînati-kumburê renders pihitana. Buddhaghosa, p. 63, gives abhiniropana as its mark, which comes to much the same thing.

[2] Anumaggana. So also Buddhaghosa, loc. cit. p. 63. The word is not in Childers, but see Morris in the Journal of the Pali Text Society, 1886, p. 118.

[3] Anuravati anusandahati. Not in Childers. Hînatikumburê says pasuwa anurâwanâ kere da anuwa pihitâ da.

[4] The following two sections form an appendix to this chapter corresponding to that formed by the last three sections of Book III, Chapter 7. The numbering of the sections is therefore carried on in both cases.

Book II. Chapter 3.

15. The king said: 'When those conditions (whose marks you have just specified) have run together, is it possible, by bending them apart one to one side and one to the other[1], to make the distinction between them clear, so that one can say: "This is contact, and this sensation, and this idea, and this intention, and this perception, and this reflection, and this investigation[2]"?'

'No: that cannot be done.'

'Give me an illustration.'

'Suppose, O king, the cook in the royal household were to make a syrup or a sauce, and were to put into it curds, and salt, and ginger, and cummin seed[3], and pepper, and other ingredients. And suppose the king were to say to him: " Pick out for me the flavour of the curds, and of the salt, and of the ginger, and of the cummin seed, and of the pepper, and of all the things you have put into it." Now would it be possible, great king, separating off one from another those flavours that had thus run together, to pick out each one, so that one could say: " Here is the sourness, and here the saltness, and here the pungency, and here the acidity, and here the astringency, and here the sweetness[4] "?'

---

[1] Vinibbhug̥itvā vinibbhug̥itvā. This question is identical with the one asked of the Buddha at Mag̥g̥hima Nikâya 43, p. 293. Compare also p. 233 and Tela Ka/âha Gâthâ 59.

[2] This list differs from that in II, 3, 8, by the addition of viññāna.

[3] G̥iraka. Compare G̥âtaka I, 244; II, 181, 363. Hina/i-kumburê translates it by duru, and Hardy by 'onions' (p. 439).

[4] This is the same list as is found above, II, 3, 6; and below, III, 4, 2, and the items are not intended to correspond with the condiments in the list above.

'No, that would not be possible [64]. But each flavour would nevertheless be distinctly present by its characteristic sign.'

'And just so, great king, with respect to those conditions we were discussing.'

'Very good, Nâgasena!'

---

16. The Elder said: 'Is salt, O king, recognisable by the eye?'

'Yes, Sir, it is.'

'But be careful, O king.'

'Well then, Sir, is it perceptible by the tongue?'

'Yes, that is right.'

'But, Sir, is it only by the tongue that every kind of salt is distinguished?'

'Yes, every kind.'

'If that be so, Sir, why do bullocks bring whole cart-loads of it? Is it not salt and nothing else that ought to be so brought?'

'It is impossible to bring salt by itself. But all these conditions [1] have run together into one, and produced the distinctive thing called salt [2]. (For instance): salt is heavy, too. But is it possible, O king, to weigh salt?'

---

[1] Not saltness only, but white colour, &c. &c.

[2] He means the king to draw the conclusion that that distinct thing is only recognisable by the tongue; so the senses are not interchangeable. In other words it is true that salt seems to be recognised by the sight, as when people load it into carts they do not stop to taste it. But what they see is not salt, what they weigh is not salt, it is whiteness and weight. And the fact of its being salt is an inference they draw. So, great king, your simile of the soul being inside the body, and using the five senses, as a man inside a house uses windows, does not hold good. See the conclusion above of II, 3, 6, p. 88.

'Certainly, Sir.'

'Nay, great king, it is not the salt you weigh, it is the weight.'

'You are ready, Nâgasena, in argument.'

Here ends the questioning of Nâgasena by Milinda[1].

---

[1] This is again most odd. One would expect, 'Here ends the questioning as to characteristic signs.' See the note at the end of last chapter.

BOOK III.

VIMATI-*KKH*EDANA-PAÑHO.
THE REMOVAL OF DIFFICULTIES.

CHAPTER 4[1].

1. [65] The king said: 'Are the five Âyatanas, Nâgasena, (eye, ear, nose, tongue, and body,) produced by various actions, or by one action?' (that is, the result of various Karmas, or of one Karma.)

'By various actions, not by one.'

'Give me an illustration.'

'Now, what do you think, O king? If I were to sow in one field five kinds of seed, would the produce of those various seeds be of different kinds?'

'Yes, certainly.'

'Well, just so with respect to the production of Âyatanas.'

'Very good, Nâgasena[2]!'

---

2. The king said: 'Why is it, Nâgasena, that all men are not alike, but some are short-lived and some long-lived, some sickly and some healthy, some ugly and some beautiful, some without influence and some of great power, some poor and some wealthy, some low born and some high born, some stupid and some wise?'

---

[1] The chapters go straight on because Books II and III are really only parts of one Book. See above, p. 4.

[2] The meaning here is not easy to follow, as the word Âyatana is used either for the organs of sense, or for the objects of sense; and there is nothing in the context to show which is meant. Probably the idea is that good sight, hearing, &c. in one birth are each the result of a separate Karma in the last birth. But I am by no means sure of this, and the Si*m*halese (p. 76) is just as ambiguous as the Pâli.

The Elder replied: 'Why is it that all vegetables are not alike, but some sour, and some salt, and some pungent, and some acid, and some astringent, and some sweet?'

'I fancy, Sir, it is because they come from different kinds of seeds.'

'And just so, great king, are the differences you have mentioned among men to be explained. For it has been said by the Blessed One: "Beings, O brahmin, have each their own Karma, are inheritors of Karma, belong to the tribe of their Karma, are relatives by Karma, have each their Karma as their protecting overlord. It is Karma that divides them up into low and high and the like divisions[1]."'

'Very good, Nâgasena!'

---

3. The king said: 'You told me, Nâgasena, that your renunciation was to the end that this sorrow might perish away, and no further sorrow might spring up[2].'

[66] 'Yes, that is so.'

'But is that renunciation brought about by previous effort, or to be striven after now, in this present time?'

The Elder replied: 'Effort is now concerned with what still remains to be done, former effort has accomplished what it had to do.'

'Give me an illustration[3].'

---

[1] Mr. Trenckner points out that this quotation is from the Magg*h*ima, No. 135. The doctrine is laid down frequently elsewhere also in the Pi*t*akas. See, for instance, Anguttara IV, 197 (pp. 202–203 of Dr. Morris's edition for the Pâli Text Society).

[2] Above, II, 1, 5, p. 50, and compare I, 38.

[3] These three illustrations recur (nearly) below, III, 7, 3, pp. 125–126.

'Now what do you think, O king? Is it when you feel thirst that you would set to work to have a well or an artificial lake dug out, with the intention of getting some water to drink?'

'Certainly not, Sir.'

'Just so, great king, is effort concerned now with what still remains to be done, former effort has accomplished what it had to do.'

'Give me a further illustration.'

'Now what do you think, O king? Is it when you feel hungry that you set to work to have fields ploughed and seed planted and crops reaped with the intention of getting some food to eat?'

'Certainly not, Sir.'

'Just so, great king, is effort concerned now with what still remains to be done, former effort has accomplished what it had to do.'

'Give me a further illustration.'

'Now what do you think, O king? Is it when the battle is set in array against you that you set to work to have a moat dug, and a rampart put up, and a watch tower built, and a stronghold formed, and stores of food collected? Is it then that you would have yourself taught the management of elephants, or horsemanship, or the use of the chariot and the bow, or the art of fencing?'

'Certainly not, Sir.'

'Just so, great king, is effort concerned now with what still remains to be done, former effort has accomplished what it had to do. For it has been thus said, O king, by the Blessed One:

"Betimes let each wise man work out
   That which he sees to be his weal!
   Not with the carter's mode of thought, but firm

Let him, with resolution, step right out.
As a carter who has left the smooth high road,
. And turned to byways rough, broods ill at ease [1]—
(Like him who hazards all at dice, and fails)—
So the weak mind who still neglects the good,
And follows after evil, grieves at heart,
When fallen into the power of death, as he,
The ruined gamester, in his hour of need [2]."'
[**67**] 'Very good, Nâgasena!'

---

4. The king said: 'You (Buddhists [3]) say thus: "The fire of purgatory is very much more fierce than an ordinary fire. A small stone cast into an ordinary fire may smoke for a day without being destroyed; but a rock as big as an upper chamber cast into the furnace of purgatory would be that moment destroyed." That is a statement I cannot believe. Now, on the other hand you say thus: "Whatsoever beings are there reborn, though they

---

[1] *Ghâyati*. It is an odd coincidence that this word, which means either to burn or to meditate, according to the root from which it is derived, can be rendered here either 'burn' or 'brood' in English. In fact it is the second, not the first, root that is here intended, as is plain from such passages as *G*âtaka III, 354, where the compound pa*ggh*âyati means 'to brood over a thing.'

[2] Quoted from the Sa*m*yutta Nikâya II, 3, 2 (p. 57 in M. Feer's edition, published by the Pâli Text Society). The readings there differ slightly from those of our text here, and the verses are put into the mouth of Khema, the god, instead of being ascribed to the Buddha. Hîna*t*i-kumburê (p. 79) agrees with M. Léon Feer in reading mando for mano in the last line; and I have followed them in my translation. There are several stanzas in the *G*âtaka book of carters lost in the desert, but there is nothing to identify any one of them with the story referred to.

[3] 'You' in the plural: that is, 'you Bhikkhus.' So also above, pp. 30, 50.

burn for hundreds of thousands of years in purgatory, yet are they not destroyed." That too is a statement I don't believe.'

The Elder said: 'Now what do you think, O king? Do not the females of sharks[1] and crocodiles and tortoises and peacocks and pigeons eat hard bits of stone and gravel?'

'Yes, Sir. They do.'

'What then? Are these hard things, when they have got into the stomach, into the interior of the abdomen, destroyed?'

'Yes, they are destroyed.'

'And the embryo that may be inside the same animals,—is that too destroyed?'

'Certainly not.'

'But why not.'

'I suppose, Sir, it escapes destruction by the influence of Karma.'

'Just so, great king, it is through the influence of Karma that beings, though they have been for thousands of years in purgatory, are not destroyed. If they are reborn there, there do they grow up, and there do they die. For this, O king, has been declared by the Blessed One: "He does not die until that evil Karma is exhausted[2]."'

'Give me a further illustration.'

---

[1] It may be noticed that the particular feminine forms chosen are in each case unusual, being in inî instead of the simple î. The first animal, the Makarinî, is said by Childers to be a mythical animal, but it is clear from Buddhaghosa on *K*ullavagga V, 1, 4, that an ordinary animal is meant, and that is so I think here, though the translation 'shark' is conjectural.

[2] From Aṅguttara III, 35, 4 (p. 141 of Dr. Morris's edition for the Pâli Text Society).

'Now what do you think, O king? Do not the females of lions and tigers and panthers and dogs eat hard bits of bone and flesh?'

'Yes, they eat such things.'

'What then? are such hard things, [68] when they have got into the stomach, into the interior of the abdomen, destroyed?'

'Yes, they are destroyed?'

'And the embryo that may be inside the same animals,—is that too destroyed?'

'Certainly not.'

'But why not?'

'I suppose, Sir, it escapes destruction by the influence of Karma.'

'Just so, great king, it is by the influence of Karma that beings in purgatory, though they burn for thousands of years, are not destroyed.'

'Give me a further illustration.'

'Now what do you think, O king? Do not the tender women—wives of the Yonakas, and nobles, and brahmins, and householders—eat hard cakes and meat?'

'Yes, they eat such hard things.'

'And when those hard things have got into the stomach, into the interior of the abdomen, are not they destroyed?'

'Yes, they are.'

'But the children in their womb,—are they destroyed?'

'Certainly not.'

'And why not?'

'I suppose, Sir, they escape destruction by the influence of Karma?'

'Just so, great king, it is through the influence

of Karma that beings in purgatory, though they burn for thousands of years, yet are they not destroyed. If they are reborn there, there do they grow up, and there do they die. For this, O king, has been declared by the Blessed One: "He does not die until that evil Karma is exhausted."'

'Very good, Nâgasena!'

5. The king said: 'Venerable Nâgasena, your people say that the world rests on water, the water on air, the air on space[1]. This saying also I cannot believe.'

Then the Elder brought water in a regulation water-pot[2], and convinced king Milinda, saying: 'As this water is supported by the atmosphere, so is that water supported by air.'

'Very good, Nâgasena!'

6. The king said: 'Is cessation Nirvâna[3]?'

'Yes, your Majesty' [69].

'How is that, Nâgasena?'

'All foolish individuals, O king, take pleasure in

---

[1] This is not a distinctively Buddhist belief. It was commonly held at the time by other teachers. Compare 'Book of the Great Decease,' III, 13 (in 'Buddhist Suttas,' Sacred Books of the East, vol. xi, p. 45).

[2] Dhamma-karakena. The passages show that this was a pot so made, that no water could pass from it except through a filtering medium. When not being actually used the water was no doubt kept at a certain height in it by the pressure of the atmosphere. I do not know of any specimen preserved in our modern museums or figured on ancient bas-reliefs, and the exact shape is unknown. It must be different from the one represented in plate xlviii of Cunningham's 'Bhilsa Tope.' See Kullavagga V, 13, 1 (note); VI, 21, 3; XII, 2, 1; Mahâvamsa, p. 60.

[3] Nirodho nibbânan ti.

the senses and in the objects of sense, find delight in them, continue to cleave to them[1]. Hence are they carried down by that flood (of human passions), they are not set free from birth, old age, and death, from grief, lamentation, pain, sorrow, and despair,—they are not set free, I say, from suffering. But the wise, O king, the disciple of the noble ones, neither takes pleasure in those things, nor finds delight in them, nor continues cleaving to them. And inasmuch as he does not, in him craving[2] ceases, and by the cessation of craving grasping[2] ceases, and by the cessation of grasping becoming[2] ceases, and when becoming has ceased birth ceases, and with its cessation birth, old age, and death, grief, lamentation, pain, sorrow, and despair cease to exist. Thus is the cessation brought about the end of all that aggregation of pain. Thus is it that cessation is Nirvâna.'

'Very good, Nâgasena!'

7. The king said: 'Venerable Nâgasena, do all men receive Nirvâna?'

'Not all, O king. But he who walks righteously, who admits those conditions which ought to be admitted, perceives clearly those conditions which ought to be clearly perceived, abandons those conditions which ought to be abandoned, practises himself in those conditions which ought to be practised, realises those conditions which ought to be realised—he receives Nirvâna.'

'Very good, Nâgasena!'

---

[1] Agghosâya titthanti. Compare Anguttara II, 4, 6, and Theri Gâthâ, 794.

[2] Tanhâ, Upâdâna, Bhava.

8. The king said: 'Venerable Nâgasena, does he who does not receive Nirvâna know how happy a state Nirvâna is [1]?'

'Yes, he knows it.'

'But how can he know that without his receiving Nirvâna?'

'Now what do you think, O king? Do those whose hands and feet have not been cut off know how sad a thing it is to have them cut off?'

'Yes, Sir, that they know.'

'But how do they know it?'

'Well, by hearing the sound of the lamentation of those whose hands and feet have been cut off, they know it.'

[70] 'Just so, great king, it is by hearing the glad words of those who have seen Nirvâna, that they who have not received it know how happy a state it is.'

'Very good, Nâgasena!'

Here ends the Fourth Chapter.

---

[1] The opposite point (whether he who has Nirvâna, knows that he has it) is discussed above, II, 2.

Book III. Chapter 5.

1. The king said: 'Have you, Nâgasena, seen the Buddha?'

'No, Sire.'

'Then have your teachers seen the Buddha?'

'No, Sire.'

'Then, venerable Nâgasena, there is no Buddha[1]!'

'But, great king, have you seen the river Ûhâ in the Himâlaya mountains?'

'No, Sir.'

'Or has your father seen it?'

'No, Sir.'

'Then, your Majesty, is there therefore no such river?'

'It is there. Though neither I nor my father has seen it, it is nevertheless there.'

'Just so, great king, though neither I nor my teachers have seen the Blessed One, nevertheless there was such a person.'

'Very good, Nâgasena!'

2. The king said: 'Is the Buddha, Nâgasena, pre-eminent?'

'Yes, he is incomparable.'

'But how do you know of one you have never seen that he is pre-eminent.'

'Now what do you think, O king? They who have never seen the ocean would they know con-

---

[1] This dialogue is so far identical with VI, 1, 1. It is a kind of parody on Gotama's own argument about the Brahmans and Brahma ('Have they seen God,' &c.) in the Tevigga Sutta I, 12–15, translated in my 'Buddhist Suttas,' pp. 172–174.

cerning it: "Deep, unmeasurable, unfathomable is the mighty ocean. Into it do the five great rivers flow—the Ganges, the Jumna, the A*k*iravatî, the Sarabhû, and the Mahî—and yet is there in it no appearance of being more empty or more full!"?'

'Yes, they would know that.'

'Just so, great king, when I think of the mighty disciples who have passed away then do I know that the Buddha is incomparable.' [71]

'Very good, Nâgasena!'

---

3. The king said: 'Is it possible, Nâgasena, for others to know how incomparable the Buddha is?'

'Yes, they may know it.'

'But how can they?'

'Long, long ago, O king, there was a master of writing, by name Tissa the Elder, and many are the years gone by since he has died. How can people know of him?'

'By his writing, Sir.'

'Just so, great king, whosoever sees what the Truth [1] is, he sees what the Blessed One was, for the Truth was preached by the Blessed One.'

'Very good, Nâgasena!'

---

4. The king said: 'Have you, Nâgasena, seen what the Truth is?'

'Have not we disciples, O king, to conduct ourselves our lives long as under the eye of the Buddha, and under his command [2]?'

'Very good, Nâgasena!'

---

[1] Dhamma*m*, here nearly = Buddhism. See below, III, 5, 10.

[2] Mr. Trenckner thinks there is a lacuna here; and Hîna*t*i-kumburê's version perhaps supports this. He renders the passage, 'How can a man use a path he does not know? And have not we

5. The king said: 'Where there is no transmigration, Nâgasena, can there be rebirth?'

'Yes, there can.'

'But how can that be? Give me an illustration.'

'Suppose a man, O king, were to light a lamp from another lamp, can it be said that the one transmigrates from, or to, the other?'

'Certainly not.'

'Just so, great king, is rebirth without transmigration.'

'Give me a further illustration.'

'Do you recollect, great king, having learnt, when you were a boy, some verse or other from your teacher?'

'Yes, I recollect that.'

'Well then, did that verse transmigrate from your teacher?'

'Certainly not.'

'Just so, great king, is rebirth without transmigration.'

'Very good, Nâgasena!'

---

6. The king said: 'Is there such a thing, Nâgasena, as the soul[1]?'

'In the highest sense, O king, there is no such thing[2].'

---

our lives long to conduct ourselves according to the Vinaya (the rules of the Order), which the Buddha preached, and which are called the eye of the Buddha, and according to the Sikkhâpada (ethics) which he laid down, and which are called his command?' But there are other passages, no less amplified in the Simhalese, where there is evidently no lacuna in the Pâli; and the passage may well have been meant as a kind of riddle, to which the Simhalese supplies the solution.

[1] Vedagû. See above, II, 3, 6, p. 86 (note).

[2] Mr. Trenckner thinks there is a lacuna here. The Simhalese follows the Pâli word for word.

'Very good, Nâgasena!'

7. [**72**] The king said: 'Is there any being, Nâgasena, who transmigrates from this body to another?'

'No, there is not.'

'But if so, would it not get free from its evil deeds.'

'Yes, if it were not reborn; but if it were, no[1].'

'Give me an illustration.'

'Suppose, O king, a man were to steal another man's mangoes, would the thief deserve punishment?'

'Yes.'

'But he would not have stolen the mangoes the other set in the ground. Why would he deserve punishment?'

'Because those he stole were the result of those that were planted.'

'Just so, great king, this name-and-form commits deeds, either pure or impure, and by that Karma another name-and-form is reborn. And therefore is it not set free from its evil deeds?'

'Very good, Nâgasena!'

8. The king said: 'When deeds are committed, Nâgasena, by one name-and-form, what becomes of those deeds?'

'The deeds would follow it, O king, like a shadow that never leaves it[2].'

'Can any one point out those deeds, saying: "Here are those deeds, or there"?'

'No.'

---

[1] This is an exact repetition of what we had above, II, 2, 6.

[2] These last words are a quotation of those that recur at Saṃyutta III, 2, 10, 10, and Dhammapada, verse 2.

'Give me an illustration.'

'Now what do you think, O king? Can any one point out the fruits which a tree has not yet produced, saying: "Here they are, or there"?'

'Certainly not, Sir.'

'Just so, great king, so long as the continuity of life is not cut off, it is impossible to point out the deeds that are done.'

'Very good, Nâgasena!'

9. [73] The king said: 'Does he, Nâgasena, who is about to be reborn know that he will be born?'

'Yes, he knows it, O king.'

'Give me an illustration.'

'Suppose a farmer, O king, a householder, were to put seed in the ground, and it were to rain well, would he know that a crop would be produced.'

'Yes, he would know that.'

'Just so, great king, does he who is about to be reborn know [1] that he will be born.'

'Very good, Nâgasena [2]!'

10. The king said: 'Is there such a person as the Buddha, Nâgasena?'

'Yes.'

'Can he then, Nâgasena, be pointed out as being here or there?'

'The Blessed One, O king, has passed away by that kind of passing away in which nothing remains which could tend to the formation of another indi-

---

[1] That is before he is born.
[2] This is all very parallel to II, 2, 2.

vidual[1]. It is not possible to point out the Blessed One as being here or there.'

'Give me an illustration.'

'Now what do you think, O king? When there is a great body of fire blazing, is it possible to point out any one flame that has gone out, that it is here or there?'

'No, Sir. That flame has ceased, it has vanished.'

'Just so, great king, has the Blessed One passed away by that kind of passing away in which no root remains for the formation of another individual. The Blessed One has come to an end, and it cannot be pointed out of him, that he is here or there. But in the body of his doctrine he can, O king, be pointed out. For the doctrine[2] was preached by the Blessed One?'

'Very good, Nâgasena!'

Here ends the Fifth Chapter.

---

[1] Anupâdisesâya nibbânadhâtuyâ.
[2] Dhamma. See above, III, 5, 3.

Book III. Chapter 6.

1. The king said: 'Is the body, Nâgasena, dear to you recluses?'

'No, they love not the body.'

'Then why do you nourish it and lavish attention upon it?'

'In all the times and places, O king, that you have gone down to battle, did you never get wounded by an arrow?'

'Yes, that has happened to me.'

'In such cases, O king, [74] is not the wound anointed with salve, and smeared with oil, and bound up in a bandage.'

'Yes, such things are done to it.'

'What then? Is the wound dear to you that you treat it so tenderly, and lavish such attention upon it?'

'No, it is not dear to me in spite of all that, which is only done that the flesh may grow again.'

'Just so, great king, with the recluses and the body. Without cleaving to it do they bear about the body for the sake of righteousness of life. The body, O king, has been declared by the Blessed One to be like a wound. And therefore merely as a sore, and without cleaving to it, do the recluses bear about the body. For it has been said by the Blessed One:

"Covered with clammy skin, an impure thing and foul,
Nine-apertured, it oozes, like a sore [1]."'

'Well answered, Nâgasena!'

---

[1] I have not been able to trace this couplet. On the sentiment compare the eloquent words of the young wife at vol. i, p. 200 of my 'Buddhist Birth Stories,' and Sutta Nipâta I, 11.

2. The king said: 'Did the Buddha, Nâgasena, the omniscient one, foresee all things?'

'Yes. The Blessed One was not only omniscient. He foresaw all things.'

'Then why was it that he was in the habit only from time to time, and as occasion arose, of laying down rules for the members of the Order[1]?'

'Is there any physician, O king, who knows all the medicinal drugs to be found on the earth?'

'Yes, there may be such a man.'

'Well, O king, does he give his decoctions to the patient to drink at a time when illness has already set in, or before that?'

'When the malady has arisen.'

'Just so, great king, the Blessed One, though he was omniscient and foresaw all things, laid down no rule at an unseasonable time, but only when need arose did he establish a regulation which his disciples were not to transgress as long as they lived.'

'Well answered, Nâgasena!'

---

3. [**75**] The king said: 'Is it true, Nâgasena, that the Buddha was endowed with the thirty-two bodily marks of a great man, and graced with the eighty subsidiary characteristics; that he was golden in colour with a skin like gold, and that there spread around him a glorious halo of a fathom's length?'

'Such, O king, was the Blessed One.'

'But were his parents like that?'

'No, they were not.'

'In that case you must say that he was born so. But surely a son is either like his mother, or those on

---

[1] This is how Hînati-kumburê understands the passage.

the mother's side, or he is like his father, or those on the father's side!'

The Elder replied: 'Is there such a thing, O king, as a lotus flower with a hundred petals?'

'Yes, there is.'

'Where does it grow up?'

'It is produced in mud, and in water it comes to perfection [1].'

'But does the lotus resemble the mud of the lake, whence it springs up, either in colour, or in smell, or in taste?'

'Certainly not.'

'Then does it resemble the water?'

'Nor that either.'

'Just so, great king, is it that the Blessed One had the bodily signs and marks you have mentioned, though his parents had them not.'

'Well answered, Nâgasena!'

---

4. The king said: 'Was the Buddha, Nâgasena, pure in conduct (was he a Brahma-kârin)?'

'Yes, the Blessed One was pure.'

'Then, Nâgasena, it follows that he was a follower of Brahmâ [2].'

---

[1] Âsîyati. See Dr. Morris in the 'Journal of the Pâli Text Society,' 1884, p. 72.

[2] There is an untranslatable play here upon the name of the god, which is used in its sense of 'pure, best,' in the expression 'pure in conduct.' The first question really amounts to: Was the Buddha's conduct 'Brahma,' that is, 'best,' which has come to have the meaning 'pure' for the same reason that our expression 'a moral man' has often that particular connotation? It is quite true that the etymological meaning of the word is neither 'best' nor 'pure'; but when our author wrote the secondary sense had completely, in Pâli, driven out the etymological sense.

'Have you a state elephant, O king?'

'Certainly.' [76]

'Well now, does that elephant ever trumpet (literally "cry the heron's cry[1]")?'

'Oh, yes.'

'But is he, then, on that account a follower of the herons?'

'Of course not.'

'Now tell me, great king, has Brahmâ wisdom (Buddhi), or has he not?'

'He is a being with wisdom.'

'Then (on your argument) he is surely a follower of Buddha[2].'

'Well answered, Nâgasena!'

---

5. The king said: 'Is ordination[3] a good thing?'

'Yes, a good thing and a beautiful.'

'But did the Buddha obtain it, or not?'

'Great king, when the Blessed One attained omniscience at the foot of the tree of Knowledge, that was to him an ordination. There was no conferring of ordination upon him at the hands of others—in the way that the Blessed One laid down regulations for his disciples, never to be transgressed by them their lives long[4]!'

'Very true, Nâgasena!'

---

[1] This technical term for an elephant's trumpeting is not infrequent. See, for instance, *Gâtaka* I, 50.

[2] As a matter of fact Brahmâ, the nearest approach in the Indian thought of that time to our idea of God, is always represented, in Buddhism, as a good Buddhist. See, for instance, 'Buddhist Suttas,' p. 116, and my note at p. 117.

[3] Upasampadâ. Admission to the higher grade in the Order.

[4] Mr. Trenckner again suspects something dropped out in this reply. But the connection of ideas seems to me quite sufficient.

6. The king said: 'To which of these two, Nâgasena,—the man who weeps at the death of his mother, and the man who weeps out of love for the Truth (Dhamma),—are his tears a cure?'

'The tears of the one, O king, are stained and hot with the three fires of passion. The tears of the other are stainless and cool. Now there is cure in coolness and calm, but in heat and passion there can be no cure [1].'

'Very good, Nâgasena!'

---

7. The king said: 'What is the distinction, Nâgasena, between him who is full of passion, and him who is void of passion?'

'The one is overpowered by craving, O king, and the other not.'

'But what does that mean?'

'The one is in want, O king, and the other not.'

'I look at it, Sir, in this way. He who has passion and he who has not—both of them alike—desire what is good to eat, either hard or soft. And neither of them desires what is wrong.'

'The lustful man, O king, in eating his food enjoys both the taste and the lust that arises from taste, [**77**] but the man free from lusts experiences the taste only, and not the lust arising therefrom.'

'Well answered, Nâgasena!'

The Siṃhalese follows the Pâli, but that of course only shows that the text before the translator was here the same as in Mr. Trenckner's edition.

[1] The point of this lies in the allusion to the coolness and calm of Nirvâna, or Arahatship, which is the dying out of the three fires of lust, ill-will, and delusion. The word used for coolness, Sîtala, is one of the many epithets of Arahatship.

8. The king said: 'Venerable Nâgasena, where does wisdom dwell?'

'Nowhere, O king.'

'Then, Sir, there is no such thing as wisdom.'

'Where does the wind dwell, O king?'

'Not anywhere, Sir.'

'So there is no such thing as wind.'

'Well answered, Nâgasena!'

---

9. The king said: 'When you speak of transmigration[1], Nâgasena, what does that mean?'

'A being born here, O king, dies here. Having died here, it springs up elsewhere. Having been born there, there it dies. Having died there, it springs up elsewhere. That is what is meant by transmigration.'

'Give me an illustration.'

'It is like the case of a man who, after eating a mango, should set the seed in the ground. From that a great tree would be produced and give fruit. And there would be no end to the succession, in that way, of mango trees.'

'Very good, Nâgasena!'

---

10. The king said: 'By what, Nâgasena, does one recollect what is past and done long ago?'

'By memory.'

'But is it not by the mind[2], not by the memory[2], that we recollect?'

'Do you recollect any business, O king, that you have done and then forgotten?'

'Yes.'

'What then? Were you then without a mind?'

---

[1] Sa*m*sâra.   [2] *K*ittena, no satiyâ.

'No. But my memory failed me.'

'Then why do you say that it is by the mind, not by the memory, that we recollect?'

'Very good, Nâgasena!'

---

11. The king said: 'Does memory, Nâgasena, always arise subjectively, [**78**] or is it stirred up by suggestion from outside[1]?'

'Both the one and the other.'

'But does not that amount to all memory being subjective in origin, and never artificial?'

'If, O king, there were no artificial (imparted) memory, then artisans would have no need of practice, or art, or schooling, and teachers would be useless. But the contrary is the case.'

'Very good, Nâgasena!'

Here ends the Sixth Chapter.

---

[1] I follow Hîna/i-kumburê's interpretation of the difficult words in the text, which Mr. Trenckner says is corrupt. Ka/umika is 'artificial,' like the Sanskrit k*r*/*r*/trima. It has only been found as yet in our author.

Book III. Chapter 7.

1. The king said: 'In how many ways, Nâgasena, does memory spring up?'

'In sixteen ways, O king. That is to say: by personal experience[1], as when the venerable Ananda, or the devoted woman Khuggutarâ, or any others who had that power, called to mind their previous births—[79] or by outward aid[2], as when others continue to remind one who is by nature forgetful—or by the impression made by the greatness of some occasion[3], as kings remember their coronation day, or as we remember the day of our conversion—by the impression made by joy[4], as when one remembers that which gave him pleasure—or by the impression made by sorrow[5], as when one remembers that which pained him—or from similarity of appearance[6], as on seeing one like them we call to mind the mother or father or sister or brother, or on seeing a camel or an ox or an ass we call to mind others like them—or by difference of appearance[7], as when we remember that such and such a colour, sound, smell, taste, or touch belong to such and such a thing—or by the knowledge of speech[8], as when one who is by nature forgetful is reminded by others and then himself remembers—or by a sign[9], as when we recognise a draught bullock by a brand mark or some other sign—or from effort to recollect[10], as when one by

---

[1] Abhigânato. [2] Ka/umikâya. [3] O/ârika-viññânato.
[4] Hita-viññânato. [5] Ahita-viññânato.
[6] Sabhâga-nimittato. [7] Visabhâga-nimittato.
[8] Kathâbhiññânato. [9] Lakkhanato. [10] Saranato.

nature forgetful is made to recollect by being urged again and again : "try and think of it"—or by calculation [11], as when one knows by the training he has received in writing that such and such a letter ought to follow after such and such a one—or by arithmetic [12], as when accountants do big sums by their knowledge of figures—or by learning by heart [13], as the repeaters of the scriptures by their skill in learning by heart recollect so much—[80] or by meditation [14], as when a Bhikkhu calls to mind his temporary states in days gone by—by reference to a book [15], as when kings calling to mind a previous regulation, say: " Bring the book here," and remind themselves out of that—or by a pledge [16], as when at the sight of goods deposited a man recollects (the circumstances under which they were pledged)—or by association [17], as when one remembers a thing because one has seen it, or a sound because one has heard it, or an odour because one has smelt it, or a touch because one has felt it, or a concept because one has perceived it.'

' Very good, Nâgasena!'

2. The king said: 'Your people say, Nâgasena, that though a man should have lived a hundred

---

[11] Muddâto (see above, p. 6). [12] Gananâto.

[13] Dharanato. The noun dhâranakâ is only found here (where I follow the Simhalese interpretation) and at Gâtaka II, 203 (where it means ' debtor,' as in Sanskrit).

[14] Bhâvanato. For a translation of the full text, here abridged in the text, see ' Buddhist Suttas,' pp. 215, 216 (§ 17).

[15] Potthaka-nibandhanato. [16] Upanikkhepato.

[17] Anubhûtato, perhaps ' experience.' There are really seventeen, not sixteen, so some two must have been regarded by the author as forming one between them. These may be Nos. 1 and 14, or more likely Nos. 4 and 5.

years an evil life, yet if, at the moment of death, thoughts of the Buddha should enter his mind, he will be reborn among the gods. This I don't believe. And thus do they also say: " By one case of destruction of life a man may be reborn in purgatory." That, too, I cannot believe.'

'But tell me, O king. Would even a tiny stone float on the water without a boat?'

'Certainly not.'

'Very well; but would not a hundred cart-loads of stones float on the water if they were loaded in a boat?'

'Yes, they would float right enough.'

'Well, good deeds are like the boat.'

'Very good, Nâgasena!'

---

3. The king said: 'Do you (recluses), Nâgasena, strive after the removal of past sorrow?'

'No.'

'What then? Is it future sorrow you strive to remove?'

'No.'

'Present sorrow, then?' [81]

'Not that either.'

'Then if it be neither past, nor future, nor present sorrow that you strive to remove, whereunto is it that you strive?'

'What are you asking, O king? That this sorrow should cease and no other sorrow should arise—that is what we strive after.'

'But, Nâgasena, is there (now) such a thing as future sorrow?'

'No. I grant that.'

'Then you are mighty clever people to strive after the removal of that which does not exist!'

'Has it ever happened to you, O king, that rival kings rose up against you as enemies and opponents?'

'Yes, certainly.'

'Then you set to work, I suppose, to have moats dug, and ramparts thrown up, and watch towers erected, and strongholds built, and stores of food collected[1]?'

'Not at all. All that had been prepared beforehand.'

'Or you had yourself trained in the management of war elephants, and in horsemanship, and in the use of the war chariot, and in archery and fencing?'

'Not at all. I had learnt all that before.'

'But why?'

'With the object of warding off future danger.'

'How so? Is there such a thing (now) as future danger?'

'No. I must grant that.'

'Then you kings are mighty clever people to trouble yourselves about the warding off of that which does not exist!'

'Give me a further illustration.'

'Tell me, O king. Is it when you are athirst that you set to work to have wells dug, or ponds hollowed out, or reservoirs formed, with the object of getting something to drink?'

'Certainly not. All that has been prepared beforehand.'

'But to what end?'

'With the object of preventing future thirst.'

'How so? Is there such a thing as future thirst?'

---

[1] All that follows only differs by slight additions from III, 4, 3 above, pp. 100–102.

'No, Sir.'

'So you are mighty clever people, O king, [82] to take all that trouble to prevent the future thirst which all the time does not exist!'

'Give me a further illustration.'

[Then the Elder referred, as before, to the means people always took of warding against future hunger, and the king expressed his pleasure at the way in which the puzzle had been solved.]

4. The king said: 'How far is it, Nâgasena, from here to the Brahma world[1]?'

'Very far is it, O king. If a rock, the size of an upper chamber, were to fall from there, it would take four months to reach the earth, though it came down eight-and-forty thousand leagues[2] each day and night.'

'Good, Nâgasena! Now do not your people say that a Bhikkhu, who has the power of Iddhi and the mastery over his mind[3], can vanish from Gambu-dîpa, and appear in the Brahma world, as quickly as a strong man could stretch forth his bent up arm, or bend it in again if it were stretched out? That is a saying I cannot believe. How is it possible that he could traverse so quickly so many hundreds of leagues?'

The Elder replied: 'In what district, O king, were you born?'

---

[1] One of the highest heavens.
[2] Yogana, a league of seven miles.
[3] Ketovasippatto, which Hînati-kumburê renders mano vasi prâpta wû. I know of no passage in the Pitakas where the phrase occurs in connection with Iddhi; but it is often used by our author. See, for instance, just below, III, 7, 9.

'There is an island called Alasanda[1]. It was there I was born.'

'And how far is Alasanda from here?'

'About two hundred leagues.'

'Do you know for certain of any business you once did there and now recollect?'

'Oh, yes.'

'So quickly, great king, have you gone about two hundred leagues.'

'Very good, Nâgasena!'

5. The king said: 'If one man, Nâgasena, were to die here and be reborn in the Brahma world, and another were to die here and be reborn in Kashmîr, which of the two would arrive first?'

'Both together, O king.'

'Give me an illustration.'

'In what town [**83**], O king, were you born?'

'There is a village called Kalasi. It was there I was born.'

'And how far is Kalasi from here?'

'About two hundred leagues.'

'How far is Kashmîr from here?'

'Twelve leagues.'

'Now, great king, think of Kalasi.'

'I have done so.'

'And now, think of Kashmîr.'

'I have done so.'

'Well, which did you think of quickest?'

'Of each in the same time.'

'Just so, great king, would it take no longer to be reborn in the Brahma world than to be reborn in Kashmîr. And tell me, O king. Suppose two

---

[1] Alexandria (in Baktria) built on an island in the Indus.

birds were flying, and one were to alight on a tall tree, and the other on a small shrub. If they settled both at the same moment, whose shadow would first fall to the ground?'

'The two shadows would fall together.'

'Just so, great king, in the case you put.'

'Very good, Nâgasena!'

6. The king said: 'Venerable Nâgasena, how many kinds of wisdom are there?'

'Seven, O king.'

'And by how many kinds of wisdom does one become wise?'

'By one: that is to say by the kind of wisdom called "the investigation of the Truth[1]."'

'Then why is it said there are seven?'

'Tell me, O king. Suppose a sword were lying in its sheath and not taken in the hand, could it cut off anything you wanted to cut off with it?'

'Certainly not.'

'Just so, great king, by the other kinds of wisdom can nothing be understood without investigation of the Truth.'

'Very good, Nâgasena!'

7. The king said: 'Which, Nâgasena, is there more of, merit or demerit?'

'Merit.' [84]

'But why?'

'He who does wrong, O king, comes to feel remorse, and acknowledges his evil-doing. So demerit does not increase. But he who does well feels no remorse, and feeling no remorse gladness will

---

[1] Dhamma-vikaya-sambogghaṅgena.

spring up within him, and joy will arise to him thus gladdened, and so rejoicing all his frame will be at peace, and being thus at peace he will experience a blissful feeling of content, and in that bliss his heart will be at rest, and he whose heart is thus at rest knows things as they really are [1]. For that reason merit increases. A man, for example, though his hands and feet are cut off, if he gave to the Blessed One merely a handful of lotuses, would not enter purgatory for ninety-one Kalpas. That is why I said, O king, that there is more merit than demerit.'

'Very good, Nâgasena!'

8. The king said: 'Whose, Nâgasena, is the greater demerit—his who sins consciously, or his who sins inadvertently?'

'He who sins inadvertently, O king, has the greater demerit.'

'In that case, reverend Sir, we shall punish doubly any of our family or our court who do wrong unintentionally.'

'But what do you think, O king? If one man were to seize hold intentionally of a fiery mass of metal glowing with heat, and another were to seize hold of it unintentionally, which would be more burnt?'

'The one who did not know what he was doing.'

'Well, it is just the same with the man who does wrong.'

'Very good, Nâgasena!'

9. The king said: 'Is there any one, Nâgasena,

---

[1] The above is a paragraph constantly recurring in the Pâli Piṭakas. See, for instance, Digha II, 75; Aṅguttara III, 104; and Mahâvagga VIII, 15, 13 (where I have annotated the details).

who can go with this bodily frame to Uttara-kuru or to the Brahma world, or to any other of the four great continents (into which the world is divided)?'

'Yes, there are such people.'

'But how can they?' [85]

'Do you recollect, O king, having ever jumped a foot or two feet across the ground?'

'Yes, Nâgasena, I can jump twelve feet.'

'But how?'

'I fix my mind on the idea of alighting there, and at the moment of my determination my body comes to seem light to me.'

'Just so, O king, can the Bhikkhu, who has the power of Iddhi, and has the mastery over his mind, when he has made his mind rise up to the occasion, travel through the sky by means of his mind.'

'Very good, Nâgasena!'

---

10. The king said: 'Your people say there are bones even a hundred leagues long. Now there is no tree even one hundred leagues in length, how then can there be bones so long?'

'But tell me, O king. Have you not heard of fishes in the sea five hundred leagues in length?'

'Yes. I have heard of such.'

'If so, could they not have bones a hundred leagues long?'

'Very good, Nâgasena!'

---

11. The king said: 'Your people, Nâgasena, say that it is possible to suppress the inhaling and exhaling (of one's breath).'

'Yes, that can be done.'

'But how?'

'Tell me, O king. Have you ever heard of a man snoring[1]?'

'Yes.'

'Well, would not that sound stop if he bent his body?'

'Yes.'

'Then surely if that sound would stop at the mere bending of the body of one who is untrained alike in body, in conduct, in mind, and in wisdom—why should it not be possible for the breathing of one trained in all these respects, and who has besides reached up to the fourth stage of the ecstatic contemplation[2], to be suppressed?'

'Very good, Nâgasena!'

12. The king said: 'There is the expression ocean, Nâgasena. Why is the water called ocean?'

The Elder replied [86]: 'Because there is just as much salt as water, O king, and just as much water as salt, therefore is it called ocean[3].'

'Very good, Nâgasena!'

13. The king said: 'Why, Nâgasena, is the ocean all of one taste, the taste of salt?'

---

[1] Kâka*kkh*amâno. See *G*âtaka I, 60, 24; 160, 18. Hîna*t*i-kumburê renders it 'sleeping with a snore (gorawamin) like the sound of crows (kâka).' [2] *Gh*âna.

[3] Samudda. The answer (to give opportunity for which the question is invented) is a kind of punning etymology of this Pâli word for ocean. Our author seems to take it as meaning 'equal water-ness,' from sama and ud(aka). The real derivation is very different. It is from the root ud, which is allied to our 'wet' and the Greek ὑετός, and the prefix sam in the sense of completeness. It is difficult to reconcile the reply to this. There is a kind of conversation condemned in the Dîgha I, 1, 17, and elsewhere as samuddakkhâyika, which is explained in the Sumangala, p. 91, as deriving samudda from sa, 'with,' and muddâ, 'a seal ring.'

'Because the water in it has stood so long, therefore it is all of one taste, the taste of salt [1].'

'Very good, Nâgasena!'

---

14. The king said: 'Can even the most minute thing, Nâgasena, be divided?'

'Yes, it can.'

'And what, Sir, is the most minute of all things.'

'Truth (Dhamma), O king, is the most minute and subtle. But this is not true of all qualities (Dhammâ). Subtleness or the reverse are epithets of qualities. But whatever can be divided that can wisdom (Paññâ) divide, and there is no other quality which can divide wisdom.'

'Very good, Nâgasena!'

---

15. The king said: 'These three, Nâgasena,—perception, and reason, and the soul in a being,—are they all different both in letter and in essence, or the same in essence differing only in the letter?'

'Recognition, O king, is the mark of perception, and discrimination of reason [2], and there is no such thing as a soul in beings [3].'

---

[1] In the same way the Buddhist religion (the Dhamma-Vinaya) is said in the Kullavagga IX, 1, 4, to be 'all of one taste, the taste of salvation, emancipation' (Vimutti).

[2] So also above, II, 3, 12. Here the words are Viñânana-lakkhanam viññânam, pagânanâ-lakkhana paññâ, which the Ceylon translator amplifies into 'As a peasant, on seeing grains of gold, would recognise them as valuable, so is it the characteristic of viññâna to recognise aramunu (objects of sense) when it sees them. As a goldsmith, on seeing grains of gold, would not only know they were valuable, but also discriminate their value (as large or small), so is it the characteristic of paññâ, not only to recognise, but also to discriminate between the objects of sense.'

[3] See above, II, 3, 6, and II, 3, 16. Hinati-kumburê here renders

' But if there be no such thing as a soul, what is it then which sees forms with the eye, and hears sounds with the ear, and smells odours with the nose, and tastes tastes with the tongue, and feels touch with the body, or perceives qualities with the mind ?'

The Elder replied: ' If there be a soul (distinct from the body) which does all this, then if the door of the eye were thrown down (if the eye were plucked out) could it stretch out its head, as it were, through the larger aperture and (with greater range) see forms much more clearly than before? Could one hear sounds better if the ears were torn away, or smell better if the nose were cut off, or taste better if the tongue were pulled out, or feel touch better if the body were destroyed ?'

[87] ' Certainly not, Sir.'

' Then there can be no soul inside the body.'

'Very good, Nâgasena !'

---

16. The Elder said: 'A hard thing there is, O king, which the Blessed One has done.'

' And what is that ?'

'The fixing of all those mental conditions which depend on one organ of sense, telling us that such is contact, and such sensation, and such idea, and such intention, and such thought[1].'

' Give me an illustration.'

' Suppose, O king, a man were to wade down into the sea, and taking some water in the palm of his hand, were to taste it with his tongue. Would he

---

*g*îvo by the 'life (or perhaps living principle, *g*îvitâ) inside the forms produced out of the four elements.'

[1] Phasso, vedanâ, sa*ññ*â, *k*etanâ, *k*itta*m*.

distinguish whether it were water from the Ganges, or from the Jumna, or from the A*k*iravatî, or from the Sarabhû, or from the Mahî?'

'Impossible, Sir.'

'More difficult than that, great king, is it to have distinguished between the mental conditions which follow on the exercise of any one of the organs of sense!'

'Very good, Nâgasena!'

Here ends the Seventh Chapter [1].

17. The Elder said: 'Do you know, O king, what time it is now?'

'Yes, Sir, I know. The first watch of the night is now passed. The middle watch is now going on. The torches are lit. The four banners are ordered to be raised, and appropriate gifts to be issued to you from the treasury.'

The Yonakas said: 'Very good, great king. Most able is the Bhikkhu.'

'Yes, my men. Most able is the Bhikkhu. Were the master like him and the pupil like me, [88] a clever scholar would not take long in getting at the truth.'

Then the king, pleased with the explanations given of the questions he had put, had Nâgasena robed in an embroidered cloak worth a hundred thousand [2], and said to him: 'Venerable Nâgasena, I hereby order that you shall be provided with your daily meal for eight hundred days, and give you the

---

[1] See the note at the end of Book II, Chapter 3, § 14.

[2] That is kahâpa*n*as, 'half-pennies.'

choice of anything in the palace that it is lawful for you to take.' And when the Elder refused, saying he had enough to live on, the king rejoined : ' I know, Sir, you have enough to live on. But you should both protect me and protect yourself—yourself from the possibility of a public rumour to the effect that you convinced me but received nothing from me, and me from the possibility of a public rumour that though I was convinced I would give nothing in acknowledgement.'

' Let it be as you wish, great king,' was the reply.

Then the king said : ' As the lion, the king of beasts, when put into a cage, though it were of gold, would turn his face longingly to the outside ; even so do I, though I dwell in the world, turn my thoughts longingly to the higher life of you recluses. But, Sir, if I were to give up the household life and renounce the world it would not be long I should have to live, so many are my foes.'

Then the venerable Nâgasena, having thus solved the questions put by Milinda the king, arose from his seat and departed to the hermitage.

---

18. Not long after Nâgasena had gone, Milinda the king thought over to himself whether he had propounded his questions rightly, and whether the replies had been properly made. And he came to the conclusion that to questions well put replies had been well given. And Nâgasena likewise, when he reached the hermitage, thought the matter over to himself, and concluded that to questions well put right replies had been given.

Now Nâgasena robed himself early in the morning, and went with his bowl in his hand to the palace, and sat down on the seat prepared for him. And Milinda saluted the venerable Nâgasena, [89] and sat down respectfully at his side, and said to him: 'Pray do not think, Sir, that I was kept awake all the rest of the night exulting in the thought of having questioned you. I was debating with myself as to whether I had asked aright, and had been rightly answered. And I concluded that I had.'

And the Elder on his part said: 'Pray do not suppose, great king, that I passed the rest of the night rejoicing at having answered all you asked. I too was thinking over what had been said by us both. And I came to the result that you had questioned well, and that I had rightly answered.'

Thus did these two great men congratulate each the other on what he had spoken well.

Here ends the answering of the problems of
the questions of Milinda.

BOOK IV.

Me*n*daka-pañho.

The Solving of Dilemmas.

Chapter 1. [90]

1. Master of words and sophistry, clever and wise
   Milinda tried to test great Nâgasena's skill.
   Leaving him not[1], again and yet again,
   He questioned and cross-questioned him, until
   His own skill was proved foolishness.
   Then he became a student of the Holy Writ.
   All night, in secrecy, he pondered o'er
   The ninefold Scriptures, and therein he found
   Dilemmas hard to solve, and full of snares.
   And thus he thought: 'The conquering Buddha's words
   Are many-sided, some explanatory,
   Some spoken as occasion rose to speak,
   Some dealing fully with essential points.
   Through ignorance of what, each time, was meant
   There will be strife hereafter as to what
   The King of Righteousness has thus laid down
   In these diverse and subtle utterances.
   Let me now gain great Nâgasena's ear,
   And putting to him that which seems so strange
   And hard—yea contradictory—get him
   To solve it. So in future times, when men
   Begin to doubt, the light of his solutions
   Shall guide them, too, along the path of Truth.'

---

[1] Vasanto tassa *kh*âyâya, literally 'abiding under his shadow.' Compare *G*âtaka I, 91.

2. Now Milinda the king, when the night was turning into day, and the sun had risen, bathed, and with hands clasped and raised to his forehead, called to mind the Buddhas of the past, the present, and the future, and solemnly undertook the observance of the eightfold vow, saying to himself: 'For seven days from now will I do penance by taking upon myself the observance of the eight rules, and when my vow is accomplished will I go to the teacher and put to him, as questions, these dilemmas.' So Milinda the king laid aside his usual dress, and put off his ornaments; and clad in yellow robes, with only a recluse's turban[1] on his head, in appearance like a hermit, did he carry out the eightfold abstinence, keeping in mind the vow—'For this seven days I am to decide no case at law. I am to harbour no lustful thought, no thought of ill-will, no thought tending to delusion. Towards all slaves, servants, and dependents I am to show a meek and lowly disposition. [91] I am to watch carefully over every bodily act, and over my six organs of sense. And I am to fill my heart with thoughts of love towards all beings.' Keeping this eightfold vow, establishing his heart in this eightfold moral law, for seven days he went not forth. But as the night was passing into day, at sunrise of the eighth day, he took his breakfast early, and then with downcast eyes and measured words, gentle in manner, collected in thought, glad and pleased and rejoicing in heart, did he go to Nâgasena. And bowing down at his feet, he stood respectfully on one side, and said:

3. 'There is a certain matter, venerable Nâgasena,

---

[1] Pa/isîsaka*m*. See *Gâtaka* II, 197.

that I desire to talk over with you alone. I wish no third person to be present. In some deserted spot, some secluded place in the forest, fit in all the eight respects for a recluse, there should this point of mine be put. And therein let there be nothing hid from me, nothing kept secret. I am now in a fit state to hear secret things when we are deep in consultation. And the meaning of what I say can be made clear by illustration. As it is to the broad earth, O Nâgasena, that it is right to entrust treasure when occasion arises for laying treasure by, so is it to me that it is right to entrust secret things when we are deep in consultation.'

4. Then having gone with the master to a secluded spot he further said: 'There are eight kinds of places, Nâgasena, which ought to be altogether avoided by a man who wants to consult. No wise man will talk a matter over in such places, or the matter falls to the ground and is brought to no conclusion. And what are the eight? Uneven ground, spots unsafe by fear of men, windy places, hiding spots, sacred places, high roads, light bambû bridges, and public bathing places.'

The Elder asked: 'What is the objection to each of these?'

The king replied: 'On uneven ground, Nâgasena, [92] the matter discussed becomes jerky, verbose, and diffuse, and comes to nothing. In unsafe places the mind is disturbed, and being disturbed does not follow the point clearly. In windy spots the voice is indistinct. In hiding places there are eaves-droppers. In sacred places the question discussed is apt to be diverted to the serious surroundings. On a high road it is apt to become frivolous, on a bridge unsteady and wavering, at a public bathing place the discussion would be matter of common talk. Therefore is it said [1]:

"Uneven ground, unsafe and windy spots,
And hiding places, and god-haunted shrines,
High roads, and bridges, and all bathing ghâts—
These eight avoid when talking of high things."'

5. 'There are eight kinds of people, Nâgasena, who when talking a matter over, spoil the discussion. And who are the eight? He who walks in lust, he who walks in ill-will, he who walks in delusion, he who walks in pride, the greedy man, the sluggard, the man of one idea, and the fool.'

'What is the objection to each of these?' asked the Elder.

'The first spoils the discussion by his lust, the next by his ill-will, the third by his delusions, the fourth by his pride, the fifth by his greed, the sixth by his sloth, the seventh by his narrowness, and the last by his folly. Therefore is it said:

"The lustful, angry, or bewildered man,
The proud, the greedy, or the slothful man,
The man of one idea, and the poor fool—
These eight are spoilers of high argument."'

6. 'There are nine kinds of people, Nâgasena, who let out a secret that has been talked over with them, and treasure it not up in their hearts. And who are the nine? The lustful man reveals it in obedience to some lust, the ill-tempered man in con-

---

[1] It is not known where the verses here (or the others quoted in these two pages) are taken from.

sequence of some ill-will, the deluded man under some mistake. [93] The timid man reveals it through fear, and the man greedy for gain to get something out of it. A woman reveals it through infirmity, a drunkard in his eagerness for drink, a eunuch because of his imperfection, and a child through fickleness. Therefore is it said :

" The lustful, angry, or bewildered man,
The timid man, and he who seeks for gain,
A woman, drunkard, eunuch, or a child—
These nine are fickle, wavering, and mean.
When secret things are talked over to them
They straightway become public property." '

7. ' There are eight causes, Nâgasena, of the advance, the ripening of insight. And what are the eight ? The advance of years, the growth of reputation, frequent questioning, association with teachers, one's own reflection, converse with the wise, cultivation of the loveable, and dwelling in a pleasant land. Therefore is it said :

" By growth in reputation, and in years,
By questioning, and by the master's aid,
By thoughtfulness, and converse with the wise,
By intercourse with men worthy of love,
By residence within a pleasant spot—
By these nine is one's insight purified.
They who have these, their wisdom grows[1]." '

8. ' This spot, Nâgasena, is free from the objections to talking matters over. And I am a model companion for any one desiring to do so. I can keep a

---

[1] Pabhiggati in the text appears not to be an old error. The Si*m*halese repeats it, but leaves it untranslated.

secret, and will keep yours as long as I live. In all the eight ways just described my insight has grown ripe. It would be hard to find such a pupil as you may have in me.

[94] 'Now towards a pupil who conducts himself thus aright the teacher ought to conduct himself in accordance with the twenty-five virtues of a teacher. And what are the twenty-five? He must always and without fail keep guard over his pupil. He must let him know what to cultivate, and what to avoid; about what he should be earnest, and what he may neglect. He must instruct him as to sleep, and as to keeping himself in health, and as to what food he may take, and what reject. He should teach him discrimination[1] (in food), and share with him all that is put, as alms, into his own bowl. He should encourage him, saying: "Be not afraid. You will gain advantage (from what is here taught you)." He should advise him as to the people whose company he should keep, and as to the villages and Vihâras he should frequent. He should never indulge in (foolish) talk[2] with him. When he sees any defect in him he should easily pardon it. He should be zealous, he should teach nothing partially, keep nothing secret, and hold nothing back[3]. He should look upon him in his heart as a son, saying to himself: "I have begotten him in

---

[1] Viseso. It does not say in what, and the Simhalese simply repeats the word.

[2] Sallâpo na kâtabbo. The Simhalese merely repeats the word, which is often used without any bad connotation. See, for instance, *G*âtaka I, 112.

[3] So that, in the author's opinion, there is no 'Esoteric Doctrine' in true Buddhism. See the note, below, on IV, 4, 8.

learning ¹." He should strive to bring him forward, saying to himself: "How can I keep him from going back?" He should determine in himself to make him strong in knowledge, saying to himself: "I will make him mighty." He should love him, never desert him in necessity, never neglect him in anything he ought to do for him, always befriend him—so far as he can rightly do so ²—when he does wrong. These, Sir, are the twenty-five good qualities in a teacher. Treat me altogether in accordance therewith. Doubt, Lord, has overcome me. There are apparent contradictions in the word of the Conqueror. About them strife will hereafter arise, and in future times it will be hard to find a teacher with insight such as yours. Throw light for me on these dilemmas, to the downfall of the adversaries.'

9. Then the Elder agreed to what he had said, and in his turn set out the ten good qualities which ought to be found in a lay disciple: 'These ten, O king, are the virtues of a lay disciple. He suffers like pain and feels like joy as the Order does. He takes the Doctrine (Dhamma) as his master. He delights in giving so far as he is able to give. On seeing the religion (Dhamma) of the Conqueror decay, he does his best to revive it. He holds right views. Having no passion for excitement ³, he runs

---

[1] So also in the Vinaya (Mahâvagga I, 25, 6).

[2] In the well-known passage in the Vinaya in which the mutual duties of pupils and teachers are set out in full (Mahâvagga I, 25, 26, translated in the 'Vinaya Texts,' vol. i, pp. 154 and foll.) there is a similar injunction (25, 22 = 26, 10) which throws light on the meaning of dhammena here.

[3] Apagata-ko/ûhala-mangaliko. 'Laying aside the erroneous views and discipline called ko/ûhala and mangalika,' says the Si*m*halese.

not after any other teacher his life long. He keeps guard over himself in thought and deed. He delights in peace, is a lover of peace. He feels no jealousy, [95] and walks not in religion in a quarrelsome spirit. He takes his refuge in the Buddha, he takes his refuge in the Doctrine, he takes his refuge in the Order. These, great king, are the ten good qualities of a lay disciple. They exist all of them in you. Hence is it fit, and right, and becoming in you that, seeing the decay of the religion of the Conqueror, you desire its prosperity. I give you leave. Ask of me whatever you will.'

[Here ends the introduction to the solving of dilemmas.]

THE DILEMMAS.

[ON HONOURS PAID TO THE BUDDHA.]

10. Then Milinda the king, having thus been granted leave, fell at the feet of the teacher, and raising his clasped hands to his forehead, said: 'Venerable Nâgasena, these leaders of other sects say thus: "If the Buddha accepts gifts he cannot have passed entirely away. He must be still in union with the world, having his being somewhere in it, in the world, a shareholder in the things of the world; and therefore any honour paid to him becomes empty and vain[1]. On the other hand if he

---

[1] 'Because honours should be paid, in the way of worship, to those who have so passed away, and to them only,' is the implied suggestion, as if it were common ground to the Buddhists and their opponents. But there is no such doctrine in the Pâli Piṭakas, and could not be. The whole discussion breathes the spirit of a later time.

be entirely passed away (from life), unattached to the world, escaped from all existence, then honours would not be offered to him. For he who is entirely set free accepts no honour, and any act done to him who accepts it not becomes empty and vain." This is a dilemma which has two horns. It is not a matter within the scope of those who have no mind [1], it is a question fit for the great. Tear asunder this net of heresy, put it on one side. To you has this puzzle been put. Give to the future sons of the Conqueror eyes wherewith to see the riddle to the confusion of their adversaries.'

'The Blessed One, O king,' replied the Elder, 'is entirely set free. And the Blessed One accepts no gift. Even at the foot of the Tree of Wisdom he abandoned all accepting of gifts, how much more then now when he has passed entirely away by that kind of passing away which leaves no root over (for the formation of a new existence). For this, O king, has been said by Sâriputta, the commander of the faith [2]:

"Though worshipped, these Unequalled Ones, alike
By gods and men, unlike them all they heed
Neither a gift nor worship. They accept
It not, neither refuse it. Through the ages
All Buddhas were so, so wil. ever be [3]!"'

---

[1] Apatta-mânâsana*m*. 'Of those who have not attained to the insight of the Arahats,' says the Si halese by way of gloss.

[2] This verse is not found in our printed texts. The Thera Gâthâ (981–1017) has preserved thirty-seven of the verses attributed to Sâriputta, but this is not one of them.

[3] Hina/i-kumburê, who quotes the Pâli verses, reads pûga-yantâ, and sâdîyanti.

11. The king said: 'Venerable Nâgasena, a father may speak in praise of his son, or a son of his father. But that is no ground for putting the adversaries to shame. It is only an expression of their own belief. Come now! Explain this matter to me fully to the establishing of your own doctrine, [96] and to the unravelling of the net of the heretics.'

The Elder replied: 'The Blessed One, O king, is entirely set free (from life). And the Blessed One accepts no gift. If gods or men put up a building to contain the jewel treasure of the relics of a Tathâgata who does not accept their gift, still by that homage paid to the attainment of the supreme good under the form of the jewel treasure of his wisdom do they themselves attain to one or other of the three glorious states [1]. Suppose, O king, that though a great and glorious fire had been kindled, it should die out, would it then again accept any supply of dried grass or sticks?'

'Even as it burned, Sir, it could not be said to accept fuel, how much less when it had died away, and ceased to burn, could it, an unconscious thing, accept it?'

'And when that one mighty fire had ceased, and gone out, would the world be bereft of fire?'

'Certainly not. Dry wood is the seat, the basis of fire, and any men who want fire can, by the exertion of their own strength and power, such as resides in individual men, once more, by twirling the fire-stick, produce fire, and with that fire do any work for which fire is required.'

---

[1] Tisso sampattiyo. That is, to another life as a man, or as a god, or to Arahatship here, on earth, in this birth.

'Then that saying of the sectarians that "an act done to him who accepts it not is empty and vain" turns out to be false. As that great and glorious fire was set alight, even so, great king, was the Blessed One set alight in the glory of his Buddhahood over the ten thousand world systems. As it went out, so has he passed away into that kind of passing away in which no root remains. As the fire, when gone out, accepted no supply of fuel, just so, and for the good of the world, has his accepting of gifts ceased and determined. As men, when the fire is out, and has no further means of burning, then by their own strength and effort, such as resides in individual men, twirl the fire-stick and produce fire, and do any work for which fire is required—so do gods and men, though a Tathâgata has passed away and no longer accepts their gifts, yet put up a house for the jewel treasure of his relics, and doing homage to the attainment of supreme good under the form of the jewel treasure of his wisdom, they attain to one or other of the three glorious states. [97] Therefore is it, great king, that acts done to the Tathâgata, notwithstanding his having passed away and not accepting them, are nevertheless of value and bear fruit.'

12. 'Now hear, too, another reason for the same thing. Suppose, O king, there were to arise a great and mighty wind, and that then it were to die away. Would that wind acquiesce in being produced again?'

'A wind that has died away can have no thought or idea of being reproduced. And why? Because the element wind is an unconscious thing.'

'Or even, O king, would the word "wind" be

still applicable to that wind, when it had so died away?'

'Certainly not, Sir. But fans and punkahs are means for the production of wind. Any men who are oppressed by heat, or tormented by fever, can by means of fans and punkahs, and by the exertion of their own strength and power, such as resides in individual men, produce a breeze, and by that wind allay their heat, or assuage their fever.'

'Then that saying of the sectarians that "an act done to him who accepts it not is empty and vain" turns out to be false. As the great and mighty wind which blew, even so, great king, has the Blessed One blown over the ten thousand world systems with the wind of his love, so cool, so sweet, so calm, so delicate. As it first blew, and then died away, so has the Blessed One, who once blew with the wind so cool, so sweet, so calm, so delicate, of his love, now passed away with that kind of passing away in which no root remains. As those men were oppressed by heat and tormented with fever, even so are gods and men tormented and oppressed with threefold fire and heat[1]. As fans and punkahs are means of producing wind, so the relics and the jewel treasure of the wisdom of a Tathâgata are means of producing the threefold attainment. [98] And as men oppressed by heat and tormented by fever can by fans and punkahs produce a breeze, and thus allay the heat and assuage the fever, so can gods and men by offering reverence to the relics, and the

---

[1] That is, the three fires of lust, ill-will, and delusion, the going out of which is the state called, par excellence, 'the going out' (Nirvâna).

jewel treasure of the wisdom of a Tathâgata, though he has died away and accepts it not, cause goodness to arise within them, and by that goodness can assuage and can allay the fever and the torment of the threefold fire. Therefore is it, great king, that acts done to the Tathâgata, notwithstanding his having passed away and not accepting them, are nevertheless of value and bear fruit.'

13. 'Now hear another reason for the same thing. Suppose, O king, a man were to make a drum sound, and then that sound were to die away. Would that sound acquiesce in being produced again?'

'Certainly not, Sir. The sound has vanished. It can have no thought or idea of being reproduced. The sound of a drum when it has once been produced and died away, is altogether cut off. But, Sir, a drum is a means of producing sound. And any man, as need arises, can by the effort of power residing in himself, beat on that drum, and so produce a sound.'

'Just so, great king, has the Blessed One—except the teacher and the instruction he has left in his doctrine and discipline, and the jewel treasure of his relics whose value is derived from his righteousness, and contemplation, and wisdom, and emancipation, and insight given by the knowledge of emancipation—just so has he passed away by that kind of passing away in which no root remains. But the possibility of receiving the three attainments is not cut off because the Blessed One has passed away. Beings oppressed by the sorrow of becoming can, when they desire the attainments, still receive them by means of the jewel treasure of his relics and of his doctrine and discipline and teaching. Therefore is it, great king, that all acts done to the Tathâgata, notwithstanding his having passed away and not accepting, are nevertheless of value and bear fruit. And this future possibility, great king, has been foreseen by the Blessed One, and spoken of, and declared, and made known, when he said: "It may be, Ânanda, that in some of you the thought may arise: [99] 'The word of the Master is ended. We have no Teacher more!' But it is not thus, Ânanda, that you should regard it. The Truth which I have preached to you, the Rules which I have laid down for the Order, let them, when I am gone, be the Teacher to you [1]." So that because the Tathâgata has passed away and consents not thereto, that therefore any act done to him is empty and vain—this saying of the enemy is proved false. It is untrue, unjust, not according to fact, wrong, and perverse. It is the cause of sorrow, has sorrow as its fruit, and leads down the road to perdition!'

14. 'Now hear another reason for the same thing. Does the broad earth acquiesce, O king, in all kinds of seeds being planted all over it?'

'Certainly not, Sir.'

'Then how is it those seeds, planted without the earth's consent, do yet stand fast and firmly rooted, and expand into trees with great trunks and sap and branches, and bearing fruits and flowers?'

'Though the earth, Sir, gives no consent, yet it acts as a site for those seeds, as a means of their development. Planted on that site they grow, by

---

[1] Book of the Great Decease, VI, 1, translated in 'Buddhist Suttas,' p. 112.

its means, into such great trees with branches, flowers, and fruit.'

'Then, great king, the sectaries are destroyed, defeated, proved wrong by their own words when they say that " an act done to him who accepts it not is empty and vain." As the broad earth, O king, is the Tathâgata, the Arahat, the Buddha supreme. Like it he accepts nothing. Like the seeds which through it attain to such developments are the gods and men who, through the jewel treasures of the relics and the wisdom of the Tathâgata—though he have passed away and consent not to it—being firmly rooted by the roots of merit, become like unto trees casting a goodly shade by means of the trunk of contemplation, the sap of true doctrine, and the branches of righteousness, and bearing the flowers of emancipation, and the fruits of Sama*n*a-ship. [100] Therefore is it, great king, that acts done to the Tathâgata, notwithstanding his having passed away and not accepting them, are still of value and bear fruit.'

15. 'Now hear another and further reason for the same thing. Do camels, buffaloes, asses, goats, oxen, or men acquiesce in the birth of worms inside them?'

'Certainly not, Sir.'

'Then how is it then, that without their consent worms are so born, and spread by rapid reproduction of sons and grandsons?'

'By the power of evil Karma, Sir.'

'Just so, great king, is it by the power of the relics and the wisdom of the Tathâgata, who has passed away and acquiesces in nothing, that an act done to him is of value and bears fruit.'

16. 'Now hear another and further reason for the same thing. Do men consent, O king, that the ninety-eight diseases should be produced in their bodies?'

'Certainly not, Sir.'

'Then how is it the diseases come?'

'By evil deeds done in former births.'

'But, great king, if evil deeds done in a former birth have to be suffered here and now, then both good and evil done here or done before has weight and bears fruit. Therefore is it that acts done to the Tathâgata, notwithstanding his having passed away and not consenting, are nevertheless of value and bear fruit.'

17. 'Now hear another and further reason for the same thing. Did you ever hear, O king, of the ogre named Nandaka, who, having laid hands upon the Elder Sâriputta, was swallowed up by the earth?'

'Yes, Sir, that is matter of common talk among men.'

'Well, did Sâriputta acquiesce in that?'

[101] 'Though the world of gods and men, Sir, were to be destroyed, though the sun and moon were to fall upon the earth, though Sineru the king of mountains were to be dissolved, yet would not Sâriputta the Elder have consented to any pain being inflicted on a fellow creature. And why not? Because every condition of heart which could cause him to be angry or offended has been in him destroyed and rooted out. And as all cause thereof had thus been removed, Sir, therefore could not Sâriputta be angered even with those who sought to deprive him of his life.'

'But if Sâriputta, O king, did not consent to it, how was it that Nandaka was so swallowed up?'

'By the power of his evil deeds.'

'Then if so, great king, an act done to him who consents not is still of power and bears fruit. And if this is so of an evil deed, how much more of a good one? Therefore is it, O king, that acts done to the Tathâgata, notwithstanding his having passed away and not accepting them, are nevertheless of value and bear fruit.'

18. 'Now how many, O king, are those men who, in this life, have been swallowed up by the earth? Have you heard anything on that point?'

'Yes, Sir, I have heard how many there are.'

'Then tell me.'

'*Kiñk*a the Brahmin woman, and Suppabuddha the Sâkyan, and Devadatta the Elder, and Nandaka the ogre, and Nanda the Brahman—these are the five people who were swallowed up by the earth.'

'And whom, O king, had they wronged?'

'The Blessed One and his disciples.'

'Then did the Blessed One or his disciples consent to their being so swallowed up?'

'Certainly not, Sir.'

'Therefore is it, O king, that an act done to the Tathâgata, notwithstanding his having passed away and not consenting thereto, is nevertheless of value and bears fruit.'

'Well has this deep question been explained by you, venerable Nâgasena, and made clear. You have made the secret thing [102] plain, you have loosed the knot, you have made in the jungle an open space, the adversaries are overthrown, the wrong opinion has been proved false, the sectaries have been covered with darkness when they met you, O best of all the leaders of schools!'

[Here ends the question as to not consenting to honours paid [1].]

[THE OMNISCIENCE OF THE BUDDHA.]

19. 'Venerable Nâgasena, was the Buddha omniscient?'

'Yes, O king, he was. But the insight of knowledge was not always and continually (consciously) present with him. The omniscience of the Blessed One was dependent on 'reflection.' But if he did reflect he knew whatever he wanted to know [2].

'Then, Sir, the Buddha cannot have been omniscient, if his all-embracing knowledge was reached through investigation.'

'[If so, great king, our Buddha's knowledge must have been less in degree of fineness than that of the other Buddhas. And that is a conclusion hard to draw. But let me explain a little further.] Suppose, O king, you had a hundred cart-loads of rice in the husk, and each cart-load was of seven ammanas [3] and a half. Would a man without consideration be able to tell you in a moment how many laks of grains there were in the whole [4]?'

---

[1] This title and the subsequent ones to the various questions are added from the Simhalese. They are probably the same titles as those referred to by Mr. Trenckner in his preface as being in his Burmese MS.

[2] So again below, § 27.

[3] An ammana is about four bushels.

[4] Mr. Trenckner has marked this passage as corrupt, and I do not pretend to understand it either. The Simhalese is also very

20. 'Now there are these seven classes of minds. Those, great king, who are full of lust, ill-will, delusion, or wrong doing, who are untrained in the management of their body, or in conduct, or in thought, or in wisdom,—their thinking powers are brought into play with difficulty, and act slowly. And why is it so? Because of the untrained condition of their minds. It is like the slow and heavy movements of a giant bambû—when it is being dragged along with its wide-spreading, extensive, overgrown, and interlaced vegetation, and with its branches intricately entangled one with the other. So slow and heavy are the movements of the minds of those men, O king. And why? Because of the intricate entanglements of wrong dispositions. This is the first class of minds.'

21. 'From it the second class is to be distinguished. Those, O king, who have been converted, for whom the gates of purgatory are closed, who have attained to right views, who have grasped the doctrine of the Master—their thinking powers, so far as the three lower stages [1] are concerned, are brought quickly

---

involved and confused. I have added the words in brackets from the Siṁhalese, and translated the rest according to the general sense of the Siṁhalese and the figures of the Pâli. Hardy gives his 'version' at p. 386 of the 'Manual of Buddhism.' It says, ' In one load of rice there are 63,660,000 grains. Each of these grains can be separately considered by Buddha in a moment of time. In that moment the seven-times gifted mind exercises this power.' The last sentence is a misunderstanding of the opening words of our next section (IV, 1, 20).

[1] That is, of the Excellent Way. They are the three Fetters— Delusion of self, Doubt, and Dependence on r tes and eremonies and outward morality—which the Sotâpanno has conquered, broken.

into play, [**103**] and act with ease. But as regards the higher regions they are brought into play with difficulty, and act slowly. And why is this so? Because of their minds having been made clear as regards those three stages, and because of the failings (to be vanquished in the higher stages) still existing within them. It is like the movement of a giant bambû which has a clean trunk as far as the third knot, but above that has its branches intricately entangled. So far as regards the smooth trunk it would travel easily when dragged along, but it would stick obstinately as regards its upper branches. This is the second class of minds.'

22. 'From these the third class is to be distinguished. Those, O king, who are Sakad Âgâmins[1], in whom lust, ill-will, and delusion are reduced to a minimum,—their thinking powers, so far as the five lower stages are concerned, are brought quickly into play, and act with ease. But as regards the higher regions they are brought into play with difficulty, and act slowly. And why is this so? Because of their minds having been made clear as regards those five stages, and because of the failings (to be vanquished in the higher stages) still existing within them. It is like the movement of a giant bambû which has a clean trunk as far as the fifth knot, but above that has its branches intricately entangled. So far as regards the smooth trunk it would travel easily when dragged along, but it would be moved with difficulty as far as its upper branches are concerned. This is the third class of minds.'

---

[1] Disciples who will return only once to this world, there attain Arahatship, and therefore pass away.

23. 'From these the fourth class is to be distinguished. Those, O king, who are Anâgâmins[1], who have completely got rid of the five lower fetters,—their thinking powers, so far as the ten stages[2] are concerned, are brought quickly into play, and act with ease. [104] But as regards the higher regions they are brought into play with difficulty, and act slowly. And why is this so? Because of their minds having been made clear as regards those ten stages, and because of the failings (to be vanquished in the higher stages) still existing within them. It is like the movement of a giant bambû which has a smooth trunk as far as the tenth knot, but above that has its branches intricately entangled. This is the fourth class of minds.'

24. 'From these the fifth class is to be distinguished. Those, O king, who are Arahats, in whom the four Great Evils[3] have ceased, whose stains have been washed away, whose predispositions to evil[4] have been put aside, who have lived the life, and accomplished the task, and laid aside every burden, and reached up to that which is good, for whom the Fetter of the craving after any kind of future life has been broken to pieces[5], who have reached the higher insight[6], who are purified as regards all those conditions of heart in which a

---

[1] Who will not return even once to this world, but attain Arahatship in heaven.

[2] This is noteworthy, for their mind is not yet quite clear as regards the higher five stages. But it is on all fours with the last section.

[3] Lust, becoming, delusion, and ignorance.   [4] Kilesâ.

[5] Parikkî*n*a-bhava-sa*m*yo*g*anâ.

[6] Patta-pa*t*isambhidâ.

hearer can be pure,—their thinking powers, as regards all that a disciple can be or do, are brought quickly into play, and act with ease. But as to those things which are within the reach of the Pa*kk*eka-Buddhas (of those who are Buddhas, but for themselves alone) they are brought into play with difficulty, and act slowly. And why is this so? Because of their having been made pure as regards all within the province of a hearer, but not as regards that within the reach of those who are Buddhas (though for themselves alone). It is like the movement of a giant bambû which has been pruned of the branches arising out of all its knots—and which, therefore, when dragged along moves quickly and with ease, because of its smoothness all along, and because of its being unencumbered with the jungly growth of vegetation. This is the fifth class of minds.'

25. [**105**] 'From these the sixth class is to be distinguished. Those, O king, who are Pa*kk*eka-Buddhas, dependent on themselves alone, wanting no teacher, dwellers alone like the solitary horn of the rhinoceros, who so far as their own higher life is concerned, have pure hearts free from stain,—their thinking powers, so far as their own province is concerned, are brought quickly into play, and act with ease. But as regards all that is specially within the province of a perfect Buddha (one who is not only Buddha, that is enlightened, himself, but can lead others to the light) they are brought with difficulty into play, and move slowly. And why is this so? Because of their purity as regards all within their own province, and because of the immensity of the province of the omniscient Buddhas. It is like a man, O king, who would fearlessly cross, and at will,

by day or night, a shallow brook on his own property. But when he comes in sight of the mighty ocean, deep and wide and ever-moving, and sees no further shore to it, then would he stand hesitating and afraid, and make no effort even to get over it. And why? Because of his familiarity with his own, and because of the immensity of the sea. This is the sixth class of minds.'

26. 'From these the seventh class is to be distinguished. Those, O king, who are complete Buddhas[1], having all knowledge, bearing about in themselves the tenfold power (of the ten kinds of insight), confident in the four modes of just self-confidence, endowed with the eighteen characteristics of a Buddha, whose mastery knows no limit, from whose grasp nothing is hid,—their thinking powers are on every point brought quickly into play, and act with ease. Suppose, O king, a dart well burnished, free from rust, perfectly smooth, with a fine edge, straight, without a crook or a flaw in it, were to be set on a powerful crossbow. Would there be any clumsiness in its action, any retarding in its movement, if it were discharged by a powerful man against a piece of fine linen, or cotton stuff, or delicate woolwork?'

'Certainly not, Sir. And why? Because the stuff is so fine, and the dart so highly tempered, and the discharge so powerful.'

[106] 'And just in the same way, great king, are the thinking powers of the Buddhas I have described brought quickly into play, and act with ease.

---

[1] That is as distinguished from the last—not only themselves enlightened, but able to teach, leaders of men.

And why? Because of their being purified in every respect. This is the seventh class of minds.'

27. 'Now of these, O king, the last — the thinking powers of the omniscient Buddhas — altogether outclasses the other six, and is clear and active in its high quality that is beyond our ken. It is because the mind of the Blessed One is so clear and active that the Blessed One, great king, displays the double miracle. From that we may get to know, O king, how clear and active His mental powers are. And for those wonders there is no further reason that can be alleged. (Yet) those wonders, O king, [caused by means of the mind (alone) of the omniscient Buddhas [1]] cannot be counted, or calculated, or divided, or separated, (For) the knowledge of the Blessed One, O king, is dependent upon reflection[2], and it is on reflection that he knows whatever he wishes to know. (But) it is as when a man passes something he already has in one hand to the other, or utters a sound when his mouth is open, or swallows some food that he has already in his mouth, or opens his eyes when they are shut, or shuts them when open, or stretches forth his arm when it is bent in, or bends it in when stretched out— more rapid than that, great king, and more easy in its action, is the all-embracing knowledge of the Blessed One, more rapid than that his reflection. And although it is by reflection that they know whatever they want to know, yet even when they

---

[1] There is surely something wrong here; either in the Pâli, or in my interpretation of it, which follows the Si*m*halese (p. 130).

[2] Here the opening argument of § 17 is again taken up.

are not reflecting the Blessed Buddhas are not, even then, anything other than omniscient.'

'But, venerable Nâgasena, reflection is carried on for the purpose of seeking (that which is not clear when the reflection begins). Come now. Convince me in this matter by some reason.'

'Suppose, O king, there were a rich man, great in wealth and property—one who had stores of gold and silver and valuables, and stores of all kinds of wheat, one who had rice, and paddy, and barley, and dry grain, and oilseed, and beans, and peas, and every other edible seed, who had ghee, and oil, and butter, and milk, and curds, and honey, and sugar, and molasses, [107] all put away in store-rooms in jars, and pots, and pans, and every sort of vessel. Now if a traveller were to arrive, one worthy of hospitality, and expecting to be entertained; and all the prepared food in the house had been finished, and they were to get out of the jar some rice ready for cooking, and prepare a meal for him. Would that wealthy man merely by reason of the deficiency in eatable stuff at that unusual time be rightly called poor or needy?'

'Certainly not, Sir. Even in the palace of a mighty king of kings there might be no food ready out of time, how much less in the house of an ordinary man.'

'Just so, great king, with the all-embracing knowledge of a Tathâgata when reflection only is wanting; but which on reflection grasps whatever he wants. Now suppose, O king, there were a tree in full fruit, with its branches bending this way and that by the weight of the burden of the bunches of its fruit, but no single fruit had fallen from it.

Could that tree rightly, under the circumstances of the case, be called barren, merely because of the want of a fallen fruit?'

'No, Sir. For though the falling of the fruit is a condition precedent to its enjoyment, yet when it has fallen one can take as much as one likes.'

'Just so, great king, though reflection is a necessary condition of the knowledge of the Tathâgata, yet on reflection it perceives whatever he wants to know.'

'Does that happen always, Nâgasena, at the moment of reflection?'

'Yes, O king. Just as when the mighty king of kings (the *K*akkavatti) calling to mind his glorious wheel of victory wishes it to appear, and no sooner is it thought of than it appears—so does the knowledge of the Tathâgata follow continually on reflection.'

'Strong is the reason you give, Nâgasena, for the omniscience of the Buddha. I am convinced that that is so.'

[Here ends the question as to the omniscience of the Buddha being dependent on reflection[1].]

[WHY DEVADATTA WAS ADMITTED TO THE ORDER.]

28. 'Venerable Nâgasena, who was it that admitted Devadatta[2] to the Order?'

---

[1] At III, 6, 2 there is another problem raised as to the omniscience of the Buddha.

[2] He is the Judas of the Buddhist story, who tried to have the Buddha killed, and to seduce his disciples from him.

'Those six young nobles, O king, Bhaddiya and Anuruddha and Ânanda and Bhagu and Kimbila and Devadatta, [108] together with Upâli the barber as a seventh—they all, when the Master had attained to Buddhahood, left the Sâkya home out of the delight they felt in him, and following the Blessed One renounced the world[1]. So the Blessed One admitted them all to the Order.'

'But was it not Devadatta who, after he had entered the Order, raised up a schism within it?'

'Yes. No layman can create a schism, nor a sister of the Order, nor one under preparatory instruction, nor a novice of either sex. It must be a Bhikkhu, under no disability, who is in full communion, and a co-resident[2].'

'And what Karma does a schismatical person gain?'

'A Karma that continues to act for a Kalpa (a very long period of time).'

'What then, Nâgasena! Was the Buddha aware that Devadatta after being admitted to the Order would raise up a schism, and having done so would suffer torment in purgatory for a Kalpa?'

'Yes, the Tathâgata knew that.'

'But, Nâgasena, if that be so, then the statement that the Buddha was kind and pitiful, that he sought after the good of others, that he was the remover of that which works harm, the provider of that which works well to all beings—that statement must be wrong. If it be not so—if he knew not that Deva-

---

[1] Hînaṭi-kumburê takes kulâ as an ablative.
[2] These are all termini technici in Buddhist canon law. The meaning is that other divisions in the Order do not amount technically to schism. See the Kullavagga VII, 1, 27, &c.

datta after he had been admitted to the Order would stir up a schism—then he cannot have been omniscient. This other double-pointed dilemma is put to you. Unravel this tough skein, break up the argument of the adversaries. In future times it will be hard to find Bhikkhus like to you in wisdom. Herein then show your skill!'

29. 'The Blessed One, O king, was both full of mercy and had all knowledge. It was when the Blessed One in his mercy and wisdom considered the life history of Devadatta that he perceived how, having heaped up Karma on Karma, he would pass for an endless series of Kalpas from torment to torment, and from perdition to perdition. And the Blessed One knew also that the infinite Karma of that man would, because he had entered the Order, become finite, and the sorrow caused by the previous Karma would also therefore become limited. [109] But that if that foolish person were not to enter the Order then he would continue to heap up Karma which would endure for a Kalpa. And it was because he knew that that, in his mercy, he admitted him to the Order.'

'Then, Nâgasena, the Buddha first wounds a man and then pours oil on the wound, first throws a man down a precipice and then reaches out to him an assisting hand, first kills him and then seeks to give him life, first gives pain and then adds a subsequent joy to the pain he gave.'

'The Tathâgata, O king, wounds people but to their good, he casts people down but to their profit, he kills people but to their advantage. Just as mothers and fathers, O king, hurt their children and even knock them down, thinking the while of their good; so by whatsoever method an increase in the virtue of living things can be brought about, by that method does he contribute to their good. If Devadatta, O king, had not entered the Order, then as a layman he would have laid up much Karma leading to states of woe, and so passing for hundreds of thousands of Kalpas from torment to misery, and from one state of perdition to another, he would have suffered constant pain. It was knowing that, that in his mercy, the Blessed One admitted Devadatta to the Order. It was at the thought that by renouncing the world according to His doctrine Devadatta's sorrow would become finite that, in his mercy, he adopted that means of making his heavy sorrow light.

30. 'As a man of influence, O king, by the power of his wealth or reputation or prosperity or birth, when a grievous penalty has been imposed by the king on some friend or relative of his, would get it made light by the ability arising from the trust reposed in him; [110] just so did the Blessed One, by admitting him to the Order, and by the efficacy of the influence of righteousness and meditation and wisdom and emancipation of heart, make light the heavy sorrow of Devadatta, who would have had to suffer many hundreds of thousands of Kalpas. As a clever physician and surgeon, O king, would make a grievous sickness light by the aid of a powerful medicinal drug, just so did the Blessed One, in his knowledge of the right means to an end, admit Devadatta to the Order and thus make his grievous pain light by the aid of the medicine of the Dhamma, strong by the power of mercy[1]. Was then, O king,

---

[1] Karuññabalopatthaddha. Compare Gâtaka, vol. i, verse 267, and Sutta Vibhaṅga I, 10, 7.

the Blessed One guilty of any wrong in that he turned Devadatta from being a man of much sorrow into being a man of less sorrow?'

'No indeed, Sir. He committed no wrong, not even in the smallest degree[1].'

'Then accept this, great king, to the full as the reason for which the Blessed One admitted Devadatta to the Order.'

31. 'Hear another and further reason, O king, for the Blessed One's having admitted Devadatta. Suppose men were to seize and hurry before the king some wicked robber, saying: "This is the wicked robber, your Majesty. Inflict upon him such punishment as you think fit!" And thereupon the king were to say to them: "Take this robber then, my men, outside the town, and there on the place of execution cut off his head." And they in obedience to his orders were to take that man accordingly towards the place of execution. And some man who was high in office near the king, and of great reputation and wealth and property, whose word was held of weight[2], and whose influence was great, should see him. And he were to have pity on him, and were to say to those men: "Stay, good fellows. What good will cutting off his head do to you? Save him alive, and cut off only a hand or a foot. I will speak on his behalf to the king." And they at the word of that influential person were to do so. Now would the officer who had acted so towards him have been a benefactor to that robber?'

---

[1] Gaddûhanam pi. It is the Sanskrit dadrûghna.
[2] Âdeyya-vakano. See my note, Kullavagga VI, 4, 8, and also Puggala Paññatti III, 12, and Pañka Gati Dîpana, 98.

'He would have saved his life, Sir. And having done that, what would he not have done?'

'But would he have done no wrong on account of the pain the man suffered [111] when his hand or foot was cut off?'

'The pain the thief suffered, Sir, was his own fault. But the man who saved his life did him no harm.'

'Just so, great king, was it in his mercy that the Blessed One admitted Devadatta, with the knowledge that by that his sorrow would be mitigated.'

32. 'And Devadatta's sorrow, O king, was mitigated. For Devadatta at the moment of his death took refuge in Him for the rest of his existences when he said:

"In him, who of the best is far the best [1],
The god of gods, the guide of gods and men,
Who see'th all, and bears the hundred marks
Of goodness,—'tis in him I refuge take
Through all the lives that I may have to live."

[2] 'If you divide this Kalpa, O king, into six parts, it was at the end of the first part that Devadatta created schism in the Order. After he has suffered the other five in purgatory he will be released, and will become a Pakkeka-Buddha [3] under the name of Atthissara.'

'Great is the gift bestowed, Nâgasena, by the Blessed One on Devadatta. In that the Tathâgata

---

[1] Literally, 'is the best of these eight'—the eight being those walking in the Excellent Way, the four magga-samaṅgino and the four phala-samaṅgino. See Puggala Paññatti VIII, 1.

[2] The Siṃhalese inserts a paragraph here not found in Mr. Trenckner's text.

[3] See above, p. 158.

has caused him to attain to the state of a Pakkeka-Buddha, what has he not done for him?'

'But inasmuch as Devadatta, O king, having made a schism in the Order, suffers pain in purgatory, has not therefore the Blessed One done him wrong?'

'No, Sir. That is Devadatta's own fault; and the Blessed One who mitigated his suffering has done him no harm.'

'Then accept this, O king, to the full as the reason for the Blessed One admitting Devadatta to the Order.

33. 'Hear another and further reason, O king, for his having done so. [112] Suppose in treating a wound full of matter and blood, in whose grievous hollow the weapon which caused it remained, which stank of putrid flesh, and was made worse by the pain that varied with constantly changing symptoms, by variations in temperature, and by the union of the three humours,—windy, bilious, and phlegmatic [1],—an able physician and surgeon were to anoint it with a rough, sharp, bitter, stinging ointment, to the end that the inflammation should be allayed. And when the inflammation had gone down, and the wound had become sweet, suppose he were then to cut into it with a lancet, and burn it with caustic. And when he had cauterised it, suppose he were to prescribe an alkaline wash, and anoint it with some drug to the end that the wound might heal up, and the sick man recover his health—now tell me, O king, would it be out of cruelty that the surgeon thus smeared with ointment, and cut with the lancet, and cauterised

---

[1] The interpretation of some of the medical terms in this paragraph is very uncertain. See pp. 134, 252, 304 of the text.

with the stick of caustic, and administered a salty wash?'

'Certainly not, Sir; it would be with kindness in his heart, and intent on the man's weal, that he would do all those things.'

'And the feelings of pain produced by his efforts to heal—would not the surgeon be guilty of any wrong in respect of them?'

'How so? Acting with kind intent and for the man's weal, how could he therein incur a wrong? It is of heavenly bliss rather that that kindly surgeon would be worthy.'

'Just so, great king, was it in his mercy that the Blessed One admitted Devadatta, to the end to release him from pain.'

34. 'Hear another and further reason, O king, why the Blessed One did so. Suppose a man had been pierced by a thorn. And another man with kindly intent and for his good were to cut round the place with another sharp thorn or with a lancet, and the blood flowing the while, were to extract that thorn. Now would it be out of cruelty that he acted so?'

'Certainly not, Sir. For he acted with kindly intent, and for the man's good. And if he had not done so the man might have died, or might have suffered such pain that he would have been nigh to death.'

'Just even so, great king, was it of his mercy that the Tathâgata admitted Devadatta, to the end to release him of his pain. If he had not done so [113] Devadatta would have suffered torment in purgatory through a succession of existences, through hundreds of thousands of Kalpas.'

'Yes, Nâgasena, the Tathâgata turned Devadatta, who was being carried down with the flood, with his head against the stream; he again pointed out the road to Devadatta when he was lost in the jungle; he gave a firm foothold to Devadatta when he was falling down the precipice: he restored Devadatta to peace when he was swallowed up of desolation. But the reason and the meaning of these things could no one have pointed out, Nâgasena, unless he were wise as you!'

[Here ends the dilemma about Devadatta.]

[VESSANTARA'S EARTHQUAKE.]

35. 'Venerable Nâgasena, the Blessed One said thus: "There are these eight causes, O Bhikkhus, proximate or remote, for a mighty earthquake [1]." This is an inclusive statement, a statement which leaves no room for anything to be supplemented, a statement to which no gloss can be added. There can be no ninth reason for an earthquake. If there were, the Blessed One would have mentioned it. It is because there is no other, that he left it unnoticed. But we find another, and a ninth reason, when we are told that on Vessantara's giving his mighty largesse the earth shook seven times [2]. If, Nâgasena, there are eight causes for an earthquake, then what we hear of the earthquake at Vessantara's largesse is false. And if that is true, then the statement as to the eight

---

[1] From the Book of the Great Decease, III, 13, translated at p. 45 of my 'Buddhist Suttas,' vol. xi in this series.
[2] See the Vessantara Gâtaka, and compare Gâtaka I, p. 74.

causes of earthquakes is false. This double-headed question, too, is subtle, hard to unravel, dark, and profound. It is now put to you. [114] No one of less knowledge can solve it, only one wise as you.'

36. 'The Blessed One made the statement you refer to, O king, and yet the earth shook seven times at Vessantara's largesse. But that was out of season, it was an isolated occurrence, it was not included in the eight usual causes, and was not therefore reckoned as one of them. Just, O king, as there are three kinds of well-known rains reckoned in the world—that of the rainy season, that of the winter months, and that of the two months Âsâḷha and Sâvana. If, besides these, any other rain falls, that is not reckoned among the usual rains, but is called "a rain out of season." And again, O king, just as there are five hundred rivers which flow down from the Himâlayas, but of these ten only are reckoned in enumerations of rivers—the Ganges, the Jumna, the Akiravatî, the Sarabhû, the Mahî, the Indus, the Sarasvatî, the Vetravatî, the Vîtaṃsâ, and the Kandabhâgâ—the others not being included in the catalogue because of their intermittent flow of water. And again, O king, just as there are a hundred or two of officers under the king, but only six of them are reckoned as officers of state—the commander-in-chief, the prime minister, and the chief judge, and the high treasurer, and the bearer of the sunshade of state, and the state sword-bearer. And why? Because of their royal prerogatives. The rest are not reckoned, they are all called simply officers. [115] Just as in all these cases, great king, the seven times repeated earthquake at the largesse of Vessantara was, as an isolated and extra-

ordinary occurrence, and distinct from the eight usual ones, not reckoned among those eight causes.'

37. 'Now have you heard, O king, in the history of our faith of any act of devotion being done so as to receive its recompense even in this present life, the fame of which has reached up to the gods?'

'Yes, Lord, I have heard of such. There are seven cases of such actions.'

'Who were the people who did those things?'

'Sumana the garland maker, and Eka-sâ*l*aka the brahman, and Pu*nn*a the hired servant, and Mallikâ the queen, and the queen known as the mother of Gopâla, and Suppiyâ the devoted woman, and Pu*nn*â the slave-girl. It was these seven who did acts of devotion which bare fruit even in this life, and the fame of which reached even to the gods.'

'And have you heard of others, O king, who, even in their human body, mounted up to the blessed abode of the great Thirty-three?'

'Yes, I have heard, too, of them.'

'And who were they?'

'Guttila the musician, and Sâdhîna the king, and king Nimi, and king Mandhâtâ—these four. Long ago was it done, this glorious deed and difficult.'

'But have you ever heard, O king, of the earth shaking, either now or in the past, and either once or twice or thrice, when a gift had been given?'

'No, Sir, that I have not heard of.'

'And I too, O king—though I have received the traditions, and been devoted to study, and to hearing the law, and to learning by heart, and to the acquirements of discipleship, and though I have been ready to learn, and to ask and to answer questions, and to sit at the feet of teachers—I too have never heard of such a thing, except only in the case of the splendid gift of Vessantara the glorious king. And between the times of Kassapa the Blessed One, and of the Blessed One the Sâkya sage, there have rolled by hundreds of thousands of years, but in all that period I have heard of no such case. [116] It is at no common effort, O king, at no ordinary struggle, that the great earth is moved. It is when overborne by the weight of righteousness, overpowered by the burden of the goodness of acts which testify of absolute purity, that, unable to support it, the broad earth quakes and trembles and is moved. Then it is as when a wagon is overladen with a too heavy weight, and the nave and the spokes are split, and the axletree is broken in twain. Then it is as when the heavens, overspread with the waters of the tempest driven by the wind, and overweighted with the burden of the heaped-up rain-clouds, roar and creak and rage at the onset of the whirlwind. Thus was it, great king, that the broad earth, unable to support the unwonted burden of the heaped-up and wide-reaching force of king Vessantara's largesse, quaked and trembled and was moved. For the heart of king Vessantara was not turned in the way of lust, nor of ill-will, nor of dullness, nor of pride, nor of delusion, nor of sin, nor of disputation, nor of discontent, but it was turned mightily to generosity. And thinking: "Let all those who want, and who have not yet come, now arrive! Let all who come receive whate'er they want, and be filled with satisfaction!" it was on giving, ever and without end, that his mind was set. And on these ten conditions of heart, O king, was his mind too fixed—on self-control, and on inward calm, and on long-suffering, and on self-restraint, and on temperance, and on voluntary subjugation to meritorious vows, and on freedom from all forms of wrath and cruelty, and on truthfulness, and on purity of heart. He had abandoned, O king, all seeking after the satisfaction of his animal lusts, he had overcome all craving after a future life, his strenuous effort was set only towards the higher life. He had given up, O king, the caring for himself, and devoted himself thenceforth to caring for others alone. His mind was fixed immovably on the thought: "How can I make all beings to be at peace, healthy, and wealthy, and long lived?" [117] And when, O king, he was giving things away, he gave not for the sake of rebirth in any glorious state, he gave not for the sake of wealth, nor of receiving gifts in return, nor of flattery, nor of long life for himself, nor of high birth, nor of happiness, nor of power, nor of fame, nor of offspring either of daughters or of sons—but it was for the sake of supreme wisdom and of the treasure thereof that he gave gifts so immense, so immeasurable, so unsurpassed. It was when he had attained to that supreme wisdom that he uttered the verse:

"*G*âli, my son, and the Black Antelope,
My daughter, and my queen, my wife, Maddî,
I gave them all away without a thought—
And 'twas for Buddhahood I did this thing[1]."

38. 'The angry man, O king, did the great king Vessantara conquer by mildness, and the wicked man by goodness, and the covetous by generosity,

---

[1] From the *K*ariyâ Pi*t*aka I, ix, 52. See Dr. Morris's edition for the Pâli Text Society, p. 81.

and the speaker of falsehood by truth, and all evil did he overcome by righteousness [1]. When he was thus giving away—he who was seeking after righteousness, who had made righteousness his aim—then were the great winds, on which the earth rests below, agitated by the full force of the power of the influence that resulted from his generosity, and little by little, one by one, the great winds began to blow confusedly, and up and down and towards each side the earth swayed, and the mighty trees rooted in the soil [2] began to totter, and masses of cloud were heaped together in the sky, and terrible winds arose laden with dust, and the heavens rushed together, and hurricanes blew with violent blasts, and a great and terrible mighty noise was given forth. And at the raging of those winds, the waters little by little began to move, and at the movement of the waters the great fish and the scaly creatures were disturbed, and the waves began to roll in double breakers, and the beings that dwell in the waters were seized with fear and as the breakers rushed together in pairs the roar of the ocean grew loud, and the spray was lashed into fury, and garlands of foam arose, and the great ocean opened to its depths, and the waters rushed hither and thither, the furious crests of their waves meeting this way and that; and the Asuras, and Garu/as, and Yakkhas, and Nâgas [3] shook with fear, and thought in their alarm: "What now! How now! is the great ocean being turned upside down?"

---

[1] On this sentiment Mr. Trenckner calls attention to the analogous phrases at Dhammapada, verse 223.
[2] Sînapattâ: which the Si*m*halese renders po/o talehi kal gewî patra wœ/îma/a pœminiyâwu w*r*/kshayo.
[3] Fabulous beings supposed to occupy these fabulous waters.

and sought, with terrified hearts, for a way of escape. And as the water on which it rests [1] was troubled and agitated, then the broad earth began to shake, and with it the mountain ranges and the ocean depths, [118] and Sineru began to revolve, and its rocky mountain crest became twisted. And at the trembling of the earth, the serpents, and mungooses, and cats, and jackals, and boars, and deer, and birds became greatly distressed, and the Yakkhas of inferior power wept, while those of greater power were merry.'

39. 'Just, O king, as when a huge and mighty cauldron [2] is placed in an oven full of water, and crowded with grains of rice, then the fire burning beneath heats first of all the cauldron, and when that has become hot the water begins to boil, and as the water boils the grains of rice are heated and dive hither and thither in the water, and a mass of bubbles arises, and a garland of foam is formed—just so, O king, king Vessantara gave away whatsoever is in the world considered most difficult to bestow, and by reason of the nature of his generosity the great winds beneath were unable to refrain from being agitated throughout, and on the great winds being thrown into confusion the waters were shaken, and on the waters being disturbed the broad earth trembled, and so then the winds and the waters and the earth became all three, as it were, of one accord by the immense and powerful influence that

---

[1] This conception of the earth resting on water and the water on air is Indian, and forms no part of distinctively Buddhist teaching.

[2] Mahati-mahâ-pariyogo; not in Childers nor in the Sanskrit Petersburg Dictionary. Hînaṭi-kumburê renders it itâ mahat wu mahâ bhâganayak.

resulted from that mighty giving. And there was never another giving, O king, which had such power as that generosity of the great king Vessantara.

40. 'And just, O king, as there are many gems of value found in the earth—the sapphire, and the great sapphire, and the wish-conferring gem, and the cat's eye, and the flax gem [1], and the Acacia gem [2], and the entrancing gem, and the favourite of the sun [3], and the favourite of the moon [4], and the crystal, and the ka*gg*opakkamaka [5], and the topaz, and the ruby, and the Masâra stone [6]—but the glorious gem of the king of kings is acknowledged to be the chief of all these and surpassing all, for the sheen of that jewel, O king, spreads round about for a league on every side [7]—just so, O king, of all the gifts that

---

[1] Ummâ-puppha; rendered diya-me*n*d̃iri-pushpa in the Si*m*halese. Clough gives diyameneri as a plant 'commelina cucullata.'

[2] Sirîsa-puppha; rendered mârâ-pushpa in the Si*m*halese, mârâ being the seed of the 'adenanthera pavonia.'

[3] Suriya-kanto, which the Si*m*halese merely repeats.

[4] *K*anda-kanta; and so also in the Si*m*halese. These are mythic gems, supposed to be formed out of the rays of the sun and moon respectively, and visible only when they shine.

[5] The Si*m*halese has ka*gg*opakramaya, which is not in Clough.

[6] Masâra-galla, which the Si*m*halese renders by masâra-galya, which Böhtlingk-Roth think is sapphire or smaragd, and Clough renders 'emerald,' and the commentary on the Abhidhâna Padîpikâ, quoted by Childers, says is a stone produced in the hill of Masâra (otherwise unknown).

On similar lists of gems elsewhere see the *K*ullavagga IX, 1, 3, and my note at pp. 249, 250 of the 'Buddhist Suttas' (vol. xi of the 'Sacred Books of the East').

[7] So also in the Mahâ-Sudassana Sutta I, 32, translated in the 'Buddhist Suttas,' p. 256. Compare above, p. 35 of the text.

have ever been given upon earth, even the greatest and the most unsurpassed, that giving of the good king Vessantara is acknowledged to surpass them all. And it was on the giving of that gift, O king, that the broad earth shook seven times[1].'

41. 'A marvellous thing is it, Nâgasena, of the Buddhas, and a most wonderful, that the Tathâgata even when a Bodisat (in the course of becoming a Buddha) [119] was so unequalled in the world, so mild, so kind, and held before him aims so high, and endeavours so grand. You have made evident, Nâgasena, the might of the Bodisats, a most clear light have you cast upon the perfection of the Conquerors, you have shown how, in the whole world of gods and men, a Tathâgata, as he continues the practice of his noble life, is the highest and the best. Well spoken, venerable Nâgasena. The doctrine of the Conqueror has been exalted, the perfection of the Conqueror has been glorified, the knot of the arguments of the adversaries has been unravelled, the jar of the theories of the opponents has been broken in pieces, the dilemma so profound has been made clear, the jungle has been turned into open country, the children of the Conqueror have received the desire of their hearts[2]. It is so, as you say, O best of the leaders of schools, and I accept that which you have said!'

[Here ends the dilemma as to the earthquake at Vessantara's gift.]

---

[1] There is here a long paragraph in the Si*m*halese omitted in the Pâli.

[2] Nibbâhana; rendered abhiwarddhiya in the Si*m*halese.

[KING SIVI [1].]

42. 'Venerable Nâgasena, your people say thus: "King Sivi gave his eyes to the man who begged them of him, and when he had thus become blind, new eyes were given to him from heaven [2]." This statement is unpalatable [3], it lays its speaker open to rebuke, it is faulty. For it is said in the Sutta: "When the cause has been utterly destroyed, when there is no longer any cause, any basis left, then the divine eye cannot arise [4]." So if he gave his eyes away, the statement that he received new (divine) ones must be false: and if divine eyes arose to him, then the statement that he gave his eyes away must be false. This dilemma too is a double-pointed one, more knotty than a knot, more piercing than an arrow, more confusing than a jungle. It is now put to you. Rouse up in yourself the desire to accomplish the task that is set to you, to the refutation of the adversaries!'

---

[1] The story is given at length in the Sivi *G*âtaka, No. 499 (vol. iv, pp. 401–412 of Professor Fausböll's edition).

[2] There is nothing in the text of the *G*âtaka (p. 410) of the new eyes being 'divine' or 'from heaven.' There new, ordinary eyes arose to him as the result of his virtue.

[3] Sa-kasa*l*a*m*. Kasa*l*a cannot mean simply 'insipid' as Dr. Edward Müller suggests at p. 43 of his 'Pâli Grammar,' for it is opposed to dullness, insipidity (manda) at Anguttara II, 5, 5. It must mean there 'wrong, not only by omission, but by commission.' Compare its use in the Dhammapada Commentary, p. 275; *G*âtaka I, 108, II, 97; and in the commentary on the Puggala IV, 24. Mr. Trenckner points out in his note that it is often written saka*l*a, and is no doubt the same as the Sanskrit word so spelt, and given by Wilson. (It is not in Böhtlingk-Roth.)

[4] I don't know which Sutta is referred to.

'King Sivi gave his eyes away, O king. Harbour no doubt on that point. And in stead thereof divine eyes were produced for him. Neither on that point should you harbour doubt.'

'But then, Nâgasena, can the divine eye arise when the cause of it has been utterly destroyed, when no cause for it, no basis, remains?'

'Certainly not, O king.'

'What then is the reason [**120**] by which in this case it arose, notwithstanding that its cause had been utterly destroyed, and no cause for it, no basis, remained. Come now. Convince me of the reason of this thing.'

43. 'What then, O king? Is there in the world such a thing as Truth, by the asseveration of which true believers can perform the Act of Truth[1]?'

'Yes, Lord, there is. And by it true believers make the rain to fall, and fire to go out[2], and ward off the effects of poison, and accomplish many other things they want to do.'

'Then, great king, that fits the case, that meets it on all fours. It was by the power of Truth that those divine eyes were produced for Sivi the king. By the power of the Truth the divine eye arose when no other cause was present, for the Truth itself was, in that case, the cause of its production. Sup-

---

[1] This paragraph is very different in the Siṃhalese, and much longer than the Pâli.

[2] See the beautiful story of the Holy Quail (translated in my 'Buddhist Birth Stories,' p. 302), where even so weak a creature as a baby quail is able, by such a mystic Act of Truth, to drive back the great and powerful Agni, the god of fire, whom the Brahmans so much feared and worshipped.

pose, O king, any Siddha (accomplished one[1]) on intoning a charm[2], and saying: "Let a mighty rain now fall!" were to bring about a heavy rainfall by the intoning of his charm—would there in that case be any cause for rain accumulated in the sky by which the rain could be brought about?'

'No, Sir. The charm itself would be the cause.'

'Just so, great king, in the case put. There would be no ordinary cause. The Truth itself would be sufficient reason for the growth of the divine eye!'

44. 'Now suppose, O king, a Siddha were to intone a charm, and say: "Now let the mighty blazing, raging mass of fire go back!" and the moment the charm were repeated it were to retreat—would there be any cause laid by which would work that result?'

'No, Sir. The charm itself would be the cause.'

'Just so, great king, would there in our case be no ordinary cause. The power of the Truth would be sufficient cause in itself!'

45. 'Now suppose, O king, one of those Siddhas were to intone a charm, [121] and were then to say: "Let this malignant poison become as a healing drug!" and the moment the charm were repeated that would be so—would there be any cause in reserve for that effect to be produced?'

'Certainly not, Sir. The charm itself would cause the warding off of that malignant poison.'

'Just so, great king, without any ordinary cause the Truth itself was, in king Sivi's case, a sufficient reason for the reproduction of his eyes.'

---

[1] 'One who knows a powerful charm (or perhaps Vedic verse, mantra),' says Hîna/i-kumburê.

[2] Sa*kk*a, literally truth. (Satya-gâyanâ in the Si*m*halese.)

46. 'Now there is no other cause, O king, for the attainment of the four Noble Truths. It is only by means of an Act of Truth that they are attained. In the land of China, O king, there is a king of China, who when he wants to charm the great ocean, performs at intervals of four months a solemn Act of Truth, and then on his royal chariot drawn by lions, he enters a league's distance into the great ocean. Then in front of the head of his chariot the mighty waves roll back, and when he returns they flow once more over the spot. But could the ocean be so drawn back by the ordinary bodily power of all gods and men combined?'

'Sir, even the water in a small tank could not be so made to retire, how much less the waters of the great ocean!'

'By this know then the force of Truth. There is no place to which it does not reach.'

47. 'When Asoka the righteous ruler, O king, as he stood one day at the city of Pâṭaliputta in the midst of the townsfolk and the country people, of his officers and his servants, and his ministers of state, beheld the Ganges river as it rolled along filled up by freshets from the hills, full to the brim and overflowing—that mighty stream five hundred leagues in length, and a league in breadth—he said to his officers: "Is there any one, my good friends, who is able to make this great Ganges flow backwards and up stream?"

'" Nay, Sire, impossible," said they.

'Now a certain courtesan, Bindumatî by name, was in the crowd there at the river side, [122] and she heard people repeat the question that the king had asked. Then she said to herself: "Here am I, a harlot, in this city of Pâṭaliputta, by the sale of my body do I gain my livelihood, I follow the meanest of vocations. Let the king behold the power of an Act of Truth performed even by such as I." And she performed an Act of Truth [1]. And that moment the mighty Ganges, roaring and raging, rolled back, up stream, in the sight of all the people!

'Then when the king heard the din and the noise of the movement of the waves of the whirlpools of the mighty Ganges, amazed, and struck with awe and wonder, he said to his officers: "How is this, that the great Ganges is flowing backwards?"

'And they told him what had happened. Then filled with emotion the king went himself in haste and asked the courtesan: "Is it true what they say, that it is by your Act of Truth that this Ganges has been forced to flow backwards?"

'"Yes, Sire," said she.

'And the king asked: "How have you such power in the matter? Or who is it who takes your words to heart (and carries them out)? By what authority is it that you, insignificant as you are [2], have been able to make this mighty river flow backwards?"

'And she replied: "It is by the power of Truth, great king."

'But the king said: "How can that power be in you—you, a woman of wicked and loose life,

---

[1] That is to say, in the words of the Quail story (loc. cit. p. 305), she 'called to mind the attributes of the Buddhas who had passed away, and made a solemn asseveration of the faith' that she had in the truth they had taught.

[2] Anummatto, which the Siṃhalese translates as a feminine.

devoid of virtue, under no restraint [1], sinful, who have overstepped all limits, and are full of transgression, and live on the plunder of fools?"

'"It is true, O king, what you say. That is just the kind of creature I am. But even in such a one as I so great is the power of the Act of Truth that I could turn the whole world of gods and men upside down by it."

'Then the king said: "What is this Act of Truth? Come now, let me hear about it."

'"Whosoever, O king, gives me gold—be he a noble or a brahman or a tradesman or a servant—I regard them all alike. When I see he is a noble I make no distinction in his favour. If I know him to be a slave I despise him not. Free alike from fawning and from dislike do I do service to him who has bought me. This, your Majesty, is the basis of the Act of Truth by the force of which I turned the Ganges back."'

48. 'Thus, O king, is it that there is nothing which those who are stedfast to the truth may not enjoy. And so king Sivi gave his eyes away to him who begged them of him, [123] and he received eyes from heaven, and that happened by his Act of Truth. But what is said in the Sutta that when the eye of flesh is destroyed, and the cause of it, the basis of it, is removed, then can no divine eye arise, that is only said of the eye, the insight, that arises out of contemplation. And thus, O king, should you take it.'

'Well said, Nâgasena! You have admirably

---

[1] *Kh*innikâya. Compare Gâtaka II, 114, and the Sutta Vibhanga on Pâ*k*ittiya 26.

solved the dilemma I put to you; you have rightly explained the point in which I tried to prove you wrong; you have thoroughly overcome the adversary. The thing is so, and I accept it thus[1].'

[Here ends the dilemma as to king Sivi's Act of Truth.]

[THE DILEMMA AS TO CONCEPTION.

49. This dilemma goes into details which can be best consulted in the Pâli.]

[THE DURATION OF THE FAITH.]

55. 'Venerable Nâgasena, it has been said by the Blessed One: " But now the good law, Ânanda, will only stand fast for five hundred years[2]." But on the other hand the Blessed One declared, just before

---

[1] This idea of the power of an Act of Truth which Nâgasena here relies on is most interesting and curious. The exact time at which it was introduced into Buddhism is as yet unknown. It has not been found in the Pi/akas themselves, and is probably an incorporation of an older, pre-Buddhistic, belief. The person carrying it out is supposed to have some goodness, to call that virtue (and perhaps, as in the case of the quail, the goodness of the Buddhas also) to mind, and then to wish something, and that thing, however difficult, and provided there is nothing cruel in it, then comes to pass. It is analogous to the mystic power supposed to reside in names. Childers very properly points out that we have a very remarkable instance of an Act of Truth (though a very un-Buddhistic one) in the Hebrew book of the Kings II. i. 10: 'And Elijah answered and said to the captain of fifty: " If I be a man of God, then let fire come down from heaven, and consume thee and thy fifty!" And there came down fire from heaven, and consumed him and his fifty.' A great point, both in this legend and in the story of the quail, is that the power of nature to be overcome is one looked upon by the Brahmans as divine.

[2] *K*ullavagga X, 1, 6, translated in 'Vinaya Texts,' vol. iii, p. 325.

his death, in response to the question put by Subhadda the recluse: "But if in this system the brethren live the perfect life, then the world would not be bereft of Arahats[1]." This last phrase is absolute, inclusive; it cannot be explained away. If the first of these statements be correct, the second is misleading, if the second be right the first must be false. [131] This too is a double-pointed question, more confused than the jungle, more powerful than a strong man, more knotty than a knot. It is now put to you. Show the extent of the power of your knowledge, like a leviathan in the midst of the sea.'

56. 'The Blessed One, O king, did make both those statements you have quoted. But they are different one from the other both in the spirit and in the letter. The one deals with the limit of the duration of the doctrine[2], the other with the practice of a religious life—two things widely distinct, as far removed one from the other as the zenith is from the surface of the earth, as heaven is from purgatory, as good is from evil, and as pleasure is from pain. But though that be so, yet lest your enquiry should be vain, I will expound the matter further in its essential connection.'

57. 'When the Blessed One said that the good law[3] would only endure for five hundred years, he said so declaring the time of its destruction, limiting the remainder of its existence. For he said: "The good law, Ânanda, would endure for a thousand years if no women had been admitted to the

---

[1] Book of the Great Decease, V, 62, translated in 'Buddhist Suttas.' p. 108.
[2] Sâsana.   [3] Saddhammo.

Order. But now, Ânanda, it will only last five hundred years." But in so saying, O king, did the Blessed One either foretell the disappearance of the good law, or throw blame on the clear understanding thereof?'

'Certainly not, Sir.'

'Just so. It was a declaration of injury done, an announcement of the limit of what remained. As when a man whose income had been diminished might announce publicly, making sure of what remained: "So much property have I lost; so much is still left"—[132] so did the Blessed One make known to gods and men what remained when he announced what had been lost by saying: "The good law will now, Ânanda, endure for five hundred years." In so saying he was fixing a limit to religion. But when in speaking to Subhadda, and by way of proclaiming who were the true Samanas, he said: "But if, in this system, the brethren live the perfect life, then the world would not be bereft of Arahats"—in so saying he was declaring in what religion consisted. You have confounded the limitation of a thing with the statement of what it is. But if you like I will tell you what the real connection between the two is. Listen carefully, and attend trustfully to what I say.'

58. 'Suppose, O king, there were a reservoir quite full of fresh cool water, overflowing at the brim, but limited in size and with an embankment running all round it. Now if, when the water had not abated in that tank, a mighty cloud were to rain down rain continually, and in addition, on to the water already in it, would the amount of water in the tank decrease or come to an end?'

'Certainly not, Sir.'

'But why not, O king?'

'Because of the continual downpour of the rain.'

'Just so, O king, is the glorious reservoir of the good law of the teaching of the Conqueror ever full of the clear fresh cool water of the practice of duty and virtue and morality and purity of life, and continues overflowing all limits even to the very highest heaven of heavens. And if the children of the Buddha rain down into it continuously, and in addition, the rainfall of still further practice of duty and virtue and morality and purity of life, then will it endure for long, and the world will not be bereft of Arahats. This was the meaning of the Master's words when he said: "But if, Subhadda, in this system the brethren continue in perfectness of life, then will the world not be bereft of Arahats."'

59. 'Now suppose again, O king, that people were to continually supply a mighty fiery furnace with dried cow-dung, and dry sticks, and dry leaves—would that fire go out?'

[133] 'No indeed, Sir. Rather would it blaze more fiercely, and burn more brightly.'

'Just so, O king, does the glorious teaching of the Conqueror blaze and shine over the ten thousand world systems by the practice of duty and virtue and morality and purity of life. And if, O king, in addition to that, the children of the Buddha, devoting themselves to the five[1] kinds of spiritual exertion, continue zealous in effort—if cultivating a longing for the threefold discipline, they train themselves therein—

---

[1] Pañka-padhânaṅgani. This is curious. In the Piṭakas there are four kinds only.

if without ceasing they carry out to the full the conduct that is right, and absolutely avoid all that is wrong, and practise righteousness of life—then will this glorious doctrine of the Conqueror stand more and more stedfast as the years roll on, and the world will not be bereft of Arahats. It was in reference to this, O king, that the Master spake when he said: "But if, Subhadda, in this system the brethren continue in perfectness of life, then will the world not be bereft of Arahats."'

60. 'Again, O king, suppose people were to continually polish with fine soft red powder a stainless mirror that was already bright and shining, well polished, smooth, and glossy, would dirt and dust and mud arise on its surface?'

'No indeed, Sir. Rather would it become to a certainty even more stainless than before.'

'Just so, O king, is the glorious doctrine of the Conqueror stainless by nature, and altogether free from the dust and dirt of evil. And if the children of the Buddha cleanse it by the virtue arising from the shaking off, the eradication of evil, from the practice of duty and virtue and morality and purity of life, then will this glorious doctrine endure for long, and the world will not be bereft of Arahats. It was in reference to this that the Blessed One spake when he said: "But if, Subhadda, in this system the brethren continue in righteousness of life, then will not the world be bereft of Arahats." For the teaching of the Master, O king, has its root in conduct, has conduct as its essence, and stands fast so long as conduct does not decline [1].'

---

[1] There is a paragraph here in the Siṃhalese not found in the Pāli.

61. 'Venerable Nâgasena, when you speak of the disappearance of the good law, what do you mean by its disappearance?'

'There are three modes of the disappearance, O king, of a system of doctrine. And what are the three? The decline of attainment to an intellectual grasp of it, the decline of conduct in accordance with it, and the decline of its outward form [1]. [134] When the attainment of it ceases, then even the man who conducts himself aright in it has no clear understanding of it. By the decline of conduct the promulgation of the rules of discipline ceases, only the outward form of the religion remains. When the outward form has ceased, the succession of the tradition is cut off. These are the three forms of the disappearance of a system of doctrine.'

'You have well explained, venerable Nâgasena, this dilemma so profound, and have made it plain. You have loosed the knot; you have destroyed the arguments of the adversary, broken them in pieces, proved them wrong—you, O best of the leaders of schools!'

[Here ends the dilemma as to the duration of the faith.]

[THE BUDDHA'S SINLESSNESS.]

62. 'Venerable Nâgasena, had the Blessed One, when he became a Buddha, burnt out all evil in himself, or was there still some evil remaining in him?'

---

[1] Liṅga, possibly 'uniform.' Either the Order or the yellow robe, for instance, if the system were Buddhism. See below, IV, 3, 2.

'He had burnt out all evil. There was none left.'

'But how, Sir? Did not the Tathâgata get hurt in his body?'

'Yes, O king. At Râgagaha a splinter of rock pierced his foot [1], and once he suffered from dysentery [2], and once when the humours of his body were disturbed a purge was administered to him [3], and once when he was troubled with wind the Elder who waited on him (that is Ânanda) gave him hot water [4].'

'Then, Sir, if the Tathâgata, on his becoming a Buddha, has destroyed all evil in himself—this other statement that his foot was pierced by a splinter, that he had dysentery, and so on, must be false. But if they are true, then he cannot have been free from evil, for there is no pain without Karma. All pain has its root in Karma, it is on account of Karma that suffering arises [5]. This double-headed dilemma is put to you, and you have to solve it.'

63. 'No, O king. It is not all suffering that has its root in Karma. There are eight causes by which sufferings arise, by which many beings suffer pain. And what are the eight? Superabundance of wind, [135] and of bile, and of phlegm, the union of these humours, variations in temperature, the avoiding of

---

[1] See Kullavagga VII, 3, 9.
[2] See Mahâparinibbâna Sutta IV, 21.
[3] Mahâvagga VIII, 1, 30–33.
[4] This is, no doubt, the occurrence recounted in the Mahâvagga VI, 17, 1–4. Childers translates vâtâbâdha by 'rheumatism,' but I adhere here to the translation adopted there. It is said in the Mahâvagga that Ânanda gave him, not hot water, but gruel. But the two are very similar, and in the Theri Gâthâ 185, referring to the same event, it is hot water that is mentioned.
[5] That is, there can be no suffering without sin. Compare the discussion in St. John's Gospel, ch. ix.

dissimilarities, external agency, and Karma. From each of these there are some sufferings that arise, and these are the eight causes by which many beings suffer pain. And therein whosoever maintains that it is Karma that injures beings, and besides it there is no other reason for pain, his proposition is false.'

'But, Sir, all the other seven kinds of pain have each of them also Karma as its origin, for they are all produced by Karma.'

'If, O king, all diseases were really derived from Karma then there would be no characteristic marks by which they could be distinguished one from the other. When the wind is disturbed, it is so in one or other of ten ways—by cold, or by heat, or by hunger, or by thirst, or by over eating, or by standing too long, or by over exertion, or by walking too fast, or by medical treatment, or as the result of Karma. Of these ten, nine do not act in a past life or in a future life, but in one's present existence. Therefore it is not right to say that all pain is due to Karma. When the bile, O king, is deranged it is so in one or other of three ways—by cold, or by heat, or by improper food. When the phlegm is disturbed it is so by cold, or by heat, or by food and drink. When either of these three humours are disturbed or mixed, it brings about its own special, distinctive pain. Then there are the special pains arising from variations in temperature, avoidance of dissimilarities, and external agency[1]. And there is the act that has Karma as its fruit, and the pain so brought about arising from the act done. So what

---

[1] As was pointed out above, IV, 1, 33, many of these medical terms are very doubtful.

arises as the fruit of Karma is much less than that which arises from other causes. And the ignorant go too far [136] when they say that every pain is produced as the fruit of Karma. No one without a Buddha's insight can fix the extent of the action of Karma.'

64. 'Now when the Blessed One's foot was torn by a splinter of rock, the pain that followed was not produced by any other of the eight causes I have mentioned, but only by external agency. For Devadatta, O king, had harboured hatred against the Tathâgata during a succession of hundreds of thousands of births[1]. It was in his hatred that he seized hold of a mighty mass of rock, and pushed it over with the hope that it would fall upon his head. But two other rocks came together, and intercepted it before it had reached the Tathâgata; and by the force of their impact a splinter was torn off, and fell upon the Blessed One's foot, and made it bleed. Now this pain must have been produced in the Blessed One either as the result of his own Karma, or of some one else's act. For beyond these two there can be no other kind of pain. It is as when a seed does not germinate—that must be due either to the badness of the soil, or to a defect in the seed. Or it is as when food is not digested—that must be due either to a defect in the stomach, or to the badness of the food.'

65. 'But although the Blessed One never suffered pain which was the result of his own Karma, or brought about the avoidance of dissimilarity[2], yet

---

[1] So below, IV, 3, 28.
[2] Visama-parihâra-gâ both in the Siṃhalese and the Pâli.

he suffered pain from each of the other six causes. And by the pain he could suffer it was not possible to deprive him of life. There come to this body of ours, O king, compounded of the four elements[1], sensations desirable and the reverse, pleasant and unpleasant. Suppose, O king, a clod of earth were to be thrown into the air, and to fall again on to the ground. Would it be in consequence of any act it had previously done that it would so fall?'

'No, Sir. There is no reason in the broad earth by which it could experience the result of an act either good or evil. It would be by reason of a present cause [137] independent of Karma that the clod would fall to earth again.'

'Well, O king, the Tathâgata should be regarded as the broad earth. And as the clod would fall on it irrespective of any act done by it, so also was it irrespective of any act done by him that that splinter of rock fell upon his foot.'

66. 'Again, O king, men tear up and plough the earth. But is that a result of any act previously done?'

'Certainly not, Sir.'

'Just so with the falling of that splinter. And the dysentery which attacked him was in the same way the result of no previous act, it arose from the union of the three humours. And whatsoever bodily disease fell upon him, that had its origin, not in Karma, but in one or other of the six causes referred to. For it has been said, O king, by the Blessed One, by him who is above all gods, in the glorious collection called the Saṃyutta Nikâya in

---

[1] Water, fire, air, and earth (âpo, tego, vayo, paṭhavî).

the prose Sutta, called after Moliya Sîvaka: "There are certain pains which arise in the world, Sîvaka, from bilious humour. And you ought to know for a certainty which those are, for it is a matter of common knowledge in the world which they are. But those Samaṇas and Brahmans, Sîvaka, who are of the opinion and proclaim the view that whatsoever pleasure, or pain, or indifferent sensation, any man experiences, is always due to a previous act—they go beyond certainty, they go beyond knowledge, and therein do I say they are wrong. And so also of those pains which arise from the phlegmatic humour, or from the windy humour, or from the union of the three, or from variation in temperature, or from avoidance of dissimilarity, [**138**] or from external action, or as the result of Karma. In each case you should know for a certainty which those are, for it is a matter of common knowledge which they are. But those Samaṇas or Brahmans who are of the opinion or the view that whatsoever pleasure, or pain, or indifferent sensation, any man may experience, that is always due to a previous act—they go beyond certainty, they go beyond common knowledge. And therein do I say they are wrong." So, O king, it is not all pain that is the result of Karma. And you should accept as a fact that when the Blessed One became a Buddha he had burnt out all evil from within him.'

'Very good, Nâgasena! It is so; and I accept it as you say.'

[Here ends the dilemma as to the Buddha's sinlessness]

[ON THE ADVANTAGES OF MEDITATION[1].]

67. 'Venerable Nâgasena, your people say that everything which a Tathâgata has to accomplish that had the Blessed One already carried out when he sat at the foot of the Tree of Wisdom[2]. There was then nothing that he had yet to do, nothing that he had to add to what he had already done. But then there is also talk of his having immediately afterwards remained plunged for three months in ecstatic contemplation[3]. If the first statement be correct, then the second must be false. And if the second be right, then the first must be wrong. There is no need of any contemplation to him who has already accomplished his task. It is the man who still has something left to do, who has to think about it. [139] It is the sick man who has need of medicine, not the healthy; the hungry man who has need of food, not the man whose hunger is quenched. This too is a double-headed dilemma, and you have to solve it!'

68. 'Both statements, O king, are true. Con-

---

[1] Pa/isallâ*n*a (not samâdhi), rendered throughout in the Si*m*halese by wiweka.

[2] I have not been able to find this statement in any of the Pi/aka texts.

[3] Here again our author seems to be referring to a tradition later than the Pi/akas. In the Mahâvagga (see our version in the 'Vinaya Texts,' vol. i, pp. 74–81) there is mention only of four periods of seven days, and even during these not of pa/isallâ*n*a, but of samâdhi. The former of these two terms only occurs at the conclusion of the twenty-eight days (Mahâvagga I, 5, 2). Even in the later orthodox literature the period of meditation is still not three months, but only seven times seven days. See the passages quoted in Professor Oldenberg's note at p. 75 of the 'Vinaya Texts,' vol. i.

templation has many virtues. All the Tathâgatas attained, in contemplation, to Buddhahood, and practised it in the recollection of its good qualities. And they did so in the same way as a man who had received high office from a king would, in the recollection of its advantages, of the prosperity he enjoyed by means of it, remain constantly in attendance on that king—in the same way as a man who, having been afflicted and pained with a dire disease, and having recovered his health by the use of medicine, would use the same medicine again and again, calling to mind its virtue.'

69. 'And there are, O king, these twenty and eight good qualities of meditation in the perception of which the Tathâgatas devoted themselves to it. And which are they? Meditation preserves him who meditates, it gives him long life, and endows him with power, it cleanses him from faults, it removes from him any bad reputation giving him a good name, it destroys discontent in him filling him with content, it releases him from all fear endowing him with confidence, it removes sloth far from him filling him with zeal, it takes away lust and ill-will and dullness, it puts an end to pride, it breaks down all doubt, it makes his heart to be at peace, it softens his mind, [140] it makes him glad, it makes him grave, it gains him much advantage, it makes him worthy of reverence, it fills him with joy, it fills him with delight, it shows him the transitory nature of all compounded things, it puts an end to rebirth, it obtains for him all the benefits of renunciation. These, O king, are the twenty and eight virtues of meditation on the perception of which the Tathâgatas devote themselves to it. But it is because

the Tathâgatas, O king, long for the enjoyment of the bliss of attainment, of the joy of the tranquil state of Nirvâna, that they devote themselves to meditation, with their minds fixed on the end they aim at.

70. 'And there are four reasons for which the Tathâgatas, O king, devote themselves to meditation. And what are the four? That they may dwell at ease, O king—and on account of the abundance of the advantages of meditation, advantages without drawback—and on account of its being the road to all noble things without exception—and because it has been praised and lauded and exalted and magnified by all the Buddhas. These are the reasons for which the Tathâgatas devote themselves to it. So it is not, great king, because they have anything left to do, or anything to add to what they have already accomplished, but because they have perceived how diversified are the advantages it possesses, that they devote themselves to meditation.'

'Very good, Nâgasena! That is so, and I accept it as you say.'

[Here ends the dilemma as to meditation.]

[THE LIMIT OF THREE MONTHS.]

71. 'Venerable Nâgasena, it has been said by the Blessed One: "The Tathâgata, Ânanda, has thought out and thoroughly practised, developed, accumulated, and ascended to the very height of the four paths to saintship [1], and so mastered them as to be able to use them as a means of mental advancement, and as a basis for edification—and he therefore, Ânanda,

---

[1] Kattâro iddhi-pâdâ.

should he desire it, might remain alive for a Kalpa, or for that portion of a Kalpa which has yet to run[1]." And again he said: "At the end of three months from this time the Tathâgata will die[2]." If the first of these statements were true, then the limit of three months must have been false. If the second were true, [141] then the first must have been false. For the Tathâgatas boast not without an occasion, the Blessed Buddhas speak no misleading words, but they utter truth, and speak sincerely. This too is a double-headed dilemma, profound, subtle, hard to expound. It is now put to you. Tear in sunder this net of heresy, put it on one side, break in pieces the arguments of the adversary!'

72. 'Both these statements, O king, were made by the Blessed One. But Kalpa in that connection means the duration of a man's life. And the Blessed One, O king, was not exalting his own power when he said so, but he was exalting the power of saintship. It was as if a king were possessed of a horse most swift of foot, who could run like the wind. And in order to exalt the power of his speed the king were to say in the presence of all his court—townsfolk and country folk, hired servants and men of war, brahmins, nobles, and officers: "If he wished it this noble steed of mine could cross the earth to its ocean boundary, and be back here again, in a moment[3]!"

---

[1] Mahâparinibbâna Sutta III, 60, translated in my 'Buddhist Suttas,' pp. 57, 58.
[2] Ibid. III, 63, translated loc. cit. p. 59.
[3] So it is said of the 'Horse-treasure' of the Great King of Glory in the Mahâsudassana Sutta I, 29 (translated in my 'Buddhist Suttas,' p. 256), that 'it passed over along the broad earth to its very ocean boundary, and then returned again, in time for the

Now though he did not try to test the horse's speed in the presence of the court, yet it had that speed, and was really able to go along over the earth to its ocean boundary in a moment. Just so, O king, the Blessed One spake as he did in praise of the power of saintship, and so spake seated in the midst of gods and men, and of the men of the threefold wisdom and the sixfold insight—the Arahats pure and free from stain—when he said: "The Tathâgata, Ânanda, has thought out and practised, developed, accumulated, and ascended to the very height of the four powers of saintship, and so mastered them as to be able to use them as a means of mental advancement, as a basis for edification. And he therefore, Ânanda, should he desire it, might remain alive for a Kalpa, or the part of a Kalpa that has yet to run." And there was that power, O king, in the Tathâgata, he could have remained alive for that time: and yet he did not show that power in the midst [142] of that assembly. The Blessed One, O king, is free from desire as respects all conditions of future life, and has condemned them all. For it has been said, O king, by the Blessed One: "Just, O Bhikkhus, as a very small quantity of excrement is of evil smell, so do I find no beauty in the very smallest degree of future life, not even in such for the time of the snapping of the fingers [1]." Now would the Blessed One, O king, who thus looked upon all sorts and conditions of future life

---

morning meal, to the royal city of Kusâvatî.' It is, of course, the sun horse which is meant.

[1] I have not traced this quotation in the Pi/akas, but it is probably there.

as dung have nevertheless, simply because of his power of Iddhi, harboured a craving desire for future life?'

'Certainly not, Sir.'

'Then it must have been to exalt the power of Iddhi that he gave utterance to such a boast.'

'Very good, Nâgasena! It is so, and I accept it as you say.'

[Here ends the dilemma as to the three months.]

Here ends the First Chapter.

Book IV. Chapter 2.

[THE ABOLITION OF REGULATIONS.]

1. 'Venerable Nâgasena, it has been said by the Blessed One: "It is by insight, O Bhikkhus, that I preach the law, not without insight[1]." On the other hand he said of the regulations of the Vinaya: "When I am gone, Ânanda, let the Order, if it should so wish, abolish all the lesser and minor precepts[2]." Were then these lesser and minor precepts wrongly laid down, or established in ignorance and without due cause, that the Blessed One allowed them to be revoked after his death? If the first statement had been true, the second would have been wrong. If the second statement were really made, [143] then the first was false. This too is a double-headed problem, fine, subtle, abstruse, deep, profound, and hard to expound. It is now put to you, and you have to solve it.'

2. 'In both cases, O king, the Blessed One said as you have declared. But in the second case it was to test the Bhikkhus that he said it, to try whether, if leave were granted them, they would, after his death, revoke the lesser and minor regulations, or still adhere to them. It runs as if a

---

[1] Not traced as yet.
[2] Mahâparinibbâna Sutta VI, 3 (translated in my 'Buddhist Suttas,' p. 112). The incident is referred to in the Kullavagga XI, 1, 9, 10, and in his commentary on that passage Buddhaghosa mentions the discussion between Milinda and Nâgasena, and quotes it as an authority in support of his interpretation.

king of kings were to say to his sons: " This great country, my children, reaches to the sea on every side. It is a hard thing to maintain it with the forces we have at our disposal. So when I am gone you had better, my children, abandon the outlying districts along the border." Now would the princes, O king, on the death of their father, give up those outlying districts, provinces already in their power?'

'No indeed, Sir. Kings are grasping. The princes might, in the lust of power, subjugate an extent of country twice or thrice the size of what they had, but they would never give up what they already possessed.'

'Just so was it, O king, that the Tathâgata to test the Bhikkhus said : " When I am gone, Ânanda, let the Order, if it should so wish, abolish all the lesser and minor precepts." But the sons of the Buddha, O king, in their lust after the law, and for emancipation from sorrow, might keep two hundred and fifty regulations[1], but would never give up any one that had been laid down in ordinary course.'

3. 'Venerable Nâgasena, when the Blessed One referred to " lesser and minor precepts," this people might therein [144] be bewildered, and fall into doubt, and find matter for discussion, and be lost in hesitation, as to which were the lesser, and which the minor precepts.'

'The lesser errors in conduct[2], O king, are the lesser precepts, and the lesser errors in speech[3] are the minor precepts : and these two together make up therefore " the lesser and minor precepts." The

---

[1] The regulations in the Pâtimokkha, which include all the most important ones, are only 220 in number.
[2] Dukka*ta*m. [3] Dubbhâsita*m*.

leading Elders too of old, O king, were in doubt about this matter, and they were not unanimous on the point at the Council held for the fixing of the text of the Scriptures [1]. And the Blessed One foresaw that this problem would arise.'

'Then this dark saying of the Conquerors, Nâgasena, which has lain hid so long, has been now to-day uncovered in the face of the world, and made clear to all.'

[Here ends the problem as to the revocation of rules.]

[ESOTERIC TEACHING.]

4. 'Venerable Nâgasena, it was said by the Blessed One: "In respect of the truths, Ânanda, the Tathâgata has no such thing as the closed fist of a teacher who keeps something back [2]." But on the other hand he made no reply to the question put by the son of the Mâlunkya woman [3]. This problem, Nâgasena, will be one of two ends, on one of which it must rest, for he must have refrained from answering either out of ignorance, or out of wish to conceal something. If the first statement be true it must have been out of ignorance. But

---

[1] In the *K*ullavagga XI, 1, 10, it is one of the faults laid to Ânanda's charge, at the Council of Râgagaha, that he had not asked for a definition of these terms.

[2] Mahâparinibbâna Sutta II, 32 (another passage from the same speech is quoted below, IV, 2, 29).

[3] See the two Mâlunkya Suttantas in the Ma*ggh*ima Nikâya (vol. i, pp. 426–437 of Mr. Trenckner's edition for the Pâli Text Society). With regard to the spelling of the name, which is doubtful, it may be noticed that Hîna*t*i-kumburê has Mâlunka throughout.

if he knew, and still did not reply, then the first statement must be false. This too is a double-pointed dilemma. It is now put to you, and you have to solve it.'

5. 'The Blessed One, O king, made that first statement to Ânanda, and he did not reply to Mâluṅkyâ-putta's question. But that was neither out of ignorance, nor for the sake of concealing anything. There are four kinds of ways in which a problem may be explained. And which are the four? There is the problem to which an explanation can be given that shall be direct and final. There is the problem which can be answered by going into details. There is the problem which can be answered by asking another. And there is the problem which can be put on one side.

'And which, O king, is the problem to which a direct and final solution can be given? It is such as this—" Is form impermanent?" [145] " Is sensation impermanent?" " Is idea impermanent?" "Are the Confections impermanent?" " Is consciousness impermanent?"

'And which is the problem which can be answered by going into details? It is such as this—" Is form thus impermanent?" and so on.

'And which is the problem which can be answered by asking another? It is such as this—"What then? Can the eye perceive all things?"

'And which is the problem which can be put on one side? It is such as this—" Is the universe everlasting?" " Is it not everlasting?" " Has it an end?" " Has it no end?" " Is it both endless and unending?" " Is it neither the one nor the other?" " Are the soul and the body the same thing?" "Is the soul distinct from the body?" "Does a Tathâgata exist after death?" "Does he not exist after death?" "Does he both exist and not exist after death?" "Does he neither exist nor not exist after death?"

'Now it was to such a question, one that ought to be put on one side, that the Blessed One gave no reply to Mâlunkyâ-putta. And why ought such a question to be put on one side? Because there is no reason or object for answering it. That is why it should be put aside. For the Blessed Buddhas lift not up their voice without a reason and without an object.'

'Very good, Nâgasena! Thus it is, and I accept it as you say?'

[Here ends the dilemma as to keeping some things back [1].]

[DEATH.]

6. 'Venerable Nâgasena, this too was said by the Blessed One: "All men tremble at punishment, all are afraid of death [2]." But again he said: "The Arahat has passed beyond all fear [3]." How then, Nâgasena? does the Arahat tremble with the fear of punishment? [146] Or are the beings in purgatory, when they are being burnt and boiled and scorched and tormented, afraid of that death which would release them from the burning fiery pit of that awful place of woe [4]? If the Blessed One, Nâgasena,

---

[1] See my note below on IV, 4, 8.   [2] Dhammapada 129.
[3] Not traced in these words, but identical in meaning with Dhammapada 39.
[4] Maha-nirayâ *k*avamânâ, 'when they are on the point of passing away from it.' For in Buddhism the time comes to each

really said that all men tremble at punishment, and all are afraid of death, then the statement that the Arahat has passed beyond fear must be false. But if that last statement is really by him, then the other must be false. This double-headed problem is now put to you, and you have to solve it.'

7. 'It was not with regard to Arahats, O king, that the Blessed One spake when he said: "All men tremble at punishment, all are afraid of death." The Arahat is an exception to that statement, for all cause for fear has been removed from the Arahat [1]. He spoke of those beings in whom evil still existed, who are still infatuated with the delusion of self, who are still lifted up and cast down by pleasures and pains. To the Arahat, O king, rebirth in every state has been cut off, all the four kinds of future existence have been destroyed, every re-incarnation has been put an end to, the rafters [2] of the house of life have broken, and the whole house completely pulled down, the Confections have altogether lost their roots, good and evil have ceased, ignorance has been demolished, consciousness has no longer any seed (from which it could be renewed), all sin has been burnt away [3], and all worldly conditions have been overcome [4]. Therefore is it that the Arahat is not made to tremble by any fear.'

---

being in Niraya (often translated 'hell') when he will pass away from it.

[1] That is from him who attained Nirvâna in this life. Compare 1 John iv. 18.

[2] Phâsû for Phâsukâ. Compare Dhammapada 154, Manu VI, 79-81, and Sumangala, p. 16.

[3] Hînaṭi-kumburê adds 'by the fire of tapas.'

[4] Eight are meant—gain, loss, fame, dishonour, praise, blame, pleasures, pains.

8. 'Suppose, O king, a king had four chief ministers, faithful, famous, trustworthy, placed in high positions of authority. And the king, on some emergency arising, were to issue to them an order touching all the people in his realm, saying: "Let all now pay up a tax, and do you, as my four officers, carry out what is necessary in this emergency." Now tell me, O king, would the tremor which comes from fear of taxation arise in the hearts of those ministers?'

'No, Sir, it would not.'

'But why not?'

'They have been appointed by the king to high office. Taxation does not affect them, they are beyond taxation. It was the rest that the king referred to when he gave the order: [147] "Let all pay tax."'

'Just so, O king, is it with the statement that all men tremble at punishment, all are afraid of death. In that way is it that the Arahat is removed from every fear.'

9. 'But, Nâgasena, the word "all" is inclusive, none are left out when it is used. Give me a further reason to establish the point.'

'Suppose, O king, that in some village the lord of the village were to order the crier, saying: "Go, crier, bring all the villagers quickly together before me." And he in obedience to that order were to stand in the midst of the village and were thrice to call out: "Let all the villagers assemble at once in the presence of the lord!" And they should assemble in haste, and have an announcement made to the lord, saying: "All the villagers, Sire, have assembled. Do now whatsoever you require." Now when the lord, O king, is thus summoning all the heads of houses, he issues his order to all the villagers, but it is not they who assemble in obedience to the order; it is the heads of houses. And the lord is satisfied therewith, knowing that such is the number of his villagers. There are many others who do not come—women and men, slave girls and slaves, hired workmen, servants, peasantry, sick people, oxen, buffaloes, sheep, and goats, and dogs—but all those do not count. It was with reference to the heads of houses that the order was issued in the words: "Let all assemble." Just so, O king, it is not of Arahats that it was said that all are afraid of death. [148] The Arahat is not included in that statement, for the Arahat is one in whom there is no longer any cause that could give rise to fear.'

10. 'There is the non-inclusive expression, O king, whose meaning is non-inclusive, and the non-inclusive expression whose meaning is inclusive; there is the inclusive expression whose meaning is non-inclusive, and the inclusive expression whose meaning is inclusive. And the meaning, in each case, should be accepted accordingly. And there are five ways in which the meaning should be ascertained—by the connection, and by taste, and by the tradition of the teachers, and by the meaning, and by abundance of reasons. And herein "connection" means the meaning as seen in the Sutta itself, "taste" means that it is in accordance with other Suttas, "the tradition of the teachers" means what they hold, "the meaning" means what they think, and "abundance of reasons" means all these four combined [1].'

---

[1] This is much more obscure in Pâli than in English. In the Pâli the names of each of the five methods are ambiguous. 'Connection,' for instance, is in Pâli âhakka-pada, which is only

11. 'Very well, Nâgasena! I accept it as you say. The Arahat is an exception in this phrase, and it is the rest of beings who are full of fear. But those beings in purgatory, of whom I spoke, who are suffering painful, sharp, and severe agonies, who are tormented with burnings all over their bodies and limbs, whose mouths are full of lamentation, and cries for pity, and cries of weeping and wailing and woe, who are overcome with pains too sharp to be borne, who find no refuge nor protection nor help, who are afflicted beyond measure, who in the worst and lowest of conditions are still destined to a certainty to further pain, who are being burnt with hot, sharp, fierce, and cruel flames, who are giving utterance to mighty shouts and groans born of horror and fear, who are embraced by the garlands of flame which intertwine around them from all the six directions, and flash in fiery speed through a hundred leagues on every side—can those poor burning wretches be afraid of death?'

'Yes, they can.'

'But, venerable Nâgasena, is not purgatory a place of certain pain? And, if so, why should the beings in it be afraid of death, which would release them from that certain pain? What! Are they fond of purgatory?'

'No, indeed. They like it not. They long to be released from it. It is the power of death of which they are afraid.'

'Now this, Nâgasena, I cannot believe, that they, who want to be released, should be afraid of rebirth.

---

found elsewhere (see *K*ullava*g*ga VI, 4, 3, and my note there) as the name of a kind of chair. And there is similar ambiguity in the other words.

[149] They must surely, Nâgasena, rejoice at the prospect of the very condition that they long for. Convince me by some further reason [1].'

12. 'Death, great king, is a condition which those who have not seen the truth[2] are afraid of. About it this people is anxious and full of dread. Whosoever is afraid of a black snake, or an elephant or lion or tiger or leopard or bear or hyena or wild buffalo or gayal, or of fire or water, or of thorns or spikes or arrows, it is in each case of death that he is really in dread, and therefore afraid of them. This, O king, is the majesty of the essential nature of death. And all being not free from sin are in dread and quake before its majesty. In this sense it is that even the beings in purgatory, who long to be released from it, are afraid of death.'

13. 'Suppose, O king, a boil were to arise, full of matter, on a man's body, and he, in pain from that disease, and wanting to escape from the danger of it, were to call in a physician and surgeon. And the surgeon, accepting the call, were to make ready some means or other for the removal of his disease—were to have a lancet sharpened, or to have sticks put into the fire to be used as cauterisers, or to have something ground on a grindstone to be mixed in a salt lotion. Now would the patient begin to be in dread of the cutting of the sharp lancet, or of the burning of the pair of caustic sticks, or of the application of the stinging lotion?'

'Yes, he would.'

---

[1] Kâranena, perhaps he means 'by an example.'
[2] Adittha-sakkânam. It may also mean 'who have not perceived the (Four Noble) Truths.'

'But if the sick man, who wants to be free from his ailment, can fall into dread by the fear of pain, just so can the beings in purgatory, though they long to be released from it, fall into dread by the fear of death.'

14. 'And suppose, O king, a man who had committed an offence against the crown, when bound with a chain, and cast into a dungeon, were to long for release. And the ruler, wishing to release him, were to send for him. Now would not that man, who had thus offended, and knew it, be in dread [150] of the interview with the king?'

'Yes, Sir.'

'But if so, then can also the beings in purgatory, though they long to be released from it, yet be afraid of death.'

'Give me another illustration by which I may be able to harmonise [1] (this apparent discrepancy).'

'Suppose, O king, a man bitten by a poisonous snake should be afraid, and by the action of the poison should fall and struggle, and roll this way and that. And then that another man, by the repetition of a powerful charm, should compel that poisonous snake to approach to suck the poison back again [2]. Now when the bitten man saw the poisonous snake coming to him, though for the object of curing him, would he not still be in dread of it?'

'Yes, Sir.'

'Well, it is just so with the beings in purgatory.

---

[1] Okappeyya*m*. See the Old Commentary at Pâ*k*ittiya I, 2, 6.

[2] On this belief the 69th *G*âtaka is founded. See Fausböll, vol. i, pp. 310, 311 (where, as Mr. Trenckner points out, we must read in the verse the same word pa*kkâk*am as we have here).

Death is a thing disliked by all beings. And therefore are they in dread of it though they want to be released from purgatory.'

'Very good, Nâgasena! That is so, and I accept it as you say.'

[Here ends the dilemma as to the fear of death.]

[PIRIT.]

15. 'Venerable Nâgasena, it was said by the Blessed One:

"Not in the sky, not in the ocean's midst,
Not in the most secluded mountain cleft,
Not in the whole wide world is found the spot
Where standing one could 'scape the snare of death[1]."

But on the other hand the Pirit service was promulgated by the Blessed One[2]—that is to say, the Ratana Sutta and the Khanda-parittâ and the Mora-parittâ and the Dhagagga-parittâ [151] and the Â/ânâ/iya-parittâ and the Anguli-mala-parittâ. If, Nâgasena, a man can escape death's snare neither by going to heaven, nor by going into the midst of the sea, nor by going to the summits of lofty palaces,

---

[1] Either Dhammapada 127, which is the same except the last word (there 'an evil deed'), or Dhammapada 128, except the last line (which is there ' where standing death would not overtake one ').

[2] This is a service used for the sick. Its use so far as the Pi/akas are known has been nowhere laid down by the Buddha, or by words placed in his mouth. This is the oldest text in which the use of the service is referred to. But the word Parittâ (Pirit) is used in Kullavagga V, 6, of an asseveration of love for snakes, to be used as what is practically a charm against snake bite, and that is attributed to the Buddha. The particular Suttas and passages here referred to are all in the Pi/akas.

nor to the caves or grottoes or declivities or clefts or holes in the mountains, then is the Pirit ceremony useless. But if by it there is a way of escape from death, then the statement in the verse I quoted is false. This too is a double-headed problem, more knotty than a knot. It is now put to you, and you have to solve it.'

16. 'The Blessed One, O king, said the verse you have quoted, and he sanctioned Pirit[1]. But that is only meant for those who have some portion of their life yet to run, who are of full age, and restrain themselves from the evils of Karma. And there is no ceremony or artificial means[2] for prolonging the life of one whose allotted span of existence has come to an end. Just, O king, as with a dry and dead log of wood, dull[3], and sapless, out of which all life has departed, which has reached the end of its allotted period of life,— you might have thousands of pots of water poured over it, but it would never become fresh again or put forth sprouts or leaves. Just so there is no ceremony or artificial means, no medicine and no Pirit, which can prolong the life of one whose allotted period has come to an end. All the medicines in the world are useless, O king, to such a one, but Pirit is a protection and assistance to those who have a period yet to live, who are full of life, and restrain themselves from the evil of Karma. And it is for that use that Pirit was appointed by the

---

[1] See last note. Hina/i-kumburê renders 'preached Pirit,' which is quite in accordance with the Pi/akas, as the Suttas of which it is composed are placed in his mouth.

[2] Upakkamo. Compare the use of the word at *K*ullavagga VII, 3, 10; Sumangala 69, 71. Utpatti-kramayek says the Si*m*halese.

[3] Ko/âpa. See *G*âtaka III, 495, and the commentary there.

Blessed One. Just, O king, as a husbandman guards the grain when it is ripe and dead and ready for harvesting from the influx of water, but makes it grow by giving it water when it is young, and dark in colour like a cloud, and full of life—just so, O king, should the Pirit ceremony be put aside and neglected in the case of one who has reached his allotted term of life, [152] but for those who have a period yet to run and are full of vigour, for them the medicine of Pirit may be repeated, and they will profit by its use.'

17. 'But, Nâgasena, if he who has a term of life yet to run will live, and he who has none will die, then medicine and Pirit are alike useless.'

'Have you ever seen, O king, a case of a disease being turned back by medicine?'

'Yes, several hundred times.'

'Then, O king, your statement as to the inefficiency of Pirit and medicine must be wrong.'

'I have seen, Nâgasena, doctors administer medicines by way of draughts or outward applications, and by that means the disease has been assuaged.'

'And when, O king, the voice of those who are repeating Pirit is heard, the tongue may be dried up, and the heart beat but faintly, and the throat be hoarse, but by that repetition all diseases are allayed, all calamities depart. Again, have you ever seen, O king, a man who has been bitten by a snake having the poison resorbed under a spell (by the snake who gave the bite[1]) or destroyed (by an antidote) or having a lotion applied above or below the spot[2]?'

---

[1] See above, IV, 2, 14.
[2] All this sentence is doubtful. Dr. Morris has a learned note on the difficult words used (which only occur here) in the 'Journal

'Yes, that is common custom to this day in the world.'

'Then what you said that Pirit and medicine are alike useless is wrong. And when Pirit has been said over a man, a snake, ready to bite, will not bite him, but close his jaws—the club which robbers hold aloft to strike him with will never strike; they will let it drop, and treat him kindly—the enraged elephant rushing at him will suddenly stop—the burning fiery conflagration surging towards him will die out—the malignant poison he has eaten will become harmless, and turn to food—assassins who have come to slay him will become as the slaves who wait upon him—and the trap into which he has trodden will hold him not.

18. 'Again, have you never heard, O king, of that hunter who during seven hundred years failed to throw his net over the peacock who had taken Pirit, but snared him the very day [153] he omitted to do so[1]?'

'Yes, I have heard of it. The fame of it has gone through all the world.'

'Then what you said about Pirit and medicine being alike useless must be wrong. And have you never heard of the Dânava[2] who, to guard his wife,

---

of the Pâli Text Society' for 1884, p. 87. Hînaṭi-kumburê, p. 191, translates as follows: Mahâ ragâneni, wisha winâsa karannâwû mantra padayakin wishaya baswana laddâwû, wisha sanhinduwana laddâwû, ûrddhâdho bhâgayehi awushadha galayen temana laddâwû, nayaku wisin dashṭa karana laddâwû kisiwek topa wisin daknâ ladde d œyi wikâla seka.

[1] This is the Mora-Gâtaka, Nos. 159, 491, or (which is the same thing) the Mora-Parittâ.

[2] An Asura, enemy of the gods, a Titan. Rakshasa says the Simhalese.

put her into a box, and swallowing it, carried her about in his stomach. And how a Vidyâdhara [1] entered his mouth, and played games with his wife. And how the Dânava when he became aware of it, vomited up the box, and opened it, and the moment he did so the Vidyâdhara escaped whither he would [2]?'

'Yes, I have heard that. The fame of it too has gone throughout the world.'

'Well, did not the Vidyâdhara escape capture by the power of Pirit?'

'Yes, that was so.'

'Then there must be power in Pirit. And have you heard of that other Vidyâdhara who got into the harem of the king of Benares, and committed adultery with the chief queen, and was caught, and then became invisible, and got away [3]?'

'Yes, I heard that story.'

'Well, did not he too escape capture by the power of Pirit?'

'Yes, Sir.'

'Then, O king, there must be power in Pirit.'

19. 'Venerable Nâgasena, is Pirit a protection to everybody?'

---

[1] They are a kind of genii, with magical powers, who are attendants on the god *S*iva (and therefore, of course, enemies of the Dânavas). They are not mentioned in the Pi*t*akas.

[2] I don't know where this story comes from. It is not in the Pi*t*akas anywhere. But Hîna*t*i-kumburê gives the fairy tale at full length, and in the course of it calls the Vidyâdharas by name Wâyassa-putra, 'Son of the Wind.' He quotes also a gâthâ which he places, not in the mouth of the Bodisat, but of Buddha himself. I cannot find the tale either in the *G*âtaka book, as far as published by Professor Fausböll, or in the Kathâ Sarit Sâgara, though I have looked all through both.

[3] See last note.

'To some, not to others.'

'Then it is not always of use?'

'Does food keep all people alive?'

'Only some, not others.'

'But why not?'

'Inasmuch as some, eating too much of that same food, die of cholera.'

'So it does not keep all men alive?'

'There are two reasons which make it destroy life—over-indulgence in it, and weakness of digestion. And even life-giving food may be made poisonous by an evil spell.'

'Just so, O king, is Pirit a protection to some and not to others. And there are three reasons [154] for its failure—the obstruction of Karma, and of sin, and of unbelief. That Pirit which is a protection to beings loses its protecting power by acts done by those beings themselves. Just, O king, as a mother lovingly nourishes the son who has entered her womb, and brings him forth with care[1]. And after his birth she keeps him clean from dirt and stains and mucus, and anoints him with the best and most costly perfumes, and when others abuse or strike him she seizes them and, full of excitement, drags them before the lord of the place. But when her son is naughty, or comes in late, she strikes him with rods or clubs on her knee or with her hands. Now, that being so, would she get seized and dragged along, and have to appear before the lord?'

'No, Sir.'

'But why not?'

---

[1] Upakârena, which the Si*m*halese repeats and construes with poseti.

'Because the boy was in fault.'

'Just in the same way, O king, will Pirit which is a protection to beings, yet, by their own fault, turn against them.'

'Very good, Nâgasena! The problem has been solved, the jungle made clear, the darkness made light, the net of heresy unravelled—and by you, O best of the leaders of schools!'

[Here ends the dilemma as to Pirit.]

[MÂRA, THE EVIL ONE.]

20. 'Venerable Nâgasena, your people say thus: "The Tathâgata was in the constant receipt of the things necessary for a recluse—robes, food, lodging, and the requisites for the sick." And again they say: "When the Tathâgata entered the Brahman village called the Five Sâla trees he received nothing, and had to return with his bowl as clean as before." If the first passage is true the second is false, and if the second passage is true [155] the first is false. This too is a double-headed problem, a mighty crux hard to unravel. It is now put to you. It is for you to solve it.'

21. 'Both statements are true, but when he received nothing that day, that was the work of Mâra, the evil one.'

'Then, Nâgasena, how was it that the merit laid up by the Blessed One through countless æons of time came to end that day? How was it that Mâra, who had only just been produced, could overcome the strength and influence of that merit? In that case, Nâgasena, the blame must fall in one of two ways—either demerit must be more powerful than merit, or the power of Mâra be greater than that of the Buddha. The root of the tree must be heavier than the top of it, or the sinner stronger than he who has heaped up virtue.'

22. 'Great king, that is not enough to prove either the one or the other of your alternatives. Still a reason is certainly desirable in this matter. Suppose, O king, a man were to bring a complimentary present to a king of kings—honey or honeycomb or something of that kind. And the king's doorkeeper were to say to him: "This is the wrong time for visiting the king. So, my good fellow, take your present as quickly as ever you can, and go back before the king inflicts a fine upon you." And then that man, in dread and awe, should pick up his present, and return in great haste. Now would the king of kings, merely from the fact that the man brought his gift at the wrong time, be less powerful than the doorkeeper, or never receive a complimentary present any more?'

'No, Sir. The doorkeeper turned back the giver of that present out of the surliness of his nature, and one a hundred thousand times as valuable [156] might be brought in by some other device.'

'Just so, O king, it was out of the jealousy of his nature that Mâra, the evil one, possessed the Brahmans and householders at the Five Sâla trees. And hundreds of thousands of other deities came up to offer the Buddha the strength-giving ambrosia from heaven, and stood reverencing him with clasped hands and thinking to themselves that they would thus imbue him with vigour.'

23. 'That may be so, Nâgasena. The Blessed

One found it easy to get the four requisites of a recluse—he, the best in the world—and at the request of gods and men he enjoyed all the requisites. But still Mâra's intention to stop the supply of food to the Blessed One was so far carried out. Herein, Sir, my doubt is not removed. I am still in perplexity and hesitation about this. My mind is not clear how the Tathâgata, the Arahat, the supreme Buddha, the best of all the best in the world of gods and men, he who had so glorious a treasure of the merit of virtue, the unequalled one, unrivalled and peerless,—how so vile, mean, insignificant, sinful, and ignoble a being as Mâra could put any obstacle in the way of gifts to Him.'

24. 'There are four kinds, O king, of obstacles—the obstacle to a gift not intended for any particular person, to a gift set apart for some one, to the gift got ready, and to the enjoyment of a gift. And the first is when any one puts an obstacle in the way of the actual gift of a thing put ready to be given away, but not with a view to or having seen any particular donee,—an obstacle raised, for instance, by saying: "What is the good of giving it away to any one else?" The second is when any one puts an obstacle in the way of the actual gift of food intended to be prepared to be given to a person specified. The third is when any one puts an obstacle in the way when such a gift has been got ready, but not yet accepted. And the fourth is when any one puts an obstacle in the way of the enjoyment of a gift already given (and so the property of the donee).'

25. 'Now when Mâra, the evil one, possessed the

Brahmans and householders at the Five Sâla trees, the food in that case was neither the property of, nor got ready for, nor intended to be prepared specially for the Blessed One. [157] The obstacle was put in the way of some one who was yet to come, who had not arrived, and for whom no gift was intended. That was not against the Blessed One alone. But all who had gone out that day, and were coming to the village, failed to receive an alms. I know no one, O king, in the world of men and gods, no one among Mâras or Brahmas, no one of the class of Brahmans or recluses, who could put any obstacle in the way of an alms intended for, or got ready for, or already given to the Blessed One. And if any one, out of jealousy, were to raise up any obstacle in that case, then would his head split into a hundred or into a thousand pieces.'

26. 'There are four things, O king, connected with the Tathâgatas, to which no one can do any harm. And what are the four? To the alms intended for, and got ready for the Blessed One—to the halo of a fathom's length when it has once spread out from him—to the treasure of the knowledge of his omniscience—and to his life. All these things, O king, are one in essence—they are free from defect, immovable, unassailable by other beings, unchangeable by other circumstances[1]. And Mâra, the evil one, lay in ambush, out of sight, when he possessed the Brahmans and householders at the Five Sâla trees. It was as when robbers, O king,

---

[1] Aphusâni kiriyâni, which I do not pretend to understand, and Mr. Trenckner says is unintelligible to him. Hîna/i-kumburê has: Anya kriyâwak no wœdagannâ bœwin apusana (sic) kriyâyo ya.

hiding out of sight in the inaccessible country over the border, beset the highways. But if the king caught sight of them, do you think those robbers would be safe?'

'No, Sir, he might have them cut into a hundred or a thousand pieces with an axe.'

'Well, just so it was, hiding out of sight, that Mâra possessed them. It was as when a married woman, in ambush, and out of sight, frequents the company of her paramour. [158] But if, O king, she were to carry on her intrigues in her husband's presence, do you think she would be safe?'

'No, Sir, he might slay her, or wound her, or put her in bonds, or reduce her to slavery.'

'Well. It was like that, hiding out of sight, that Mâra possessed them. But if, O king, he had raised any obstacle in the case of an alms intended for, got ready for, or in possession of the Blessed One, then his head would have split into a hundred or a thousand pieces.'

'That is so, Nâgasena. Mâra, the evil one, acted after the manner of robbers, he lay in ambush, possessing the Brahmans and householders of the Five Sâla trees. But if the same Mâra, the evil one, had interfered with any alms intended for, or made ready for the Blessed One, or with his partaking thereof, then would his head have been split into a hundred or a thousand pieces, or his bodily frame have been dissipated like a handful of chaff.'

'Very good, Nâgasena! That is so, and I accept it as you say.'

[Here ends the dilemma as to Mâra's interference with alms.]

[UNCONSCIOUS CRIME.]

27. 'Venerable Nâgasena, your people say: "Whosoever deprives a living being of life, without knowing that he does so, he accumulates very serious demerit[1]." But on the other hand it was laid down by the Blessed One in the Vinaya: "There is no offence to him who acts in ignorance[2]." If the first passage is correct, the other must be false; and if the second is right, the first must be wrong. This too is a double-pointed problem, hard to master, hard to overcome. It is now put to you, and you have to solve it.'

28. 'Both the passages you quote, O king, were spoken by the Blessed One. But there is a difference between the sense of the two. And what is that difference? [159] There is a kind of offence which is committed without the co-operation of the mind[3], and there is another kind which has that co-operation. It was with respect to the first of the

---

[1] Not traced as yet, in so many words. And though there are several injunctions in the Vinaya against acts which might haply, though unknown to the doer, destroy life (such, for instance, as drinking water without the use of a strainer), when these are all subjects of special rule, and in each case there is an exception in favour of the Bhikkhu who acts in ignorance of there being living things which could be killed. (See, for instance, Pâkittiya 62, on the drinking of water.)

[2] Agânantassa nâpatti. Pâkittiya LXI, 2, 3 (in the Old Commentary, not ascribed to the Buddha).

[3] Saññâ-vimokkhâ. I am not sure of the exact meaning of this difficult compound, which has only been found in this passage. Hînati-kumburê (p. 199) has: Mahâ ragâneni, kittângayen abhâwayen midena bœwin saññâ-wimoksha-namwû âpattit atteya, &c. (mid = muk).

two that the Blessed One said: "There is no offence to him who acts in ignorance[1]."'

'Very good, Nâgasena! That is so, and I accept it as you say.'

[Here ends the dilemma as to sins in ignorance.]

[THE BUDDHA AND HIS FOLLOWERS.]

29. 'Venerable Nâgasena, it was said by the Blessed One: "Now the Tathâgata thinks not, Ânanda, that is he who should lead the brotherhood, or that the Order is dependent upon him[2]." But on the other hand when describing the virtues and the nature of Metteyya, the Blessed One, he said thus: "He will be the leader of a brotherhood several thousands in number, as I am now the leader of a brotherhood several hundreds in number[3]." If the first statement be right, then the second is wrong. If the second passage is right, the first must be false. This too is a double-pointed problem now put to you, and you have to solve it.'

30. 'You quote both passages correctly, O king. But in the dilemma that you put the sense in the one passage is inclusive, in the other it is not. It is not the Tathâgata, O king, who seeks after a following, but the followers who seek after him.

---

[1] The Simhalese has here a further page, giving examples of the two kinds of offences referred to, and drawing the conclusion for each.

[2] Book of the Great Decease, II, 32 (translated in my 'Buddhist Suttas,' p. 37), just after the passage quoted above, IV, 2, 4.

[3] Not in any of the published texts. Metteyya is, of course, the Buddha to come, the expected messiah.

[160] It is a mere commonly received opinion, O king, that "This is I," or "This is mine," it is not a transcendental truth[1]. Attachment is a frame of mind put away by the Tathâgata, he has put away clinging, he is free from the delusion that "This is mine," he lives only to be a help to others[2]. Just as the earth, O king, is a support to the beings in the world, and an asylum to them, and they depend upon it, but the broad earth has no longing after them in the idea that "These belong to me"—just so is the Tathâgata a support and an asylum to all beings, but has no longing after them in the idea that "These belong to me." And just as a mighty rain cloud, O king, pours out its rain, and gives nourishment to grass and trees, to cattle and to men, and maintains the lineage thereof, and all these creatures depend for their livelihood upon its rain, but the cloud has no feelings of longing in the idea that "These are mine"—just so does the Tathâgata give all beings to know what are good qualities and maintains them in goodness, and all beings have their life in him, but the Tathâgata has no feelings of longing in the idea that "These are mine." And why is it so? Because of his having abandoned all self-regard[3].'

'Very good, Nâgasena! The problem has been well solved by variety of examples. The jungle has been made open, the darkness has been turned

---

[1] Sammuti .... na paramattho.
[2] Upâdâya avassayo hoti.
[3] Attânudi*tth*iyâ pahînattâ. See the passages quoted by Dr. Morris in the 'Journal of the Pâli Text Society,' 1886, pp. 113, 114.

to light, the arguments of the adversaries have been broken down, insight has been awakened in the sons of the Conqueror.'

[Here ends the dilemma as to the Buddha and his following.]

[SCHISM.]

31. 'Venerable Nâgasena, your people say: "The Tathâgata is a person whose following can never be broken up." And again they say: "At one stroke Devadatta seduced five hundred of the brethren[1]." If the first be true the second is false, but if the second be correct then the first is wrong. [161] This too is a double-pointed problem, profound, hard to unravel, more knotty than a knot. By it these people are veiled, obstructed, hindered, shut in, and enveloped. Herein show your skill as against the arguments of the adversaries.'

32. 'Both statements, O king, are correct. But the latter is owing to the power of the breach maker. Where there is one to make the breach, a mother will be separated from her son, and the son will break with the mother, or the father with the son and the son with the father, or the brother from the sister and the sister from the brother, or friend from friend. A ship pieced together with timber of all sorts is broken up by the force of the violence of the waves, and a tree in full bearing and full of sap is broken down by the force of the violence of the wind, and gold of the finest sort is divided by

---

[1] Neither of these phrases is to be found in the published texts in these words. But the latter sums up the episode related in the *K*ullavagga VII, 4, 1.

bronze. But it is not the intention of the wise, it is not the will of the Buddhas, it is not the desire of those who are learned that the following of the Tathâgata should be broken up. And there is a special sense in which it is said that that cannot be. It is an unheard-of thing, so far as I know, that his following could be broken up by anything done or taken, any unkindly word, any wrong action, any injustice, in all the conduct, wheresoever or whatsoever, of the Tathâgata himself. In that sense his following is invulnerable. And you yourself, do you know of any instance in all the ninefold word of the Buddha of anything done by a Bodisat which broke up the following of the Tathâgata?'

'No, Sir. Such a thing has never been seen or heard in the world. It is very good, Nâgasena, what you say: and I accept it so.'

[Here ends the dilemma as to schism.]

Here ends the Second Chapter.

Book IV. Chapter 3.

[PRECEDENCE OF THE DHARMA.]

1. 'Venerable Nâgasena, it was said by the Blessed One: " For it is the Dhamma, O Vâsettha, which is 'the best in the world[1],' as regards both what we now see, and what is yet to come[2]." But again (according to your people) the devout layman who has entered the Excellent Way, for whom the possibility of rebirth in any place of woe has passed away, who has attained to insight, and to whom the doctrine is known, even such a one ought to salute and to rise from his seat in token of respect for, and to revere, any member of the Order, though a novice, and though he be unconverted[3]. Now if the Dhamma be the best that rule of conduct is wrong, but if that be right then the first statement must be wrong.

---

[1] This is a quotation from a celebrated verse, which is, as it were, the national anthem of those who, in the struggle for religious and ceremonial supremacy between the Brahmans and the nobles, took the side of the nobles (the Khattiyas). As might be expected it is not seldom found in the Buddhist Suttas, and is often put in the mouth of the Buddha, the most distinguished of these Khattiyas who were transcendental rather than military. It runs: 'The Khattiya is the best in the world of those who observe the rules of exogamous marriage, but of the whole race of men and gods he who has wisdom and righteousness is the best.' See, for instance, the Amba*ttha* Sutta, in the Dîgha Nikâya, and the Sumaṅgala Vilâsinî on that passage. By 'best in the world' is meant 'entitled to take precedence before all others,' not best in the moral sense.

[2] From the Aggañña Sutta in the Digha Nikâya.

[3] I cannot give any authority for this, but it is no doubt correct Buddhism according to the spirit of the Pi*t*akas.

This too is a double-pointed problem. It is now put to you, and you have to solve it.' [162]

2. 'The Blessed One said what you have quoted, and you have rightly described the rule of conduct. But there is a reason for that rule, and that is this. There are these twenty personal qualities, making up the Samaṇaship of a Samaṇa, and these two outward signs[1], by reason of which the Samaṇa is worthy of salutation, and of respect, and of reverence. And what are they? The best form of self-restraint, the highest kind of self-control[2], right conduct, calm manners[3], mastery over (his deeds and words[4]), subjugation (of his senses[5]), long-suffering[6], sympathy[7],

---

[1] Liṅgâni. See above, IV, 1, 61.

[2] Aggo niyamo. Hînaṭi-kumburê takes agga in the sense of Arahatship: 'Niwan dena pratipattiyen yukta bawa.' Niyama is a self-imposed vow.

[3] Vihâra, which the Siṃhalese glosses by: 'Sansun iriyâpatha wiharaṇayen yukta bawa,' ('because he continues in the practice of tranquil deportment.')

[4] Saṃyama. 'Kâya wâk saṃyamayen yukta bawa.'

[5] Saṃvaro. 'Indriya saṃvarayen yukta bawa.'

[6] Khanti, which the Siṃhalese repeats.

[7] Sorakkaṃ. 'Because he is docile and pleasant of speech,' says the Siṃhalese: 'Suwaka kîkaru bhâwayen yukta bawa.' It is an abstract noun formed from surata, and does not occur in Sanskrit, though Böhtlingk-Roth give one authority for it (under sauratya) from a Buddhist work, the Vyutpatti. It is one of the many instances in which the Buddhist ethics has put new and higher meaning into current phrases, for in Sanskrit literature surata (literally 'high pleasure') is used frequently enough, but almost without exception in an obscene sense. The commentary on Gâtaka III, 442 only repeats the word. It is there, as here, and in the Vyutpatti, and at Aṅguttara II, 15, 3, always allied with khanti. My translation follows Childers (who probably follows Böhtlingk-Roth); but the Siṃhalese gloss here makes me very doubtful as to the exact connotation which the early Buddhists associated with 'high pleasure.'

the practice of solitude[1], love of solitude[2], meditation[3], modesty and fear of doing wrong[4], zeal[5], earnestness[6], the taking upon himself of the precepts[7], recitation (of the Scriptures)[8], asking questions (of those wise in the Dhamma and Vinaya), rejoicing in the Sîlas and other (rules of morality), freedom from attachment (to the things of the world), fulfilment of the precepts—and the wearing of the yellow robe, and the being shaven. [163] In the practice of all these things does the member of the Order live. By being deficient in none of them, by being perfect in all, accomplished in all, endowed with all of them does he reach forward to the condition of Arahatship, to the condition of those who have nothing left to learn; he is marching towards the highest of all lands[9]. Thus it is because he sees him to be in the company of the Worthy Ones (the Arahats) that the layman who has already entered on the Excellent Way thinks it worthy in him[10] to

---

[1] Ekatta-kariyâ='Ekalâwa hœsirîmen yukta bawa.'

[2] Ekattâbhirati.

[3] Palisallanam, not samâdhi. Kittekâgratâ says the Simhalese.

[4] Hiri-otappam.

[5] Viriyam, 'the zeal of the fourfold effort (pradhâna) towards the making of Arahatship,' is the Simhalese gloss.

[6] Appamâdo, 'in the search for Arahatship,' says Hînatikumburê.

[7] Sikkhâ-samâdanam. 'Learning them, investigating their meaning, love of the virtuous law laid down in them,' expands Hînati-kumburê.

[8] Uddero. There is a lacuna here in the Simhalese. It has nothing more till we come to the shaven head.

[9] Amrita mahâ avakâsa bhûmiyata says the Simhalese (p. 205).

[10] Arahati. I have endeavoured to imitate the play upon the words.

reverence and to show respect to the Bhikkhu, though be may be, as yet, unconverted. It is because he sees him to be in the company of those in whom all evil has been destroyed, because he feels that he is not in such society[1], that the converted layman thinks it worthy of him to do reverence and to show respect to the unconverted Bhikkhu. It is because he knows that he has joined the noblest brotherhood, and that he himself has reached no such state, that the converted layman holds it right to do reverence and to show respect to the unconverted Bhikkhu—because he knows that he listens to the recitation of the Pâtimokkha, while he himself can not—because he knows that he receives men into the Order, and thus extends the teaching of the Conqueror, which he himself is incapable of doing—because he knows that he carries out innumerable precepts, which he himself cannot observe—because he knows that he wears the outward signs of Samaṇaship, and carries out the intention of the Buddha, while he himself is gone away far from that—because he knows that he, though he has given up his hair and beard, and is unanointed and wears no ornaments, yet is anointed with the perfume of righteousness, while he is himself addicted to jewelry and fine apparel—that the converted layman thinks it right to do reverence, and to show respect to the unconverted Bhikkhu.'

3. 'And moreover, O king, it is because he knows that not only are all these twenty personal qualities which go to make a Samaṇa, and the two outward signs, found in the Bhikkhu, but that he carries them

---

[1] N'atthi me so samayo ti: E sâmâgrî lâbhaya maṭa nœtœyi sitâ.

on, and trains others in them, that the converted layman, realising that he has no part in that tradition [1], in that maintenance of the faith, thinks it right to reverence and to show respect to the converted Bhikkhu. [164] Just, O king, as a royal prince who learns his knowledge, and is taught the duties of a Khattiya, at the feet of the Brahman who acts as family chaplain [2], when after a time he is anointed king, pays reverence and respect to his master in the thought of his being the teacher, and the carrier on of the traditions of the family, so is it right for the converted Bhikkhu to do reverence and to pay respect to the unconverted Bhikkhu.'

4. 'And moreover, O king, you may know by this fact the greatness and the peerless glory of the condition of the Bhikkhus—that if a layman, a disciple of the faith, who has entered upon the Excellent Way, should attain to the realisation of Arahatship, one of two results must happen to him, and there is no other—he must either die away on that very day, or take upon himself the condition of a Bhikkhu. For immovable, O king, is that state of renunciation, glorious, and most exalted—I mean the condition of being a member of the Order!'

'Venerable Nâgasena, this subtle problem has been thoroughly unravelled by your powerful and great wisdom. No one else could solve it so unless he were wise as you.'

[Here ends the problem as to the precedence of the Dharma.]

---

[1] Âgamo, which the Si*m*halese repeats.
[2] Purohita, which the Si*m*halese repeats.

[THE HARM OF PREACHING.]

5. 'Venerable Nâgasena, you Bhikkhus say that the Tathâgata averts harm from all beings, and does them good[1]. And again you say that when he was preaching the discourse based on the simile of the burning fire[2] hot blood was ejected from the mouths of about sixty Bhikkhus. By his delivery of that discourse he did those Bhikkhus harm and not good. So if the first statement is correct, the second is false; and if the second is correct, the first [165] is false. This too is a double-pointed problem put to you, which you have to solve.'

6. 'Both are true. What happened to them was not the Tathâgata's doing, but their own.'

'But, Nâgasena, if the Tathâgata had not delivered that discourse, then would they have vomited up hot blood?'

'No. When they took wrongly what he said, then was there a burning kindled within them, and hot blood was ejected from their mouths.'

'Then that must have happened, Nâgasena, through the act of the Tathâgata, it must have been the Tathâgata who was the chief cause[3] to destroy them. Suppose a serpent, Nâgasena, had crept into an anthill, and a man in want of earth were to break into the anthill, and take the earth of it away. And by his doing so the entrance-hole to the anthill

---

[1] I cannot give chapter and verse for the words, but the sentiment is common enough.

[2] This is not the Âditta-pariyâya given in the Mahâvagga I, 21, and the Aggikkhandûpama Sutta in the 7th Book of the Aṅguttara.

[3] Adhikâra. Pradhâna is the Siṃhalese translation.

were closed up, and the snake were to die in consequence from want of air. Would not the serpent have been killed by that man's action?'

'Yes, O king.'

'Just so, Nâgasena, was the Tathâgata the prime cause of their destruction.'

7. 'When the Tathâgata delivered a discourse, O king, he never did so either in flattery or in malice. In freedom both from the one and from the other did he speak. And they who received it aright were made wise[1], but they who received it wrongly, fell. Just, O king, as when a man shakes a mango tree or a jambu tree or a mee tree[2], such of the fruits on it as are full of sap and strongly fastened to it remain undisturbed, but such as have rotten stalks, and are loosely attached, fall to the ground—[166] so was it with his preaching. It was, O king, as when a husbandman, wanting to grow a crop of wheat, ploughs the field, but by that ploughing many hundreds and thousands of blades of grass are killed—or it was as when men, for the sake of sweetness, crush sugarcane in a mill, and by their doing so such small creatures as pass into the mouth of the mill are crushed also—so was it that the Tathâgata making wise those whose minds were prepared, preached the Dhamma without flattery and without malice. And they who received it aright were made wise, but they who received it wrongly, fell.'

8. 'Then did not those Bhikkhus fall, Nâgasena, just because of that discourse?'

---

[1] Bu*ggh*anti: unto Arahatship adds Hina/i-kumburê.
[2] Madhuka. See *G*âtaka IV, 434. The Si*m*halese (p. 208) has mîgahak (Bassia Latifolia).

'How, then, could a carpenter by doing nothing to a piece of timber, and simply laying it by [1], make it straight and fit for use?'

'No, Sir. He would have to get rid of the bends out of it, if he wanted it straight and ready for use.'

'Just so, O king, the Tathâgata could not, by merely watching over his disciples, have opened the eyes of those who were ready to see. But by getting rid of those who took the word wrongly he saved those prepared to be saved. And it was by their own act and deed, O king, that the evil-minded fell; just as a plantain tree, or a bambû, or a she-mule are destroyed by that to which they themselves give birth [2]. And just, O king, as it is by their own acts that robbers come to have their eyes plucked out, or to impalement, or to the scaffold, just so were the evil-minded destroyed by their own act, and fell from the teaching of the Conqueror.'

9. 'And so [**167**] with those sixty Bhikkhus, they fell neither by the act of the Tathâgata nor of any one else, but solely by their own deed [3]. Suppose, O king, a man were to give ambrosia [4] to all the people, and they, eating of it, were to become healthy and long-lived and free from every bodily ill. But one man, on eating it, were by his own bad digestion, to

---

[1] Rakkhanto, which Hînaṭi-kumburê expands in the sense adopted above.

[2] Plantains and bambûs die when they flower. And it was popular belief in India that she-mules always died if they foaled. See Kullavagga VI, 4, 3; VII, 2, 5; Vimâna Vatthu 43, 8; Saṃyutta Nikâya VI, 2, 2.

[3] Hînaṭi-kumburê here inserts a translation of the whole of the Sutta referred to.

[4] Amatam, with reference, no doubt, to Arahatship, of which this is also an epithet.

die. Would then, O king, the man who gave away the ambrosia be guilty therein of any offence?'

'No, Sir.'

'Just so, O king, does the Tathâgata present the gift of his ambrosia to the men and gods in the ten thousand world systems; and those beings who are capable of doing so are made wise by the nectar of his law, while they who are not are destroyed and fall. Food, O king, preserves the lives of all beings. But some who eat of it die of cholera[1]. Is the man who feeds the hungry guilty therein of any offence?'

'No, Sir.'

'Just so, O king, does the Tathâgata present the gift of his ambrosia to the men and gods in the ten thousand world systems; and those beings who are capable of doing so are made wise by the nectar of his law, while they who are not are destroyed and fall.'

'Very good, Nâgasena! That is so, and I accept it as you say.'

[Here ends the dilemma on the harm resulting from preaching.]

[THE SECRETS OF A TATHÂGATA.]

11. [This dilemma treats of one of the thirty bodily signs of a 'great man' (Mahâpurusha) supposed to be possessed by every Tathâgata, but as it deals with matters not usually spoken of in this century, it is best read in the original.]

[THE FOOLISH FELLOW.]

15. [170] 'Venerable Nâgasena, it was said by the Elder Sâriputta, the commander of the faith: " The

[1] Visû*k*ikâya, which Hîna*t*i-kumburê renders: A*g*îr*n*a wa wiwekâbâdhayen. So above, IV, 2, 18.

Tathâgata, brethren, is perfect in courtesy of speech. There is no fault of speech in the Tathâgata concerning which he should have to take care that no one else should know it [1]." And on the other hand the Tathâgata, when promulgating the first Pârâgika on the occasion of the offence of Sudinna the Kalanda [2], addressed him with harsh words, calling him a useless fellow [3]. And that Elder, on being so called, terrified with the fear of his teacher [4], and overcome with remorse, was unable to comprehend the Excellent Way [5]. Now if the first statement be correct, the allegation that the Tathâgata called Sudinna the Kalanda a useless fellow must be false. But if that be true, then the first statement must be false. [171] This too is a double-pointed problem now put to you, and you have to solve it.'

16. 'What Sâriputta the Elder said is true, O king. And the Blessed One called Sudinna a useless fellow on that occasion. But that was not out of rudeness of disposition [6], it was merely pointing out the real nature (of his conduct) in a way that would do him no harm [7]. And what herein is meant by

---

[1] I don't know where such a phrase is put into Sâriputta's mouth: but a similar one, as Mr. Trenckner points out, is ascribed to the Buddha at Aṅguttara VII, 6, 5.

[2] Kalanda-putto, where Kalanda (or Kalandaka as some MSS. of the Vinaya spell it) is the name of the clan (see Pârâgika I, 5, 1), not of the father.

[3] See the whole speech at Pârâgika I, 5, 11.

[4] Garuttâsena. Tâso is not in Childers, but occurs Gâtaka III, 177, 202.

[5] There is nothing in the Vinaya account of this result.

[6] Du*tth*a-*k*ittena, which Hîna*t*i-kumburê repeats.

[7] Asârambhena yâthâva-lakkha*n*ena. For yâthâva, which is not in Childers, see Buddhaghosa in the Sumaṅgala Vilâsinî, p. 65, and Dhammapâla on Theri Gâthâ, 387. Hîna*t*i-kumburê

"pointing out the real nature." If any man, O king, in this birth does not attain to the perception of the Four Truths, then is his manhood (his being born as a man) in vain[1], but if he acts differently he will become different. Therefore is it that he is called a useless fellow[2]. And so the Blessed One addressed Sudinna the Kalanda with words of truth, and not with words apart from the facts.'

17. 'But, Nâgasena, though a man in abusing another speaks the truth, still we should inflict a small[3] fine upon him. For he is guilty of an offence, inasmuch as he, although for something real, abused him by the use of words that might lead to a breach (of the peace)[4].'

'Have you ever heard, O king, of a people bowing down before, or rising up from their seats in respect for, or showing honour to, or bringing the complimentary presents (usually given to officials) to a criminal?'

'No, if a man have committed a crime of whatever sort or kind, if he be really worthy of reproof and punishment, they would rather behead him, or tor-

---

translates: Upadra kara*n*a sitakin ut no wanneya, swabhâwa laksha*n*ayen maya ehi wadâla kisiwek œt nam, ê swabhâwa laksha*n*aya maya.

[1] Mogham. So at *G*âtaka III, 24.

[2] Mogha-puriso, the same word as I have translated elsewhere 'foolish fellow,' following Childers. But I never think that the word means always and only 'in vain, useless.' See *G*âtaka I, 14; III, 24, 25; Sutta Nipâta III, 7, 20; Mahâvagga VIII, 1, 5; *K*ullavagga V, 11, 3; Aṅguttara II, 5, 10; Sumaṅgala Vilâsinî, p. 55.

[3] Literally, 'a fine of a kahâpa*n*a,' a copper coin worth in our money about a penny. See my 'Ancient Coins and Measures,' p. 3.

[4] Visu*m* vohâra*m* â*k*aranto. The Si*m*halese (p. 224) has Wen wû wa*k*ana wû wyawahârayekin hœsiremin.

ture him [1], or bind him with bonds, or put him to death, or deprive him of his goods [2].'

'Did then the Blessed One, O king, act with justice or not?'

'With justice, Sir, and in a most fit and proper way. And when, Nâgasena, they hear of it the world of men and gods will be made tender of conscience, and afraid of falling into sin, struck with awe at the sight of it, and still more so when they themselves associate with wrong-doers, or do wrong.'

18. [**172**] 'Now would a physician, O king, administer pleasant things as a medicine in a case where all the humours of the body were affected, and the whole frame was disorganised and full of disease?'

'No. Wishing to put an end to the disease he would give sharp and scarifying drugs.'

'In the same way, O king, the Tathâgata bestows admonition for the sake of suppressing all the diseases of sin. And the words of the Tathâgata, even when stern, soften men and make them tender. Just as hot water, O king, softens and makes tender anything capable of being softened, so are the words of the Tathâgata, even when stern, yet as full of benefit, and as full of pity as the words of a father would be to his children. Just, O king, as the drinking of evil-smelling decoctions, the swallowing of nasty drugs, destroys the weaknesses of men's bodies, so are the words of the Tathâgata, even when stern, bringers of advantage and laden with pity. And

---

[1] Hananti. But hi*m*sât kereti says the Si*m*halese.

[2] *G*âpenti. Dr. Edward Müller thinks this a misprint for *gh*âpenti (Pâli Grammar, p. 37). Dhanaya hânayen nirddhanîka kereti is the Si*m*halese version.

just, O king, as a ball of cotton falling on a man raises no bruise, so do the words of the Tathâgata, even when stern, do no harm.'

'Well have you made this problem clear by many a simile. Very good, Nâgasena! That is so, and I accept it as you say.'

[End of the dilemma as to the Buddha's harsh words to Sudinna.]

[THE TREE TALKING.]

19. 'Venerable Nâgasena, the Tathâgata said:
"Brahman! why do you ask an unconscious thing,
Which cannot hear you, how it does to-day?
Active, intelligent, and full of life,
How can you speak to this so senseless thing—
This wild Palâsa tree[1]?"
[173] And on the other hand he said:
"And thus the Aspen tree then made reply:
'I, Bhâradvâga, can speak too. Listen to me[2].'"
'Now if, Nâgasena, a tree is an unconscious thing, it must be false that the Aspen tree spoke to Bhâradvâga. But if that is true, it must be false to say that a tree is unconscious. This too is a double-edged problem now put to you, and you have to solve it.'

20. 'The Master said, Nâgasena, that a tree is unconscious. And the Aspen tree conversed with Bhâradvâga. But that last is said, O king, by a common form of speech. For though a tree being unconscious cannot talk, yet the word "tree" is used

---

[1] *Gâtaka* III, 24. It is not the Tathâgata, but the Bodisat, who speaks.

[2] *Gâtaka* IV, 210, where the verses are ascribed to the Buddha.

as a designation of the dryad who dwells therein, and in that sense that "the tree talks" is a well-known expression. Just, O king, as a waggon laden with corn is called a corn-waggon. But it is not made of corn, it is made of wood, yet because of the corn being heaped up in it the people use the expression "corn-waggon." Or just, O king, as when a man is churning sour milk the common expression is that he is churning butter. But it is not butter that he is churning, but milk. Or just, O king, as when a man is making something that does not exist the common expression is that he is making that thing which all the while as yet is not, [174] but people talk of the work as accomplished before it is done. And the Tathâgata, when expounding the Dhamma, does so by means of the phraseology which is in common use among the people.'

'Very good, Nâgasena! That is so, and I accept it as you say.'

[Here ends the dilemma as to the talking tree.]

[THE BUDDHA'S LAST ILLNESS.]

21. 'Venerable Nâgasena, it was said by the Elders who held the Recitation[1]:

"When he had eaten Kunda's alms,
 The coppersmith's,—thus have I heard,—
 The Buddha felt that sickness dire,
 That sharp pain even unto death[2]."

---

[1] The Council of Râgagaha is meant, at which the Pitakas were recited. All the so-called Councils are exclusively 'Recitations' (Samgîtiyo) in Buddhist phraseology. But 'Council' is the best rendering of the word, as Recitation implies so much that would be unintelligible to the ordinary reader.

[2] Book of the Great Decease, IV, 23.

And afterwards the Blessed One said: "These two offerings of food, Ânanda, equal, of equal fruit, and of equal result, are of much greater fruit and much greater result than any others[1]." Now if sharp sickness fell upon the Blessed One, Nâgasena, after he had partaken of *K*unda's alms, and sharp pains arose within him even unto death, then that other statement must be wrong. But if that is right then the first must be wrong. How could that alms, Nâgasena, be of great fruit when it turned to poison, gave rise to disease, [175] put an end to the period of his then existence, took away his life? Explain this to me to the refutation of the adversaries. The people are in bewilderment about this, thinking that the dysentery must have been caused by his eating too much, out of greediness.'

22. 'The Blessed One said, O king, that there were two almsgivings equal, of equal fruit, and equal result, and of much greater fruit, and much greater result than any others,—that which, when a Tathâgata has partaken of it, he attains to supreme and perfect Buddhahood (Enlightenment), and that when he has partaken of which, he passes away by that utter passing away in which nothing whatever remains behind[2]. For that alms is full of virtue, full of advantage. The gods, O king, shouted in joy and gladness at the thought: "This is the last meal the Tathâgata will take," and communicated a divine power of nourishment to that tender

---

[1] Book of the Great Decease, IV, 57, but with a slightly different reading.

[2] Book of the Great Decease, loc. cit. The Si*m*halese gives the whole context in full.

pork[1]. And that was itself in good condition, light, pleasant, full of flavour, and good for digestion[2]. It was not because of it that any sickness fell upon the Blessed One, but it was because of the extreme weakness of his body, and because of the period of life he had to live having been exhausted, that the disease arose, and grew worse and worse—just as when, O king, an ordinary fire is burning, if fresh fuel be supplied, it will burn up still more—or [176] as when a stream is flowing along as usual, if a

---

[1] Sûkara-maddava. There is great doubt as to the exact meaning of this name of the last dish the Buddha partook of. Maddati is 'to rub,' or 'to press,' or 'to trample,' and just as 'pressed beef' is ambiguous, so is 'boar-pressed' or 'pork-tender' capable of various interpretations. The exegetical gloss as handed down in the Mahâ Vihâra in Anurâdhapure, Ceylon, in the now lost body of tradition called the Mahâ A*tth*akathâ, has been preserved by Dhammapâla in his comment on Udâna VIII, 5 (p. 81 of Dr. Steinthal's edition for the Pâli Text Society). It means, I think, 'Meat pervaded by the tenderness and niceness of boar's (flesh).' But that is itself ambiguous, and Dhammapâla adds that others say the word means not pork or meat at all, but 'the tender top sprout of the bambû plant after it has been trampled upon by swine'—others again that it means a kind of mushroom that grows in ground trodden under foot by swine—others again that it means only a particular kind of flavouring, or sauce. As Maddana is rendered by Childers 'withered,' I have translated it in my 'Buddhist Suttas' (pp. 71–73) 'dried boar's flesh.' But the fact is that the exact sense is not known. (Maddavâni pupphâni at Dhammapada 377 is 'withered flowers,' according to Fausböll. But it may be just as well 'tender flowers,' especially as Mârdava in Sanskrit always means 'tender, pitiful,' &c. This is the only passage where the word is known to occur in Pâli apart from those in which sûkara-maddava is mentioned.) The Si*m*halese here (p. 230) repeats the word and adds the gloss: E taru*n*u wû ûru ma*m*sayehi.

[2] *G*atharaggi-te*g*assa hitam. On this curious old belief in an internal fire see my 'Buddhist Suttas,' p. 260.

heavy rain falls, it will become a mighty river with a great rush of water—or as when the body is of its ordinary girth, if more food be eaten, it becomes broader than before. So this was not, O king, the fault of the food that was presented, and you can not impute any harm to it.'

23. 'But, venerable Nâgasena, why is it that those two gifts of food are so specially meritorious?'

'Because of the attainment of the exalted conditions which resulted from them[1].'

'Of what conditions, Nâgasena, are you speaking?'

'Of the attainment of the nine successive states which were passed through at first in one order, and then in the reverse order[2].'

'It was on two days, was it not, Nâgasena, that the Tathâgata attained to those conditions in the highest degree?'

'Yes, O king[3].'

'It is a most wonderful thing, Nâgasena, and a most strange, that of all the great and glorious gifts which were bestowed upon our Blessed One[4] not one can be compared with these two alms-givings. Most marvellous is it, that even as those

---

[1] Dhammânumaggana-samâpatti-varena: which the Simhalese merely repeats. For Anumaggan â see the text above, p. 62, and Sumangala Vilâsinî, p. 65.

[2] See the full description in the Book of the Great Decease, VI, 11-13. ('Buddhist Suttas,' pp. 115, 116.) The Simhalese is here greatly expanded (pp. 230-233).

[3] So our author must have thought that the nine Anupubba-vihâras occurred also after the alms given to Gotama before he sat under the Bo Tree, but I know of no passage in the Pitakas which would support this belief. Compare the note 2 in vol. i, p. 74 of the 'Vinaya Texts,' and the passages there quoted.

[4] Buddha-khette dânam, 'gifts which had the Buddha as the field in which they were bestowed, or sown.'

nine successive conditions are glorious, even so are those gifts made, by their glory, [177] of greater fruit, and of greater advantage than any others. Very good, Nâgasena! That is so, and I accept it as you say.'

[Here ends the dilemma as to the Buddha's last illness.]

[ADORATION OF RELICS.]

24. 'Venerable Nâgasena, the Tathâgata said: "Hinder not yourselves, Ânanda, by honouring the remains of the Tathâgata[1]." And on the other hand he said:

"Honour that relic of him who is worthy of honour,
Acting in that way you go from this world to heaven[2]."

'Now if the first injunction was right the second must be wrong, and if the second is right the first must be wrong. This too is a double-edged problem now put to you, and you have to solve it.'

25. 'Both the passages you quote were spoken by the Blessed One. But it was not to all men, it was to the sons of the Conqueror[3] that it was said: "Hinder not yourselves, Ânanda, by honouring the remains of the Tathâgata[4]." Paying reverence is not the work of the sons of the Conqueror, [178] but rather the grasping of the true nature of all

---

[1] Book of the Great Decease, V, 24.
[2] Not found in any of the Piṭaka texts as yet published.
[3] *G*ina-puttânam. That is, the members of the Order.
[4] Here again Hînaṭi-kumburê goes into a long account of the attendant circumstances (pp. 233, 234).

compounded things, the practice of thought, contemplation in accordance with the rules of Satipa-*tth*âna, the seizing of the real essence of all objects of thought, the struggle against evil, and devotion to their own (spiritual) good. These are things which the sons of the Conqueror ought to do, leaving to others, whether gods or men, the paying of reverence [1].'

26. 'And that is so, O king, just as it is the business of the princes of the earth to learn all about elephants, and horses, and chariots, and bows, and rapiers, and documents, and the law of property [2], to carry on the traditions of the Khattiya clans, and to fight themselves and to lead others in war, while husbandry, merchandise, and the care of cattle are the business of other folk, ordinary Vessas and Suddas.—Or just as the business of Brahmins and their sons is concerned with the Rig-veda, the Ya*g*ur-veda, the Sâma-veda, the Atharva-veda, with the knowledge of lucky marks (on the body), of legends [3], Purâ*n*as, lexicography [4], prosody, phonology, verses, grammar, etymology, astrology, interpretation of omens, and of dreams, and of signs, study of the six Vedângas, of eclipses of the sun and moon, of the prognostications to be drawn from the flight of comets, the thunderings of the gods, the junctions of planets, the fall of meteors, earthquakes, conflagrations, and signs in the heavens and on the earth, the study of arithmetic, of cas-

---

[1] This is really only an expansion and a modernisation of the context of the passage quoted.
[2] Lekha-muddâ. See the note above on I, 1, 10.
[3] Itihâsa, 'the Bhârata and the Râmâya*n*a,' says the Si*m*halese.
[4] 'Of names of trees and so on,' says Hîna*t*i-kumburê.

uistry, of the interpretation of the omens to be drawn from dogs, and deer, and rats, and mixtures of liquids, and the sounds and cries of birds—while husbandry, merchandise, and the care of cattle are the business of other folk, ordinary Vessas and Suddas. So it was, O king, in the sense of "Devote not yourselves to such things as are not your business, but to such things as are so" that the Tathâgata was speaking [179] when he said: "Hinder not yourselves, Ânanda, by honouring the remains of the Tathâgata." And if, O king, he had not said so, then would the Bhikkhus have taken his bowl and his robe, and occupied themselves with paying reverence to the Buddha through them[1]!'

'Very good, Nâgasena! That is so, and I accept it as you say.'

[Here ends the dilemma as to reverence to relics.]

[THE SPLINTER OF ROCK.]

27. 'Venerable Nâgasena, you Bhikkhus say that: "When the Blessed One walked along, the earth, unconscious though it is, filled up its deep places, and made its steep places plain[2]." And on the other hand you say that a splinter of

---

[1] This certainly looks as if our author did not know anything of the worship paid to the supposed bowl of the Buddha, or of the feast, the Patta-maha, held in its honour. The passage may therefore be used as an argument for the date of the book. Fâ-Hien saw this bowl-worship in full force at Peshawar about 400 A.D. See Chapter xii of his travels (Dr. Legge's translation, pp. 35-37).

[2] Not found as yet in the Pi/akas.

rock grazed his foot[1]. When that splinter was falling on his foot why did it not, then, turn aside? If it be true that the unconscious earth makes its deep places full and its steep places plain for him, then it must be untrue that the splinter of rock hurt his foot. But if the latter statement be true, then the first must be false. This too is a double-edged problem now put to you, and you have to solve it.'

28. 'Both statements, O king, are true. But that splinter of rock did not fall of itself[2], it was cast down through the act of Devadatta. Through hundreds of thousands of existences, O king, had Devadatta borne a grudge against the Blessed One[3]. It was through that hatred that he seized hold of a mighty mass of rock, and pushed it over with the hope that it would fall upon the Buddha's head. But two other rocks came together, and intercepted it before it reached the Tathâgata, and by the force of their impact a splinter was torn off, and fell in such a direction that it struck [180] the Blessed One's foot.'

29. 'But, Nâgasena, just as two rocks intercepted that mighty mass, so could the splinter have been intercepted.'

'But a thing intercepted, O king, can escape, slip through, or be lost—as water does, through the fingers, when it is taken into the hand—or milk, or buttermilk, or honey, or ghee, or oil, or fish curry,

---

[1] *K*ullavagga VII, 3, 9. Compare the Sa*m*yutta Nikâya I, 4, 8; IV, 2, 3 (pp. 27 and 110 of M. Léon Feer's edition for the Pâli Text Society).

[2] Attaro dhammatâya.

[3] So above, IV, 2, 64, and below, IV, 4, 41.

or gravy—or as fine, subtle, minute, dusty grains of sand do, through the fingers, if you close your fist on them—or as rice will escape sometimes when you have taken it into your fingers, and are putting it into your mouth.'

30. 'Well, let that be so, Nâgasena. I admit that the rock was intercepted. But the splinter ought at least to have paid as much respect to the Buddha as the earth did.'

'There are these twelve kinds of persons, O king, who pay no respect—the lustful man in his lust, and the angry man in his malice, and the dull man in his stupidity, and the puffed-up man in his pride, and the bad man in his want of discrimination, and the obstinate man in his want of docility, and the mean man in his littleness, and the talkative man in his vanity, and the wicked man in his cruelty, and the wretched man in his misery, and the gambler [181] because he is overpowered by greed, and the busy man in his search after gain. But that splinter, just as it was broken off by the impact of the rocks, fell by chance[1] in such a direction that it struck against the foot of the Blessed One—just as fine, subtle, and minute grains of sand, when carried away by the force of the wind, are sprinkled down by chance in any direction they may happen to take. If the splinter, O king, had not been separated from the rock of which it formed a part, it too would have been intercepted by their meeting together. But, as it was, it was neither fixed on the earth, nor did it remain stationary in the air, but fell whithersoever

---

[1] Animitta-kata-disâ, which the Simhalese (p. 238) merely repeats.

chance directed it, and happened to strike against the Blessed One's foot—just as dried leaves might fall if caught up in a whirlwind. And the real cause of its so striking against his foot was the sorrow-working deed [1] of that ungrateful, wicked, Devadatta.'

'Very good, Nâgasena! That is so, and I accept it as you say.'

[Here ends the dilemma as to the splinter grazing the Buddha's foot.]

[THE SAMAṆA.]

31. 'Venerable Nâgasena, the Blessed One said: "A man becomes a Samaṇa by the destruction of the Âsavas [2]." But on the other hand he said:
"The man who has these dispositions four
Is he whom the world knows as Samaṇa [3]."
And in that passage these are the four dispositions referred to—long-suffering, temperance in food, renunciation [4], and the being without the attachments [5] (arising from lust, ill-will, and dulness). Now these four dispositions are equally found in those who are still defective, in whom [182] the

---

[1] Dukkhânubhâvanâ—the sorrow being Devadatta's subsequent existence in purgatory.

[2] That is 'of sensuality, individuality, delusion, and ignorance.' I don't know which is the passage referred to.

[3] Also not traced as yet in the texts.

[4] Vippahânâ, not in Childers, but see Sutta Nipâta V, 14, 4, 5. Hînaṭi-kumburê (p. 239) renders it âlaya hœrîma.

[5] Âkinkaññâ, not having the three kiñkanas mentioned. Hînaṭi-kumburê (p. 239) takes it to mean the practice of the Âkiñkâyatana meditation. But if so that would surely have been the word used.

Âsavas have not yet been completely destroyed. So that if the first statement be correct, the second is wrong, and if the second be right the first must be wrong. This too is a double-edged problem now put to you, and you have to solve it.'

32. 'Both statements, O king, were made by the Blessed One. But the second was said of the characteristics of such and such men; the first is an inclusive statement—that all in whom the Âsavas are destroyed are Sama*n*as. And moreover, of all those who are made perfect by the suppression of evil, if you take them in regular order one after the other, then the Sama*n*a in whom the Âsavas are destroyed is acknowledged to be the chief—just, O king, as of all flowers produced in the water or on the land, the double jasmine [1] is ackowledged to be the chief, all other kinds of flowers of whatever sort are merely flowers, and taking them in order it is the double jasmine that people most desire and like. Or just, O king, as of all kinds of grain, rice is acknowledged to be the chief, all other kinds of grain, of whatever sort, [183] are useful for food and for the support of the body, but if you take them in order, rice is acknowledged as the best.'

'Very good, Nâgasena! That is so, and I accept it as you say.'

[Here ends the dilemma as to what constitutes a Sama*n*a.]

---

[1] Varsikâ (Dŏ̄saman mal, jasminum zambac).

[THE BUDDHA'S EXULTATION.]

33. 'Venerable Nâgasena, the Blessed One said: " If, O Bhikkhus, any one should speak in praise of me, or of our religion (Dhamma), or of the Order, you should not thereupon indulge in joy, or delight, or exultation of mind[1]". And on the other hand the Tathâgata was so delighted, and pleased, and exultant at the deserved praise bestowed on him by Sela the Brahman, that he still further magnified his own goodness in that he said:

" A king am I, Sela, the king supreme
 Of righteousness. The royal chariot wheel
 In righteousness do I set rolling on—
 That wheel that no one can turn back again[2]!"

Now if the passage first quoted be right then must the second be wrong, but if that be right then must the first be wrong. This too is a double-edged problem now put to you, and you have to solve it.'

34. [184] 'Both your quotations, O king, are correct. But the first passage was spoken by the Blessed One with the intention of setting forth truthfully, exactly, in accordance with reality, and fact, and

---

[1] From the Brahma-gâla Sutta in the Dîgha Nikâya (I, 1, 5).

[2] From the Sela Sutta in the Sutta Nipâta (III, 7, 7). Professor Fausböll in his translation of this stanza (at vol. x, p. 102 of the 'Sacred Books of the East') draws attention to the parallel at John xviii. 37. 'Thou sayest that I am a king. To this end was I born. And for this cause came I into the world that I should bear witness unto the truth '—where 'truth,' if one translated the verse into Pâli, would be correctly rendered by Dhamma, 'righteousness, religion, truth, essential quality.' Professor Fausböll's version of the stanza runs: 'I am a king, O Sela, an incomparable religious (Dhamma-râga) king, with justice (Dhamma). I turn the wheel, a wheel that is irresistible.'

sense, the real nature, and essence, and characteristic marks of the Dhamma. And the second passage was not spoken for the sake of gain or fame, nor out of party spirit, nor in the lust of winning over men to become his followers. But it was in mercy and love, and with the welfare of others in view, conscious that thereby three hundred young Brahmans would attain to the knowledge of the truth, that he said: "A king am I, Sela, the king supreme of righteousness."'

'Very good, Nâgasena! That is so, and I accept it as you say.'

[Here ends the problem as to exultation of mind.]

[KINDNESS AND PUNISHMENT.]

35. 'Venerable Nâgasena, the Blessed One said:
"Doing no injury to any one
Dwell full of love and kindness in the world [1]."
And on the other hand he said: " Punish him who deserves punishment [2], favour him who is worthy of favour." [185] Now punishment, Nâgasena, means the cutting off of hands or feet, flogging [3], casting into bonds, torture [4], execution, degradation in rank [5].

---

[1] From the 521st Gâtaka.
[2] The crux lies in the ambiguity of this phrase as will be seen below.
[3] Vadha, which is ambiguous, and means also 'killing.' The Simhalese repeats the word.
[4] Kâranâ, which Hînati-kumburê renders toelîmaya, 'flogging.'
[5] Santati-vikopanam, literally 'breach of continuity.' Hînati-kumburê explains it to mean 'injury to the duration of life,' and this may be the author's meaning, as he is fond of heaping together a string of words, some of which mean the same thing. But as

Such a saying is therefore not worthy of the Blessed One, and he ought not to have made use of it. For if the first injunction be right then this must be wrong, and if this be right then the injunction to do no injury to any one, but to dwell full of love and kindness in the world, must be wrong. This too is a double-edged problem now put to you, and you have to solve it.'

36. 'The Blessed One, great king, gave both the commands you quote. As to the first, to do no injury to any one, but to live full of love and kindness in the world—that is a doctrine approved by all the Buddhas. And that verse is an injunction, an unfolding of the Dhamma, for the Dhamma has as its characteristic that it works no ill. And the saying is thus in thorough accord with it. But as to the second command you quote that is a special use of terms [which you have misunderstood. The real meaning of them is: "Subdue that which ought to be subdued, strive after, cultivate, favour what is worthy of effort, cultivation, and approval"]. The proud heart, great king, is to be subdued, and the lowly heart cultivated—the wicked heart to be subdued, and the good heart to be cultivated—carelessness of thought is to be subdued, and exactness of thought to be cultivated—[186] he who is given over to wrong views is to be subdued, and he who has attained to right views is to be cultivated—he who is not noble[1] is to be subdued, and the noble one is

---

santati means also 'lineage, descent,' the phrase may equally well refer to the sort of punishment I have ventured to put into the text.

[1] Ariyo and anariyo used technically in the sense of one who has not, and one who has, entered upon the Noble Eightfold Path.

to be cultivated—the robber [1] is to be subdued, and the honest brother is to be cultivated.'

37. 'Let that be so, Nâgasena. But now, in that last word of yours, you have put yourself into my power, you have come round to the sense in which I put my question. For how, venerable Nâgasena, is the robber to be subdued by him who sets to work to subdue him?'

'Thus, great king—if deserving of rebuke let him be rebuked, if of a fine let him be fined, if of banishment let him be banished, if of death let him be put to death.'

'Is then, Nâgasena, the execution of robbers part of the doctrine laid down by the Tathâgatas?'

'Certainly not, O king.'

'Then why have the Tathâgatas laid down that the robber is to be taught better?'

'Whosoever, great king, may be put to death, he does not suffer execution by reason of the opinion put forth by the Tathâgatas. He suffers by reason of what he himself has done. But notwithstanding that the doctrine of the Dhamma has been taught (by the Buddhas)[2], would it be possible, great king, for a man who had done nothing wrong, and was walking innocently along the streets, to be seized and put to death by any wise person?'

'Certainly not.'

---

[1] Coro probably here used figuratively of a member of the Order who is unworthy of it, and injures believing laymen. So the word is used, for instance, in the introductory story (in the Sutta Vibhaṅga) to the fourth Pârâgikâ—where four sorts of such religious 'robbers' are distinguished (compare our 'wolf in sheep's clothing'). But the king takes it literally.

[2] The three words in brackets are Hînaṭi-kumburê's gloss.

'But why?'

'Because of his innocence.'

'Just so, great king, since the thief is not put to death through the word of the Tathâgata, but only through his own act, how can any fault be rightly found on that account with the Teacher?'

'It could not be, Sir.'

'So you see the teaching of the Tathâgatas is a righteous teaching.'

'Very good, Nâgasena! That is so, and I accept it as you say.'

[Here ends the problem as to kindness and punishment.]

[THE DISMISSAL OF THE ELDERS.]

38. 'Venerable Nâgasena, it was said by the Blessed One:

"Anger I harbour not, nor sulkiness[1]."

But on the other hand the Tathâgata dismissed the Elders Sâriputta and Moggallâna, together with the brethren who formed their company of disciples[2].

---

[1] From the Dhaniya Sutta in the Sutta Nipâta (I, 2, 2).

[2] The episode here referred to will be found in the Magghima Nikâya, No. 67. Hînati-kumburê gives it in full. The Buddha was staying at the Âmalakî garden near the Sâkya town called Kâtumâ. There the two elders with their attendant 500 disciples came to call upon him. The resident Bhikkhus received them with applause, and a great hubbub arose. The Buddha enquired what that noise was, like the chattering of fishermen when a net full of fishes was drawn to shore. Ânanda told him. Thereupon the Buddha called the brethren together, made a discourse to them on the advantages of quiet, and 'sent away' the visitors. They went to the public rest-house in the town. The town's folk enquired why, and

How now, Nâgasena, [187] was it in anger that the Tathâgata sent away[1] the disciples, or was it in pleasure? Be so good as to explain to me how this was[2]. For if, Nâgasena, he dismissed them in anger, then had the Tathâgata not subdued all liability to anger in himself. But if it was in pleasure, then he did so ignorantly, and without due cause. This too is a double-edged problem now put to you, and you have to solve it.'

39. 'The Blessed One did say, O king:
"Anger I harbour not, nor sulkiness."
And he did dismiss the Elders with their disciples. But that was not in anger. Suppose, O king, that a man were to stumble against some root, or stake, or stone, or potsherd, or on uneven ground, and fall upon the broad earth. Would it be that the broad earth, angry with him, had made him fall?'

'No, indeed, Sir. The broad earth feels neither anger against any man nor delight. It is altogether

---

when they heard the reason, went to the Buddha, and obtained his forgiveness for the offending brethren. The incident is the basis of another question below, IV, 4, 41.

[1] Pa*n*âmesi means, in the technical legal phraseology of the Buddhist canon law, 'formally dismissed, sent away, did not allow them any more to be his disciples.' On this technical meaning of the term, compare Mahâvagga I, 2, 27, and *K*ullavagga XII, 2, 3. (Childers does not give this use of the word.) But it is difficult to imagine the circumstances under which the Buddha could so have dismissed his two principal disciples. So I think we must take the word in a less formal sense—such, for instance, as we find in Thera Gâthâ 511, 557.

[2] Eta*m* tâva *g*ânâhi ima*m* nâmâti. I follow Hîna*t*i-kumburê's rendering (p. 244) of this difficult phrase, according to which there ought to be a full stop in the text after pa*n*âmesi, and these words are supposed to be addressed to Nâgasena by Milinda. But I am not at all satisfied that he is right, and the text may be corrupt.

free from ill-will, neither needs it to fawn on any one. It would be by reason of his own carelessness that that man stumbled and fell.'

'Just so, great king, do the Tathâgatas experience neither anger against, nor pride in any man. Altogether free are the Tathâgatas, the Arahat-Buddhas, alike from ill-will, and from the need to fawn on any one. And those disciples were sent away by reason of what they themselves had done. So also the great ocean endures not association with any corpse. Any dead body there may be in it that does it promptly cast up, and leave high and dry on the shore[1]. But is it in anger that it casts it up?'

'Certainly not, Sir. The broad ocean feels neither anger against any, nor does it take delight in any. It seeks not in the least to please any, and is altogether free from the desire to harm.'

'Just so, great king, do the Tathâgatas feel neither anger against any man, nor do they place their faith in any man. The Tathâgatas, the Arahat-Buddhas, are quite set free from the desire either to gain the goodwill of any man, or to do him harm. And it was by reason of what they themselves had done that those disciples were sent away. Just as a man, great king, who stumbles against the ground is made to fall, so is he who stumbles in the excellent teaching of the Conqueror made to go away. Just as a corpse in the great ocean is cast up, [188] so is he who stumbles in the excellent teaching of the Conqueror sent away. And when the Tathâgata sent those disciples away it was for their good, and their

---

[1] This supposed fact is already the ground of a comparison in the *K*ullavagga IX, 1, 3, 4 ('Vinaya Texts,' III, 303).

gain, their happiness, and their purification, and in order that in that way they should be delivered from birth, old age, disease, and death.'

'Very good, Nâgasena! That is so, and I accept it as you say.'

[Here ends the problem as to the dismissal of the Elders.]

Here ends the Third Chapter.

Book IV. Chapter 4.

[The Murder of Moggallâna.]

1. 'Venerable Nâgasena, it has been said by the Blessed One: "This is the chief, O Bhikkhus, of those of my disciples in the Order who are possessed of the power of Iddhi, I mean Moggallâna[1]." But on the other hand they say his death took place by his being beaten to death with clubs, so that his skull was broken, and his bones ground to powder, and all his flesh and nerves bruised and pounded together[2]. Now, Nâgasena, if the Elder, the great Moggallâna, had really attained to supremacy in the magical power of Iddhi, then it cannot be true that he was beaten to death with clubs[3]. But if his death was on that wise, then the saying that he was chief of those possessed of Iddhi must be wrong. How could he who was not even able, by his power of Iddhi, to prevent his own murder, be worthy nevertheless to stand as succour to the world of gods and men? This too is a double-edged problem now put to you, and you have to solve it.'

2. 'The Blessed One did declare, O king, that Moggallâna was chief among the disciples in power

---

[1] From the Anguttara Nikâya I, xiv, 1 (page 23 of Dr. Morris's edition for the Pâli Text Society)

[2] Parikatto, which the Siṃhalese version renders garhâ wemin.

[3] 'By robbers,' adds Hînaṭi-kumburê, so there is no question of martyrdom.

of Iddhi. And he was nevertheless beaten to death by clubs. But that was through his being then possessed by the still greater power of Karma [1].'

3. 'But, venerable Nâgasena, [189] are not both of these things appurtenant to him who has the power of Iddhi—that is the extent of his power, and the result of his Karma—both alike unthinkable? And cannot the unthinkable be held back by the unthinkable? Just, Sir, as those who want the fruits will knock a wood apple [2] down with a wood apple, or a mango with a mango, so ought not the unthinkable in like manner to be subject to restraint by the unthinkable?'

'Even among things beyond the reach of the imagination, great king, still one is in excess above the other, one more powerful than the other. Just, O king, as the monarchs of the world are alike in kind, but among them, so alike in kind, one may overcome the rest, and bring them under his command—just so among things beyond the grasp of the imagination is the productive effect of Karma by far the most powerful. It is precisely the effect of Karma which overcomes all the rest, and has them under its rule; and no other influence is of any avail to the man in whom Karma is working out its inevitable end [3]. It is as when, O king, any man has committed an offence against the law [4].

---

[1] Kammâdhigahitenâpi, which the Simhalese merely repeats. Compare the use of adhiga*n*hâti at Anguttara Nikâya V, 31 (adhiga*n*hâti ta*m* tena, 'surpasses him in that'), and see below.

[2] Kapittham (Feronia Elephantum), which the Simhalese renders Diwul ge*d*i.

[3] 'No good action has an opportunity at the time when evil Karma is in possession of a man,' says Hîna*t*i-kumburê (p. 250).

[4] Pakara*n*e apara*ggh*ati, literally 'against the book,' the book

Neither his mother nor his father, neither his sisters nor his brother, neither his friends nor his intimate associates can protect him then. He has fallen therein under the power of the king who will issue his command respecting him. And why is that so? Because of the wrong that he has done. So is it precisely the effect of Karma which overcomes all other influences, and has them under its command, and no other influence can avail the man in whom Karma is working out its inevitable end. It is as when a jungle fire has arisen on the earth, then can not even a thousand pots of water avail to put it out, but the conflagration overpowers all, and brings it under its control. And why is that so? Because of the fierceness of its heat. So is it precisely the effect of Karma which overcomes all other influences, and has them under its command; and no other influence can avail the man in whom Karma is working out its inevitable end. That is why the venerable one, great king, the great Moggallâna, when, at a time when he was possessed by Karma, he was being beaten to death with clubs, was yet unable to make use of his power of Iddhi [1].'

'Very good, Nâgasena! That is so, and I accept it as you say.'

[Here ends the problem as to the murder of Moggallâna.]

---

of the law being, no doubt, understood. But the Simhalese has 'against any one.'

[1] Iddhiyâ samannâhâro nâho si. See the use of this word, which is not in Childers, at p. 123 of the Sumangala (on Dîgha I, 3, 24). The Simhalese goes on to much greater length than the Pâli, giving the full religious life history of the famous disciple (pp. 250, 251).

[ON SECRET DOCTRINE.]

4. [190] 'Venerable Nâgasena, it was said by the Blessed One: "The Dhamma and the Vinaya (Doctrine and Canon Law) proclaimed by the Tathâgata shine forth when they are displayed, and not when they are concealed [1]." But on the other hand the recitation of the Pâtimokkha and the whole of the Vinaya Pi/aka are closed and kept secret [2]. So that if, Nâgasena, you (members of the Order) carried out what is just, and right, and held of faith in the teaching of the Conqueror then would the Vinaya shine forth as an open thing. And why would that be so? Because all the instruction therein, the discipline, the self-control, the regulations as to moral and virtuous conduct, are in their essence full of truth and righteousness, and redounding to emancipation of heart. But if the Blessed One really said that the Dhamma and Vinaya proclaimed by the Tathâgata shine forth when displayed and not when kept secret, then the saying that the recitation of the Pâtimokkha and the whole of the Vinaya must be kept secret must be wrong. And if that be right, then the saying of the Blessed One must be wrong. This too is a double-edged problem now put to you, and you have to solve it.'

5. 'It was said, O king, by the Blessed One that the Dhamma and Vinaya proclaimed by the Tathâ-

---

[1] From the Aṅguttara Nikâya III, 124 (vol. i, p. 283 of Dr. Morris's edition for the Pâli Text Society).

[2] In the Vinaya (Mahâvagga II, 16, 8) it is laid down that the Pâtimokkha (the rules of the Order) is not to be recited before laymen. I know of no passage in the Pi/akas which says that it, or the Vinaya, is to be kept secret.

gata shine forth when displayed, and not when kept secret. And on the other hand the recitation of the Pâtimokkha and the whole of the Vinaya Pi/aka are kept close and secret [1]. But this last is not the case as regards all men. They are only kept secret up to a certain limit. And the recitation of the Pâtimokkha is kept secret up to that certain limit on three grounds—firstly because that is the traditional custom [2] of previous Tathâgatas, secondly out of respect for the Truth (Dhamma), and thirdly out of respect for the position of a member of the Order [3].'

6. 'And as to the first it was the universal custom, O king, of previous Tathâgatas for the recitation of the Pâtimokkha to take place in the midst of the members of the Order only, to the exclusion of all others. Just, O king, as the Kshatriya secret formulas (of the nobles) are handed down among the nobles alone, and that this or that is so is common tradition among the nobles [4] of the world and kept secret from all others—[**191**] so was this the universal custom of previous Tathâgatas, that the recitation of the Pâtimokkha should take place among the

---

[1] This is, so far as I know, the earliest mention of this being the case. There is nothing in the Pâtimokkha itself (see my translation of this list of offences against the rules of the Order in vol. i of the 'Vinaya Texts' in the S. B. E.) as to its recitation taking place in secret, and nothing in the Vinaya as to its being kept secret. But the regulations in the Vinaya as to the recitation of the Pâtimokkha forbade the actual presence of any one not a member of the Order, and as a matter of fact any one not such a member is excluded in practice during its recitation now in Ceylon. But it would be no offence in a layman to read the Vinaya, and learned laymen who have left the Order still do so.

[2] Va*m*sa (repeated in the Si*m*halese).

[3] Bhikkhu-bhûmiyâ (also repeated in the Si*m*halese, p. 252).

[4] Kha///iyâna*m* (but the Si*m*halese has Sakyayangê).

members of the Order only, and be kept secret from all others. And again, just as there are several classes of people, O king, known as distinct in the world—such as wrestlers, tumblers, jugglers, actors, ballet-dancers, and followers of the mystic cult of the sun and moon, of the goddess of fortune and other gods[1]. And the secrets of each of these sects are handed on in the sect itself, and kept hidden from all others. Just so with the universal custom of all the Tathâgatas that the recitation of the Pâtimokkha should take place before the members of the Order only, and be kept secret from all others. This is why the recitation of the Pâtimokkha is, up to that extent, kept secret in accordance with the habit of previous Tathâgatas.'

7. 'And how is it that the Pâtimokkha is kept secret, up to that extent, out of reverence for the Dhamma? The Dhamma, great king, is venerable and weighty. He who has attained to proficiency in it may exhort another in this wise : " Let not this Dhamma so full of truth, so excellent, fall into the hands of those unversed in it, where it would be despised and contemned, treated shamefully, made a game of, and found fault with. Nor let it fall into the hands of the wicked who would deal with it in all respects as badly as they." It is thus, O king, that the recitation of the Pâtimokkha is, up to that

---

[1] There are twenty classes of these people mentioned in the text, and the meaning of most of the names is obscure. The Simhalese simply repeats them all, adding only the word bhaktiyo, 'believers in,' to the names of the various divinities. The classing together of jugglers, ballet-dancers, and followers of the numerous mystic cults, so numerous in India, is thoroughly Buddhistic, and quite in the vein of Gotama himself—as, for instance, in the Mahâ Sîla (see my 'Buddhist Suttas,' p. 196).

extent, kept secret out of reverence for the Dhamma. For if not, then it would be like the best, most costly, and most rare red sandal wood of the finest kind, which when brought to Savara (that city of the outcast *Kand*âlas[1]) is despised and contemned, treated shamefully, made game of, and found fault with.'

8. [192] 'And how is it that the Pâtimokkha is kept secret, up to that extent, out of reverence for the position of a member of the Order? The condition of a Bhikkhu, great king, is in glory beyond the reach of calculation by weight, or measure, or price. None can value it, weigh it, measure it. And the recitation of the Pâtimokkha is carried on before the Bhikkhus alone, lest any one who has occupied that position should be brought down to a level with the men of the world. Just, O king, as if there be any priceless thing, in vesture or floor covering, in elephants, chargers, or chariots, in gold or silver or jewels or pearls or women, or in unsurpassable strong drink[2], all such things are the appanage of kings—just so, O king, whatever is most priceless in the way of training, of the traditions of the Blessed One, of learning, of conduct, and of the virtues of righteousness and self-control—all these are the appanages of the Order of Bhikkhus. This is why the recitation of the Pâtimokkha is, to that extent, kept secret[3].'

---

[1] Added from the Si*m*halese.

[2] Ni*gg*ita-kamma-surâ, rendered in the Si*m*halese (p. 254), *g*aya-gr*i*hita-kr*i*tya-surâ-pânayen.

[3] It will be noticed that there is no mention here (in a connection where, if it had then existed, it would almost certainly have been referred to) of any Esoteric Buddhism. So above, at

'Very good, Nâgasena! That is so, and I accept it as you say.'

[Here ends the problem as to the secrecy in which the Vinaya is kept.]

[THE TWO KINDS OF FALSEHOOD.]

9. 'Venerable Nâgasena, it has been said by the Blessed One that a deliberate lie is an offence of the greatest kind (involving exclusion from the Order [1]).

IV, 1, 8, it is stated that a good Buddhist teacher should keep nothing secret from his pupil. And even in so old a text as the 'Book of the Great Decease' (Chap. II, § 32, p. 36 of my translalation in the 'Buddhist Suttas'), it is said of the Buddha himself that he had 'no such thing as the closed fist of a teacher who keeps some things back.' This passage is itself quoted above at IV, 2, 4, as the basis of one of Milinda's questions; and is entirely accepted by Nâgasena, that is, by our author. The fact is that there has never been any such thing as esoteric teaching in Buddhism, and that the modern so called esoteric Buddhism is neither esoteric nor Buddhism. Its tenets, so far as they are Indian at all, are perfectly accessible, are well known to all those who choose to study the books of Indian mysticism, and are Hindu, not Buddhist. They are, indeed, quite contradictory to Buddhism, of which the authors of what they ignorantly call Esoteric Buddhism know but very little—that little being only a portion of those beliefs which have been common ground to all religious teachers in India. If one doctrine—more than any other—is distinctive of Buddhism, it is the ignoring, in ethics, of the time-honoured belief in a soul—that is, in the old sense, in a separate creature inside the body, which flies out of it, like a bird out of a cage, when the body dies. Yet the Theosophists, who believe, I am told, in seven souls inside each human body (which would be worse according to true Buddhism than seven devils), still venture to call themselves Buddhists, and do not see the absurdity of their position!

[1] Sampagâna-musâvâda parâgikâ. This is curious as according to the Pâtimokkha it is Pâkittiya, not Parâgikâ. Compare Parâgikâ 4 with Pâkittiya 1. ('Vinaya Texts,' S. B. E., vol. iii, pp. 5 and 32.)

And again he said: "By a deliberate lie a Bhikkhu commits a minor offence, one that ought to be the subject of confession made before another (member of the Order)[1]." Now, venerable Nâgasena, what is herein the distinction, what the reason, that by one lie a Bhikkhu is cast out of the Order, and by another he is guilty only of an offence that can be atoned for. If the first decision be right, then the second must be wrong; but if the second be right, then the first must be wrong. This too is a double-edged problem now put to you, and you have to solve it.'

10. [193][2] 'Both your quotations, O king, are correct[3]. But a falsehood is a light or heavy offence according to the subject matter. For what do you think, great king? Suppose a man were to give another a slap with his hand, what punishment would you inflict upon him?'

'If the other refused to overlook the matter, then neither should we be able to pardon his assailant[4], but should mulct him in a penny or so[5].'

'But on the other hand, suppose it had been you

---

[1] I cannot trace these identical words in the Pitaka texts. But the general sense of them is exactly in agreement with the first Pâkittiya rule.

[2] Hînati-kumburê here inserts a summary of the Introductory Story (in the Sutta Vibhanga) to the 4th Pârâgikâ. All this (pp. 254–256) stands in his version for lines 1–3 on p. 193 of the Pâli text.

[3] The Pâli repeats them word for word. As I have pointed out above, they are not really correct.

[4] So Hînati-kumburê, who must have had a different reading, and I think a better one, before him.

[5] A kahâpana. See the discussion of the value of this coin in my 'Ancient Coins and Measures,' pp. 3, 4.

yourself that he had given the blow to, what would then be the punishment?'

'We should condemn him to have his hands cut off, and his feet cut off, and to be skinned alive[1], and we should confiscate all the goods in his house, and put to death all his family to the seventh generation on both sides.'

'But, great king, what is the distinction? Why is it that for one slap of the hand there should be a gentle fine of a penny, while for a slap given to you there should be so fearful a retribution?'

'Because of the difference in the person (assaulted).'

'Well! just so, great king, is a falsehood a light or a heavy offence according to the attendant circumstances.'

'Very good, Nâgasena! That is so, and I accept it as you say.'

[Here ends the problem as to the degree of offence in falsehood.]

[THE BODISAT'S CONSIDERATION.]

11. 'Venerable Nâgasena, it has been said by the Blessed One in the discourse on the essential conditions[2]: "Long ago have his parents been destined for each Bodisat, and the kind of tree he is to select for his Bo tree, and the

---

[1] Yâva sîsam ka/irakkheggam khedâpeyyâma, which the Simhalese merely repeats. It is literally 'We should have him "bambû-sprout-cut" up to his head.' What this technical term may mean is not exactly known—possibly having slits the shape of a bambû sprout cut all over his body.

[2] Dhammatâ-dhamma-pariyâye. I don't know where this is to be found.

Bhikkhus who are to be his two chief disciples, and the lad who is to be his son, and the member of the Order who is to be his special attendant." But on the other hand he said: "When yet in the condition of a god in the Tusita heaven the Bodisat makes the eight Great Investigations — he investigates the time (whether the right moment had come at which he ought to be re-born as a man), and the continent (in which his birth is to take place), and the country (where he is to be re-born), and the family (to which he is to belong), and the mother (who is to bear him), and the period (during which he was to remain in the womb), and the month (in which his birthday shall come), and his renunciation (when it shall be)[1]. [194] Now, Nâgasena, before knowledge is ripe there is no understanding, but when it has reached its summit there is no longer any need to wait for thinking a matter over[1], for there is nothing outside the ken of the omniscient mind. Why then should the Bodisat investigate the time, thinking to himself: "In what moment shall I be born[2]?" And for the same reason why should he investigate the family, thinking to him-

---

[1] These eight Investigations (Vilokanâni) have not yet been found in the Pi/aka texts. But, when relating the birth of the historical Buddha, the *G*âtaka commentary (vol. i, p. 48, of Professor Fausböll's edition) mentions the first six of them (substituting okâsa for desa), and calls them, oddly enough, the Five Great Investigations. In the corresponding passage in the Lalita Vistara only the first four are mentioned. The last two of the above eight seem very forced.

[2] Nimesantaram na âgameti, for which Hîna/i-kumburê (p. 256 at the end) has nivesantara. Neither word occurs elsewhere.

self: "In what family shall I be born?" And if, Nâgasena, it is a settled matter who shall be the parents of the Bodisat, then it must be false that he "investigated the family." But if that be true, then must the other saying be wrong. This too is a double-edged problem now put to you, and you have to solve it.'

12. 'It was both a settled matter, O king, who should be the parents of the Bodisat, and he did investigate into the question as to which family he was to be born into. But how did he do so? He thought over the matter as to whether his parents should be nobles or Brahmans. With respect to eight things, O king, should the future be investigated before it comes to pass. A merchant, O king, should investigate goods before he buys them—an elephant should try with its trunk a path it has not yet trod—a cartman should try a ford he has not yet crossed over—a pilot should test a shore he has not yet arrived at, and so guide the ship—a physician should find out the period of life which his patient has lasted[1] before he treats his disease—a traveller should test the stability of a bambû bridge[2] before he mounts on to it—a Bhikkhu should find out how much time has yet to run before sun turn before he begins to eat his meal—and Bodisats, before they are born, should investigate the question whether it would be right for them to be born in the family of a noble or of a Brahman.

---

[1] Âyum oloketvâ, which the Si*m*halese (p. 257) repeats. This implied meaning is doubtful.

[2] Uttara-setu, a word which does not occur elsewhere. Hîna*ṭ*i-kumburê renders it He-da*nd*a, which Clough explains as a foot-bridge usually made of a single tree.

These are the eight occasions on which investigation ought to precede action.'

'Very good, Nâgasena! That is so, and I accept it as you say.'

[Here ends the problem as to the Bodisat's consideration.]

[ON SUICIDE.]

13. [**195**] 'Venerable Nâgasena, it has been said by the Blessed One: "A brother is not, O Bhikkhus, to commit suicide. Whosoever does so shall be dealt with according to the law[1]." And on the other hand you (members of the Order) say: "On whatsoever subject the Blessed One was addressing the disciples, he always, and with various similes, preached to them in order to bring about the destruction of birth, of old age, of disease, and of death. And whosoever overcame birth, old age, disease, and death, him did he honour with the highest praise[2]." Now if the Blessed One forbade suicide that saying of yours must be wrong, but if not then the prohibition of suicide must be wrong. This too is a double-edged problem now put to you, and you have to solve it.'

14. 'The regulation you quote, O king, was laid down by the Blessed One, and yet is our saying you refer to true. And there is a reason for this, a

---

[1] Literally 'is not to throw himself down,' and I think 'from a precipice' is to be understood, especially as the nearest approach to the words quoted, that is the passage in the Sutta Vibhanga on the 3rd Pârâgika (III, 5, 13), has that meaning.

[2] Here again the passage referred to is not known.

reason for which the Blessed One both prohibited (the destruction of life), and also (in another sense) instigated us to it.'

'What, Nâgasena, may that reason be?'

'The good man, O king, perfect in uprightness, is like a medicine to men [1] in being an antidote to the poison of evil, he is like water to men in laying the dust and the impurities of evil dispositions, he is like a jewel treasure to men in bestowing upon them all attainments in righteousness, he is like a boat to men inasmuch as he conveys them to the further shore of the four flooded streams (of lust, individuality, delusion, and ignorance) [2], he is like a caravan owner to men in that he brings them beyond the sandy desert of rebirths, he is like a mighty rain cloud to men in that he fills their hearts with satisfaction, he is like a teacher to men in that he trains them in all good, he is like a good guide to men in that he points out to them the path of peace. It was in order that so good a man as that, one whose good qualities are so many, so various, so immeasurable, [196] in order that so great a treasure mine of good things, so full of benefit to all beings, might not be done away with, that the Blessed One, O king, out of his mercy towards all beings, laid down that injunction, when he said: "A brother is not, O Bhikkhus, to commit suicide. Whosoever does so shall be dealt with according to the law." This is the reason for which the Blessed One prohibited (self-slaughter). And it was said, O king,

---

[1] Sattânam, in which gods are included.
[2] The four oghas; also called Âsavas. The former term is used of them objectively, the latter subjectively.

by the Elder Kumâra Kassapa, the eloquent, when he was describing to Pâyâsi the Râganya the other world : " So long as Sama*n*as and Brahmans of uprightness of life, and beauty of character, continue to exist—however long that time may be—just so long do they conduct themselves to the advantage and happiness of the great masses of the people, to the good and the gain and the weal of gods and men[1] !" '

15. 'And what is the reason for which the Blessed One instigated us (to put an end to life) ? Birth, O king, is full of pain, and so is old age, and disease, and death. Sorrow is painful, and so is lamentation, and pain, and grief, and despair. Association with the unpleasant is painful, and separation from the pleasant[2]. The death of a mother is painful, or of a father, or a brother, or a sister, or a son, or a wife, or of any relative. Painful is the ruin of one's family, and the suffering of disease, and the loss of wealth, and decline in goodness, and the loss of in-

---

[1] This Kumâra Kassapa is said at Anguttara I, xiv, 3 to have been the most eloquent of the early disciples. Another eloquent little outburst of his is preserved for us in verses 201 and 202 of the Therâ Gâthâ. ' O for the Buddhas, and their doctrines ! O for the achievements of our Master ! Thereby may the disciple realise the Truth. Through countless æons of time has Selfness followed on Selfness. But this one is now the last. This aggregation (of mental and material qualities which forms me now again into an individuality) is at last the end, the end of the coming and going of births and deaths. There will be no rebirth for me !' But where the verses are so full of allusions to the deepest Buddhist psychology, it is impossible to reproduce in English the vigour of the original Pâli. Selfness (Sakkâya) is the condition of being a separate individual.

[2] All this is from the celebrated discourse, the ' Foundation of the Kingdom of Righteousness ' (in ' Buddhist Suttas,' p. 148).

sight. Painful is the fear produced by despots, or by robbers, or by enemies, or by famine, or by fire, or by flood, or by the tidal wave, or by earthquake, or by crocodiles or alligators. Painful is the fear of possible blame attaching to oneself, or to others, the fear of punishment, the fear of misfortune. Painful is the fear arising from shyness in the presence of assemblies of one's fellows, painful is anxiety as to one's means of livelihood, painful the foreboding of death. [**197**] Painful are (the punishments inflicted on criminals), such as being flogged with whips, or with sticks, or with split rods, having one's hands cut off, or one's feet, or one's hands and feet, or one's ears, or one's nose, or one's ears and nose. Painful are (the tortures inflicted on traitors)—being subjected to the Gruel Pot (that is, having boiling gruel poured into one's head from the top of which the skull bone has been removed [1])—or to the Chank Crown [2] (that is, having the scalp rubbed with gravel till it becomes smooth like a polished shell)—or to the Râhu's Mouth [3] (that is, having one's mouth held open by iron pins, and oil put in it, and a wick lighted therein)—or to the Fire Garland [4] or to the Hand Torch [5] (that is, being made a living torch, the whole body, or the arms only, being wrapped up in oily cloths, and set on fire)—or to the Snake Strips [6] (that is, being skinned in strips from the neck to the hips, so that the skin falls in strips round the legs)— or to the Bark Dress [7] (that is, being skinned alive from the neck downwards, and having each strip of

---

[1] Bilanga-thâlika*m*.
[2] Sankha-mu*nd*ika*m*.
[3] Râhu-mukha*m*.
[4] *G*oti-mâlaka*m*.
[5] Hattha-pa*gg*otika*m*.
[6] Eraka-vattika*m*.
[7] *K*îraka-vâsika*m*.

skin as soon as removed tied to the hair, so that these strips form a veil around one)—or to the Spotted Antelope [1] (that is, having one's knees and elbows tied together, and being made to squat on a plate of iron under which a fire is lit)—or to the Flesh-hooks [2] (that is, being hung up on a row of iron hooks)—or to the Pennies [3] (that is, having bits cut out of the flesh, all over the body, of the size of pennies)—or to the Brine Slits [4] (that is, having cuts made all over one's body by means of knives or sharp points, and then having salt and caustic liquids poured over the wounds)—or to the Bar Turn [5] (that is, being transfixed to the ground by a bar of iron passing through the root of the ear, and then being dragged round and round by the leg)—or to the Straw Seat [6] (that is, being so beaten with clubs that

---

[1] E*n*eyyaka*m*.
[2] Balisa-ma*m*sika*m* (so the Si*m*halese, Mr. Trenckner reads Ba*l*isa).
[3] Kahâpa*n*akam.   [4] Khârâpati*kkh*aka*m*.
[5] Paligha-parivattika*m*.
[6] Palâla-pî*th*aka*m*. I follow throughout Hîna*t*i-kumburê's interpretation (pp. 260, 261) of these pretty names, which could be well matched in the West. That some Indian kings were cruel in the extreme is no doubt true. But it must not be supposed that this list gives the names of well-known punishments. It is merely a string of technical terms which is repeated by rote whenever tortures have to be specified. And the meaning of its terms was most likely unknown to the very people who so used them. For the whole list (which is taken by our author from the Pâli Pi*t*akas) is explained by Buddhaghosa in his commentary, the Manoratha Pûra*n*î, on Aṅguttara II, 1, 1, as edited by Dr. Morris at pp. 113, 114 of the first edition of his Aṅguttara for the Pâli Text Society, 1884. But Buddhaghosa's explanations differ from Hîna*t*i-kumburê's in several details; and to nearly half the names he gives alternative meanings, quite contradictory to those that he gives first. So the list had its origin some centuries (say 400–500) B.C., and was certainly

the bones are broken, and the body becomes like a heap of straw)—or to be anointed with boiling oil, or to be eaten by dogs, or to be impaled alive, or to be beheaded. Such and such, O king, are the manifold and various pains which a being caught in the whirlpool of births and rebirths has to endure. Just, O king, as the water rained down upon the Himâlaya mountain flows, in its course along the Ganges, through and over rocks and pebbles and gravel, whirlpools and eddies and rapids[1], and the stumps and branches of trees which obstruct and oppose its passage,—just so has each being caught in the succession of births and rebirths to endure such and such manifold and various pains. Full of pain, then, is the continual succession of rebirths, a joy is it when that succession ends. And it was in pointing out the advantage of that end, the disaster involved in that succession, that the Blessed One, great king, instigated us to get beyond birth, and old age, and disease, and death by the realisation of the final end of that succession of rebirths. This is the sense, O king, which led the Blessed One to instigate us (to put an end to life).'

'Very good, Nâgasena! Well solved is the puzzle (I put), well set forth are the reasons (you alleged). That is so, and I accept it as you say.'

[Here ends the problem as to suicide.]

---

not understood in the fifth century A. D.; and was probably therefore unintelligible also, at least in part, to our author.

[1] Ûmika-vañka-*k*adika. I don't pretend to understand this last word. Dr. Morris, at p. 92 of the 'Pâli Text Society's Journal' for 1884, suggests velika. Perhaps it was simply adika after all, with or without *m* euphonic.

[A LOVING DISPOSITION.]

16. [198] 'Venerable Nâgasena, it has been said by the Blessed One: "Eleven advantages, O brethren, may be anticipated from practising, making a habit of, enlarging within one, using as a means of advancement, and as a basis of conduct, pursuing after, accumulating, and rising well up to the very heights of the emancipation of heart, arising from a feeling of love (towards all beings)[1]. And what are these eleven? He who does so sleeps in peace, and in peace does he awake. He dreams no sinful dreams. He becomes dear to men, and to the beings who are not men[2]. The gods watch over him. Neither fire, nor poison, nor sword works any harm to him. Quickly and easily does he become tranquillised. The aspect of his countenance is calm. Undismayed does he meet death, and should he not press through to the Supreme Condition (of Arahatship), then is he sure of rebirth in the Brahma world[3]." But on the other hand you (members of

---

[1] This same string of words, except the first, is used of the Iddhi-pâdas in the Book of the Great Decease, III, 3 (p. 40 of vol. xi of the S. B. E.). The words 'towards all beings' are not in the text. But this is the meaning of the phrase used, and not love to men only, as would be understood if they were not inserted in the translation.

[2] Amanussa. This means, not the gods, but the various spirits on the earth, nayads, dryads, fairies, &c. &c. As here, so again below, IV, 4, 41, the amanussâ are opposed to the devatâ, mentioned in the next clause here. In older texts the devatâ include the amanussâ.

[3] From the Anguttara Nikâya, Ekâdasa Nipâta; quoted in full, with the context, in the Introductory Story to the 169th Gâtaka (vol. ii, pp. 60, 61 of Professor Fausböll's edition).

the Order) say that " Sâma the Prince, while dwelling in the cultivation of a loving disposition toward all beings, and when he was (in consequence thereof) wandering in the forest followed by a herd of deer, was hit by a poisoned arrow shot by Piliyakkha the king, and there, on the spot, fainted and fell[1]." Now, venerable Nâgasena, if the passage I have quoted from the words of the Blessed One be right, then this statement of yours must be wrong. But if the story of Prince Sâma be right, then it cannot be true that neither fire, nor poison, nor sword can work harm to him who cultivates the habit of love to all beings. This too is a double-edged problem, so subtle, so abstruse, so delicate, and so profound, that the thought of having to solve it might well bring out sweat over the body even of the most subtle-minded of mortals. This problem is now put to you. Unravel this mighty knot[2]. Throw light upon this matter[3] to the accomplishment of the desire of those sons of the Conqueror who shall arise hereafter[4].'

'The Blessed One spake, O king, as you have quoted. And Prince Sâma dwelling in the cultivation of love, and thus followed by a herd of deer when he was wandering in the forest, was hit by the poisoned arrow shot by king Piliyakkha, and then and there fainted and fell. But there is a reason for that. [199] And what is the reason? Simply that those virtues (said in the passage you quoted

---

[1] Mr. Trenckner points out that this story is given in the 540th Gâtaka.

[2] See p. 105 of the text.

[3] *K*akkhum dehi. So also p. 95 of the text.

[4] Nibbâhana; not in Childers, but see p. 119 of the text.

to be in the habit of love) are virtues not attached to the personality of the one who loves, but to the actual presence of the love that he has called up in his heart[1]. And when Prince Sâma was upsetting the water-pot, that moment he lapsed from the actual feeling of love. At the moment, O king, in which an individual has realised the sense of love, that moment neither fire, nor poison, nor sword can do him harm. If any men bent on doing him an injury come up, they will not see him, neither will they have a chance of hurting him. But these virtues, O king, are not inherent in the individual, they are in the actual felt presence of the love that he is calling up in his heart.'

'Suppose, O king, a man were to take into his hand a Vanishing Root of supernatural power; and that, so long as it was actually in his hand, no other ordinary person would be able to see him. The virtue, then, would not be in the man. It would be in the root that such virtue would reside that an object in the very line of sight of ordinary mortals could, nevertheless, not be seen. Just so, O king, is it with the virtue inherent in the felt presence of love that a man has called up in his heart.'

'Or it is like the case of a man [200] who has entered into a well-formed mighty cave. No storm of rain, however mightily it might pour down, would be able to wet him. But that would be by no virtue inherent

---

[1] Bhânanâ is really more than 'cultivation.' It is the actual, present, felt sense of the particular moral state that is being cultivated (in this case, of love). I have elsewhere rendered it 'meditation': but as the ethical doctrine, and practice, are alike unknown to us, we have no word that exactly reproduces the connotation of the Pâli phrase.

in the man. It would be a virtue inherent in the cave that so mighty a downpour of rain could not wet the man. And just so, O king, is it with the virtue inherent in the felt presence of love that a man has called up in his heart[1].'

---

[1] This is no quibble. The early Buddhists did believe in the power of a subjective love over external circumstances. It is true that the best known instances in which this power is represented as having been actually exercised, are instances of the power of love over the hearts of other beings, and hence, indirectly, over their actions. Thus when Devadatta had had the fierce, manslaying elephant Nâlâgiri let loose against the Buddha (*K*ullavagga VII, 3, 11, 12), Gotama is said to have permeated him with his love, and the elephant then went up to him only to salute him, and allowed himself to be stroked, and did no harm. And when the five disciples had intended, when he went to Benares, to show him no respect, the Buddha, in like manner, is said to have ' concentrated that feeling of his love which was able to pervade generally all beings in earth and heaven,' and to have 'directed it specially towards them.' Then ' the sense of his love diffused itself through their hearts. And as he came nearer and nearer, unable any longer to adhere to their resolve, they rose from their seats, and bowed down before him, and welcomed him with every mark of reverence and of respect' ('Buddhist Birth Stories,' vol. i, p. 112).

And when he wished to convert Ro*g*a the Mallian, the Buddha is said, in like manner, to have 'suffused him with the feeling of his love.' And then Ro*g*a, ' overcome by the Blessed One by the sense of his love—just as a young calf follows the kine, so did he go from apartment to apartment' seeking the Blessed One (Mahâvagga VI, 36, 4).

And again, when the Bhikkhus told the Buddha of a brother having been killed by a snake-bite, he is represented (in the *K*ullavagga V, 6) to have said : ' Now surely that brother had not let his love flow out over the four royal kinds of serpents. Had he done so, he would not have died of the bite of a snake.' And then he is said to have enjoined the use of a poem of love to snakes (set out in the text quoted) as a safeguard against snake-bite. This goes really much further than the other instances, but no case is given of that safeguard having been actually used successfully. And I know of no case in the Pâli Pi*t*akas of the felt presence

'Most wonderful is it, Nâgasena, and most strange how the felt presence of love has the power of warding off all evil states of mind [1].'

'Yes! The practice of love is productive of all virtuous conditions of mind both in good (beings) and in evil ones. To all beings whatsoever, who are in the bonds of conscious existence [2], is this practice of love of great advantage, and therefore ought it to be sedulously cultivated.'

[Here ends the problem as to the power of love.]

[DEVADATTA.]

17. 'Venerable Nâgasena, is the consequence the same to him who does good and to him who does evil, or is there any difference in the two cases?'

'There is a difference, O king, between good and evil. Good works have a happy result, and lead to Sagga [3], and evil works have an unhappy result, and lead to Niraya [4].'

---

of the feeling of love being said to have actually counteracted either fire, or poison, or sword.

It is noteworthy that the Siṃhalese inserts here six pages (265-271) of matter not found in the Pâli. But as it gives at length the story of Prince Sâma, it is taken, I presume, from the Gâtaka book.

[1] This is something quite different from what was said before.

[2] Ye viññana-baddhâ, sabbesaṃ, which the Siṃhalese takes as a gloss on 'good and evil ones,' and renders viññâna prati wûda. But I prefer Mr. Trenckner's punctuation.

[3] That is to a temporary life in heaven.

[4] That is to life in a temporary hell (or purgatory).

'But, venerable Nâgasena, your people say that Devadatta was altogether wicked, full of wicked dispositions, and that the Bodisat[1] was altogether pure, full of pure dispositions[2]. And yet Devadatta, through successive existences[3], was not only quite equal to the Bodisat, but even sometimes superior to him, both in reputation and in the number of his adherents.

18. 'Thus, Nâgasena, when Devadatta became the Purohita (family Brâhman, royal chaplain) of Brahmadatta, the king, in the city of Benares, then the Bodisat was a wretched Ka*nd*âla (outcast)[4] who knew by heart a magic spell. And by repeating his spell he produced mango fruits out of season[5]. This

---

[1] Bodhi-satto (Wisdom-Child). The individual who (through virtue practised in successive li.es) was becoming the Buddha.

[2] 'Wicked' and 'pure' are in the Pâli ka*n*he and sukka, literally, 'dark' and 'light.' The only other passage I recollect where these names of colours are used in an ethical sense is the 87th verse of the Dhammapada. Professor Max Müller there renders: 'A wise man should lea·e the d..rk state (of ordinary life), and follow the bright state (of the Bhikshu),' (S. B. E., vol. x, p. 26.) But the words should certainly be translated: 'A wise man should put away wicked dispositions, and cultivate purity of heart.' Bhâvetha could never refer to adopting or following any outward profession. It is exclusively used of the practice, cultivation, of inward feelings. And the commentary, which is quoted by Professor Fausböll, takes the passage in the Dhammapada in that sense, just as Hina/i-kumburê (p. 271) does here.

[3] Bhave bhave, which would be more accurately rendered 'in the course of his gradual becoming.'

[4] *K*avaka-ka*nd*âla. The *K*a*nd*âlas are a well-known caste still existing in India—if indeed that can rightly be called a caste which is beneath all others. *Kh*avaka is not in Childers, but is applied below (p. 256 of our text) to Mâra, the Buddhist Satan. See also the next note.

[5] This is not a summary of the 309th *G*âtaka, for it differs from that story as published by Professor Fausböll (vol. iii, pp.

is one case in which the Bodisat was inferior to Devadatta in birth, [201] inferior to him in reputation.'

19. 'And again, when Devadatta became a king, a mighty monarch of the earth [1], living in the enjoyment of all the pleasures of sense, then the Bodisat was an elephant, decked with all manner of ornaments that the king might make use of them. And the king, being put out of temper at the sight of his graceful and pleasant style of pace and motion, said to the elephant trainer with the hope of bringing about the death of the elephant: "Trainer, this elephant has not been properly trained, make him perform the trick called 'Sky walking.'" In that case too the Bodisat was inferior to Devadatta,—was a mere foolish animal [2].'

20. 'And again, when Devadatta became a man who gained his living by winnowing grain [3], then

---

217–30), and also from the older and shorter version contained in the Old Commentary on the Pâtimokkha (on the 69th Sakhiya, Vinaya IV, pp. 203, 204). [The name of that story in Professor Fausböll's edition is *Khavaka-Gâtaka*, but throughout the story itself the word *Kandâla* is used in the passages corresponding to those in which Professor Fausböll has *Khapaka* (sic),—a coincidence which throws light on our author, *Khavaka-kandâla*.] The story here referred to is the Amba Gâtaka (No. 474) in which the word *Khavaka* does not occur.

[1] 'Of Magadha,' says Hînati-kumburê (p. 272).

[2] This is the 122nd Gâtaka, there called the Dummedha Gâtaka. The king has the elephant taken to the top of the Vepulla mountain outside Râgagaha. Then having made him stand first on three feet, then on two, then on one, he demands of the trainer to make him stand in the air. Then the elephant flies away to Benares!

[3] Pavane natthâyiko. But as Hînati-kumburê renders all this: 'a farmer in Benares who gained his living by husbandry,' I would suggest pavanena tthâyiko as the right reading.

the Bodisat was a monkey called "the broad earth." Here again we have the difference between an animal and a man, and the Bodisat was inferior in birth to Devadatta[1].'

21. 'And again, when Devadatta became a man, by name So*n*uttara, a Nesâda (one of an outcast tribe of aborigines, who lived by hunting), and was of great strength and bodily power, like an elephant, then the Bodisat was the king of elephants under the name of the "Six-tusked." And in that birth, the hunter slew the elephant. In that case too Devadatta was the superior[2].'

22. 'And again, when Devadatta became a man, a wanderer in the woods, without a home, then the Bodisat was a bird, a partridge who knew the Vedic hymns. And in that birth too the woodman killed the bird. So in that case also Devadatta was the superior by birth[3].'

23. 'And again, when Devadatta became the king of Benares, by name Kalâbu, then the Bodisat was an ascetic who preached kindness to animals. And the king (who was fond of sport), enraged with the ascetic, had his hands and feet cut off like so many bambû sprouts[4]. In that birth, too, Deva-

---

[1] I cannot unfortunately trace this story among the *G*âtakas.

[2] I do not know which *G*âtaka is here referred to.

[3] This must be the 438th *G*âtaka, there called the Tittira *G*âtaka. In the summary Devadatta is identified with the hypocritical ascetic who killed and ate the wise partridge.

[4] This is the 313th *G*âtaka, there called the Khanti-vadi *G*âtaka. The royal sportsman has first the skin, and then the hands and feet of the sage cut off, to alter his opinions. But the sage simply says that his love to animals is not in his skin, or in his limbs, but in his heart. Then the earth swallows up the cruel monarch, and the citizens bury the body of the sage with all honour. In the summary Kalâbu, the king, is identified with Devadatta.

datta was the superior, both in birth and in reputation among men.'

24. 'And again, when Devadatta became a man, a woodman, then the Bodisat was Nandiya the monkey king. And in that birth too the man killed the monkey, and his mother besides, and his younger brother. So in that case also it was Devadatta who was the superior in birth [1].'

25. 'And again, when Devadatta became a man, a naked ascetic, by name Kârambhiya, then the Bodisat was a snake king called "the Yellow one." So in that case too it was Devadatta [202] who was the superior in birth [2].'

26. 'And again, when Devadatta became a man, a crafty ascetic with long matted hair, then the Bodisat was a famous pig, by name "the Carpenter." So in that case too it was Devadatta who was the superior in birth [3].'

27. 'And again, when Devadatta became a king among the *K*etas, by name Sura Pari*k*ara [4], who had the power of travelling through the air at a level above men's heads [5], then the Bodisat was a Brah-

---

[1] This is the 222nd *G*âtaka, there called the *K*ûla Nandiya *G*âtaka.

[2] This is probably the 518th *G*âtaka. See Mr. Trenckner's note.

[3] This must be the 492nd *G*âtaka, the Ta*kkh*a-sûkara *G*âtaka, in which the hero is a learned pig who helps the carpenter in his work, and the villain of the story is a hypocrite ascetic with matted hair. But it should be added that though in the summary (Fausböll, vol. iv, p. 350) Devadatta is identified with the ascetic, the Bodisat is identified, not with the learned pig, but with the dryad.

[4] He is called Upa*k*ara both in the 422nd *G*âtaka (of which this is a summary) and in the Sumaṅgala (p. 258). The *G*âtaka (III, 454) also gives a third variation, Apa*k*ara.

[5] Purisamatto gagane vehâsaṅgamo. The *G*âtaka says simply upari*k*aro, which must mean about the same.

man named Kapila. So in that case too it was Devadatta who was the superior in birth and in reputation.'

28. 'And again, when Devadatta became a man, by name Sâma, then the Bodisat was a king among the deer, by name Ruru. So in that case too it was Devadatta who was the superior in birth [1].'

29. 'And again, when Devadatta became a man, a hunter wandering in the woods, then the Bodisat was a male elephant, and that hunter seven times broke off and took away the teeth of the elephant. So in that case too it was Devadatta who was the superior in respect of the class of beings into which he was born [2].'

30. 'And again, when Devadatta became a jackal who wanted to conquer the world [3], and brought the kings of all the countries in India under his control, then the Bodisat was a wise man, by name Vidhura. So in that case too it was Devadatta who was the superior in glory.'

31. 'And again, when Devadatta became the

---

[1] This must be the 482nd Gâtaka. It is true that the man is there called Mahâ Dhanaka (Fausböll, vol. iii, p. 255), and the Bodisat is not specially named Ruru, nor is he a king of the herd, but is only a stag of the kind of deer called Ruru, who lives alone. But a comparison of the poetical version of the same story in the Kariyâ Pitaka II, 6 (p. 87 of Dr. Morris's edition for the Pâli Text Society) shows that the same story is here referred to.

[2] This is the 72nd Gâtaka, the Sîlava Nâga Gâtaka. (Fausböll, vol. i, p. 319.)

[3] Khattiya-dhammo; literally, 'who had the nature of a Kshatriya.' This expression is not found in the Gâtaka referred to, No. 241 (vol. ii, p. 242 and foll. in Professor Fausböll's edition), and the Bodisat is there called purdhita not pandita, and his name is not given as Vidhura. The jackal also came to grief in his attempt to conquer Benares. But there is no doubt as to that story, the Sabba Dâtha Gâtaka being the one here quoted.

elephant who destroyed the young of the Chinese partridge, then the Bodisat was also an elephant, the leader of his herd. So in that case they were both on a par¹.'

32. 'And again, when Devadatta became a yakkha, by name Unrighteous, then the Bodisat too was a yakkha, by name Righteous. So in that case too they were both on a par².'

33. 'And again, when Devadatta became a sailor, the chief of five hundred families, then the Bodisat too was a sailor, the chief of five hundred families. So in that case too they were both on a par³.'

34. 'And again, when Devadatta became a caravan leader, the lord of five hundred waggons, then the Bodisat too was a caravan leader, the lord of five hundred waggons. So in that case too they were both on a par⁴.'

35. [203] 'And again, when Devadatta became a king of deer, by name Sâkha, then the Bodisat was a king of deer, by name Nigrodha. So in that case too they were both on a par⁵.'

36. 'And again, when Devadatta became a commander-in-chief, by name Sâkha, then the Bodisat

---

¹ This is the 357th Gâtaka (Fausböll, vol. iii, pp. 174) and which is one of those illustrated on the Bharhut Tope (Cunningham, Plate 109).

² In the Gâtaka text (No. 457, Fausböll, vol. iv, pp. 100 and foll.), there are both devaputtâ, 'gods,' not yakkhâ. This is by no means the only instance of the term yakkha being used of gods.

³ I cannot trace this story in the printed text of the Gâtakas.

⁴ This is the Apa*nn*aka Gâtaka (No. 1, vol. i, pp. 98 and foll. in Professor Fausböll's edition), translated in the 'Buddhist Birth Stories,' vol. i, pp. 138-145.

⁵ The Nigrodha Miga Gâtaka (No. 12, vol. i, pp. 145 and foll. in Fausböll), translated in 'Buddhist Birth Stories,' vol. i, pp. 198 and following.

was a king, by name Nigrodha. So in that case too they were both on a par[1].'

37. 'And again, when Devadatta became a brahman, by name Khandahâla, then the Bodisat was a prince, by name Kanda. So in that case that Khandahâla was the superior[2].'

38. 'And again, when Devadatta became a king, by name Brahmadatta, then the Bodisat was his son, the prince called Mahâ Paduma. In that case the king had his son cast down seven times, from the precipice from which robbers were thrown down. And inasmuch as fathers are superior to and above their sons, in that case too it was Devadatta was the superior[3].'

39. 'And again, when Devadatta became a king, by name Mahâ Patâpa, then the Bodisat was his son, Prince Dhamma-pâla; and that king had the hands and feet and head of his son cut off. So in that case too Devadatta was the superior[4].'

40. 'And now again, in this life, they were in the Sâkya clan, and the Bodisat became a Buddha, all wise, the leader of the world, and Devadatta having left the world to join the Order founded by Him who is above the god of gods, and having attained to the powers of Iddhi, was filled with lust to become himself the Buddha. Come now, most venerable Nâgasena! Is not all that I have said true, and just, and accurate?'

---

[1] The Nigrodha Gâtaka (No. 445, Fausböll, vol. iv, pp. 37 and foll.).

[2] I cannot trace this story among the published Gâtakas.

[3] This is the Mahâ Paduma Gâtaka (No. 472, Fausböll, vol. iv, pp. 187–195). It was a case of Joseph and Potiphar's wife.

[4] This tragical story is No. 358 in the Gâtaka collection (Fausböll, vol. iii, pp. 177–182).

41. 'All the many things which you, great king, have now propounded, are so, and not otherwise.'

'Then, Nâgasena, unless black and white are the same in kind, it follows that good and evil bear equal fruit.'

'Nay, not so, great king! Good and evil have not the same result. Devadatta was opposed by everybody. No one was hostile to the Bodisat. And the hostility which Devadatta felt towards the Bodisat, that came to maturity and bore fruit in each successive birth. And so also as Devadatta, when he was established in lordship over the world, [204] was a protection to the poor, put up bridges and courts of justice and rest-houses for the people, and gave gifts according to his bent to Samaṇas and Brahmans, to the poor and needy and the wayfarers, it was by the result of that conduct that, from existence to existence, he came into the enjoyment of so much prosperity. For of whom, O king, can it be said that without generosity and self-restraint, without self-control and the observance of the Uposatha[1], he can reach prosperity?

'And when, O king, you say that Devadatta and the Bodisat accompanied one another in the passage from birth to birth, that meeting together of theirs took place not only at the end of a hundred, or a thousand, or a hundred thousand births, but was in fact constantly and frequently taking place through an immeasurable period of time[2]. For you should regard that matter in the light of the comparison drawn by the Blessed One between the case of the

---

[1] The Buddhist Sabbath, on which see my 'Manual of Buddhism,' pp. 139-141.

[2] So also above, IV, 2, 64, and IV, 3, 28.

purblind tortoise and the attainment of the condition of a human being. And it was not only with Devadatta that such union took place. Sâriputta the Elder also, O king, was through thousands of births the father, or the grandfather, or the uncle [1], or the brother, or the son, or the nephew, or the friend of the Bodisat; and the Bodisat was the father, or the grandfather, or the uncle, or the brother, or the son, or the nephew, or the friend of Sâriputta the Elder.

'All beings in fact, O king, who, in various forms as creatures, are carried down the stream of transmigration, meet, as they are whirled along in it, both with pleasant companions and with disagreeable ones—just as water whirled along in a stream meets with pure and impure substances, with the beautiful and with the ugly.

'And when, O king, Devadatta as the god, had been himself Unrighteous, and had led others into unrighteousness of life, he was burnt in purgatory for an immeasurable period of time [2]. [205] But the Bodisat, who, as the god, had been himself Righteous, and had led others into righteousness of life, lived in all the bliss of heaven for a like immeasurable period of time. And whilst in this life, Devadatta, who had plotted injury against the Buddha, and had created a schism in the Order, was swallowed up by the earth, the Tathâgata,

---

[1] That is 'father's younger brother.' The Pâli has no word for uncle generally, the whole scheme of relationship being different from ours, and the various sorts of uncles having, in the Pâli scheme, different and distinct names.

[2] 'Fifty-seven ko/is and sixty hundreds of thousands of years,' says the text, with touching accuracy.

knowing all that can be known, arrived at the insight of Buddhahood[1], and was completely set free (from the necessity of becoming) by the destruction of all that leads to re-existence.'

'Very good, Nâgasena! That is so, and I accept it as you say[2].'

[Here ends the dilemma as to Devadatta's superiority to the Bodisat in previous births.]

---

[1] So Hîna/i-kumburê, who takes sabbadhamme as accusative to bugg*h*itvâ, and understands the phrase as above translated.

[2] This discussion is very interesting, both as a specimen of casuistry, and as an exposition of orthodox Buddhist belief. And it is full of suggestion if taken as a statement of the kind of reason which led the Buddhist editors of the earlier folk-lore to identify Devadatta with the characters referred to by king Milinda. But the facts are that those editors, in using the old stories and legends for their ethical purposes, always identified Devadatta with the cruel person in the story, and paid no heed to the question whether he was superior or not in birth or in the consideration of the world, to the person they identified with the Bodisat. In searching through the four volumes of the published *G*âtakas, and the proof-sheets of the fifth volume with which Professor Fausböll has favoured me, for the purpose of tracing the stories referred to by our author, I find that Devadatta appears in sixty-four of them, and that in almost every one of these sixty-four he is either superior in birth, or equal to the character identified with the Bodisat. This is not surprising, for it is not unusually the superiors in birth who are guilty of the kind of cruelty and wickedness which the Buddhist editors would ascribe to Devadatta. So that our author, had he chosen to do so, might have adduced many other instances of a similar kind to those he actually quotes. I add in an appendix the full list of the Devadatta stories in the *G*âtakas. It is clear our author had before him a version of the *G*âtaka book slightly different from our own, as will be seen from the cases pointed out in the notes in which, as to names or details, the story known to him differs from the printed text. And also that here (as at III, 6, 2) he would have been able to solve his own dilemma much better if he had known more of the history of those sacred books on the words of which it is based.

[WOMEN'S WILES.]

42. 'Venerable Nâgasena, it has been said by the Blessed One:
"With opportunity, and secrecy,
And the right woo'r, all women will go wrong—
Aye, failing others, with a cripple even [1]."
But on the other hand it is said: "Mahosadha's wife, Amarâ, when left behind in the village while her husband was away on a journey, remained alone and in privacy, and regarding her husband as a man would regard his sovran lord, she refused to do wrong, even when tempted with a thousand pieces [2]." Now if the first of these passages be correct, the second must be wrong; and if the second be right, [206] the first must be wrong. This too is a double-edged problem now put to you, and you have to solve it.'

43. 'It is so said, O king, as you have quoted, touching the conduct of Amarâ, Mahosadha's wife. But the question is would she have done wrong, on receipt of those thousand pieces, with the right man: or would she not have done so, if she had had the opportunity, and the certainty of secrecy, and a suitable wooer? Now, on considering the matter, that lady Amarâ was not certain of any of these

---

[1] It is not meant that men would not. But that is too clear to be even worthy of mention, whereas with regard to women the question is worth discussion. Our author is mistaken in ascribing this verse to the Buddha. It is only found (as has been pointed out by Mr. Trenckner) in a *G*âtaka story, No. 536, and is a specimen, not of Buddhist teaching, but of Indian folk-lore. There is a very similar sentiment in *G*âtaka, No. 62 (vol. i, p. 289).

[2] This story will be found in the Ummagga *G*âtaka, No. 546.

things. Through her fear of censure in this world the opportunity seemed to her not fit, and through her fear of the sufferings of purgatory in the next world. And because she knew how bitter is the fruit of wrong-doing, and because she did not wish to lose her loved one, and because of the high esteem in which she held her husband, and because she honoured goodness, and despised ignobleness of life, and because she did not want to break with her customary mode of life—for all these reasons the opportunity seemed to her not fit.

'And, further, she refused to do wrong because, on consideration, she was not sure of keeping the thing secret from the world. [207] For even could she have kept it secret from men, yet she could not have concealed it from spirits [1]—even could she have kept it secret from spirits, yet she could not have concealed it from those recluses who have the power of knowing the thoughts of others—even could she have kept it secret from them, yet she could not have concealed it from those of the gods who can read the hearts of men—even could she have kept it secret from the gods, yet she could not have escaped, herself, from the knowledge of her sin—even could she have remained ignorant of it herself, yet she could not have kept it secret from (the law of the result which follows on) unrighteousness[2]. Such were the

---

[1] Fairies, nayad, dryads, &c. &c.—not gods.
[2] Adhammena raho na labheyya. I am in great doubt as to the real meaning of these words, which Hînaṭi-kumburê (p. 286) renders merely adharmayen rahasak no labannê. They look very much like a kind of personification of Karma. The phrase is really very parallel to the saying in Numbers xxxii. 23, 'Be sure your sin will find you out'—namely, in its results—and is as true ethically as it is difficult grammatically.

'various reasons which led her to abstain from doing wrong because she could not be sure of secrecy.

'And, further, she refused to do wrong because, on consideration, she found no right wooer. Mahosadha the wise, O king, was endowed with the eight and twenty qualities. And which are those twenty-eight? He was brave, O king, and full of modesty, and ashamed to do wrong, he had many adherents, and many friends, he was forgiving, he was upright in life, he was truthful, he was pure in word, and deed and heart [1], he was free from malice, he was not puffed up, he felt no jealousy [2], he was full of energy, he strove after all good things [3], he was popular with all men, he was generous, he was friendly [4], he was humble in disposition, he was free from guile, he was free from deceit, he was full of insight, he was of high reputation, he had much knowledge, he sought after the good of those dependent on him, his praise was in all men's mouths, great was his wealth, and great his fame. Such were the twenty-eight qualities, O king, with which Mahosadha, the wise, was endowed. And it was because she found no wooer like unto him that she did no wrong [5].'

---

[1] Soķeyya-sampanno, which Hînaṭi-kumburê renders suvaķa guṇayen samanwibawa: that is, 'compliant, attentive to what is said.' But I prefer to take the expression in the sense explained at length in Aṅguttara III, 119. See also Gâtaka I, 214; Milinda, p. 115.

[2] Anusuyyako. See Gâtaka II, 192, and Milinda, p. 94.

[3] Âyûhako. Hînaṭi-kumburê (p. 286) renders this word, which is only found here, by Dhana piris rœs kirîm œtteya, 'one who has heaped up goods and men.' But see Milinda, p. 181, and Dr. Morris in the Pâli Text Society's Journals for 1885 and 1886.

[4] Sakhilo, 'kindly in speech,' says the Siṃhalese.

[5] This is all very well, but it does not confirm, it explains away, the supposed quotation from the Buddha's words.

'Very good, Nâgasena! That is so, and I accept it as you say.'

[Here ends the dilemma as to the wickedness of women[1].]

[ON THE FEARLESSNESS OF THE ARAHATS.]

44. 'Venerable Nâgasena, it was said by the Blessed One: " The Arahats have laid aside all fear and trembling[2]." But on the other hand when, in the city of Râgagaha, they saw Dhana-pâlaka, the man-slaying elephant, bearing down upon the Blessed

---

[1] The position of women in India, at the time when Buddhism arose, was, theoretically, very low. The folk tales are full of stories turning on the wiles of women, and the Hindoo law-books seem never tired of the theme of her uncleanness, her weakness, and her wickedness. But, except in matters of property, the bark was I think worse than the bite. Among the people, in the homes of the peasantry, the philippics of the Brahmin priests were not much regarded, and the women led lives as pleasant as those of their male relations, and shared in such mental and physical advantages as their male relations enjoyed. The influence of Buddhism must have been felt in two directions. In the first place the importance attached to the celibate life must have encouraged the kind of view taken of women among Catholics in mediæval times (the Brahmin view being much akin to those that were promulgated by Luther). On the other hand the fact that women were admitted to the Order, and that the still higher aim of Arahatship was held to be attainable by them, must have helped to encourage a high esteem for women. We have many instances of women who were credited with the insight of Arahatship. A whole treatise in the Buddhist sacred books, the Theri Gâtha, is devoted to hymns and poems ascribed to them, and many of these reach a very high level of intelligent and spiritual emotion.

[2] I do not know the exact passage referred to, but there are many of similar tendency in the sacred books. See, for instance, Dhammapada, verses 39, 188, 214, 351, and 385; and Sutta Nipâta, verses 15, 70, 212, 621, and 965.

One, all the five hundred Arahats forsook the Conqueror and fled, one only excepted, Ânanda the Elder[1]. Now how was it, Nâgasena? Did those Arahats run away from fear—or did they run away willing to let the Blessed One be destroyed, and thinking : " (Our conduct) will be clear (to him) from the way in which he himself will act[2]," [208] or did they run away with the hope of watching the immense and unequalled mighty power which the Tathâgata would exhibit ? If, Nâgasena, what the

---

[1] Here again we have a variation between our author's words and those of the Pi/akas. In the Kullavagga VII, 3, 11, 12 (translated in pp. 247–250 of vol. iii of the 'Vinaya Texts' in the 'Sacred Books of the East'), we have the oldest versions of this story; and there the elephant is called, not Dhana-pâlaka, but Nâlâgiri, and the number of attendant disciples (who are not called Arahats) is not given as five hundred. The Buddha is simply said to have entered Râgagaha 'with a number of Bhikkhus.' Nothing also is said, either of their running away, or of Ânanda's remaining behind. It is, no doubt, an easily explicable and very pretty alteration of the story, which exhibits Ânanda, the beloved disciple, as acting in this way. But it is none the less an alteration.

It should be added that Nâlâgiri (it should be Nâ/âgiri) in the Vinaya text is a personal name of the elephant, but may be derived from its place of origin. (See the references to a famous elephant named Na/âgiri in the Megha Dûta and Nadâgiri in the Kathâ Sarit Sâgara XI, 42, XII, 10, XIII, 7, 29. But Pâṇini VI, 3, 117, gives the latter as the name of a mountain.) So while there may be a variation in the legend, it may also be that we have only two names for the same elephant, just as one might speak of the Shetland pony (named) Brownie. And the stanza quoted below (p. 410 of the Pâli text) shows that the name Dhana-pâlaka was given already in older texts to the Nâ/âgiri elephant.

[2] Paññâyissati sakena kammena, 'It will be plain to the Buddha (that is, he will be able to judge of our motives) from his own kindness and goodness,' according to the Siṃhalese (p. 287). But the expression is a very strange one, and perhaps, after all, it merely means, 'The matter will turn out according to his Karma.'

Blessed One said as to the Arahats being devoid of fear be true, then this story must be false. But if the story be true, then the statement that the Arahats have put away fear and trembling must be false. This too is a double-edged problem now put to you, and you have to solve it.'

45. 'The Blessed One did say, O king, that Arahats have put away all fear and trembling, and five hundred Arahats, save only Ânanda, did, as you say, run away when the elephant Dhana-pâlaka bore down upon the Tathâgata that day in Râgagaha. But that was neither out of fear, nor from willingness to let the Blessed One be destroyed. For the cause by which Arahats could be made to fear or tremble has been destroyed in them, and therefore are they free from fear or trembling. Is the broad earth, O king, afraid at people digging into it, or breaking it up, or at having to bear the weight of the mighty oceans and the peaked mountain ranges?'

'Certainly not, Sir.'

'But why not?'

'Because there is no cause in the broad earth which could produce fear or trembling.'

'Just so, O king. And neither is there any such cause in Arahats. And would a mountain peak be afraid of being split up, or broken down, or made to fall, or burnt with fire?'

'Certainly not, Sir.'

'But why not?' [209]

'The cause of fear or trembling does not exist within it.'

'And just so, O king, with Arahats. If all the creatures of various outward form in the whole universe[1] were, together, to attack one Arahat in order to put him to fear, yet would they bring about no variation in his heart. And why? Because there is neither condition nor cause for fear (in him, whence fear could arise). Rather, O king, was it these considerations that arose in the minds of those Arahats: "To-day when the best of the best of men, the hero among conquerors, has entered into the famous city, Dhana-pâlaka the elephant will rush down the street. But to a certainty the brother who is his special attendant will not forsake him who is above the god of gods. But if we should not go away, then neither will the goodness of Ânanda be made manifest, nor will the elephant actually approach[2] the Tathâgata. Let us then withdraw. Thus will great masses of the people attain to emancipation from the bonds of evil, and the goodness of Ânanda be made manifest." It was on the realisation of the fact that those advantages would arise from their doing so, that the Arahats withdrew to every side.'

'Well, Nâgasena, have you solved the puzzle. That is so. The Arahats feared not, nor did they tremble. But for the advantages that they foresaw they withdrew on every side.'

[Here ends the problem as to the panic of the Arahats.]

---

[1] Literally, 'In the hundreds of thousands of world systems.'
[2] A*tth*ânam-anavakâsata*y*a, 'Because of the absence of condition and opportunity.'

[ON CAUSING THE OMNISCIENT ONE TO CHANGE HIS MIND.]

46. 'Venerable Nâgasena, your people say that the Tathâgata is all wise [1]. And on the other hand they say: "When the company of the members of the Order presided over by Sâriputta and Moggallâna had been dismissed by the Blessed One [2], then the Sâkyas of Kâtumâ and Brahmâ Sabanipati, by means of the parables of the seed and of the calf, gained the Buddha over, and obtained his forgiveness, and made him see the thing in the right light [3]." Now how was that, Nâgasena? Were those two parables unknown to him that he should be [210] appeased and gained over to their side, and brought to see the matter in a new light? But if he did not already know them, then, Nâgasena, he was not all-wise. If he did know them, then he must have dismissed those brethren rudely and violently [4] in order to try them; and therein is his unkindness made manifest. This too is a double-edged problem now put to you, and you have to solve it.'

47. 'The Tathâgata, O king, was all-wise, and yet, pleased at those parables, he was gained over by them, he granted pardon to the brethren he had sent

---

[1] This question is also discussed above, III, 6, 2.
[2] This episode has already been referred to above, and will be found set out in full in the *K*âtumâ Sutta, No. 67, in the Ma*ggh*ima Nikâya (pp. 456–462 of Mr. Trenckner's edition for the Pâli Text Society).
[3] Ni*ggh*atta*m* aka*m*su. Compare *G*âtaka, vol. i, p. 495.
[4] Okassa pasayha, which the Si*m*halese (p. 289) renders âka*ddh*anaya ko*t*a abhibhavanaya karanâ. See Dr. Morris in the 'Journal of the Pâli Text Society,' 1887, p. 148.

away, and he saw the matter in the light (in which the intercessors on their behalf wished him to see it). For the Tathâgata, O king, is lord of the Scriptures. It was with parables that had been first preached by the Tathâgata himself[1] that they conciliated him, pleased him, gained him over, and it was on being thus gained over that he signified his approval (of what they had said). It was, O king, as when a wife conciliates, and pleases, and gains over her husband by means of things that belong to the husband himself; and the husband signifies his approval thereof. Or it was, O king, as when the royal barber conciliates and pleases and gains over the king when he dresses the king's head with the golden comb[2] which belongs to the king himself, and the king then signifies his approval thereof. Or it was, O king, as when an attendant novice, when he serves his teacher with the food given in alms which his teacher has himself brought home, conciliates him and pleases him and gains him over, and the teacher then signifies his approval thereof.'

'Very good, Nâgasena! That is so, and I accept it as you say.'

[Here ends the problem as to the all-wise Buddha being gained over by intercession[3].]

Here ends the Fourth Chapter.

---

[1] This is quite correct. They are in the fourth book of the Aṅguttara Sutta, No. 13.

[2] Paṇaka, a word only found in this passage. Hînaṭi-kumburê (p. 280 at the end) renders it ran panâwen.

[3] Other cruxes arising out of the dogma of the Buddha's omniscience are discussed above, III, 6, 2.

APPENDIX.

DEVADATTA IN THE *GÂTAKAS*.

No. of *G*âtaka.	Character filled by Devadatta.	Character filled by the Bodisat.
1	Merchant	Merchant
3	,,	,,
11	Deer (Kâ*l*a)	His father
12	Deer (Sâkha)	Deer (Nigrodha)
20	Water sprite	Monkey
21	Hunter	Kurunga deer
33	Quail	Quail
51	Minister	King
57	Crocodile	Monkey king
58	Monkey king	His son
72	Woodman	Elephant
73	King	King
113	Jackal	Tree god
122	King	Elephant
131	Piliya	Sa*m*kha
139	Fisherman	Tree god
141	Chameleon	Iguana
142	Drunkard	Jackal
143	Jackal	Lion
160	Vinîlaka (a crow)	King of Videha
168	Hawk	Quail
174	Monkey	Brahman
184	Groom	Minister
193	Cripple	King Paduma
194	King	Countryman
204	Crow	Crow
206	Hunter	Kurunga deer
208	Crocodile	Monkey
210	Bird	Bird
220	Unjust judge	Just judge
221	Hunter	Elephant
222	,,	Nandiya (monkey king)
231	Elephant trainer	Elephant trainer

240	King Piṅgala	Prince
241	Jackal	Minister
243	Musician	Musician
277	Ascetic	Pigeon
294	Jackal	Tree god
295	„	„ „
303	Lion	Bird
313	King Kalâbu	Kuṇḍaka (a brahman)
326	Brahman	God
329	Káḷabâhu (a woodman)	Parrot
335	Jackal	Lion
342	Crocodile	Monkey
353	Piṅgiya (a purohit)	Teacher
357	Mad elephant	Elephant king
358	King Patâpa	His son
367	Doctor	Hag
389	Crow	Brahman
397	Jackal	Lion
404	Monkey king	Monkey king
416	King of Benares	His son
422	King of Ketiya	Brahman
438	Ascetic	Partridge
445	Sâkha (a minister)	Nigrodha (a king)
448	Hawk	Cock
457	Adhamma (a god)	Dhamma (a god)
466	Carpenter	Carpenter
472	King of Benares	Prince Paduma
482	Man	Ruru deer
503	Thief	Parrot
505	Ascetic	Prince Somanassa
506	Snake charmer	Snake king

64 in all.

Professor Fausböll has kindly allowed me to look at the advance sheets of his fifth volume, so that the above list is complete down to No. 513. There may be a few more instances in the remaining 37 Gâtakas not yet printed.

ADDENDA ET CORRIGENDA.

Page xiii. *Srî-wardhana-pura.* It should have been pointed out that this city is not (as stated by Emerson Tennant at vol. i, p. 414 of his 'Ceylon') the same as the modern town of Kandy, but was in the Kurunægalla district, and (as pointed out by Mr. K. James Pohath in the 'Ceylon Orientalist,' vol. iii, p. 218) about three and a half miles distant from the modern Damba-deniya.

P. 2, note 2. Mr. Trenckner in his 'Pâli Miscellany' (London, 1879) has translated and annotated the whole of Book I, that is, to the end of p. 39 of this translation.

P. 6, line 1, read 'to Tissa the Elder, the son of Moggali.'

P. 10, note 1. It is strange that when it occurred to me that §§ 10–14 are an early interpolation I failed to notice the most important, and indeed almost conclusive argument for my suggestion. It is this, that the closing words of § 14 are really in complete contradiction to the opening words, and that they look very much as if they had been inserted, after the interpolation, to meet the objection to it which would at once arise from the expression in § 16, that the venerable Assagutta 'heard those words of King Milinda.' As it originally stood the words he heard were those of § 10. After the interpolation these words had to be reinserted at the end of § 14, in spite of their being in contradiction to the context.

Pp. 14 foll., for 'Rohana' read 'Rohana.'

Pp. 15, 16. This whole episode as to the charge of lying is repeated by Buddhaghosa (in the Introduction to his Samanta Pâsâdikâ, p. 296 of vol. iii of Oldenberg's Vinaya), but as having happened to Siggava in connection with the birth of Moggali-putta Tissa. A modern author would be expected to mention his source, but Buddhaghosa makes no reference whatever to the Milinda. Perhaps the episode is common stock of Buddhist legend, and we shall find it elsewhere.

P. 32, line 1, add after 'Quietism' ' and the discourse on losses (Parâbhava Suttanta).' [See p. xxix, where the reference is supplied.]

P. 53. 'Virtue's the base.' It should have been pointed out that this is the celebrated verse given by the Ceylon scholars to Buddhaghosa as the theme of the test essay he was to write as a proof of his fitness. If he succeeded in the essay they would then entrust him with all their traditions for him to recast in Pâli. The 'Path of Purity,' which opens with this verse, was the result.

P. 185, § 49. On the question discussed in this section the curious may compare what is said by Sir Thomas Brown in his 'Enquiries into Vulgar and Common Errors,' Book VII, Chapter xvi (p. 304 of the London edition of 1686). He gives several instances of supposed cases of conception without sexual connection mentioned in western writers, and comes to the conclusion, apropos of the supposed generation of the magician Merlin by Satan, that 'generations by the devil are very improbable.'

I had desired to dedicate this translation of the Milinda to Mr. Trenckner, to whose self-denying labours, spread over many years, we owe the edition of the Pâli text on which the translation is based, and without which the translation would not have been attempted. But I am now informed that any dedication of a single volume in the series of the 'Sacred Books of the East' is not allowable, as it would conflict with the dedication of the entire series. Had I known this when the Introduction was being written, a more suitable acknowledgment of the debt due to Mr. Trenckner than the few words on page xv, would have been made at the close of the Introductory remarks. I am permitted therefore to add here what was intended to appear in the dedication as an expression of the gratitude which all interested in historical research must feel to a scholar who has devoted years of labour, and of labour rendered valuable by the highest training and critical scholarship, to a field of enquiry in which the only fruit to be gathered is knowledge.

INDEX OF PROPER NAMES.

Abhidharma Kosa Vyâkhyâ, quoted, page xxvi.
Agathokles, king of Baktria, xxii.
Agita, the teacher, 8, 41.
Akesines, the river, xliv.
Akiravatî, the river, xliv, 171.
Âlakamandâ, city of the gods, 3.
Alasanda (Alexandria), on the Indus, xxiii, 127.
Amarâ, Mahosadha's wife, 294.
Amara-sekara, Mr. C. A. M., xii.
Amara-sekara, Mr. N. M., xii.
Ânanda, the teacher, 163, 191, 257.
Anantakâya, attendant on Menander, probably = Antiochos, xix, xlii, 48.
Anuruddha, the Sâkyan, 163.
Apollodotus, king of Baktria, xix, xlii.
Archebios, king of Baktria, xxii.
Ariano-pâli, legends on coins, xxi.
Âsâlha, a month, 171.
Asiknî, the river, xliv.
Asipâsâ, a caste, xlvi.
Asoka, emperor of India, xxxvii, xlii, 182.
Asokârâma, near Patna, xliii, 26.
Assagutta of the Vattaniya hermitage, xxv, xliii.
Asvagupta, not the same as last, xxv.
Atthissara, = Devadatta, 167.
Avîki, purgatory, xl, 9.
Âyupâla, of the Sankheyya hermitage, a Buddhist teacher, xxv, xliii, 30 foll.

Barygaza, in Gujarat, xx.
Benares, 31.
Benfey, Professor, quoted, xxvi.
Bhaddasâla, the general, xliii, 292.
Bhaddi-(or Bhatti-)puttâ, a caste, xlvi.
Bhaddiya, the Sâkyan, 163.
Bhagu, the Sâkyan, 163.
Bharukakkha, men of, xliii, 331.
Bindumati, a courtesan, xliii, 182.
Bird, Major, quoted, xxvi.

Brahmâ, the god, 118, 301.
Brahma-world, heaven, 126.
Buddhaghosa's 'Path of Purity,' xi, 306; his quotations of the Milinda, xiv–xvii.
Budh Gâyâ, in Behar, 9.
Burgess, Dr., quoted, xxvi.
Burmese translations of the 'Questions of Milinda,' xi, xvi.
Burnouf, quoted, xxvi.
Bu-ston, a Tibetan work, quoted, xxvi.

Ceylon, xi, xiv; its literature, xiii.
Childers, Professor, quoted, xlv, 185, 230, 244.
Cunningham, General, quoted, xi.

Dâgabas, sepulchral heaps, xx.
Dânava, Titan, 216.
Daramitipola, a Ceylon scholar, xiii.
Devadatta, the heresiarch, 153, 163 foll., 193, 249, 282 foll., 303.
Devamantiya, = Demetrios, xix, xliii, 22, 24, 37, 47.
Dhamma-kitti, author of the Saddhamma Sangaha, xxvii.
Dhammakkhanda. See Madhurasatora.
Dhammapâla, quoted, 244.
1. Dhamma-rakkhita. See Daramitipola.
2. Dhamma-rakkhita, one of Nâgasena's teachers, xxv, xliii, 16, 18.
Dhana-phâlaka, elephant, 297.
Dinna, attendant on king Milinda, 87.
Divyâvadâna, quoted, xxv.

Ekasâtaka, a Brahman, 172.
Elijah, his 'Act of Truth,' 185.
Eukratides, king of Baktria, xxiii.

Fâ-Hien, the traveller, 248.
Fausböll, Professor, quoted, 244, 253.

308 THE QUESTIONS OF KING MILINDA.

Gandhâra, the country, xliii, 327, 331.
Gangâ, the Ganges river, xliv, 5, 171, 182.
Gardiner, Professor, quoted, xxi.
Garu*d*as, snake-eating birds, 38, 175.
Gopâla-mâtâ, queen, 172.
Gu*n*ânanda. See Moho*tt*i-watte.
Guttila, musician, 172.

Hardy, Rev. R. Spence, quoted, xxvi, 40, 61, 64, 77.
Himâlayas, mountains, 11, 171, 278.
Hîna*t*i-kumburê Sumangala, translates the Milinda into Si*m*halese, xii, xiii.
Hydaspes, the river Bihat, xliv.
Hypanis (the Sutlej), xix.

Indra, the god, 37.
Indus, river, 171.
Isamos (the Jumna), xix.
Itihâsas, 6, 247.

Jains, their founder, 8.
Jâli, Vessantara's son, 174.
Jumna, river. See Isamos, Yamunâ.
Justin, quoted, xix.

Kâbul, Menander's coins found there, xx.
Kadphises, a coin of his referred to, xxii.
Kagangala, in the Terai, 14, 18.
Kâlâbu, king, 286.
Kalanda, a clan, 238.
Kalasi, a town on an island in the Indus, xxiii, xliii, 83, 127.
Kali-devatâ, a sect so called, xlvi.
*K*andabhâgâ, the river, xliv, 171.
*K*andagutta, king, xliii, 292.
Kârambhiya, ascetic, 287.
Karisi. See Kalasi.
Kashmîr, Menander's coins found there, xx, xliii, 82.
Kassapa, the Buddha, 4, 173.
Kathâ Sarit Sâgara, quoted, 298.
*K*âtumâ, a Sâkyan town, 257, 301.
Kern, Professor, quoted, xxvi.
Ketumatî, a mansion in heaven, 11.
Khugguttarâ, 122.
Kimbila, the Sâkyan, 163.
*K*ina, perhaps China, xliii, 121, 327, 331, 359.
Ki*nk*î, a Brahman woman, 153.

Kîrtti *S*rî Râga-si*m*ha, king of Ceylon, xii, xiii.
Kola-pa*tt*ana, seaport, xliii, 359.
Ko*t*umbara, its stuffs, 3.
Kumâra Kassapa, 275.
*K*unda, the coppersmith, 242.
Kuvera, the god, 37.

Lassen, Professor, quoted, xliv.
Legge, Professor, his version of Fâ-Hien, 248.
Liwera, Mr. A., xiii.
Lokâyatas, a sect so called, 7.

Maddî, wife to Vessantara, 174.
Madhura, the city, xliii, 331.
Madhurasa-to*t*a, a Buddhist scholar, xiii.
Mahâ-bhârata, called an Itihâsa, 247.
Mahâsena, a god, 11.
Mahî, the river, xliv, 171.
Mahosadha and his wife, 294.
Makkhali (of the cowshed), 8.
Mallikâ, queen, 172.
Mâlunkyâ-putta, 204 foll.
Ma*n*ibhaddâ, a caste so called, xlvi, 191.
Mankura, attendant on Menander, xx, 29, 30, 48.
Mandhâtâ, king, 172.
Manoratha Pûra*n*î, quoted, xiv.
Mâra, the Evil One, 219.
Masâra, mountain, 177.
Mathurâ, Menander's coins found there, xx.
Megha Dûta, quoted, 298.
Menander-Milinda, identity of the names, xviii; notices of in classical writers, xix; coins of, xx-xxii; date and birthplace of, xxiii; his conversion to Buddhism, xxv-xxvii.
Mendis, Mr. L., xiii.
Milinda, the Questions of, in Ceylon, xii, xiii; in Buddhaghosa, xiv–xvi; MSS. of, xvii; is a religious romance, xvii; the charm of its style, xviii.
Milinda Prash*n*aya, xii.
Moggallâna, his death, 261 foll.
Moho*tt*i-watte Gu*n*ânanda, a Buddhist scholar, xii.
Morris, the Rev. Dr., quoted, xiv, xv, 46, 65, 174, 278, 301.

INDEX OF PROPER NAMES.

Müller, Prof. Ed., quoted, xliv, 179, 240.

Nâgârguna, founder of the Mahâyâna school, xxv; identified wrongly with Nâgasena, xxvi.
Nâgasena, xxv, xxvi, and passim.
Nâgesa, epithet of Patañgali, xxvi.
Nâḷâgiri, elephant and mountain, 298.
Nanda, the Brahman, 153.
Nandaka, an ogre, 153.
Nandiya, monkey king, 287.
Nesâda, outcasts, 286.
Nigantha Nâta-putta, founder of the Jain sect, 8.
Nikumba, the country, xliii, 327.
Nimi, king, 172.
Nyâya philosophy, 6.

Pabbatâ, a caste so called, xlvii, 191.
Pâkittiya rules, xli.
Pakudha Kakkâyana, the teacher, 8, 42.
Pâli Text Society, xxv, xxvii, xl, xliv, 46, 65.
Pânini, quoted, 298.
Papañka Sûdanî, quoted, xv.
Pâragika offences, xli.
Pâṭaliputta, the modern Patna, 26, 182.
Patañgali, not the same as Nâgasena, xxvi.
Pâtimokkha, xli.
Pâtimokkha, recitation of, 264 foll.
Pâyâsi the Râganya, 275.
Phanin, epithet of Patañgali, xxvi.
Piliyakkha, king, 280.
Piris, Mr. K., xii.
Plutarch, quoted, xix, xxii.
Pragâpati, the god, 37.
Punnâ, slave girl, 172.
Punna, a servant, 172.
Pûrana Kassapa, the teacher, 8, 9, 41.
Purânas, 6, 247.

Râgagaha, 191, 298; council held at, 242.
Râhula, son of the Buddha, 32.
Rakkhita-tala, in the Himâlayas, xliii, 6, 12, 18.
Râmâyana, called an Itihâsa, 247.
Roga, the Mallian, 282.
1. Rohana, a Buddhist teacher mentioned in the Anguttara, xxv.
2. Rohana, Nâgasena's teacher, xxv, xliii.

Sabba-dinna, attendant on Menander, xix, xliii, 20, 47, 56.
Saddhamma Samgaha, a Pâli historical work, xxvii.
Sâdhîna, king, 172.
Sâgala, capital of Baktria, xviii, xliii, 2, 23.
Saka, a country, xliii, 327, 331.
Sâkha, general, 291.
Sakka, king of the gods, 12.
Sâkyan, member of the clan, 153.
Sallet, Alfred von, quoted, xxi.
Sâma, prince, 280 foll., 288.
Sañgaya, the teacher, 8.
Saṅkheyya, a hermitage, xliii, 17, 22.
Sâṅkhya philosophy, 6.
Santushita, a god, 37.
Sarabhû, the river, xliv, 171.
Saranankara. See Wœliwita.
Sarassatî, the river, xliv, 171.
Savara, city of the Kandâlas, 267.
Schiefner, Prof., quoted, xxvi.
Siamese translations, &c., of the 'Questions of Milinda,' xi, xvi, xvii, xxiv.
Sindhu, the Indus river, xliv.
Sineru, king of mountains, 152, 176.
Sivaka, 195.
Sivi, king, 179.
1. Somuttara, a Brahman, xliii, 14.
2. Somuttara, an outcast, 286.
Srî-wardhanâ-pura, a city in Ceylon, xiii, 305.
Sthûpas. See Dâgabas.
Strabo, quoted, xix.
Strato, king of Baktria, xxii.
Subhadda, recluse, 186.
Sudinna, of the Kalanda clan, 238.
Sumana, garland maker, 172.
Sumaṅgala Vilâsinî, quoted, xiv, xv, 131, 263.
Suppabuddha, a Sâkyan, 153.
Suppiyâ, devotee, 172.
Surattha, Surat, xliii, 331, 359.
Sutta Nipâta, xlii.
Suvanna-bhûmi, the country, xliii, 359.
Suyâma, a god, 37.
Sy-Hermaios, king of Baktria, xxii.

Takkola, the place, xliii, xliv, 359.
Theosophists, sect of, 268.

Tissa, son of Moggalî, 6.
Tissa-thera, a writer, xliii, 71.
Trenckner, Mr., xv-xix, xxiv, xxxi, 25, 28, 32, 49, 80, 175, 179, 294, 306.
Tusita heaven, 271.

Ûhâ, a river, xliii, 70.
Upâli, the barber, 163.
Uposatha Ârâma, in Ceylon, xiii.
Uttarakuru, 3.

Vaiseshika philosophy, 6.
Vaṅga, Bengal, xliii, 359.
Varuna, the god, 37.
Vattaniya, a hermitage, xliii, 10-16.
Vedas, the four, 6, 247; the three, 17, 34.
Vegayanta, palace of the gods, 11.
Vessantara, the king, 170 foll.
Vessavana, king of the fairies, 38.
Vetravatî, the river, xliv, 171.
Vidhura, sage, 288.
Vigamba-vatthu, a hermitage, xliii, 12.

Vilâta, a country, xliii, 327, 331.
Vîtamsâ, the river, xliv, 171.
Vitandas, a sect so called, 7.

Weber, Prof., quoted, xxv.
Wenzel, Dr., quoted, xxv, xxvi.
Wilson, H. H., quoted, xxi.
Wœliwita Saranankara, a Buddhist scholar, xii, xiii.

Yakkha, ogre, 38, 176.
Yâma, the god, 37.
Yamunâ, the Jumna river, xliv, 171.
Yavana, Baktria, xliii, 327, 331.
Yoga philosophy, 6.
Yonakas, the Greeks (Ionians) attendant on Menander, xix, xlii, 1, 4, 20, 68.
Yugandhara, a peak of the Himâlayas, 12.

Zoilos, king of Baktria, xxii.

INDEX OF SUBJECTS.

Acrobats, page 53.
'Act of Truth,' 180 foll.
Alkaline wash, in medicine, 168.
Alms, customs of the Buddhist Order in regard to, 14–16, 20.
Alms-halls. 2. See Rest-houses.
Altruism, Buddhist, 174.
Ambrosia, 35, 236.
Animals, their reasoning powers, 51.
Arahat, the great, is Buddha, 8; others, 11, 12; their knowledge of others' thoughts, 18, 23; nature of their wisdom, 29; does not fear death, 70; description of, 157; have no fear, 206 foll., 297 foll.
Arahatship, above ordinary morality, 25; its seven conditions, 52, 58; the highest of all lands, 227.
Architects, 2, 53.
Arithmetic, 6, 91.
Army, its four divisions, 7, 54, 60, 62.
Arts and sciences, the nineteen, &c., 6.
Aspiration of reward, on doing a good act, 5; duty of, 55.
Association of ideas, 89–92.
Assurance of salvation, the Arahat's final, 65.
Astrologer, the royal, 31, 247.
Astronomy, 6.
Atonement, 14.

Baby, is it the same as the grown man? 63.
Bambû, simile of the giant-, 155 foll.; dies in reproduction, 236.
Barber, 19, 302.
Barley reapers, simile of, 51.
Bathing places, public, 140.
Becoming, 83; sorrow of, 149; freedom from, 293.
Boat, similes of, 124, 227.
Body, the thirty-two parts of the human, 42; the love of the, 114; bodily marks, the, 32, 117, 237; made of four elements, 194.

Bones, hundred leagues long, 130.
Book, 123; of the law, 262.
Brahman, works in the fields, 15; duties of a, 247.
Brand marks, on cattle, 122.
Breath, no soul in the, 48.
Bridges, 140, 272, 291.
Brooms, 4.
Buddha, the, is incomparable, 108; is not still alive, 144 foll.; gifts to, 144 foll.; distinction between Pa*kk*eka- and Perfect-Buddhas, 158; the best of men, 178; sinlessness of, 191.
Burning glass, 85.

Calf, similes of, 282, 301.
Carpenter, simile of, 236.
Carriages, 3, 91.
Carter, should test a ford, 272.
Casuists, 7; casuistry no branch of education, 17.
Cat's eye, the gem, 177.
Cattle, brand marks on, 122.
Cauterising a wound, 168, 211.
Ceremonies, observed by kings on visiting Sama*n*as, 30, 31, 37, 49.
Character, of the ideally good layman, 296.
Chariot, simile of, 43; parts of, 44.
Charms, intoning of, 181.
City, description of a wealthy, 2; foundation of, 53; with one gateway, simile of, 90.
Clocks, want of, 7.
Clod, thrown in the air, simile of, 194.
Cloth goods, 3.
Combs for the hair, 19.
Comets, 247.
'Confections,' 42, 83, 205, 207.
Contact, 92.
Conversion, what it consists in, 25.
Conveyancing, as an art, 6.
Copper ware, 3, 96.

Cotton stuffs, 159.
Counting. See Arithmetic; by the finger-joints, 91.
Courtesan, story of, 183 foll.
Courts of justice, 291.
Criminal, the condemned, similes of, 165–6, 211.
Crops, estimation of growing, 91.
Cymbals, simile of, 93.

Dacoits, 33.
Dart, simile of the perfect, 159.
Dead body, always cast up by the sea, 259.
Death, the fear of, 206–212, 278, 279.
Death of the Buddha, the legend of, explained, 242 foll.
Delusion of self, 207, 226.
Dependents, kindness to, 138.
Dice-playing, 103.
Digestion, 193, 236.
Diseases, ninety-eight kinds of, 152; caused in ten ways (one of which is medical treatment), 192; cured by Pirit, 225.
Divination, practised by Brahmans, 247.
'Divine Ear,' the, 11.
'Divine Eye,' the, 26, 179.
Divining other people's thoughts, 18, 23.
Dreams, interpretation of, 247.
Drugs, five kinds of, 69.
Drum, simile of, 149.
Dryads, 242.

Ear, the divine, 11.
Earth, the broad, similes of, 52, 150, 194, 258, 299.
Earthquakes, 170 foll.
Eclipses, 247.
Education, 17, 50, 63.
Egoism, delusion of, 207, 226.
Elements, the four, 194.
Elephants, 3, 38, 126, 211, 267, 272.
Embroidery, 134.
Embryo, four stages of the, 63, 105.
Esoteric teaching, none in Buddhism, 138, 142, 267.
Estimating growing crops, 91.
Eunuchs, cannot keep a secret, 141.
Evil, origin of. See Pain. Conquest of, by good, 174.
Excitement, condemned, 143.
Exorcism, 38.

Eye, the Divine, 26.
'Eye of the Truth,' 25.

Fairies, 38.
Faith, 52, 56.
Fans, 148.
Finger-joints, used to count with, 91.
Fire, similes of, 73, 146, 188, 234, 244.
Fire-extinguishing apparatus, 68.
Fire-stick apparatus, 85.
Flame, simile of, 64.
Flavours, the six, 88.
Flood, simile of a, 56.
Floor coverings, 267.
Food, Indian idea of, 26.
Fossil bones, 130.
Future life, the craving after, condemned, 174, 200.

Garlands, habit of wearing, 19.
Gayal, kind of buffalo, 211.
Gems, various kinds of, 177.
Generosity, the mighty power of, 173–5.
Gestation, period of, is ten months, 16.
Ghee, 65, 75, 161, 249.
Gold and silver, 3, 59, 267.
Grammar, 17.
Granary, 65, 161.
Guilds of traders, 3.

Hair, the sixteen impediments of wearing, 19; hair-dyeing and shampooing, &c., ibid.
Head-splitting, belief as to, 222.
Heads of houses, 209.
Health and wealth, explained, 97.
Hell, none in Buddhism. See Purgatory.
Hen and eggs, similes of, 76, 77, 80.
Highwaymen, 32, 222.
Honey, the man in the trough of, 88; the drink of, 95; slips through the fingers, 249.
Horripilation, 38.
Horses, 3; the swift, simile of, 199.
House-building, 57, 83; house of life, 207.
Humours, the three, in medicine, 168, 191.
Husbandry, 215, 235, 247, 285.

Iddhi, powers of, 261.
Ideas, mark of, 94; association of, 89–92.

INDEX OF SUBJECTS.

Income, simile of, 187.
Indeterminate questions, 205.
Individuality, 40–45, 50, 64, 67.
Indivisibility, denied, 132.
Insight, the eight causes of its ripening, 141, and see Conversion.
Intoxicating drinks, 41.
Investigation, characteristic of, 96; why the Buddha investigates, 272.
Invisible, story of the magician, 217; root to make one, 281.
Iron, 70.

Jasmine, the chief of flowers, 252.
Javelins, 69.

Karma, 3, 12, 18, 32, 41, 71, 80, 103, 163, 191, 214, 262–4.
King of kings, the mythical, 162, 177, 199.
Kings, their manner of discussing, 46; their tyranny, 50; their greed, 203; they take the best of everything, 267.

Lamps, 61, 64, 67, 73, 110.
Lancet, surgeon's, 168–9, 211.
Law, of property, 247. See Peace, breach of, and Conveyancing, and Punishments, and Book.
Laymen, includes the gods, 32.
Learning by heart, 17, 22, 28, 34, 123, 172.
Letter-writing, 67.
Leviathan, 187.
Lexicography, 17.
Lie, a deliberate, excludes from the Order, 268.
Lions, 135, 211.
Log, the dry, simile of, 214.
Looking-glass, 86, 189.
Lord of a village, 208.
Lotions, medicinal, 211, 215.
Lotus flower, simile of, 117.
Love to all beings, 138, 279 foll.; of teacher to pupil, 142; duty of, 254.
Lucky marks, 32, 117, 237, 247.

Magic, 6, 181, 217.
Mandolin and its parts, 84.
Market places, 2, 53.
Marks on the body, as omens of future greatness, 17.
Marriage by purchase, 74.

Medicine, 6, 191, 197, 214. See Physician, Surgery.
Meditation, 13, 18, 52, 196 foll.
Memory, 120–122.
Merchant, should test goods, 272.
Milk and butter, simile of, 65, 75.
Mindfulness, 52, 58.
Minds, seven classes of, 154.
Ministers of state, the six, 171.
Miracles at conception of Nâgasena, 14.
Money, 17, 59, 134, 267.
Mules die in giving birth, 236.
Music, 6.
Muslin, of Benares, 3.
Mutilation, of criminals, 63, 166, 270, 276.

Name, soul not implied in, 41.
'Name-and-form,' 71 foll., 77.
Nirvâna, a state of mind to be attained in, and which ends with, this life, 36, 41, 78, 106. See Arahatship.
Novice, the intractable, 4; Nâgasena becomes a, 20; his duties as, 24, 302.

Ocean, taste of, 131, 133; always casts up a dead body, 259.
Offences, conscious and unconscious, 224.
Official gratitude, 76, 93, 197.
Ogres, 38.
Oil, for the hair, 19.
Ointment, for a wound, 168.
Omens, interpretation of, 247.
Omniscience of the Buddhas, 117, 154–162, 271, 301 foll.

Pain, origin of, 83, 191, 195.
Pakkeka-Buddhas, 158.
Peace, breach of the, in law, 239.
Perception, characteristic of, 95, 132.
Perseverance, 52.
Physician, 68, 69, 112, 165, 168, 211, 240, 272.
Pilot, should test the shore, 272.
Pipers, 48.
Pirit, 213.
Pledge, deposit of, 123.
Poison, simile of, 94; antidotes to, 215; love counteracts, 279.
Pork, the Buddha's last meal of, 244 foll.

Posthumous honours, 144 foll.
Potter and the pots, simile of, 84.
Precepts, abolition of the minor, 202.
Present to a king, simile of, 220.
Prophecy, 6, 185.
Punishments, 63, 223, 239, 254, 269.
Punkahs, 148.
Pupil, his duty to his teacher, 144.
Purgatory, 94, 101, 125, 163, 167, 206, 210, 283.
Purity, the power of, 173.
Purohita, family chaplain, 282.

Rain, three seasons of, 171; produced by charms, 181.
Rain water, similes of, 90, 226, 245, 274, 278.
Rams, simile of two butting, 92.
Reasoning contrasted with wisdom, 50.
Recognition, mark of perception, 132.
Reflection, characteristic of, 95.
Re-incarnation, 207, and see next.
Re-individualisation, 50, 72–75.
Relationship, scheme of, 292.
Relics, of the Buddha, 144 foll., 246.
Renunciation, 31, 49, 98, 251, 271.
Rest-houses, public, 291.
Rhinoceros, 38.
Rice, simile of cartload of, 154; simile of boiling, 176; is the chief of all grains, 252.
Robber, figuratively, of a bad monk, 256.

Sandal-wood dust, 29.
Schism, 163, 227.
Scholars, their manner of discussing, 46.
Schooling, 63, and see Education.
Season, the rainy, 7, 24.
Secret wisdom, 139.
Sects, 3, 7, 8, 144, 266.
Seed-fruit-seed, succession of, 80.
Seed, simile of, 301.
Seeds, edible, 161.
Sensation, results of a, 82, 83, 89, 92; characteristics of, 93; kinds of, 194.
Shadow of a man, 45; abiding under another's, 137.
Shampooing the hair, 19.

Ship, simile of, 227.
Shops, 2, 3.
Shrines, god-haunted, 140.
Sins, the five, 41; will find you out, 295.
Snake-charmers, 38, 212, 215.
Snakes, 211.
Snoring, how to stop, 131.
Snow, 70.
Son in the faith, 142.
Sophists, 7.
Sorrow, 125, and see Pain.
Soul, no such thing as, 40–45, 48, 67, 86–89, 111, 132.
Spells, 6.
Splinter of rock, incident of, 193 foll., 249 foll.
State officials, the six, 171.
Suffering, cause of, see Pain; various kinds of, 275.
Sugar, 72; sugar mill, 235.
Suggestion, as source of memory, 121.
Suicide, 69, 273.
Surgery, 168.
Swallowed up by the earth, 152.
Syrups and sweetmeats, 3.

Tank, simile of the full, 187.
Taxation, 208.
Teacher, his fees, 17, 25; his duties to his pupil, 142.
Thought-perception, 89.
Tidal-wave, 276.
Time, definition of, 77; root of, 79; ultimate point of, 80–82.
To pay, 177.
Torture, 239; various kinds of death with, 276, 277.
Transmigration, 111, 118, 120.
Travellers, hospitality towards, 161.
Treasurer, the royal, 59.
Trees, disciples compared to, 151; simile of the barren, 162; talking trees, dilemma of, 241.
Trumpeters, 48.
Truth, is the most minute of all things, 132; its power, 182.
Turbans, 138.
Tutor's fees, 17.
Twirling-stick, 85, 146.

Uncle, no word for in Pâli, 292.
Unguents, for the hair, 19.

Vanishing root, 281.
Village organisation, 208-9.
Vow, the eightfold, of a layman, 138.

Waggons, 3, 27; parts of, 44; simile of path of, 91; of load of rice, 154; breaking up of, 173; reckoned among valuable things, 267.
Wandering teachers, 7, 34.
Water-clearing gem, 55.
Water, earth rests on, 106, 175.
Water-pot, the regular, 106.
Weapons, 69.
Wheel of victory, 162; of the kingdom of righteousness, 31, 253.

Wife. See Marriage.
Wind, simile of, 147-8; as medical term, 191.
Wisdom, distinct from reasoning, 50; mark of, 51, 61; of Arahats, 29; seven kinds of, 128.
Women, put before men, 83; their fickleness, 141; in the Order, 187; reckoned among valuable things, 267; their wiles, 294; their management of their husbands, 302. See Marriage.
Woollen stuffs, 3, 28, 159.
Worms in the body, 151.
Wound, treatment of, 168.
Writing a letter, 67.

TRANSLITERATION OF ORIENTAL ALPHABETS. 317

Transliteration of Oriental Alphabets adopted for the Translations of the Sacred Books of the East.

CONSONANTS.	MISSIONARY ALPHABET.			Sanskrit.	Zend.	Pehlevi.	Persian.	Arabic.	Hebrew.	Chinese.
	I Class.	II Class.	III Class.							
Gutturales.										
1 Tenuis	k			क	ﻛ	ک	ک	ک	ח ת כ ק	k
2 ,, aspirata	kh			ख	ﻫ	ن	ﺥ	ﺥ		kh
3 Media	g			ग	൧	ᑣ				
4 ,, aspirata	gh			घ						
5 Gutturo-labialis	q					൧				
6 Nasalis	ṅ (ng)			ङ	{ ɜ (ng) ʃ(ṅ) }	ๅ				
					ᵕ(ṅhv)					
7 Spiritus asper	h			ह					ה	h, hs
8 ,, lenis	ʼ								א	
9 ,, asper faucalis	ʽh								ח	
10 ,, lenis faucalis	ʽh	ʽh							ע	
11 ,, asper fricatus		ʼh								
12 ,, lenis fricatus		ʽh								
Gutturales modificatae (palatales, &c.)										
13 Tenuis		k		च	Ϩ	ک	ک	ک		k
14 ,, aspirata		kh		छ	ഴ	ള	ﺥ	ﺥ		kh
15 Media		g		ज						
16 ,, aspirata		gh		झ						
17 ,, Nasalis		ñ		ञ						

TRANSLITERATION OF ORIENTAL ALPHABETS

CONSONANTS (continued)	MISSIONARY ALPHABET			Sanskrit.	Zend.	Pehlevi.	Persian.	Arabic.	Hebrew.	Chinese.
	I Class.	II Class.	III Class.							
18 Semivocalis	y			य	init. ݵ ی	و	ی	ی	י	y
19 Spiritus asper										
20 " lenis		(ṡ)								
21 " asper assibilatus		(ż)						ۻ		z
22 " lenis assibilatus		s		श	श	ܦ	ج	ج		
		z								
Dentales.										
23 Tenuis	t			त	ت	ܬ	ت	ت	ת ת	t
24 " aspirata	th		T_H	थ	थ					th
25 " assibilata										
26 Media	d			द	द	ܕ	د	د	ד ד	
27 " aspirata	dh		D_H	ध						
28 " assibilata										
29 Nasalis	n			न	ن	ن	ن	ن	נ ן	n
30 Semivocalis	l		L	ल	ل	ل	ل	ل	ל	l
31 " mollis 1		l								
32 " mollis 2										
33 Spiritus asper 1	s		s (/)	स	س	س	س	س	ס ש	s
34 " asper 2										
35 " lenis	z									
36 " asperrimus 1			z (š)				(ث) ژ	ث		z
37 " asperrimus 2			z (ṣ)				(ذ) ژ	ذ		ṣ, ẓh

FOR THE SACRED BOOKS OF THE EAST. 319

						r	sh		p	ph			m	w		f		

(table of transliteration symbols across multiple scripts)

Dentales modificatae (linguales, &c.)

38 Tenuis ... t
39 ,, aspirata ... th
40 Media ... d
41 ,, aspirata ... dh
42 Nasalis ... n
43 Semivocalis ... r
44 ,, fricata
45 ,, diacritica
46 Spiritus asper ... sh
47 ,, lenis ... zh

Labiales.

48 Tenuis ... p
49 ,, aspirata ... ph
50 Media ... b
51 ,, aspirata ... bh
52 Tenuissima
53 Nasalis ... m
54 Semivocalis ... w
55 ,, aspirata ... hw
56 Spiritus asper ... f
57 ,, lenis ... v
58 Anusvâra ... m
59 Visarga ... h

320 TRANSLITERATION OF ORIENTAL ALPHABETS.

VOWELS.	MISSIONARY ALPHABET.			Sanskrit.	Zend.	Pehlevi.	Persian.	Arabic.	Hebrew.	Chinese.
	I Class.	II Class.	III Class.							
1 Neutralis	ŏ								־	ă
2 Laryngo-palatalis	ĕ									
3 ,, labialis	ŏ									
4 Gutturalis brevis	a	(e)		अ	ʌ	๑ fin. ๑ init	ا	ا	־	a
5 ,, longa	â	(ē)		आ	ʌʌ	๑	ٲ	ٲ	־	â
6 Palatalis brevis	i	(i)		इ	ᴧ	:	ا	ا	־׳	i
7 ,, longa	î			ई	ᴧ	๑	ي	ي	־׳	î
8 Dentalis brevis	ï									
9 ,, longa	ï									
10 Lingualis brevis	ï									
11 ,, longa	ï									
12 Labialis brevis	u	(u)		उ	ʌ	൦			־	u
13 ,, longa	û	(ū)		ऊ		൦				û
14 Gutturo-palatalis brevis	e	(e)			ε(e) ξ(e)					e
15 ,, longa	ê	(ē)		ए	ε ξ		ـي	ـي	־	ê
16 Diphthongus gutturo-palatalis	ai	(ai)		ऐ						ei, êi
17 ,,	ei (êi)									
18 ,,	oi (ou)									
19 Gutturo-labialis brevis	o	(o)							־	o
20 ,, longa	ô	(ō)		ओ	ഀൗ	๑	ـو	ـو	־	âu
21 Diphthongus gutturo-labialis	au	(au)		औ	๑൦(au)					
22 ,,	au (êu)									
23 ,,	ou (ou)									
24 Gutturalis fracta	ä									
25 Palatalis fracta	ï									ü
26 Labialis fracta	ü									

Clarendon Press, Oxford.

I. LITERATURE AND PHILOLOGY.

SECTION I.

DICTIONARIES, GRAMMARS, ETC.

ANGLO-SAXON. An Anglo-Saxon Dictionary, based on the MS. Collections of the late JOSEPH BOSWORTH, D.D., Professor of Anglo-Saxon, Oxford. Edited and enlarged by Prof. T. N. TOLLER, M.A. Parts I–III. A—SAR. 4to. 15s. each. Part IV. *In the Press.*

ARABIC. A Practical Arabic Grammar. Part I. Compiled by A. O. GREEN, Brigade Major, Royal Engineers. *Second Edition, Enlarged.* Crown 8vo. 7s. 6d.

CELTIC. Ancient Cornish Drama. Edited and translated by E. NORRIS, with a Sketch of Cornish Grammar, an Ancient Cornish Vocabulary, etc. 2 vols. 1859. 8vo. 1l. 1s.

    The Sketch of Cornish Grammar separately, stitched, 2s. 6d.

CHINESE. A Handbook of the Chinese Language. By JAMES SUMMERS. 1863. 8vo. half bound, 1l. 8s.

ENGLISH. A New English Dictionary, on Historical Principles: founded mainly on the materials collected by the Philological Society. Vol. I. A and B. Imperial 4to. half morocco, 2l. 12s. 6d.

    Part IV. Section II. C—CASS (beginning of Vol. II.) 5s.
    Part V. CASS—CLIVY. 12s. 6d.
    Part VI. *In the Press.*

    Edited by JAMES A. H. MURRAY, LL.D., with the assistance of many Scholars and men of Science.

    Vol. III (E, F, and G). Part I. Edited by HENRY BRADLEY. *In the Press.*

Oxford: Clarendon Press. London: HENRY FROWDE, Amen Corner, E.C.

I. Literature and Philology.

ENGLISH, *continued*.

ENGLISH. An Etymological Dictionary of the English Language. By W. W. SKEAT, Litt.D. *Second Edition.* 4to. 2*l*. 4*s*.

—— A Concise Etymological Dictionary of the English Language. By W. W. SKEAT, Litt.D. *Third Edition.* Crown 8vo. 5*s*. 6*d*.

—— A Concise Dictionary of Middle English, from A.D. 1150 to 1580. By A. L. MAYHEW, M.A., and W. W. SKEAT, Litt. D. Crown 8vo. half roan, 7*s*. 6*d*.

GREEK. A Greek-English Lexicon, by H. G. LIDDELL, D.D., and ROBERT SCOTT, D.D. *Seventh Edition, Revised and Augmented throughout.* 4to. 1*l*. 16*s*.

—— An intermediate Greek-English Lexicon, abridged from LIDDELL and SCOTT's Seventh Edition. Small 4to. 12*s*. 6*d*.

—— A Greek-English Lexicon, abridged from Liddell and Scott's 4to. edition, chiefly for the use of Schools. Square 12mo. 7*s*. 6*d*.

—— A copious Greek-English Vocabulary, compiled from the best authorities. 1850. 24mo. 3*s*.

—— **Etymologicon Magnum.** Ad Codd. mss. recensuit et notis variorum instruxit T. GAISFORD, S.T.P. 1848. fol. 1*l*. 12*s*.

—— **Suidae Lexicon.** Ad Codd. mss. recensuit T. GAISFORD, S.T.P. Tomi III. 1834. fol. 2*l*. 2*s*.

HEBREW. The Book of Hebrew Roots, by ABU 'L-WALÍD MARWÂN IBN JANÂH, otherwise called RABBÎ YÔNÂH. Now first edited, with an appendix, by Ad. NEUBAUER. 1875. 4to. 2*l*. 7*s*. 6*d*.

—— A Treatise on the use of the Tenses in Hebrew. By S. R. DRIVER, D.D. *Second Edition.* Extra fcap. 8vo. 7*s*. 6*d*.

ICELANDIC. An Icelandic-English Dictionary, based on the MS. collections of the late RICHARD CLEASBY. Enlarged and completed by G. VIGFÚSSON, M.A. With an Introduction, and Life of Richard Cleasby, by G. WEBBE DASENT, D.C.L. 4to. 3*l*. 7*s*.

—— A List of English Words the Etymology of which is illustrated by comparison with Icelandic. Prepared in the form of an Appendix to the above. By W. W. SKEAT, Litt.D. stitched, 2*s*.

——An Icelandic Primer, with Grammar, Notes, and Glossary. By HENRY SWEET, M.A. Extra fcap. 8vo. 3*s*. 6*d*.

——An Icelandic Prose Reader, with Notes, Grammar and Glossary, by Dr. GUDBRAND VIGFÚSSON and F. YORK POWELL, M.A. Extra fcap. 8vo. 10*s*. 6*d*.

Oxford: Clarendon Press.

Dictionaries, Grammars, etc.

LATIN. A Latin Dictionary, founded on Andrews' edition of Freund's Latin Dictionary, revised, enlarged, and in great part rewritten by CHARLTON T. LEWIS, Ph.D., and CHARLES SHORT, LL.D. 4to. 1*l*. 5*s*.

—— A School Latin Dictionary. By CHARLTON T. LEWIS, Ph.D. Small 4to. 18*s*.

—— Scheller's Dictionary of the Latin Language, revised and translated into English by J. E. RIDDLE, M.A. 1835. fol. 1*l*. 1*s*.

—— Contributions to Latin Lexicography. By HENRY NETTLESHIP, M.A. 8vo. 21*s*.

MELANESIAN. The Melanesian Languages. By ROBERT H. CODRINGTON, D.D., of the Melanesian Mission. 8vo. 18*s*.

RUSSIAN. A Grammar of the Russian Language. By W. R. MORFILL, M.A. Crown 8vo. 6*s*.

SANSKRIT. A Practical Grammar of the Sanskrit Language, arranged with reference to the Classical Languages of Europe, for the use of English Students, by Sir M. MONIER-WILLIAMS, D.C.L. *Fourth Edition.* 8vo. 15*s*.

—— A Sanskrit-English Dictionary, Etymologically and Philologically arranged, with special reference to Greek, Latin, German, Anglo-Saxon, English, and other cognate Indo-European Languages. By Sir M. MONIER-WILLIAMS, D.C.L. 4to. 4*l*. 14*s*. 6*d*.

—— Nalopákhyánam. Story of Nala, an Episode of the Mahá-Bhárata: the Sanskrit text, with a copious Vocabulary, and an improved version of Dean MILMAN's Translation, by Sir M. MONIER-WILLIAMS, D.C.L. *Second Edition, Revised and Improved.* 8vo. 15*s*.

—— Sakuntalá. A Sanskrit Drama, in Seven Acts. Edited by Sir M. MONIER-WILLIAMS, D.C.L. *Second Edition.* 8vo. 21*s*.

SYRIAC. Thesaurus Syriacus: collegerunt Quatremère, Bernstein, Lorsbach, Arnoldi, Agrell, Field, Roediger: edidit R. PAYNE SMITH, S.T.P. Vol. I, containing Fasc. I–V, sm. fol. 5*l*. 5*s*.

Fasc. VI. 1*l*. 1*s*. Fasc. VII. 1*l*. 11*s*. 6*d*. Fasc. VIII. 1*l*. 16*s*.

—— The Book of Kalīlah and Dimnah. Translated from Arabic into Syriac. Edited by W. WRIGHT, LL.D. 8vo. 21*s*.

BIBLIOGRAPHICAL DICTIONARIES.

Cotton's Typographical Gazetteer. 1831. 8vo. 12*s*. 6*d*.

—— Typographical Gazetteer. Second Series. 1866. 8vo. 12*s*. 6*d*.

Ebert's Bibliographical Dictionary, translated from the German. 4 vols. 1837. 8vo. 1*l*. 10*s*.

I. Literature and Philology.

SECTION II.

ANGLO-SAXON AND ENGLISH.

HELPS TO THE STUDY OF THE LANGUAGE AND LITERATURE.

A NEW ENGLISH DICTIONARY on Historical Principles, founded mainly on the materials collected by the Philological Society. Imperial 4to. Parts I–IV, price 12s. 6d. each.
    Vol. I (A and B), half morocco, 2l. 12s. 6d.
    Vol. II (C and D). *In the Press.*
        Part IV, Section 2, C—CASS, beginning Vol. II, price 5s.
        Part V, CASS—CLIVY, price 12s. 6d.
    Edited by JAMES A. H. MURRAY, LL.D., sometime President of the Philological Society; with the assistance of many Scholars and Men of Science.
    Vol. III (E, F, and G). Part I. Edited by Mr. HENRY BRADLEY. *In the Press.*

Bosworth and Toller. An Anglo-Saxon Dictionary, based on the MS. collections of the late JOSEPH BOSWORTH, D.D. Edited and enlarged by Prof. T. N. TOLLER, M.A., Owens College, Manchester. Parts I–III. A—SAR. 4to. stiff covers, 15s. each. Part IV. *In the Press.*

Earle. A Book for the Beginner in Anglo-Saxon. By JOHN EARLE, M.A. *Third Edition.* Extra fcap. 8vo. 2s. 6d.

—— The Philology of the English Tongue. *Fourth Edition.* Extra fcap. 8vo. 7s. 6d.

Mayhew and Skeat. A Concise Dictionary of Middle English, from A.D. 1150 to 1580. By A. L. MAYHEW, M.A., and W. W. SKEAT, Litt. D. Crown 8vo. half roan, 7s. 6d.

Skeat. An Etymological Dictionary of the English Language, arranged on an Historical Basis. By W. W. SKEAT, Litt.D. *Second Edition.* 4to. 2l. 4s.
    A Supplement to the First Edition of the above. 4to. 2s. 6d.

—— A Concise Etymological Dictionary of the English Language. *Third Edition.* Crown 8vo. 5s. 6d.

—— Principles of English Etymology. First Series. The Native Element. Crown 8vo. 9s.

Oxford: Clarendon Press.

Sweet. An Anglo-Saxon Primer, with Grammar, Notes and Glossary. By HENRY SWEET, M.A. *2nd Edition.* Extra fcap. 8vo. *2s. 6d.*

———— An Anglo-Saxon Reader. In Prose and Verse. With Grammatical Introduction, Notes, and Glossary. *Sixth Edition, Revised and Enlarged.* Extra fcap. 8vo. *8s. 6d.*

———— A Second Anglo-Saxon Reader. Extra fcap. 8vo. *4s. 6d.*

———— Old English Reading Primers:
    I. Selected Homilies of Ælfric. Stiff covers, *1s. 6d.*
    II. Extracts from Alfred's Orosius. Stiff covers, *1s. 6d.*

———— First Middle English Primer, with Grammar and Glossary. Extra fcap. 8vo. *2s.*

———— Second Middle English Primer. Extracts from Chaucer, with Grammar and Glossary. Extra fcap. 8vo. *2s.*

———— History of English Sounds from the Earliest Period. With full Word-Lists. 8vo. *14s.*

———— A Primer of Phonetics. Extra fcap. 8vo. *3s. 6d.*

———— Elementarbuch des Gesprochenen Englisch. Grammatik, Texte und Glossar. *Second Edition.* Extra fcap. 8vo., stiff covers, *2s. 6d.*

Tancock. An Elementary English Grammar and Exercise Book. By O. W. TANCOCK, M.A. *Second Edition.* Extra fcap. 8vo. *1s. 6d.*

———— An English Grammar and Reading Book, for Lower Forms in Classical Schools. *Fourth Edition.* Extra fcap. 8vo. *3s. 6d.*

Saxon Chronicles. Two of the Saxon Chronicles parallel (787–1001 A.D.). A Revised Text. Edited, with Introduction, Critical Notes, and Glossary, by CHARLES PLUMMER, M.A., on the basis of an Edition by JOHN EARLE, M.A. Crown 8vo., stiff covers, *3s.*

Specimens of Early English. A New and Revised Edition. With Introduction, Notes, and Glossarial Index.
    Part I. From Old English Homilies to King Horn (A.D. 1150 to A.D. 1300). By R. MORRIS, LL.D. *Ed. 2.* Extra fcap. 8vo. *9s.*
    Part II. From Robert of Gloucester to Gower (A.D. 1298 to A.D. 1393). By R. MORRIS, LL.D., and W. W. SKEAT, Litt. D. *Third Edition.* Extra fcap. 8vo. *7s. 6d.*

Specimens of English Literature, from the 'Ploughmans Crede' to the 'Shepheardes Calender' (A.D. 1394 to A.D. 1579). With Introduction, Notes, and Glossarial Index. By W. W. SKEAT, Litt. D. *Fourth Edition.* Extra fcap. 8vo. *7s. 6d.*

Typical Selections from the best English Writers, with Introductory Notices. In 2 vols. Extra fcap. 8vo. *3s. 6d.* each.
    Vol. I. Latimer to Berkeley.   Vol. II. Pope to Macaulay.

I. Literature and Philology.

A SERIES OF ENGLISH CLASSICS.
(CHRONOLOGICALLY ARRANGED)

Ormulum, The, with the Notes and Glossary of Dr. R. M. WHITE. Edited by R. HOLT, M.A. 2 vols. Extra fcap. 8vo. 1*l*. 1*s*.

CHAUCER.
  I. The Prologue, the Knightes Tale, The Nonne Preestes Tale; from the Canterbury Tales. Edited by R. MORRIS, LL.D. A New Edition, with Collations and Additional Notes by W. W. SKEAT, Litt.D. Extra fcap. 8vo. 2*s*. 6*d*.
  II. The Prioresses Tale; Sir Thopas; The Monkes Tale; The Clerkes Tale; The Squieres Tale, &c. Edited by W. W. SKEAT, Litt.D. *Third Edition.* Extra fcap. 8vo. 4*s*. 6*d*.
  III. The Tale of the Man of Lawe; The Pardoneres Tale; The Second Nonnes Tale; The Chanouns Yemannes Tale. By W. W. SKEAT, Litt.D. *New Edition.* Extra fcap. 8vo. 4*s*. 6*d*.
  IV. Minor Poems. Edited by W. W. SKEAT, Litt.D. Crown 8vo. 10*s*. 6*d*.
  V. The Legend of Good Women. By W. W. SKEAT, Litt.D. Crown 8vo. 6*s*.

Langland, W. The Vision of William concerning Piers the Plowman, in three Parallel Texts; together with Richard the Redeless. By WILLIAM LANGLAND (about 1362-1399 A.D.). Edited from numerous Manuscripts, with Preface, Notes, and a Glossary, by W. W. SKEAT, Litt.D. 2 vols. 8vo. 1*l*. 11*s*. 6*d*.

—— The Vision of William concerning Piers the Plowman, by WILLIAM LANGLAND. Edited, with Notes, by W. W. SKEAT, Litt.D. *Fourth Edition.* Extra fcap. 8vo. 4*s*. 6*d*.

Gamelyn, the Tale of. Edited, with Notes, Glossary, &c., by W. W. SKEAT, Litt.D. Extra fcap. 8vo. Stiff covers, 1*s*. 6*d*.

WYCLIFFE.
  I. The Books of Job, Psalms, Proverbs, Ecclesiastes, and the Song of Solomon: according to the Wycliffite Version made by NICHOLAS DE HEREFORD, about A.D. 1381, and Revised by JOHN PURVEY, about A.D. 1388. With Introduction and Glossary by W. W. SKEAT, Litt.D. Extra fcap. 8vo. 3*s*. 6*d*.
  II. The New Testament in English, according to the Version by JOHN WYCLIFFE, about A.D. 1380, and Revised by JOHN PURVEY, about A.D. 1388. With Introduction and Glossary by W. W. SKEAT, Litt.D. Extra fcap. 8vo. 6*s*.

Minot (Laurence). Poems. Edited, with Introduction and Notes, by JOSEPH HALL, M.A., Head Master of the Hulme Grammar School, Manchester. Extra fcap. 8vo. 4*s*. 6*d*.

Spenser's Faery Queene. Books I and II. Designed chiefly for the use of Schools. With Introduction and Notes by G. W. KITCHIN, D.D., and Glossary by A. L. MAYHEW, M.A. Extra fcap. 8vo. 2s. 6d. each.

Hooker. Ecclesiastical Polity, Book I. Edited by R. W. CHURCH, M.A. *Second Edition.* Extra fcap. 8vo. 2s. [See also p. 43.]

OLD ENGLISH DRAMA.

I. York Plays.—The Plays performed by the Crafts or Mysteries of York, on the day of Corpus Christi, in the 14th, 15th, and 16th centuries; now first printed from the unique manuscript in the library of Lord Ashburnham. Edited, with Introduction and Glossary, by LUCY TOULMIN SMITH. 8vo. 1l. 1s.

II. The Pilgrimage to Parnassus, with the Two Parts of the Return from Parnassus. Three Comedies performed in St. John's College, Cambridge, A.D. MDXCVII–MDCI. Edited from MSS. by W. D. MACRAY, M.A., F.S.A. Medium 8vo. Bevelled Boards, Gilt top, 8s. 6d.

III. Marlowe's Edward II. With Introduction, Notes, &c. By O. W. TANCOCK, M.A. Extra fcap. 8vo. Paper covers, 2s.; cloth, 3s.

IV. Marlowe and Greene. Marlowe's Tragical History of Dr. Faustus, and Greene's Honourable History of Friar Bacon and Friar Bungay. Edited by A. W. WARD, Litt. D. *New and enlarged Edition.* Extra fcap. 8vo. 6s. 6d.

SHAKESPEARE. Select Plays. Extra fcap. 8vo. stiff covers.

Edited by W. G. CLARK, M.A., and W. ALDIS WRIGHT, D.C.L.

The Merchant of Venice. 1s.   Macbeth. 1s. 6d.
Richard the Second. 1s. 6d.   Hamlet. 2s.

Edited by W. ALDIS WRIGHT, D.C.L.

The Tempest. 1s. 6d.   Midsummer Night's Dream. 1s. 6d.
As You Like It. 1s. 6d.   Coriolanus. 2s. 6d.
Julius Cæsar. 2s.   Henry the Fifth. 2s.
Richard the Third. 2s. 6d.   Twelfth Night. 1s. 6d.
King Lear. 1s. 6d.   King John. 1s. 6d.

Shakespeare as a Dramatic Artist; a popular Illustration of the Principles of Scientific Criticism. By R. G. MOULTON, M.A. *Second Edition, Enlarged.* Crown 8vo. 6s.

Bacon.

I. Advancement of Learning. Edited by W. ALDIS WRIGHT, D.C.L. *Third Edition.* Extra fcap. 8vo. 4s. 6d.

II. The Essays. With Introduction and Notes. By S. H. REYNOLDS, M.A. *In preparation.*

I. Literature and Philology.

MILTON.
    I. Areopagitica. With Introduction and Notes. By JOHN W. HALES, M.A. *Third Edition.* Extra fcap. 8vo. 3s.
    II. Poems. Edited by R. C. BROWNE, M.A. In two Volumes. *Fifth Edition.* Extra fcap. 8vo. 6s. 6d.
    Sold separately, Vol. I. 4s.; Vol. II. 3s.
In paper covers:
Lycidas, 3d.   L'Allegro, 3d.   Il Penseroso, 4d.   Comus, 6d.
    III. Paradise Lost. Book I. Edited by H. C. BEECHING, B.A. Extra fcap. 8vo. stiff covers, 1s. 6d.; in Parchment, 3s. 6d.
    IV. Samson Agonistes. Edited, with Introduction and Notes, by J. CHURTON COLLINS, M.A. Extra fcap. 8vo. stiff covers, 1s.

Bunyan.
    I. The Pilgrim's Progress, Grace Abounding, Relation of the Imprisonment of Mr. JOHN BUNYAN. Edited, with Biographical Introduction and Notes, by E. VENABLES, M.A. Extra fcap. 8vo. 5s. In Parchment, 6s.
    II. Holy War, &c. *In the Press.*

Clarendon.
    I. History of the Rebellion. Book VI. Edited by T. ARNOLD, M.A. Extra fcap. 8vo. 4s. 6d.
    II. Characters and Episodes of the Great Rebellion. Selections from Clarendon. Edited by G. BOYLE, M.A., Dean of Salisbury. Crown 8vo., gilt top, 7s. 6d. [See also p. 44.]

Dryden. Select Poems. (Stanzas on the Death of Oliver Cromwell; Astræa Redux; Annus Mirabilis; Absalom and Achitophel; Religio Laici; The Hind and the Panther.) Edited by W. D. CHRISTIE, M.A. *Second Edition.* Extra fcap. 8vo. 3s. 6d.

—— An Essay of Dramatic Poesy. Edited, with Notes, by THOMAS ARNOLD, M.A. Extra fcap. 8vo. 3s. 6d.

Locke. Conduct of the Understanding. Edited, with Introduction, Notes, &c., by T. FOWLER, D.D. *Second Edition.* Extra fcap. 8vo. 2s.

Addison. Selections from Papers in the Spectator. With Notes. By T. ARNOLD, M.A. Extra fcap. 8vo. 4s. 6d. In Parchment, 6s.

Steele. Selections from the Tatler, Spectator, and Guardian. Edited by AUSTIN DOBSON. Extra fcap. 8vo. 5s. In Parchment, 7s. 6d.

Pope. Select Works. With Introduction and Notes. By MARK PATTISON, B.D.
    I. Essay on Man. Extra fcap. 8vo. 1s. 6d.
    II. Satires and Epistles. Extra fcap. 8vo. 2s.

Parnell. The Hermit. Paper covers, 2d.

Oxford: Clarendon Press.

A Series of English Classics.

Gray. Selected Poems. Edited by EDMUND GOSSE, M.A. Extra fcap. 8vo. In Parchment, 3s.
—— *The same*, together with Supplementary Notes for Schools by FOSTER WATSON, M.A. *Stiff covers*, 1s. 6d.
—— Elegy, and Ode on Eton College. Paper covers, 2d.

Goldsmith.
I. Selected Poems. Edited with Introduction and Notes, by AUSTIN DOBSON. Extra fcap. 8vo. 3s. 6d. In Parchment, 4s. 6d.
II. The Traveller. Edited by G. BIRKBECK HILL, D.C.L. Stiff covers, 1s.
III. The Deserted Village. Paper covers, 2d.

JOHNSON.
I. Rasselas. Edited, with Introduction and Notes, by G. BIRKBECK HILL, D.C.L. Extra fcap. 8vo. Bevelled boards, 3s. 6d. In Parchment, 4s. 6d.
II. Rasselas; Lives of Dryden and Pope. Edited by ALFRED MILNES, M.A. (London). Extra fcap. 8vo. 4s. 6d., or Lives of DRYDEN and POPE only, stiff covers, 2s. 6d.
III. Life of Milton. By C. H. FIRTH, M.A. Extra fcap. 8vo. cloth, 2s. 6d. Stiff covers, 1s. 6d.
IV. Wit and Wisdom of Samuel Johnson. Edited by G. BIRKBECK HILL, D.C.L. Crown 8vo. 7s. 6d.
V. Vanity of Human Wishes. With Notes, by E. J. PAYNE, M.A. Paper covers, 4d.

BOSWELL.
Boswell's Life of Johnson. With the Journal of a Tour to the Hebrides. Edited by G. BIRKBECK HILL, D.C.L., Pembroke College. 6 vols. Medium 8vo. Half bound, 3l. 3s.

Cowper. Edited, with Life, Introductions, and Notes, by H. T. GRIFFITH, B.A.
I. The Didactic Poems of 1782, with Selections from the Minor Pieces, A.D. 1779-1783. Extra fcap. 8vo. 3s.
II. The Task, with Tirocinium, and Selections from the Minor Poems, A.D. 1784-1799. *Second Edition*. Extra fcap. 8vo. 3s.

Burke. Select Works. Edited, with Introduction and Notes, by E. J. PAYNE, M.A.
I. Thoughts on the Present Discontents; the two Speeches on America. *Second Edition*. Extra fcap. 8vo. 4s. 6d.
II. Reflections on the French Revolution. *Second Edition*. Extra fcap. 8vo. 5s.
III. Four Letters on the Proposals for Peace with the Regicide Directory of France. *Second Edition*. Extra fcap. 8vo. 5s.

Burns. Selected Poems. Edited, with Introduction, Notes, and a Glossary, by J. LOGIE ROBERTSON, M.A. Crown 8vo. 6s.

Keats. Hyperion, Book I. With Notes by W. T. ARNOLD, B.A. Paper covers, 4d.

Byron. Childe Harold. With Introduction and Notes, by H. F. TOZER, M.A. Extra fcap. 8vo. 3s. 6d. In Parchment, 5s.

Scott. Lay of the Last Minstrel. Edited by W. MINTO, M.A. With Map. Extra fcap. 8vo. 2s. Parchment, 3s. 6d.

—— Lay of the Last Minstrel. Introduction and Canto I, with Preface and Notes, by the same Editor. 6d.

—— Marmion. Edited, with Introduction and Notes, by T. BAYNE. Extra fcap. 8vo. 3s. 6d.

Campbell. Gertrude of Wyoming. Edited, with Introduction and Notes, by H. MACAULAY FITZGIBBON, M.A. Extra fcap. 8vo. 2s.

Shairp. Aspects of Poetry; being Lectures delivered at Oxford, by J. C. SHAIRP, LL.D. Crown 8vo. 10s. 6d.

Palgrave. The Treasury of Sacred Song. With Notes Explanatory and Biographical. By F. T. PALGRAVE, M.A. Half vellum, gilt top, 10s. 6d.

SECTION III.

EUROPEAN LANGUAGES. MEDIAEVAL AND MODERN.

(1) FRENCH AND ITALIAN.

Brachet's Etymological Dictionary of the French Language. Translated by G. W. KITCHIN, D.D. *Third Edition.* Crown 8vo. 7s. 6d.

—— Historical Grammar of the French Language. Translated by G. W. KITCHIN, D.D. *Fourth Edition.* Extra fcap. 8vo. 3s. 6d.

Saintsbury. Primer of French Literature. By GEORGE SAINTSBURY, M.A. Extra fcap. 8vo. 2s.

—— Short History of French Literature. Crown 8vo. 10s. 6d.

—— Specimens of French Literature, from Villon to Hugo. Crown 8vo. 9s.

Beaumarchais' Le Barbier de Séville. Edited, with Introduction and Notes, by AUSTIN DOBSON. Extra fcap. 8vo. 2s. 6d.

French and Italian.

Corneille's Horace. Edited, with Introduction and Notes, by GEORGE SAINTSBURY, M.A. Extra fcap. 8vo. 2s. 6d.

Molière's Les Précieuses Ridicules. Edited, with Introduction and Notes, by ANDREW LANG, M.A. Extra fcap. 8vo. 1s. 6d.

Musset's On ne badine pas avec l'Amour, and Fantasio. Edited, with Prolegomena, Notes, etc., by W. H. POLLOCK. Extra fcap. 8vo. 2s.

Racine's Esther. Edited, with Introduction and Notes, by GEORGE SAINTSBURY, M.A. Extra fcap. 8vo. 2s.

Voltaire's Mérope. Edited, with Introduction and Notes, by GEORGE SAINTSBURY, M.A. Extra fcap. 8vo. 2s.

* *The above six Plays may be had in ornamental case, and bound in Imitation Parchment, price 12s. 6d.*

MASSON'S FRENCH CLASSICS.
Edited by Gustave Masson, B.A.

Corneille's Cinna. With Notes, Glossary, etc. Extra fcap. 8vo. 2s. Stiff covers, 1s. 6d.

Louis XIV and his Contemporaries; as described in Extracts from the best Memoirs of the Seventeenth Century. With English Notes, Genealogical Tables, &c. Extra fcap. 8vo. 2s. 6d.

Maistre, Xavier de, &c. Voyage autour de ma Chambre, by XAVIER DE MAISTRE. Ourika, by MADAME DE DURAS; Le Vieux Tailleur, by MM. ERCKMANN-CHATRIAN; La Veillée de Vincennes, by ALFRED DE VIGNY; Les Jumeaux de l'Hôtel Corneille, by EDMOND ABOUT; Mésaventures d'un Écolier, by RODOLPHE TÖPFFER. *Third Edition, Revised.* Extra fcap. 8vo. 2s. 6d.

—— Voyage autour de ma Chambre. Limp. 1s. 6d.

Molière's Les Fourberies de Scapin, and **Racine's** Athalie. With Voltaire's Life of Molière. Extra fcap. 8vo. 2s. 6d.

—— Les Fourberies de Scapin. With Voltaire's Life of Molière. Extra fcap. 8vo. stiff covers, 1s. 6d.

—— Les Femmes Savantes. With Notes, Glossary, etc. Extra fcap. 8vo. cloth, 2s. Stiff covers, 1s. 6d.

Racine's Andromaque, and **Corneille's** Le Menteur. With LOUIS RACINE'S Life of his Father. Extra fcap. 8vo. 2s. 6d.

Regnard's Le Joueur, and **Brueys and Palaprat's** Le Grondeur. Extra fcap. 8vo. 2s. 6d.

Sévigné, Madame de, and her chief Contemporaries, Selections from their Correspondence. Intended more especially for Girls' Schools. Extra fcap. 8vo. 3s.

I. Literature and Philology.

Blouët. L'Éloquence de la Chaire et de la Tribune Françaises. Edited by PAUL BLOUËT, B.A. Vol. I. Sacred Oratory. Extra fcap. 8vo. 2s. 6d.

Gautier, Théophile. Scenes of Travel. Selected and Edited by GEORGE SAINTSBURY, M.A. Extra fcap. 8vo. 2s.

Perrault's Popular Tales. Edited from the Original Editions, with Introduction, etc., by ANDREW LANG, M.A. Extra fcap. 8vo., paper boards, 5s. 6d.

Quinet's Lettres à sa Mère. Selected and Edited by GEORGE SAINTSBURY, M.A. Extra fcap. 8vo. 2s.

Sainte-Beuve. Selections from the Causeries du Lundi. Edited by GEORGE SAINTSBURY, M.A. Extra fcap. 8vo. 2s.

Dante. Selections from the Inferno. With Introduction and Notes. By H. B. COTTERILL, B.A. Extra fcap. 8vo. 4s. 6d.

Tasso. La Gerusalemme Liberata. Cantos i, ii. With Introduction and Notes. By the same Editor. Extra fcap. 8vo. 2s. 6d.

(2) GERMAN AND GOTHIC.

Max Müller. The German Classics, from the Fourth to the Nineteenth Century. With Biographical Notices, Translations into Modern German, and Notes. By F. MAX MÜLLER, M.A. A New Edition, Revised, Enlarged, and Adapted to WILHELM SCHERER'S 'History of German Literature,' by F. LICHTENSTEIN. 2 vols. Crown 8vo. 21s.

Scherer. A History of German Literature by WILHELM SCHERER. Translated from the Third German Edition by Mrs. F. C. CONYBEARE. Edited by F. MAX MÜLLER. 2 vols. 8vo. 21s.

Skeat. The Gospel of St. Mark in Gothic. By W. W. SKEAT, Litt. D. Extra fcap. 8vo. cloth, 4s.

Wright. An Old High German Primer. With Grammar, Notes, and Glossary. By JOSEPH WRIGHT, Ph.D. Extra fcap. 8vo. 3s. 6d.

—— A Middle High German Primer. With Grammar, Notes, and Glossary. By JOSEPH WRIGHT, Ph.D. Extra fcap. 8vo. 3s. 6d.

LANGE'S GERMAN COURSE.

By Hermann Lange, Lecturer on French and German at the Manchester Technical School, etc.

I. **Germans at Home**; a Practical Introduction to German Conversation, with an Appendix containing the Essentials of German Grammar. Third Edition. 8vo. 2s. 6d.

II. **German Manual**; a German Grammar, Reading Book, and a Handbook of German Conversation. 8vo. 7s. 6d.

III. **Grammar of the German Language.** 8vo. 3s. 6d.

IV. **German Composition**; A Theoretical and Practical Guide to the Art of Translating English Prose into German. *Second Edition.* 8vo. 4s. 6d. [*A Key to the above*, price 5s. *Just Published.*]

German Spelling; A Synopsis of the Changes which it has undergone through the Government Regulations of 1880. 6d.

BUCHHEIM'S GERMAN CLASSICS.

Edited, with Biographical, Historical, and Critical Introductions, Arguments (to the Dramas), and Complete Commentaries, by C. A. BUCHHEIM, *Phil. Doc., Professor in King's College, London.*

Becker (the Historian). Friedrich der Grosse. Edited, with Notes, an Historical Introduction, and a Map. 3s. 6d.

Goethe:
  (*a*) Egmont. A Tragedy. 3s.
  (*b*) Iphigenie auf Tauris. A Drama. 3s.

Heine:
  (*a*) Prosa: being Selections from his Prose Writings. 4s. 6d.
  (*b*) Harzreise. Cloth, 2s. 6d.; paper covers, 1s. 6d.

Lessing:
  (*a*) Nathan der Weise. A Dramatic Poem. 4s. 6d.
  (*b*) Minna von Barnhelm. A Comedy. 3s. 6d.

Schiller:
  (*a*) Wilhelm Tell. A Drama. Large Edition. With Map. 3s. 6d.
  (*b*) Wilhelm Tell. School Edition. With Map. 2s.
  (*c*) Historische Skizzen. With Map. 2s. 6d.

Modern German Reader. A Graduated Collection of Extracts from Modern German Authors:—

  Part I. **Prose Extracts.** With English Notes, a Grammatical Appendix, and a complete Vocabulary. *Fourth Edition.* 2s. 6d.

  Part II. **Extracts in Prose and Poetry.** With English Notes and an Index. *Second Edition.* 2s. 6d.

German Poetry for Beginners. Edited with English Notes and a complete Vocabulary, by EMMA S. BUCHHEIM. Extra fcap. 8vo. 2s.

Chamisso. Peter Schlemihl's Wundersame Geschichte. Edited with Notes and a complete Vocabulary, by EMMA S. BUCHHEIM. Extra fcap. 8vo. 2s.

I. Literature and Philology.

Lessing. The Laokoon, with Introduction, English Notes, etc. By A. HAMANN, Phil. Doc., M.A. Extra fcap. 8vo. 4s. 6d.

Niebuhr: Griechische Heroen-Geschichten (Tales of Greek Heroes). With English Notes and Vocabulary, by EMMA S. BUCHHEIM. Second, Revised Edition. Extra fcap. 8vo. cloth, 2s., stiff covers, 1s. 6d.
    Edition A. *Text in German Type.*
    Edition B. *Text in Roman Type.*

Schiller's Wilhelm Tell. Translated into English Verse by E. MASSIE, M.A. Extra fcap. 8vo. 5s.

(3) SCANDINAVIAN.

Cleasby and Vigfússon. An Icelandic-English Dictionary, based on the MS. collections of the late RICHARD CLEASBY. Enlarged and completed by G. VIGFÚSSON, M.A. With an Introduction, and Life of Richard Cleasby, by G. WEBBE DASENT, D.C.L. 4to. 3l. 7s.

Sweet. Icelandic Primer, with Grammar, Notes, and Glossary. By HENRY SWEET, M.A. Extra fcap. 8vo. 3s. 6d.

Vigfússon. Sturlunga Saga, including the Islendinga Saga of Lawman STURLA THORDSSON and other works. Edited by Dr. GUDBRAND VIGFÚSSON. In 2 vols. 8vo. 2l. 2s.

Vigfússon and Powell. Icelandic Prose Reader, with Notes, Grammar, and Glossary. By G. VIGFÚSSON, M.A., and F. YORK POWELL, M.A. Extra fcap. 8vo. 10s. 6d.

—— Corpvs Poeticvm Boreale. The Poetry of the Old Northern Tongue, from the Earliest Times to the Thirteenth Century. Edited, classified, and translated, with Introduction, Excursus, and Notes, by GUDBRAND VIGFÚSSON, M.A., and F. YORK POWELL, M.A. 2 vols. 8vo. 2l. 2s.

—— The Landnáma-Bók. Edited and translated by the same. *In the Press.*

SECTION IV.
CLASSICAL LANGUAGES.
(1) LATIN.
STANDARD WORKS AND EDITIONS.

Ellis. Harleian MS. 2610; Ovid's Metamorphoses I, II, III, 1–622; XXIV Latin Epigrams from Bodleian or other MSS.; Latin Glosses on Apollinaris Sidonius from MS. Digby 172. Collated and Edited by ROBINSON ELLIS, M.A., LL.D. (Anecdota Oxon.) 4s.

King and Cookson. The Principles of Sound and Inflexion, as illustrated in the Greek and Latin Languages. By J. E. KING, M.A., and CHRISTOPHER COOKSON, M.A. 8vo. 18s.

Lewis and Short. A Latin Dictionary, founded on Andrews' edition of Freund's Latin Dictionary, revised, enlarged, and in great part rewritten by CHARLTON T. LEWIS, Ph.D., and CHARLES SHORT, LL.D. 4to. 1l. 5s.

Nettleship. Contributions to Latin Lexicography. By HENRY NETTLESHIP, M.A. 8vo. 21s.

—— Lectures and Essays on Subjects connected with Latin Scholarship and Literature. By HENRY NETTLESHIP, M.A. Crown 8vo. 7s. 6d.

—— The Roman Satura. 8vo. sewed, 1s.

—— Ancient Lives of Vergil. 8vo. sewed, 2s.

Papillon. Manual of Comparative Philology. By T. L. PAPILLON, M.A. Third Edition. Crown 8vo. 6s.

Pinder. Selections from the less known Latin Poets. By NORTH PINDER, M.A. 8vo. 15s.

Sellar. Roman Poets of the Augustan Age. VIRGIL. By W. Y. SELLAR, M.A. New Edition. Crown 8vo. 9s.

—— Roman Poets of the Republic. Third Edition. Crown 8vo. 10s.

Wordsworth. Fragments and Specimens of Early Latin. With Introductions and Notes. By J. WORDSWORTH, D.D. 8vo. 18s.

Avianus. The Fables. Edited, with Prolegomena, Critical Apparatus, Commentary, etc., by ROBINSON ELLIS, M.A., LL.D. 8vo. 8s. 6d.

Catulli Veronensis Liber. Iterum recognovit, apparatum criticum prolegomena appendices addidit, ROBINSON ELLIS, A.M. 8vo. 16s.

Catullus, a Commentary on. By ROBINSON ELLIS, M.A. Second Edition. 8vo. 18s.

Cicero. De Oratore. With Introduction and Notes. By A. S. WILKINS, Litt.D.
Book I. Second Edition. 8vo. 7s. 6d. Book II. 8vo. 5s.

—— Philippic Orations. With Notes. By J. R. KING, M.A. Second Edition. 8vo. 10s. 6d.

—— Select Letters. With English Introductions, Notes, and Appendices. By ALBERT WATSON, M.A. Third Edition. 8vo. 18s.

Horace. With a Commentary. Vol. I. The Odes, Carmen Seculare, and Epodes. By E. C. WICKHAM, M.A. Second Edition. 8vo. 12s.

I. Literature and Philology.

Livy, Book I. With Introduction, Historical Examination, and Notes. By J. R. SEELEY, M.A. *Second Edition.* 8vo. 6s.

Nonius Marcellus, de Compendiosa Doctrina (Harleian MS. 2719). Collated by J. H. ONIONS, M.A. (Anecdota Oxon.) 3s. 6d.

Ovid. P. Ovidii Nasonis Ibis. Ex Novis Codicibus edidit, Scholia Vetera Commentarium cum Prolegomenis Appendice Indice addidit, R. ELLIS, A.M. 8vo. 10s. 6d.

—— P. Ovidi Nasonis Tristium Libri V. Recensuit S. G. OWEN, A.M. 8vo. 16s.

Persius. The Satires. With a Translation and Commentary. By JOHN CONINGTON, M.A. Edited by HENRY NETTLESHIP, M.A. *Second Edition.* 8vo. 7s. 6d.

Plautus. Bentley's Plautine Emendations. From his copy of Gronovius. By E. A. SONNENSCHEIN, M.A. (Anecdota Oxon.) 2s. 6d.

Scriptores Latini rei Metricae. Edidit T. GAISFORD, S.T.P. 8vo. 5s.

Tacitus. The Annals. Books I–VI. Edited, with Introduction and Notes, by H. FURNEAUX, M.A. 8vo. 18s.

LATIN EDUCATIONAL WORKS.
GRAMMARS, EXERCISE BOOKS, &C.

ALLEN.

Rudimenta Latina. Comprising Accidence, and Exercises of a very Elementary Character, for the use of Beginners. By JOHN BARROW ALLEN, M.A. Extra fcap. 8vo. 2s.

An Elementary Latin Grammar. By the same Author. *Fifty-Seventh Thousand.* Extra fcap. 8vo. 2s. 6d.

A First Latin Exercise Book. By the same Author. *Fourth Edition.* Extra fcap. 8vo. 2s. 6d.

A Second Latin Exercise Book. By the same Author. Extra fcap. 8vo. 3s. 6d.

*** A Key to First and Second Latin Exercise Books, in one volume, price 5s. Supplied to *Teachers only* on application to the Secretary of the Clarendon Press.

An Introduction to Latin Syntax. By W. S. GIBSON, M.A. Extra fcap. 8vo. 2s.

First Latin Reader. By T. J. NUNNS, M.A. *Third Edition.* Extra fcap. 8vo. 2s.

A Latin Prose Primer. By J. Y. SARGENT, M.A. Extra fcap. 8vo. 2s. 6d.

Passages for Translation into Latin. For the use of Passmen and others. Selected by J. Y. SARGENT, M.A. *Seventh Edition.* Extra fcap. 8vo. 2s. 6d.

*** A Key to the above, price 5s. Supplied to *Teachers only* on application to the Secretary of the Clarendon Press.

Exercises in Latin Prose Composition; with Introduction, Notes, and Passages of Graduated Difficulty for Translation into Latin. By G. G. RAMSAY, M.A., LL.D. *Second Edition.* Extra fcap. 8vo. 4s. 6d.

Hints and Helps for Latin Elegiacs. By H. LEE-WARNER, M.A. Extra fcap. 8vo. 3s. 6d.

*** A Key to the above, price 4s. 6d. Supplied to *Teachers only* on application to the Secretary of the Clarendon Press.

Reddenda Minora, or Easy Passages, Latin and Greek, for Unseen Translation. For the use of Lower Forms. Composed and selected by C. S. JERRAM, M.A. Extra fcap. 8vo. 1s. 6d.

Anglice Reddenda, or Extracts, Latin and Greek, for Unseen Translation. By C. S. JERRAM, M.A. *Third Edition, Revised and Enlarged.* Extra fcap. 8vo. 2s. 6d.

Anglice Reddenda. *Second Series.* By the same Author. Extra fcap. 8vo. 3s.

A School Latin Dictionary. By CHARLTON T. LEWIS, Ph.D. Small 4to. 18s.

LATIN CLASSICS FOR SCHOOLS.

Caesar. The Commentaries (for Schools). With Notes and Maps. By CHARLES E. MOBERLY, M.A.

The Gallic War. *Second Edition.* Extra fcap. 8vo. 4s. 6d.

—— Books I and II. Extra fcap. 8vo. 2s.

—— Books III, IV, V. Extra fcap. 8vo. 2s. 6d.

—— Books VI, VII, VIII. Extra fcap. 8vo. 3s. 6d.

The Civil War. Extra fcap. 8vo. 3s. 6d.

—— Book I. Extra fcap. 8vo. 2s.

Catulli Veronensis Carmina Selecta, secundum recognitionem ROBINSON ELLIS, A.M. Extra fcap. 8vo. 3s. 6d.

CICERO. Selection of Interesting and Descriptive Passages. With Notes. By HENRY WALFORD, M.A. In three Parts. *Third Edition.* Extra fcap. 8vo. 4s. 6d.

Each Part separately, limp, 1s. 6d.

Part I. Anecdotes from Grecian and Roman History.

Part II. Omens and Dreams: Beauties of Nature.

Part III. Rome's Rule of her Provinces.

I. Literature and Philology.

CICERO. De Senectute. Edited, with Introduction and Notes, by L. HUXLEY, M.A. Extra fcap. 8vo. 2s.

—— pro Cluentio. With Introduction and Notes. By W. RAMSAY, M.A. Edited by G. G. RAMSAY, M.A. *Second Edition.* Extra fcap. 8vo. 3s. 6d.

—— Select Orations (for Schools). In Verrem Actio Prima. De Imperio Gn. Pompeii. Pro Archia. Philippica IX. With Introduction and Notes by J. R. KING, M.A. *Second Edition.* Extra fcap. 8vo. 2s. 6d.

—— In Q. Caecilium Divinatio, and In C. Verrem Actio Prima. With Introduction and Notes, by J. R. KING, M.A. Extra fcap. 8vo. limp, 1s. 6d.

—— Speeches against Catilina. With Introduction and Notes, by E. A. UPCOTT, M.A. Extra fcap. 8vo. 2s. 6d.

—— Selected Letters (for Schools). With Notes. By the late C. E. PRICHARD, M.A., and E. R. BERNARD, M.A. *Second Edition.* Extra fcap. 8vo. 3s.

—— Select Letters. Text. By ALBERT WATSON, M.A. *Second Edition.* Extra fcap. 8vo. 4s.

Cornelius Nepos. With Notes. By OSCAR BROWNING, M.A. *Third Edition.* Revised by W. R. INGE, M.A. Extra fcap. 8vo. 3s.

Horace. With a Commentary. (In a size suitable for the use of Schools.) Vol. I. The Odes, Carmen Seculare, and Epodes. By E. C. WICKHAM, M.A. *Second Edition.* Extra fcap. 8vo. 6s.

—— Selected Odes. With Notes for the use of a Fifth Form. By E. C. WICKHAM, M.A. Extra fcap. 8vo. 2s.

Juvenal. Thirteen Satires. Edited, with Introduction and Notes, by C. H. PEARSON, M.A., and HERBERT A. STRONG, M.A., LL.D. Crown 8vo. 6s.
Also separately :—
Part I. Introduction, Text, etc., 3s. Part II. Notes, 3s. 6d.

Livy. Books V–VII. With Introduction and Notes. By A. R. CLUER, B.A. *Second Edition.* Revised by P. E. MATHESON, M.A. Extra fcap. 8vo. 5s.

—— Book V. By the same Editors. Extra fcap. 8vo. 2s. 6d.

—— Books XXI–XXIII. With Introduction and Notes. By M. T. TATHAM, M.A. *Second Edition, enlarged.* Extra fcap. 8vo. 5s.

—— Book XXI. By the same Editor. Extra fcap. 8vo. 2s. 6d.

—— Book XXII. With Introduction, Notes, and Maps. By the same Editor. Extra fcap. 8vo. 2s. 6d.

Latin: Educational Works.

Livy. Selections (for Schools). With Notes and Maps. By H. LEE-WARNER, M.A. Extra fcap. 8vo. In Parts, limp, each 1s. 6d.
- Part I. The Caudine Disaster.
- Part II. Hannibal's Campaign in Italy.
- Part III. The Macedonian War.

Ovid. Selections for the use of Schools. With Introductions and Notes, and an Appendix on the Roman Calendar. By W. RAMSAY, M.A. Edited by G. G. RAMSAY, M.A. *Third Edition.* Extra fcap. 8vo. 5s. 6d.

—— Tristia. Book I. The Text revised, with an Introduction and Notes. By S. G. OWEN, B.A. Extra fcap. 8vo. 3s. 6d.

—— Tristia. Book III. With Introduction and Notes. By the same Editor. Extra fcap. 8vo. 2s.

Plautus. Captivi. Edited by WALLACE M. LINDSAY, M.A. Extra fcap. 8vo. 2s. 6d.

Plautus. Trinummus. With Notes and Introductions. (Intended for the Higher Forms of Public Schools.) By C. E. FREEMAN, M.A., and A. SLOMAN, M.A. Extra fcap. 8vo. 3s.

Pliny. Selected Letters (for Schools). With Notes. By C. E. PRICHARD, M.A., and E. R. BERNARD, M.A. Extra fcap. 8vo. 3s.

Sallust. With Introduction and Notes. By W. W. CAPES, M.A. Extra fcap. 8vo. 4s. 6d.

Tacitus. The Annals. Books I-IV. Edited, with Introduction and Notes (for the use of Schools and Junior Students), by H. FURNEAUX, M.A. Extra fcap. 8vo. 5s.

—— The Annals. Book I. With Introduction and Notes, by the same Editor. Extra fcap. 8vo. limp. 2s.

Terence. Andria. With Notes and Introductions. By C. E. FREEMAN, M.A., and A. SLOMAN, M.A. Extra fcap. 8vo. 3s.

—— Adelphi. With Notes and Introductions. (Intended for the Higher Forms of Public Schools.) By A. SLOMAN, M.A. Extra fcap. 8vo. 3s.

—— Phormio. With Notes and Introductions. By A. SLOMAN, M.A. Extra fcap. 8vo. 3s.

Tibullus and **Propertius.** Selections. Edited by G. G. RAMSAY, M.A. (In one or two parts.) Extra fcap. 8vo. 6s.

Virgil. With Introduction and Notes. By T. L. PAPILLON, M.A. Two vols. Crown 8vo. 10s. 6d. *The Text separately,* 4s. 6d.

—— Bucolics. Edited by C. S. JERRAM, M.A. In one or two Parts. Extra fcap. 8vo. 2s. 6d.

—— Georgics. By the same Editor. *In the Press.*

I. Literature and Philology.

Virgil. Aeneid I. With Introduction and Notes, by the same Editor. Extra fcap. 8vo. limp, 1s. 6d.

—— Aeneid IX. Edited, with Introduction and Notes, by A. E. HAIGH, M.A. Extra fcap. 8vo. limp, 1s. 6d. In two Parts, 2s.

(2) GREEK.

STANDARD WORKS AND EDITIONS.

Allen. Notes on Abbreviations in Greek Manuscripts. By T. W. ALLEN, Queen's College, Oxford. Royal 8vo. 5s.

Chandler. A Practical Introduction to Greek Accentuation, by H. W. CHANDLER, M.A. *Second Edition.* 10s. 6d.

Haigh. The Attic Theatre. A Description of the Stage and Theatre of the Athenians, and of the Dramatic Performances at Athens. By A. E. HAIGH, M.A. 8vo. 12s. 6d.

Head. Historia Numorum: A Manual of Greek Numismatics. By BARCLAY V. HEAD. Royal 8vo. half-bound, 2l. 2s.

Hicks. A Manual of Greek Historical Inscriptions. By E. L. HICKS, M.A. 8vo. 10s. 6d.

King and Cookson. The Principles of Sound and Inflexion, as illustrated in the Greek and Latin Languages. By J. E. KING, M.A., and CHRISTOPHER COOKSON, M.A. 8vo. 18s.

Liddell and Scott. A Greek-English Lexicon, by H. G. LIDDELL, D.D., and ROBERT SCOTT, D.D. *Seventh Edition, Revised and Augmented throughout.* 4to. 1l. 16s.

Papillon. Manual of Comparative Philology. By T. L. PAPILLON, M.A. *Third Edition.* Crown 8vo. 6s.

Veitch. Greek Verbs, Irregular and Defective. By W. VEITCH, LL.D. *Fourth Edition.* Crown 8vo. 10s. 6d.

Vocabulary, a copious Greek-English, compiled from the best authorities. 24mo. 3s.

Aeschinem et Isocratem, Scholia Graeca in. Edidit G. DINDORFIUS. 1852. 8vo. 4s.

Aeschines. See under **Oratores Attici,** and **Demosthenes.**

Aeschyli quae supersunt in Codice Laurentiano quoad effici potuit et ad cognitionem necesse est visum typis descripta edidit R. MERKEL. Small folio, 1l. 1s.

Aeschylus: Tragoediae et Fragmenta, ex recensione GUIL. DINDORFII. *Second Edition,* 1851. 8vo. 5s. 6d.

—— Annotationes GUIL. DINDORFII. Partes II. 1841. 8vo. 10s.

Greek: Standard Works.

Anecdota Graeca Oxoniensia. Edidit J. A. CRAMER, S.T.P. Tomi IV. 1835. 8vo. 1*l*. 2*s*.

—— Graeca e Codd. MSS. Bibliothecae Regiae Parisiensis. Edidit J. A. CRAMER, S.T.P. Tomi IV. 1839. 8vo. 1*l*. 2*s*.

Apsinis et **Longini** Rhetorica. E Codicibus mss. recensuit JOH. BAKIUS. 1849. 8vo. 3*s*.

Aristophanes. A Complete Concordance to the Comedies and Fragments. By HENRY DUNBAR, M.D. 4to. 1*l*. 1*s*.

—— J. Caravellae Index in Aristophanem. 8vo. 3*s*.

—— Comoediae et Fragmenta, ex recensione GUIL. DINDORFII. Tomi II. 1835. 8vo. 11*s*.

—— Annotationes GUIL. DINDORFII. Partes II. 8vo. 11*s*.

—— Scholia Graeca ex Codicibus aucta et emendata a GUIL. DINDORFIO. Partes III. 1838. 8vo. 1*l*.

ARISTOTLE.

—— Ex recensione IMMANUELIS BEKKERI. Accedunt Indices Sylburgiani. Tomi XI. 1837. 8vo. 2*l*. 10*s*.
 The volumes (except vol. IX) may be had separately, price 5*s*. 6*d*. each.

—— The **Politics**, with Introductions, Notes, etc., by W. L. NEWMAN, M.A., Fellow of Balliol College, Oxford. Vols. I and II. Medium 8vo. 28*s*.

—— The **Politics**, translated into English, with Introduction, Marginal Analysis, Notes, and Indices, by B. JOWETT, M.A. Medium 8vo. 2 vols. 21*s*.

—— **Ethica Nicomachea**, ex recensione IMMANUELIS BEKKERI. Crown 8vo. 5*s*.

—— **Aristotelian Studies.** I. On the Structure of the Seventh Book of the Nicomachean Ethics. By J. C. WILSON, M.A. 8vo. Stiff covers, 5*s*.

—— The English Manuscripts of the **Nicomachean Ethics**, described in relation to Bekker's Manuscripts and other Sources. By J. A. STEWART, M.A. (Anecdota Oxon.) Small 4to. 3*s*. 6*d*.

—— On the History of the process by which the **Aristotelian** Writings arrived at their present form. By R. SHUTE, M.A. 8vo. 7*s*. 6*d*.

—— **Physics.** Book VII. Collation of various MSS.; with Introduction by R. SHUTE, M.A. (Anecdota Oxon.) Small 4to. 2*s*.

Choerobosci Dictata in Theodosii Canones, necnon Epimerismi in Psalmos. E Codicibus mss. edidit THOMAS GAISFORD, S.T.P. Tomi III. 1842. 8vo. 15*s*.

London: HENRY FROWDE, Amen Corner, E.C.

I. Literature and Philology.

Demosthenes. Ex recensione GUIL. DINDORFII. Tomi IX. 1846-1851. 8vo. 2*l.* 6*s.*
Separately:—
Textus. 1*l.* 1*s.* Annotations. 15*s.* Scholia. 10*s.*

Demosthenes and Aeschines. The Orations of Demosthenes and Aeschines on the Crown. With Introductory Essays and Notes. By G. A. SIMCOX, M.A., and W. H. SIMCOX, M.A. 8vo. 12*s.*

Euripides. Tragoediae et Fragmenta, ex recensione GUIL. DINDORFII. Tomi II. 1833. 8vo. 10*s.*

—— Annotationes GUIL. DINDORFII. Partes II. 1839. 8vo. 10*s.*

—— Scholia Graeca, ex Codicibus aucta et emendata a GUIL. DINDORFIO. Tomi IV. 1863. 8vo. 1*l.* 16*s.*

—— Alcestis, ex recensione G. DINDORFII. 1834. 8vo. 2*s.* 6*d.*

Harpocrationis Lexicon. Ex recensione G. DINDORFII. Tomi II. 1854. 8vo. 10*s.* 6*d.*

Hephaestionis Enchiridion, Terentianus Maurus, Proclus, etc. Edidit T. GAISFORD, S.T.P. Tomi II. 1855. 10*s.*

Heracliti Ephesii Reliquiae. Recensuit I. BYWATER, M.A. Appendicis loco additae sunt Diogenis Laertii Vita Heracliti, Particulae Hippocratei De Diaeta Lib. I., Epistolae Heracliteae. 8vo. 6*s.*

HOMER.

—— A Complete Concordance to the Odyssey and Hymns of Homer; to which is added a Concordance to the Parallel Passages in the Iliad, Odyssey, and Hymns. By HENRY DUNBAR, M.D. 4to. 1*l.* 1*s.*

—— Seberi Index in Homerum. 1780. 8vo. 6*s.* 6*d.*

—— A Grammar of the Homeric Dialect. By D. B. MONRO, M.A. 8vo. 10*s.* 6*d.*

—— Ilias, cum brevi Annotatione C. G. HEYNII. Accedunt Scholia minora. Tomi II. 1834. 8vo. 15*s.*

—— Ilias, ex rec. GUIL. DINDORFII. 1856. 8vo. 5*s.* 6*d.*

—— Scholia Graeca in Iliadem. Edited by W. DINDORF, after a new collation of the Venetian MSS. by D. B. MONRO, M.A., Provost of Oriel College. 4 vols. 8vo. 2*l.* 10*s.*

—— Scholia Graeca in Iliadem Townleyana. Recensuit ERNESTUS MAASS. 2 vols. 8vo. 1*l.* 16*s.*

—— Odyssea, ex rec. G. DINDORFII. 1855. 8vo. 5*s.* 6*d.*

—— Scholia Graeca in Odysseam. Edidit GUIL. DINDORFIUS. Tomi II. 1855. 8vo. 15*s.* 6*d.*

—— Odyssey. Books I–XII. Edited with English Notes, Appendices, etc. By W. W. MERRY, D.D., and the late JAMES RIDDELL, M.A. *Second Edition.* 8vo. 16*s.*

Oxford: Clarendon Press.

Oratores Attici, ex recensione BEKKERI:
    I. Antiphon, Andocides, et Lysias. 1823. 8vo. 7s.
    II. Isocrates. 1823. 8vo. 7s.
    III. Isaeus, Aeschines, Lycurgus, Dinarchus, etc. 1823. 8vo. 7s.

Paroemiographi Graeci, quorum pars nunc primum ex Codd. mss. vulgatur. Edidit T. GAISFORD, S.T.P. 1836. 8vo. 5s. 6d.

PLATO.

—— **Apology**, with a revised Text and English Notes, and a Digest of Platonic Idioms, by JAMES RIDDELL, M.A. 8vo. 8s. 6d.

—— **Philebus**, with a revised Text and English Notes, by EDWARD POSTE, M.A. 1860. 8vo. 7s. 6d.

—— **Sophistes** and **Politicus**, with a revised Text and English Notes, by L. CAMPBELL, M.A. 1867. 8vo. 18s.

—— **Theaetetus**, with a revised Text and English Notes, by L. CAMPBELL, M.A. *Second Edition*. 8vo. 10s. 6d.

—— **The Dialogues**, translated into English, with Analyses and Introductions, by B. JOWETT, M.A. 5 vols. medium 8vo. 3l. 10s.

—— **The Republic**, translated into English, with Analysis and Introduction, by B. JOWETT, M.A. Medium 8vo. 12s. 6d.; half-roan, 14s.

—— **Index to Plato**. Compiled for Prof. Jowett's Translation of the Dialogues. By EVELYN ABBOTT, M.A. 8vo. Paper covers, 2s. 6d.

Plotinus. Edidit F. CREUZER. Tomi III. 1835. 4to. 1l. 8s.

Polybius. Selections. Edited by J. L. STRACHAN-DAVIDSON, M.A. With Maps. Medium 8vo. buckram, 21s.

SOPHOCLES.

—— The Plays and Fragments. With English Notes and Introductions, by LEWIS CAMPBELL, M.A. 2 vols.
    Vol. I. Oedipus Tyrannus. Oedipus Coloneus. Antigone. 8vo. 16s.
    Vol. II. Ajax. Electra. Trachiniae. Philoctetes. Fragments. 8vo. 16s.

—— Tragoediae et Fragmenta, ex recensione et cum commentariis GUIL. DINDORFII. *Third Edition*. 2 vols. Fcap. 8vo. 1l. 1s.
    Each Play separately, limp, 2s. 6d.

—— The Text alone, with large margin, small 4to. 8s.

—— The Text alone, square 16mo. 3s. 6d.
    Each Play separately, limp, 6d.

—— Tragoediae et Fragmenta cum Annotationibus GUIL. DINDORFII. Tomi II. 1849. 8vo. 10s.
    The Text, Vol. I. 5s. 6d. The Notes, Vol. II. 4s. 6d.

I. Literature and Philology.

Stobaei Florilegium. Ad mss. fidem emendavit et supplevit T. GAISFORD, S.T.P. Tomi IV. 1822. 8vo. 1*l.*

—— Eclogarum Physicarum et Ethicarum libri duo. Accedit Hieroclis Commentarius in aurea carmina Pythagoreorum. Ad mss. Codd. recensuit T. GAISFORD, S.T.P. Tomi II. 1850. 8vo. 11*s.*

Thucydides. Translated into English, with Introduction, Marginal Analysis, Notes, and Indices. By B. JOWETT, M.A., Regius Professor of Greek. 2 vols. Medium 8vo. 1*l.* 12*s.*

XENOPHON. Ex rec. et cum annotatt. L. DINDORFII.

I. Historia Graeca. *Second Edition.* 1853. 8vo. 10*s.* 6*d.*

II. Expeditio Cyri. *Second Edition.* 1855. 8vo. 10*s.* 6*d.*

III. Institutio Cyri. 1857. 8vo. 10*s.* 6*d.*

IV. Memorabilia Socratis. 1862. 8vo. 7*s.* 6*d.*

V. Opuscula Politica Equestria et Venatica cum Arriani Libello de Venatione. 1866. 8vo. 10*s.* 6*d.*

GREEK EDUCATIONAL WORKS.

GRAMMARS, EXERCISE BOOKS, &c.

Chandler. The Elements of Greek Accentuation: abridged from his larger work by H. W. CHANDLER, M.A. Extra fcap. 8vo. 2*s.* 6*d.*

Liddell and Scott. An Intermediate Greek-English Lexicon, abridged from LIDDELL and SCOTT's Seventh Edition. Small 4to. 12*s.* 6*d.*

Liddell and Scott. A Greek-English Lexicon, abridged from LIDDELL and SCOTT's 4to. edition. Square 12mo. 7*s.* 6*d.*

Miller. A Greek Testament Primer. An Easy Grammar and Reading Book for the use of Students beginning Greek. By the Rev. E. MILLER, M.A. Extra fcap. 8vo. 3*s.* 6*d.*

Moulton. The Ancient Classical Drama. A Study in Literary Evolution. Intended for Readers in English and in the Original. By R. G. MOULTON, M.A. Crown 8vo. 8*s.* 6*d.*

Wordsworth. A Greek Primer, for the use of beginners in that Language. By the Right Rev. CHARLES WORDSWORTH, D.C.L. *Seventh Edition.* Extra fcap. 8vo. 1*s.* 6*d.*

—— Graecae Grammaticae Rudimenta in usum Scholarum. Auctore CAROLO WORDSWORTH, D.C.L. *Nineteenth Edition.* 12mo. 4*s.*

Passages for Translation into Greek Prose. By J. YOUNG SARGENT, M.A. Extra fcap. 8vo. 3*s.*

Exemplaria Graeca. Being Selections from "Passages for Translation into Greek Prose." By the same author. Extra fcap. 8vo. 3*s.*

Models and Materials for Greek Iambic Verse. By the same author. Extra fcap. 8vo. 4*s.* 6*d.*

Oxford: Clarendon Press.

Greek: Educational Works.

Graece Reddenda. By C. S. JERRAM, M.A. Extra fcap. 8vo. 2s. 6d.

Reddenda Minora, or Easy Passages, Latin and Greek, for Unseen Translation. By C. S. JERRAM, M.A. Extra fcap. 8vo. 1s. 6d.

Anglice Reddenda, or Extracts, Latin and Greek, for Unseen Translation. By C. S. JERRAM, M.A. Extra fcap. 8vo. 2s. 6d.

Anglice Reddenda. *Second Series.* By the same Author. Extra fcap. 8vo. 3s.

Golden Treasury of Ancient Greek Poetry. By R. S. WRIGHT, M.A. *Second Edition.* Revised by EVELYN ABBOTT, M.A., LL.D. Extra fcap. 8vo. 10s. 6d.

Golden Treasury of Greek Prose, being a Collection of the finest passages in the principal Greek Prose Writers, with Introductory Notices and Notes. By R. S. WRIGHT, M.A., and J. E. L. SHADWELL, M.A. Extra fcap. 8vo. 4s. 6d.

GREEK READERS.

Easy Greek Reader. By EVELYN ABBOTT, M.A. In one or two Parts. Extra fcap. 8vo. 3s.

First Greek Reader. By W. G. RUSHBROOKE, M.L. *Second Edition.* Extra fcap. 8vo. 2s. 6d.

Second Greek Reader. By A. M. BELL, M.A. Extra fcap. 8vo. 3s. 6d.

Specimens of Greek Dialects; being a Fourth Greek Reader. With Introductions, etc. By W. W. MERRY, D.D. Extra fcap. 8vo. 4s. 6d.

Selections from Homer and the Greek Dramatists; being a Fifth Greek Reader. With Explanatory Notes and Introductions to the Study of Greek Epic and Dramatic Poetry. By EVELYN ABBOTT, M.A. Extra fcap. 8vo. 4s. 6d.

GREEK CLASSICS FOR SCHOOLS.

Aeschylus. In Single Plays. Extra fcap. 8vo.
  I. Agamemnon. With Introduction and Notes, by ARTHUR SIDGWICK, M.A. *Third Edition.* 3s.
  II. Choephoroi. By the same Editor. 3s.
  III. Eumenides. By the same Editor. 3s.
  IV. Prometheus Bound. With Introduction and Notes, by A. O. PRICKARD, M.A. *Second Edition.* 2s.

London: HENRY FROWDE, Amen Corner, E.C.

I. Literature and Philology.

Aristophanes. In Single Plays. Edited, with English Notes, Introductions, &c., by W. W. MERRY, D.D. Extra fcap. 8vo.
   I. The Acharnians. *Third Edition*, 3s.
   II. The Clouds. *Third Edition*, 3s.
   III. The Frogs. *Second Edition*, 3s.
   IV. The Knights. *Second Edition*, 3s.
   V. The Birds. 3s. 6d.

Cebes. Tabula. With Introduction and Notes. By C. S. JERRAM, M.A. Extra fcap. 8vo. 2s. 6d.

Demosthenes. Orations against Philip. With Introduction and Notes, by EVELYN ABBOTT, M.A., and P. E. MATHESON, M.A.
   Vol. I. Philippic I. Olynthiacs I–III. Extra fcap. 8vo. 3s.
   Vol. II. De Pace, Philippic II, De Chersoneso, Philippic III. Extra fcap. 8vo. 4s. 6d.

Euripides. In Single Plays. Extra fcap. 8vo.
   I. Alcestis. Edited by C. S. JERRAM, M.A. 2s. 6d.
   II. Hecuba. Edited by C. H. RUSSELL, M.A. 2s. 6d.
   III. Helena. Edited, with Introduction, Notes, etc., for Upper and Middle Forms. By C. S. JERRAM, M.A. 3s.
   IV. Heracleidae. By C. S. JERRAM, M.A. 3s.
   V. Iphigenia in Tauris. By the same Editor. 3s.
   VI. Medea. By C. B. HEBERDEN, M.A. 2s.

Herodotus. Book IX. Edited, with Notes, by EVELYN ABBOTT, M.A. Extra fcap. 8vo. 3s.

—— Selections. Edited, with Introduction and Notes, by W. W. MERRY, D.D. Extra fcap. 8vo. 2s. 6d.

Homer.
   I. Iliad, Books I–XII. With an Introduction and a brief Homeric Grammar, and Notes. By D. B. MONRO, M.A. *Second Edition*. Extra fcap. 8vo. 6s.
   II. Iliad, Books XIII–XXIV. With Notes. By the same Editor. Extra fcap. 8vo. 6s.
   III. Iliad, Book I. By D. B. MONRO, M.A. *Second Edition*. Extra fcap. 8vo. 2s.
   IV. Iliad, Books VI and XXI. With Introduction and Notes. By HERBERT HAILSTONE, M.A. Extra fcap. 8vo. 1s. 6d. each.

Homer (*continued*).

V. Odyssey, Books I–XII. By W. W. MERRY, D.D. *Fortieth Thousand.* Extra fcap. 8vo. 5*s.*
Books I and II, separately, each 1*s.* 6*d.*

VI. Odyssey, Books XIII–XXIV. By the same Editor. Extra fcap. 8vo. 5*s.*

Lucian. Vera Historia. By C. S. JERRAM, M.A. *Second Edition.* Extra fcap. 8vo. 1*s.* 6*d.*

Lysias. Epitaphios. Edited, with Introduction and Notes, by F. J. SNELL, B.A. Extra fcap. 8vo. 2*s.*

Plato. Meno. With Introduction and Notes. By St. GEORGE STOCK, M.A. Extra fcap. 8vo. 2*s.* 6*d.*

—— The Apology. With Introduction and Notes. By St. GEORGE STOCK, M.A. Extra fcap. 8vo. 2*s.* 6*d.*

Sophocles. For the use of Schools. Edited with Introductions and English Notes. By LEWIS CAMPBELL, M.A., and EVELYN ABBOTT, M.A. *New and Revised Edition.* 2 vols. Extra fcap. 8vo. 10*s.* 6*d.*
Sold separately: Vol. I, Text, 4*s.* 6*d.*; Vol. II, Explanatory Notes, 6*s.*

Or in single Plays:—

Oedipus Coloneus, Antigone, 1*s.* 9*d.* each; Oedipus Tyrannus, Ajax, Electra, Trachiniae, Philoctetes, 2*s.* each.

Sophocles. Oedipus Rex: Dindorf's Text, with Notes by the present Bishop of St. David's. Extra fcap. 8vo. limp, 1*s.* 6*d.*

Theocritus (for Schools). With English Notes. By H. KYNASTON, D.D. (late SNOW). *Third Edition.* Extra fcap. 8vo. 4*s.* 6*d.*

XENOPHON. Easy Selections (for Junior Classes). With a Vocabulary, Notes, and Map. By J. S. PHILLPOTTS, B.C.L., and C. S. JERRAM, M.A. *Third Edition.* Extra fcap. 8vo. 3*s.* 6*d.*

—— Selections (for Schools). With Notes and Maps. By J. S. PHILLPOTTS, B.C.L. *Fourth Edition.* Extra fcap. 8vo. 3*s.* 6*d.*

—— Anabasis, Book I. Edited for the use of Junior Classes and Private Students. With Introduction, Notes, etc. By J. MARSHALL, M.A. Extra fcap. 8vo. 2*s.* 6*d.*

—— Anabasis, Book II. With Notes and Map. By C. S. JERRAM, M.A. Extra fcap. 8vo. 2*s.*

—— Anabasis, Book III. With Introduction, Analysis, Notes, etc. By J. MARSHALL, M.A. Extra fcap. 8vo. 2*s.* 6*d.*

London: HENRY FROWDE, Amen Corner, E.C.

Xenophon (*continued*).

—— Vocabulary to the Anabasis. By J. MARSHALL, M.A. Extra fcap. 8vo. 1s. 6d.

—— Cyropaedia, Book I. With Introduction and Notes. By C. BIGG, D.D. Extra fcap. 8vo. 2s.

—— Cyropaedia, Books IV and V. With Introduction and Notes. By C. BIGG, D.D. Extra fcap. 8vo. 2s. 6d.

—— Hellenica, Books I, II. With Introduction and Notes. By G. E. UNDERHILL, M.A. Extra fcap. 8vo. 3s.

—— Memorabilia. By J. MARSHALL, M.A. *In the Press.*

SECTION V.

ORIENTAL LANGUAGES*.

THE SACRED BOOKS OF THE EAST.

TRANSLATED BY VARIOUS ORIENTAL SCHOLARS, AND EDITED BY F. MAX MÜLLER.

First Series, Vols. I—XXIV. Demy 8vo. cloth.

Vol. I. The Upanishads. Translated by F. MAX MÜLLER. Part I. 10s. 6d.

Vol. II. The Sacred Laws of the Âryas, as taught in the Schools of Âpastamba, Gautama, Vâsishtha, and Baudhâyana. Translated by Prof. GEORG BÜHLER. Part I. 10s. 6d.

Vol. III. The Sacred Books of China. The Texts of Confucianism. Translated by JAMES LEGGE. Part I. 12s. 6d.

Vol. IV. The Zend-Avesta. Part I. The Vendidâd. Translated by JAMES DARMESTETER. 10s. 6d.

Vol. V. The Pahlavi Texts. Translated by E. W. WEST. Part I. 12s. 6d.

Vols. VI and IX. The Qur'ân. Translated by E. H. PALMER. 21s.

Vol. VII. The Institutes of Vishnu. Translated by JULIUS JOLLY. 10s. 6d.

Vol. VIII. The Bhagavadgîtâ, with The Sanatsugâtîya, and The Anugîtâ. Translated by KÂSHINÂTH TRIMBAK TELANG. 10s. 6d.

* See also ANECDOTA OXON., Series II, III, pp. 32, 33, below.

The Sacred Books of the East (*continued*).

Vol. X. The Dhammapada, translated from Pâli by F. MAX MÜLLER; and The Sutta-Nipâta, translated from Pâli by V. FAUSBÖLL; being Canonical Books of the Buddhists. 10*s.* 6*d.*

Vol. XI. Buddhist Suttas. Translated from Pâli by T. W. RHYS DAVIDS. 10*s.* 6*d.*

Vol. XII. The Satapatha-Brâhmana, according to the Text of the Mâdhyandina School. Translated by JULIUS EGGELING. Part I. Books I and II. 12*s.* 6*d.*

Vol. XIII. Vinaya Texts. Translated from the Pâli by T. W. RHYS DAVIDS and HERMANN OLDENBERG. Part I. 10*s.* 6*d.*

Vol. XIV. The Sacred Laws of the Âryas, as taught in the Schools of Âpastamba, Gautama, Vâsish*th*a and Baudhâyana. Translated by GEORG BÜHLER. Part II. 10*s.* 6*d.*

Vol. XV. The Upanishads. Translated by F. MAX MÜLLER. Part II. 10*s.* 6*d.*

Vol. XVI. The Sacred Books of China. The Texts of Confucianism. Translated by JAMES LEGGE. Part II. 10*s.* 6*d.*

Vol. XVII. Vinaya Texts. Translated from the Pâli by T. W. RHYS DAVIDS and HERMANN OLDENBERG. Part II. 10*s.* 6*d.*

Vol. XVIII. Pahlavi Texts. Translated by E. W. WEST. Part II. 12*s.* 6*d.*

Vol. XIX. The Fo-sho-hing-tsan-king. A Life of Buddha by Asvaghosha Bodhisattva, translated from Sanskrit into Chinese by Dharmaraksha, A.D. 420, and from Chinese into English by SAMUEL BEAL. 10*s.* 6*d.*

Vol. XX. Vinaya Texts. Translated from the Pâli by T. W. RHYS DAVIDS and HERMANN OLDENBERG. Part III. 10*s.* 6*d.*

Vol. XXI. The Saddharma-pu*nd*arîka; or, the Lotus of the True Law. Translated by H. KERN. 12*s.* 6*d.*

Vol. XXII. Gaina-Sûtras. Translated from Prâkrit by HERMANN JACOBI. Part I. 10*s.* 6*d.*

Vol. XXIII. The Zend-Avesta. Part II. Translated by JAMES DARMESTETER. 10*s.* 6*d.*

Vol. XXIV. Pahlavi Texts. Translated by E. W. WEST. Part III. 10*s.* 6*d.*

I. Literature and Philology.

THE SACRED BOOKS OF THE EAST. (Second Series.)

Vol. XXV. Manu. Translated by GEORG BÜHLER. 21s.

Vol. XXVI. The Satapatha-Brâhmaṇa. Translated by JULIUS EGGELING. Part II. 12s. 6d.

Vols. XXVII and XXVIII. The Sacred Books of China. The Texts of Confucianism. Translated by JAMES LEGGE. Parts III and IV. 25s.

Vols. XXIX and XXX. The Gṛihya-Sûtras, Rules of Vedic Domestic Ceremonies. Translated by HERMANN OLDENBERG.
Part I (Vol. XXIX). 12s. 6d.
Part II (Vol. XXX). *In the Press.*

Vol. XXXI. The Zend-Avesta. Part III. Translated by L. H. MILLS. 12s. 6d.

Vol. XXXIII. Nârada, and some Minor Law-books. Translated by JULIUS JOLLY. 10s. 6d.

Vol. XXXIV. The Vedânta-Sûtras, with Saṅkara's Commentary. Translated by G. THIBAUT. 12s. 6d.

The following Volumes are in the Press:—

Vol. XXXII. Vedic Hymns. Translated by F. MAX MÜLLER. Part I.

Vol. XXXV. Milinda. Translated by T. W. RHYS DAVIDS.

ARABIC. A Practical Arabic Grammar. Part I. Compiled by A. O. GREEN, Brigade Major, Royal Engineers. *Second Edition, Enlarged.* Crown 8vo. 7s. 6d.

CHINESE. Catalogue of the Chinese Translation of the Buddhist Tripiṭaka, the Sacred Canon of the Buddhists in China and Japan. Compiled by BUNYIU NANJIO. 4to. 1l. 12s. 6d.

—— Handbook of the Chinese Language. Parts I and II. Grammar and Chrestomathy. By JAMES SUMMERS. 8vo. 1l. 8s.

CHINESE. Record of Buddhistic Kingdoms; being an Account by the Chinese Monk FÂ-HIEN of his travels in India and Ceylon (A.D. 399–414) in search of the Buddhist Books of Discipline. Translated and annotated, with a Corean recension of the Chinese Text, by JAMES LEGGE, M.A., LL.D. Crown 4to., boards, 10s. 6d.

Oxford: Clarendon Press.

Oriental Languages. 31

CHALDEE. Book of Tobit. A Chaldee Text, from a unique MS. in the Bodleian Library; with other Rabbinical Texts, English Translations, and the Itala. Edited by AD. NEUBAUER, M.A. Crown 8vo. 6s.

COPTIC. Libri Prophetarum Majorum, cum Lamentationibus Jeremiae, in Dialecto Linguae Aegyptiacae Memphitica seu Coptica. Edidit cum Versione Latina H. TATTAM. S.T.P. Tomi II. 1852. 8vo. 17s.

—— Libri duodecim Prophetarum Minorum in Ling. Aegypt. vulgo Coptica. Edidit H. TATTAM, A.M. 1836. 8vo. 8s. 6d.

—— Novum Testamentum Coptice, cura D. WILKINS. 1716. 4to. 12s. 6d.

HEBREW. Psalms in Hebrew (without points). Cr. 8vo. 2s.

Driver. Notes on the Hebrew Text of the Books of Samuel. By S. R. DRIVER, D.D. 8vo. 14s. *Just Published.*

—— Treatise on the use of the Tenses in Hebrew. By S. R. DRIVER, D.D. *Second Edition.* Extra fcap. 8vo. 7s. 6d.

—— Commentary on the Book of Proverbs. Attributed to Abraham Ibn Ezra. Edited from a Manuscript in the Bodleian Library by S. R. DRIVER, D.D. Crown 8vo. paper covers, 3s. 6d.

Neubauer. Book of Hebrew Roots, by Abu 'l-Walîd Marwân ibn Janâh, otherwise called Rabbi Yônâh. Now first edited, with an Appendix, by AD. NEUBAUER. 4to. 2l. 7s. 6d.

Spurrell. Notes on the Hebrew Text of the Book of Genesis. By G. J. SPURRELL, M.A. Crown 8vo. 10s. 6d.

Wickes. Hebrew Accentuation of Psalms, Proverbs, and Job. By WILLIAM WICKES, D.D. 8vo. 5s.

—— Hebrew Prose Accentuation. 8vo. 10s. 6d.

SANSKRIT.—Sanskrit-English Dictionary, Etymologically and Philologically arranged, with special reference to Greek, Latin, German, Anglo-Saxon, English, and other cognate Indo-European Languages. By Sir M. MONIER-WILLIAMS, D.C.L. 4to. 4l. 14s. 6d.

—— Practical Grammar of the Sanskrit Language, arranged with reference to the Classical Languages of Europe, by Sir M. MONIER-WILLIAMS, D.C.L. *Fourth Edition.* 8vo. 15s.

—— Nalopákhyánam. Story of Nala, an Episode of the Mahábhárata: the Sanskrit Text, with a copious Vocabulary, and an improved version of Dean Milman's Translation, by Sir M. MONIER-WILLIAMS, D.C.L. *Second Edition, Revised and Improved.* 8vo. 15s.

—— Sakuntalá. A Sanskrit Drama, in seven Acts. Edited by SIR M. MONIER-WILLIAMS, D.C.L. *Second Edition.* 8vo. 1l. 1s.

SYRIAC.—Thesaurus Syriacus: collegerunt Quatremère, Bernstein, Lorsbach, Arnoldi, Agrell, Field, Roediger: edidit R. PAYNE SMITH, S.T.P. Vol. I. containing Fasc. I–V. Sm. fol. 5l. 5s. Fasc. VI. 1l. 1s. Fasc. VII. 1l. 11s. 6d. Fasc. VIII. 1l. 16s.

I. Literature and Philology.

SYRIAC (*continued.*)

—— The Book of Kalīlah and Dimnah. Translated from Arabic into Syriac. Edited by W. WRIGHT, LL.D. 8vo. 1*l.* 1*s.*

—— Cyrilli Archiepiscopi Alexandrini Commentarii in Lucae Evangelium quae supersunt Syriace. E MSS. apud Mus. Britan. edidit R. PAYNE SMITH, A.M. 4to. 1*l.* 2*s.*

—— —— Translated by R. PAYNE SMITH, M.A. 2 vols. 8vo. 14*s.*

—— Ephraemi Syri, Rabulae Episcopi Edesseni, Balaei, etc., Opera Selecta. E Codd. Syriacis mss. in Museo Britannico et Bibliotheca Bodleiana asservatis primus edidit J. J. OVERBECK. 8vo. 1*l.* 1*s.*

—— John, Bishop of Ephesus. The Third Part of his Ecclesiastical History. [In Syriac.] Now first edited by WILLIAM CURETON, M.A. 4to. 1*l.* 12*s.*

—— —— Translated by R. PAYNE SMITH, M.A. 8vo. 10*s.*

SECTION VI.
ANECDOTA OXONIENSIA.
(Crown 4to., stiff covers.)

I. CLASSICAL SERIES.

I. The English Manuscripts of the Nicomachean Ethics. By J. A. STEWART, M.A. 3*s.* 6*d.*

II. Nonius Marcellus, de Compendiosa Doctrina, Harleian MS. 2719. Collated by J. H. ONIONS, M.A. 3*s.* 6*d.*

III. Aristotle's Physics. Book VII. With Introduction by R. SHUTE, M.A. 2*s.*

IV. Bentley's Plautine Emendations. From his copy of Gronovius. By E. A. SONNENSCHEIN, M.A. 2*s.* 6*d.*

V. Harleian MS. 2610; Ovid's Metamorphoses I, II, III. 1–622; XXIV Latin Epigrams from Bodleian or other MSS.; Latin Glosses on Apollinaris Sidonius from MS. Digby 172. Collated and Edited by ROBINSON ELLIS, M.A., LL.D. 4*s.*

II. SEMITIC SERIES.

I. Commentary on Ezra and Nehemiah. By Rabbi Saadiah. Edited by H. J. MATHEWS, M.A. 3*s.* 6*d.*

II. The Book of the Bee. Edited by ERNEST A. WALLIS BUDGE, M.A. 21*s.*

III. A Commentary on the Book of Daniel. By Japhet Ibn Ali. Edited and Translated by D. S. MARGOLIOUTH, M.A. 21*s.*

IV. Mediaeval Jewish Chronicles and Chronological Notes. Edited by AD. NEUBAUER, M.A. 14*s.*

Oxford: Clarendon Press.

ANECDOTA OXONIENSIA (*continued*).

III. ARYAN SERIES.

I. Buddhist Texts from Japan. 1. Va*grakkh*edikâ. Edited by F. MAX MÜLLER. 3*s.* 6*d.*

II. Buddhist Texts from Japan. 2. Sukhâvatî Vyûha. Edited by F. MAX MÜLLER, M.A., and BUNYIU NANJIO. 7*s.* 6*d.*

III. Buddhist Texts from Japan. 3. The Ancient Palm-leaves containing the Pra*gñ*â-Pâramitâ-H*r*idaya-Sûtra and the Ush*n*isha-Vi*g*aya-Dhâra*n*i, edited by F. MAX MÜLLER, M.A., and BUNYIU NANJIO, M.A. With an Appendix by G. BÜHLER. 10*s.*

IV. Kâtyâyana's Sarvânukrama*n*î of the *R*igveda. With Extracts from Sha*dg*uru*s*ishya's Commentary entitled Vedârthadîpikâ. Edited by A. A. MACDONELL, M.A., Ph.D. 16*s.*

V. The Dharma Sa*m*graha. Edited by KENJIU KASAWARA, F. MAX MÜLLER, and H. WENZEL. 7*s.* 6*d.*

IV. MEDIAEVAL AND MODERN SERIES.

I. Sinonoma Bartholomei. Edited by J. L. G. MOWAT, M.A. 3*s.* 6*d.*

II. Alphita. Edited by J. L. G. MOWAT, M.A. 12*s.* 6*d.*

III. The Saltair Na Rann. Edited from a MS. in the Bodleian Library, by WHITLEY STOKES, D.C.L. 7*s.* 6*d.*

IV. The Cath Finntrága, or Battle of Ventry. Edited by KUNO MEYER, Ph.D., M.A. 6*s.*

V. Lives of Saints, from the Book of Lismore. Edited, with Translation, by WHITLEY STOKES, D.C.L. 1*l.* 11*s.* 6*d.* *Just Published.*

II. THEOLOGY.

A. THE HOLY SCRIPTURES, ETC.

COPTIC. Libri Prophetarum Majorum, cum Lamentationibus Jeremiae, in Dialecto Linguae Aegyptiacae Memphitica seu Coptica. Edidit cum Versione Latina H. TATTAM, S.T.P. Tomi II. 1852. 8vo. 17*s.*

—— Libri duodecim Prophetarum Minorum in Ling. Aegypt. vulgo Coptica. Edidit H. TATTAM, A.M. 1836. 8vo. 8*s.* 6*d.*

—— Novum Testamentum Coptice, cura D. WILKINS. 1716. 4to. 12*s.* 6*d.*

II. Theology.

ENGLISH. The Holy Bible in the Earliest English Versions, made from the Latin Vulgate by JOHN WYCLIFFE and his followers: edited by FORSHALL and MADDEN. 4 vols. 1850. Royal 4to. 3*l*. 3*s*.

Also reprinted from the above, with Introduction and Glossary by W. W. SKEAT, Litt. D.

I. The Books of Job, Psalms, Proverbs, Ecclesiastes, and the Song of Solomon. Extra fcap. 8vo. 3*s*. 6*d*.

II. The New Testament. Extra fcap. 8vo. 6*s*.

—— **The Holy Bible : an exact reprint, page for page, of the** Authorised Version published in the year 1611. Demy 4to. half bound. 1*l*. 1*s*.

—— **The Holy Bible, Revised Version*.**

Cheap editions for School Use.

Revised Bible. Pearl 16mo., cloth boards, 1*s*. 6*d*.
Revised New Testament. Nonpareil 32mo., 6*d*.; Brevier 16mo., 1*s*.; Long Primer 8vo., 1*s*. 6*d*.

—— **The Oxford Bible for Teachers,** containing supplementary. HELPS TO THE STUDY OF THE BIBLE, including summaries of the several Books, with copious explanatory notes; and Tables illustrative of Scripture History and the characteristics of Bible Lands with a complete Index of Subjects, a Concordance, a Dictionary of Proper Names, and a series of Maps. Prices in various sizes and bindings from 3*s*. to 2*l*. 5*s*.

—— **Helps to the Study of the Bible,** taken from the OXFORD BIBLE FOR TEACHERS. Crown 8vo., 3*s*. 6*d*.

—— **The Psalter, or Psalms of David, and certain Canticles,** with a Translation and Exposition in English, by RICHARD ROLLE of Hampole. Edited by H. R. BRAMLEY, M.A., Fellow of S. M. Magdalen College, Oxford. With an Introduction and Glossary. Demy 8vo. 1*l*. 1*s*.

—— **Studia Biblica.** Essays in Biblical Archæology and Criticism, and kindred subjects. By Members of the University of Oxford. 8vo. 10*s*. 6*d*.

—— **Lectures on the Book of Job.** Delivered in Westminster Abbey by the Very Rev. G. G. BRADLEY, D.D. Crown 8vo. 7*s*. 6*d*.

—— **Lectures on Ecclesiastes.** By the same Author. Cr. 8vo. 4*s*. 6*d*.

—— **The Book of Wisdom :** the Greek Text, the Latin Vulgate, and the Authorised English Version; with an Introduction, Critical Apparatus, and a Commentary. By W. J. DEANE, M.A. 4to. 12*s*. 6*d*.

—— **The Five Books of Maccabees,** in English, with Notes and Illustrations by HENRY COTTON, D.C.L. 1832. 8vo. 10*s*. 6*d*.

* *The Revised Version is the joint property of the Universities of Oxford and Cambridge.*

The Holy Scriptures, etc.

ENGLISH (*continued*).

——— **List of Editions of the Bible in English.** By HENRY COTTON, D.C.L. *Second Edition.* 1852. 8vo. 8s. 6d.

——— **Rhemes and Doway.** An attempt to shew what has been done by Roman Catholics for the diffusion of the Holy Scriptures in English. By HENRY COTTON, D.C.L. 1855. 8vo. 9s.

GOTHIC. Evangeliorum Versio Gothica, cum Interpr. et Annott. E. BENZELII. Edidit E. LYE, A.M. 4to. 12s. 6d.

——— **The Gospel of St. Mark in Gothic,** according to the translation made by WULFILA in the Fourth Century. Edited by W. W. SKEAT, Litt. D. Extra fcap. 8vo. 4s.

GREEK. Old Testament. Vetus Testamentum ex Versione Septuaginta Interpretum secundum exemplar Vaticanum Romae editum. Accedit potior varietas Codicis Alexandrini. Tomi III. 18mo. 18s.

——— Vetus Testamentum Graece cum Variis Lectionibus. Editionem a R. HOLMES, S.T.P. inchoatam continuavit J. PARSONS, S.T.B. Tomi V. 1798-1827. folio, 7l.

——— Origenis Hexaplorum quae supersunt; sive, Veterum Interpretum Graecorum in totum Vetus Testamentum Fragmenta. Edidit FRIDERICUS FIELD, A.M. 2 vols. 1875. 4to. 5l. 5s.

——— **Essays in Biblical Greek.** By EDWIN HATCH, M.A., D.D. 8vo. 10s. 6d.

——— **New Testament.** Novum Testamentum Graece. Antiquissimorum Codicum Textus in ordine parallelo dispositi. Edidit E. H. HANSELL, S.T.B. Tomi III. 8vo. 24s.

——— Novum Testamentum Graece. Accedunt parallela S. Scripturae loca, etc. Edidit CAROLUS LLOYD, S.T.P.R. 18mo. 3s. On writing paper, with wide margin, 10s. 6d.

  Critical Appendices to the above, by W. SANDAY, M.A. Extra fcap. 8vo. cloth, 3s. 6d.

——— Novum Testamentum Graece juxta Exemplar Millianum. 18mo. 2s. 6d. On writing paper, with wide margin, 9s.

——— Evangelia Sacra Graece. Fcap. 8vo. limp, 1s. 6d.

——— **The Greek Testament,** with the Readings adopted by the Revisers of the Authorised Version:—
  (1) Pica type, with Marginal References. Demy 8vo. 10s. 6d.
  (2) Long Primer type. Fcap. 8vo. 4s. 6d.
  (3) The same, on writing paper, with wide margin, 15s.

——— **The New Testament in Greek and English.** Edited by E. CARDWELL, D.D. 2 vols. 1837. Crown 8vo. 6s.

London: HENRY FROWDE, Amen Corner, E.C.

II. Theology.

GREEK (*continued*).

—— The Parallel New Testament, Greek and English; being the Authorised Version, 1611; the Revised Version, 1881; and the Greek Text followed in the Revised Version. 8vo. 12s. 6d.

—— Diatessaron; sive Historia Jesu Christi ex ipsis Evangelistarum verbis apte dispositis confecta. Ed. J. WHITE. 3s. 6d.

—— Outlines of Textual Criticism applied to the New Testament. By C. E. HAMMOND, M.A. Extra fcap. 8vo. 3s. 6d.

—— A Greek Testament Primer. An Easy Grammar and Reading Book for the use of Students beginning Greek. By E. MILLER, M.A. Extra fcap. 8vo. 3s. 6d.

—— Canon Muratorianus: the earliest Catalogue of the Books of the New Testament. Edited with Notes and a Facsimile of the MS. in the Ambrosian Library at Milan, by S. P. TREGELLES, LL.D. 1867. 4to. 10s. 6d.

HEBREW, etc. Notes on the Hebrew Text of the Book of Genesis. By G. J. SPURRELL, M.A. Crown 8vo. 10s. 6d.

—— Notes on the Hebrew Text of the Books of Samuel. By S. R. DRIVER, D.D. 8vo. 14s.

—— The Psalms in Hebrew without points. Stiff covers, 2s.

—— A Commentary on the Book of Proverbs. Attributed to ABRAHAM IBN EZRA. Edited from a MS. in the Bodleian Library by S. R. DRIVER, D.D. Crown 8vo. paper covers, 3s. 6d.

—— The Book of Tobit. A Chaldee Text, from a unique MS. in the Bodleian Library; with other Rabbinical Texts, English Translations, and the Itala. Edited by AD. NEUBAUER, M.A. Crown 8vo. 6s.

—— Hebrew Accentuation of Psalms, Proverbs, and Job. By WILLIAM WICKES, D.D. 8vo. 5s.

—— Hebrew Prose Accentuation. By the same. 8vo. 10s. 6d.

—— Horae Hebraicae et Talmudicae, a J. LIGHTFOOT. A new Edition, by R. GANDELL, M.A. 4 vols. 1859. 8vo. 1l. 1s.

LATIN. Libri Psalmorum Versio antiqua Latina, cum Paraphrasi Anglo-Saxonica. Edidit B. THORPE, F.A.S. 1835. 8vo. 10s. 6d.

—— Nouum Testamentum Domini Nostri Iesu Christi Latine, secundum Editionem Sancti Hieronymi. Ad Codicum Manuscriptorum fidem recensuit IOHANNES WORDSWORTH, S.T.P., Episcopus Sarisburiensis; in operis societatem adsumto HENRICO IULIANO WHITE, A.M. *Partis Prioris Fasciculus Primus. Euangelium Secundum Mattheum.* Quarto, Paper covers, 12s. 6d.

—— Old-Latin Biblical Texts: No. I. The Gospel according to St. Matthew, from the St. Germain MS. (g_1). Edited with Introduction and Appendices by JOHN WORDSWORTH, D.D. Small 4to., stiff covers, 6s.

LATIN (*continued*).

—— Old-Latin Biblical Texts: No. II. Portions of the Gospels according to St. Mark and St. Matthew, from the Bobbio MS. (k), &c. Edited by JOHN WORDSWORTH, D.D., W. SANDAY, M.A., D.D., and H. J. WHITE, M.A. Small 4to., stiff covers, 21s.

—— Old-Latin Biblical Texts: No. III. The Four Gospels, from the Munich MS. (q), now numbered Lat. 6224 in the Royal Library at Munich. With a Fragment from St. John in the Hof-Bibliothek at Vienna (Cod. Lat. 502). Edited, with the aid of Tischendorf's transcript (under the direction of the Bishop of Salisbury), by H. J. WHITE, M.A. Small 4to. stiff covers, 12s. 6d.

OLD-FRENCH. Libri Psalmorum Versio antiqua Gallica e Cod. ms. in Bibl. Bodleiana adservato, una cum Versione Metrica aliisque Monumentis pervetustis. Nunc primum descripsit et edidit FRANCISCUS MICHEL, Phil. Doc. 1860. 8vo. 10s. 6d.

B. FATHERS OF THE CHURCH, ETC.

St. Athanasius: Orations against the Arians. With an Account of his Life by WILLIAM BRIGHT, D.D. Crown 8vo. 9s.

—— Historical Writings, according to the Benedictine Text. With an Introduction by W. BRIGHT, D.D. Crown 8vo. 10s. 6d.

St. Augustine: Select Anti-Pelagian Treatises, and the Acts of the Second Council of Orange. With an Introduction by WILLIAM BRIGHT, D.D. Crown 8vo. 9s.

Barnabas, The Editio Princeps of the Epistle of, by Archbishop Ussher, as printed at Oxford, A.D. 1642, and preserved in an imperfect form in the Bodleian Library. With a Dissertation on the Literary History of that Edition, by J. H. BACKHOUSE, M.A. Small 4to. 3s. 6d.

Canons of the First Four General Councils of Nicaea, Constantinople, Ephesus, and Chalcedon. Crown 8vo. 2s. 6d.

—— Notes on the above. By WILLIAM BRIGHT, D.D. Crown 8vo. 5s. 6d.

Catenae Graecorum Patrum in Novum Testamentum. Edidit J. A. CRAMER, S.T.P. Tomi VIII. 8vo. 2l. 4s.

Clementis Alexandrini Opera, ex recensione Guil. Dindorfii. Tomi IV. 8vo. 3l.

Cyrilli Archiepiscopi Alexandrini in XII Prophetas. Edidit P. E. PUSEY, A.M. Tomi II. 8vo. 2l. 2s.

—— in D. Joannis Evangelium. Accedunt Fragmenta Varia necnon Tractatus ad Tiberium Diaconum Duo. Edidit post Aubertum P. E. PUSEY, A.M. Tomi III. 8vo. 2l. 5s.

II. Theology.

Cyrilli Commentarii in Lucae Evangelium quae supersunt Syriace. E MSS. apud Mus. Britan. edidit R. PAYNE SMITH, A.M. 4to. 1*l*. 2*s*.

—— —— Translated by R. PAYNE SMITH, M.A. 2 vols. 8vo. 14*s*.

Dowling (J. G.). Notitia Scriptorum SS. Patrum aliorumque vet. Eccles. Mon. quae in Collectionibus Anecdotorum post annum Christi MDCC. in lucem editis continentur. 8vo. 4*s*. 6*d*.

Ephraemi Syri, Rabulae Episcopi Edesseni, Balaei, aliorumque Opera Selecta. E Codd. Syriacis mss. in Museo Britannico et Bibliotheca Bodleiana asservatis primus edidit J. J. OVERBECK. 8vo. 1*l*. 1*s*.

Eusebii Pamphili Evangelicae Praeparationis Libri XV. Ad Codd. mss. recensuit T. GAISFORD, S.T.P. Tomi IV. 8vo. 1*l*. 10*s*.

—— Evangelicae Demonstrationis Libri X. Recensuit T. GAISFORD, S.T.P. Tomi II. 8vo. 15*s*.

—— contra Hieroclem et Marcellum Libri. Recensuit T. GAISFORD, S.T.P. 8vo. 7*s*.

Eusebius' Ecclesiastical History, according to the text of BURTON, with an Introduction by W. BRIGHT, D.D. Crown 8vo. 8*s*. 6*d*.

—— —— Annotationes Variorum. Tomi II. 8vo. 17*s*.

Evagrii Historia Ecclesiastica, ex recensione H. VALESII. 1844. 8vo. 4*s*.

Irenaeus: The Third Book of St. Irenaeus, Bishop of Lyons, against Heresies. With short Notes and a Glossary by H. DEANE, B.D. Crown 8vo. 5*s*. 6*d*.

Origenis Philosophumena; sive omnium Haeresium Refutatio. E Codice Parisino nunc primum edidit EMMANUEL MILLER. 1851. 8vo. 10*s*.

Patrum Apostolicorum, S. Clementis Romani, S. Ignatii, S. Polycarpi, quae supersunt. Edidit GUIL. JACOBSON, S.T.P.R. Tomi II. *Fourth Edition*. 8vo. 1*l*. 1*s*.

Reliquiae Sacrae secundi tertiique saeculi. Recensuit M. J. ROUTH, S.T.P. Tomi V. *Second Edition*. 8vo. 1*l*. 5*s*.

Scriptorum Ecclesiasticorum Opuscula. Recensuit M. J. ROUTH, S.T.P. Tomi II. *Third Edition*. 8vo. 10*s*.

Socratis Scholastici Historia Ecclesiastica. Gr. et Lat. Edidit R. HUSSEY, S.T.B. Tomi III. 1853. 8vo. 15*s*.

Socrates' Ecclesiastical History, according to the Text of HUSSEY, with an Introduction by WILLIAM BRIGHT, D.D. Crown 8vo. 7*s*. 6*d*.

Sozomeni Historia Ecclesiastica. Edidit R. Hussey, S.T.B. Tomi III. 1860. 8vo. 15s.

Tertulliani Apologeticus adversus Gentes pro Christianis. Edited, with Introduction and Notes, by T. Herbert Bindley, M.A. Crown 8vo. 6s.

Theodoreti Ecclesiasticae Historiae Libri V. Recensuit T. Gaisford, S.T.P. 1854. 8vo. 7s. 6d.

—— Graecarum Affectionum Curatio. Ad Codices mss. recensuit T. Gaisford, S.T.P. 1839. 8vo. 7s. 6d.

C. ECCLESIASTICAL HISTORY, ETC.

Baedae Historia Ecclesiastica. Edited, with English Notes, by G. H. Moberly, M.A. Crown 8vo. 10s. 6d.

Bigg. The Christian Platonists of Alexandria; being the Bampton Lectures for 1886. By Charles Bigg, D.D. 8vo. 10s. 6d.

Bingham's Antiquities of the Christian Church, and other Works. 10 vols. 8vo. 3l. 3s.

Bright. Chapters of Early English Church History. By W. Bright, D.D. *Second Edition.* 8vo. 12s.

Burnet's History of the Reformation of the Church of England. *A new Edition.* Carefully revised, and the Records collated with the originals, by N. Pocock, M.A. 7 vols. 8vo. 1l. 10s.

Cardwell's Documentary Annals of the Reformed Church of England; being a Collection of Injunctions, Declarations, Orders, Articles of Inquiry, &c. from 1546 to 1716. 2 vols. 8vo. 18s.

Councils and Ecclesiastical Documents relating to Great Britain and Ireland. Edited, after Spelman and Wilkins, by A. W. Haddan, B.D., and W. Stubbs, D.D. Vols. I and III. Medium 8vo. each 1l. 1s.

Vol. II, Part I. Medium 8vo. 10s. 6d.

Vol. II, Part II. Church of Ireland; Memorials of St. Patrick. Stiff covers, 3s. 6d.

Formularies of Faith set forth by the King's authority during the Reign of Henry VIII. 8vo. 7s.

Fuller's Church History of Britain. Edited by J. S. Brewer, M.A. 6 vols. 8vo. 1l. 19s.

Gibson's Synodus Anglicana. Edited by E. Cardwell, D.D. 8vo. 6s.

Hamilton's (Archbishop John) Catechism, 1552. Edited, with Introduction and Glossary, by Thomas Graves Law, Librarian of the Signet Library, Edinburgh. With a Preface by the Right Hon. W. E. Gladstone. Demy 8vo. 12s. 6d.

II. Theology.

Hussey. Rise of the Papal Power, traced in three Lectures. By ROBERT HUSSEY, B.D. *Second Edition.* Fcap. 8vo. 4s. 6d.

Inett's Origines Anglicanae (in continuation of Stillingfleet). Edited by J. GRIFFITHS, M.A. 3 vols. 8vo. 15s.

John, Bishop of Ephesus. The Third Part of his Ecclesiastical History. [In Syriac.] Now first edited by WILLIAM CURETON, M.A. 4to. 1l. 12s.

—— The same, translated by R. PAYNE SMITH, M.A. 8vo. 10s.

Le Neve's Fasti Ecclesiae Anglicanae. Corrected and continued from 1715 to 1853 by T. DUFFUS HARDY. 3 vols. 8vo. 1l. 1s.

Noelli (A.) Catechismus sive prima institutio disciplinaque Pietatis Christianae Latine explicata. Editio nova cura GUIL. JACOBSON, A.M. 8vo. 5s. 6d.

Prideaux's Connection of Sacred and Profane History. 2 vols. 8vo. 10s.

Primers put forth in the Reign of Henry VIII. 8vo. 5s.

Records of the Reformation. The Divorce, 1527–1533. Mostly now for the first time printed from MSS. in the British Museum and other Libraries. Collected and arranged by N. POCOCK, M.A. 2 vols. 8vo. 1l. 16s.

Reformatio Legum Ecclesiasticarum. The Reformation of Ecclesiastical Laws, as attempted in the reigns of Henry VIII, Edward VI, and Elizabeth. Edited by E. CARDWELL, D.D. 8vo. 6s. 6d.

Shirley. Some Account of the Church in the Apostolic Age. By W. W. SHIRLEY, D.D. *Second Edition.* Fcap. 8vo. 3s. 6d.

Shuckford's Sacred and Profane History connected (in continuation of Prideaux). 2 vols. 8vo. 10s.

Stillingfleet's Origines Britannicae, with LLOYD's Historical Account of Church Government. Edited by T. P. PANTIN, M.A. 2 vols. 8vo. 10s.

Stubbs. Registrum Sacrum Anglicanum. An attempt to exhibit the course of Episcopal Succession in England. By W. STUBBS, D.D. Small 4to. 8s. 6d.

Strype's Memorials of Cranmer. 2 vols. 8vo. 11s.
    Life of Aylmer. 8vo. 5s. 6d.
    Life of Whitgift. 3 vols. 8vo. 16s. 6d.
    General Index. 2 vols. 8vo. 11s.

Sylloge Confessionum sub tempus Reformandae Ecclesiae editarum. Subjiciuntur Catechismus Heidelbergensis et Canones Synodi Dordrechtanae. 8vo. 8s.

D. LITURGIOLOGY.

Cardwell's Two Books of Common Prayer, set forth by authority in the Reign of King Edward VI, compared with each other. *Third Edition.* 8vo. 7s.

—— History of Conferences on the Book of Common Prayer from 1551 to 1690. *Third Edition.* 8vo. 7s. 6d.

Hammond. Liturgies, Eastern and Western. Edited, with Introduction, Notes, and a Liturgical Glossary, by C. E. HAMMOND, M.A. Crown 8vo. 10s. 6d.

    An Appendix to the above, crown 8vo. paper covers, 1s. 6d.

Leofric Missal, The, as used in the Cathedral of Exeter during the Episcopate of its first Bishop, A.D. 1050–1072; together with some Account of the Red Book of Derby, the Missal of Robert of Jumièges, and a few other early MS. Service Books of the English Church. Edited, with Introduction and Notes, by F. E. WARREN, B.D., F S.A. 4to. half morocco, 1l. 15s.

Maskell. Ancient Liturgy of the Church of England, according to the uses of Sarum, York, Hereford, and Bangor, and the Roman Liturgy arranged in parallel columns, with preface and notes. By W. MASKELL, M.A. *Third Edition.* 8vo. 15s.

—— Monumenta Ritualia Ecclesiae Anglicanae. The occasional Offices of the Church of England according to the old use of Salisbury, the Prymer in English, and other prayers and forms, with dissertations and notes. *Second Edition.* 3 vols. 8vo. 2l. 10s.

Warren. The Liturgy and Ritual of the Celtic Church. By F. E. WARREN, B.D. 8vo. 14s.

E. ENGLISH THEOLOGY.

Beveridge's Discourse upon the XXXIX Articles. 8vo. 8s.

Biscoe's Boyle Lectures on the Acts of the Apostles. 8vo. 9s. 6d.

Bradley. Lectures on the Book of Job. By GEORGE GRANVILLE BRADLEY, D.D., Dean of Westminster. Crown 8vo. 7s. 6d.

Bradley. Lectures on Ecclesiastes. By G. G. BRADLEY, D.D., Dean of Westminster. Crown 8vo. 4s. 6d.

Bull's Works, with NELSON's Life. Edited by E. BURTON, D.D. 8 vols. 8vo. 2l. 9s.

II. Theology.

Burnet's Exposition of the xxxix Articles. 8vo. 7s.

Burton's (Edward) Testimonies of the Ante-Nicene Fathers to the Divinity of Christ. 1829. 8vo. 7s.

—— Testimonies of the Ante-Nicene Fathers to the Doctrine of the Trinity and of the Divinity of the Holy Ghost. 1831. 8vo. 3s. 6d.

Butler's Works. 2 vols. 8vo. 11s.

—— Sermons. 5s. 6d. Analogy of Religion. 5s. 6d.

Chandler's Critical History of the Life of David. 8vo. 8s. 6d.

Chillingworth's Works. 3 vols. 8vo. 1l. 1s. 6d.

Clergyman's Instructor. *Sixth Edition.* 8vo. 6s. 6d.

Comber's Companion to the Temple; or a Help to Devotion in the use of the Common Prayer. 7 vols. 8vo. 1l. 11s. 6d.

Cranmer's Works. Collected and arranged by H. JENKYNS, M.A., Fellow of Oriel College. 4 vols. 8vo. 1l. 10s.

Enchiridion Theologicum Anti-Romanum.
> Vol. I. JEREMY TAYLOR'S Dissuasive from Popery, and Treatise on the Real Presence. 8vo. 8s.
>
> Vol. II. BARROW on the Supremacy of the Pope, with his Discourse on the Unity of the Church. 8vo. 7s. 6d.
>
> Vol. III. Tracts selected from WAKE, PATRICK, STILLINGFLEET, CLAGETT, and others. 8vo. 11s.

[Fell's] Paraphrase, etc. on the Epistles of St. Paul. 8vo. 7s.

Greswell's Harmonia Evangelica. *Fifth Edition.* 8vo. 9s. 6d.

—— Prolegomena ad Harmoniam Evangelicam. 8vo. 9s. 6d.

—— Dissertations on the Principles and Arrangement of a Harmony of the Gospels. 5 vols. 8vo. 3l. 3s.

Hall's Works. Edited by P. WYNTER, D.D. 10 vols. 8vo. 3l. 3s.

Hammond's Paraphrase on the Book of Psalms. 2 vols. 8vo. 10s.

—— Paraphrase etc. on the New Testament. 4 vols. 8vo. 1l.

Heurtley. Harmonia Symbolica: Creeds of the Western Church. By C. HEURTLEY, D.D. 8vo. 6s. 6d.

Homilies appointed to be read in Churches. Edited by J. GRIFFITHS, M.A. 8vo. 7s. 6d.

Oxford: Clarendon Press.

HOOKER'S WORKS, with his Life by WALTON, arranged by JOHN KEBLE, M.A. *Seventh Edition*. Revised by R. W. CHURCH, M.A., Dean of St. Paul's, and F. PAGET, D.D. 3 vols. medium 8vo. 1*l*. 16*s*.

—— the Text as arranged by J. KEBLE, M.A. 2 vols. 8vo. 11*s*.

Hooper's Works. 2 vols. 8vo. 8*s*.

Jackson's (Dr. Thomas) Works. 12 vols. 8vo. 3*l*. 6*s*.

Jewel's Works. Edited by R. W. JELF, D.D. 8 vols. 8vo. 1*l*. 10*s*.

Martineau. A Study of Religion: its Sources and Contents. By JAMES MARTINEAU, D.D. *Second Edition*. 2 vols. crown 8vo. 15*s*.

Patrick's Theological Works. 9 vols. 8vo. 1*l*. 1*s*.

Pearson's Exposition of the Creed. Revised and corrected by E. BURTON, D.D. *Sixth Edition*. 8vo. 10*s*. 6*d*.

—— Minor Theological Works. Edited with a Memoir, by EDWARD CHURTON, M.A. 2 vols. 8vo. 10*s*.

Sanderson's Works. Edited by W. JACOBSON, D.D. 6 vols. 8vo. 1*l*. 10*s*.

Stanhope's Paraphrase and Comment upon the Epistles and Gospels. *A new Edition*. 2 vols. 8vo. 10*s*.

Stillingfleet's Origines Sacrae. 2 vols. 8vo. 9*s*.

—— Rational Account of the Grounds of Protestant Religion; being a vindication of ARCHBISHOP LAUD's Relation of a Conference, &c. 2 vols. 8vo. 10*s*.

Wall's History of Infant Baptism. *A New Edition*, by HENRY COTTON, D.C.L. 2 vols. 8vo. 1*l*. 1*s*.

Waterland's Works, with Life, by Bp. VAN MILDERT. *A new Edition*, with copious Indexes. 6 vols. 8vo. 2*l*. 11*s*.

—— Review of the Doctrine of the Eucharist, with a Preface by the late Bishop of London. Crown 8vo. 6*s*. 6*d*.

Wheatly's Illustration of the Book of Common Prayer. 8vo. 5*s*.

Wyclif. A Catalogue of the Original Works of John Wyclif. By W. W. SHIRLEY, D.D. 8vo. 3*s*. 6*d*.

—— Select English Works. By T. ARNOLD, M.A. 3 vols. 8vo. 1*l*. 1*s*.

—— Trialogus. With the Supplement now first edited. By GOTTHARD LECHLER. 8vo. 7*s*.

London: HENRY FROWDE, Amen Corner, E.C.

III. POLITICAL SCIENCE.

A. HISTORY, BIOGRAPHY, CHRONOLOGY, ETC.

Baker's Chronicle. Chronicon Galfridi le Baker de Swynebroke. Edited with Notes by EDWARD MAUNDE THOMPSON, Hon. LL.D. St. Andrews; Hon. D.C.L. Durham; F.S.A.; Principal Librarian of the British Museum. Small 4to., stiff covers, 18s., cloth, gilt top, 21s.

Bluntschli. The Theory of the State. By J. K. BLUNTSCHLI. Translated from the Sixth German Edition. 8vo. half bound, 12s. 6d.

Boswell's Life of Samuel Johnson, LL.D.; including BOSWELL'S Journal of a Tour to the Hebrides, and JOHNSON'S Diary of a Journey into North Wales. Edited by G. BIRKBECK HILL, D.C.L. In six volumes, medium 8vo. With Portraits and Facsimiles. Half bound, 3l. 3s.

Burnet's History of His Own Time, with the suppressed Passages and Notes. 6 vols. 8vo. 2l. 10s.

—— History of James II, with Additional Notes. 8vo. 9s. 6d.

—— Life of Sir M. Hale, and **Fell's** Life of Dr. Hammond. Small 8vo. 2s. 6d.

Calendar of the Clarendon State Papers, preserved in the Bodleian Library. In three volumes. 1869-76.

Vol. I. From 1523 to January 1649. 8vo. 18s.

Vol. II. From 1649 to 1654. 8vo. 16s.

Vol. III. From 1655 to 1657. 8vo. 14s.

Calendar of Charters and Rolls preserved in the Bodleian Library. 8vo. 1l. 11s. 6d.

Carte's Life of James Duke of Ormond. A new Edition, carefully compared with the original MSS. 6 vols. 8vo. 1l. 5s.

Casauboni Ephemerides, cum praefatione et notis J. RUSSELL. S.T.P. Tomi II. 8vo. 15s.

CLARENDON'S History of the Rebellion and Civil Wars in England. Re-edited from a fresh collation of the original MS. in the Bodleian Library, with marginal dates and occasional notes, by W. DUNN MACRAY, M.A., F.S.A. 6 vols. Crown 8vo. 2l. 5s.

—— History of the Rebellion and Civil Wars in England. To which are subjoined the Notes of BISHOP WARBURTON. 1849. 7 vols. medium 8vo. 2l. 10s.

—— History of the Rebellion and Civil Wars in England. Also his Life, written by himself, in which is included a Continuation of his History of the Grand Rebellion. Royal 8vo. 1l. 2s.

Oxford : Clarendon Press.

History, Biography, Chronology, etc. 45

Clarendon's Life, including a Continuation of his History. 2 vols. 1857. medium 8vo. 1*l*. 2*s*.

Clinton's Fasti Hellenici. The Civil and Literary Chronology of Greece, from the LVIth to the CXXIIIrd Olympiad. *Third Edition.* 4to. 1*l*. 14*s*. 6*d*.

Clinton's Fasti Hellenici. The Civil and Literary Chronology of Greece, from the CXXIVth Olympiad to the Death of Augustus. *Second Edition.* 4to. 1*l*. 12*s*.

—— Epitome of the Fasti Hellenici. 8vo. 6*s*. 6*d*.

—— Fasti Romani. The Civil and Literary Chronology of Rome and Constantinople, from the Death of Augustus to the Death of Heraclius. 2 vols. 4to. 2*l*. 2*s*.

—— Epitome of the Fasti Romani. 8vo. 7*s*.

Cramer's Geographical and Historical Description of Asia Minor. 2 vols. 8vo. 11*s*.

—— Description of Ancient Greece. 3 vols. 8vo. 16*s*. 6*d*.

Earle. Handbook to the Land-Charters, and other Saxonic Documents. By JOHN EARLE, M.A., Professor of Anglo-Saxon in the University of Oxford. Crown 8vo. 16*s*.

Finlay. A History of Greece from its Conquest by the Romans to the present time, B.C. 146 to A.D. 1864. By GEORGE FINLAY, LL.D. A new Edition, revised throughout, and in part re-written, with considerable additions, by the Author, and edited by H. F. TOZER, M.A. 7 vols. 8vo. 3*l*. 10*s*.

Fortescue. The Governance of England: otherwise called The Difference between an Absolute and a Limited Monarchy. By Sir JOHN FORTESCUE, Kt. A Revised Text. Edited, with Introduction, Notes, etc., by CHARLES PLUMMER, M.A. 8vo. half bound, 12*s*. 6*d*.

Freeman. History of the Norman Conquest of England; its Causes and Results. By E. A. FREEMAN, D.C.L. In Six Volumes. 8vo. 5*l*. 9*s*. 6*d*.

—— The Reign of William Rufus and the Accession of Henry the First. 2 vols. 8vo. 1*l*. 16*s*.

—— A Short History of the Norman Conquest of England. *Second Edition.* Extra fcap. 8vo. 2*s*. 6*d*.

Gardiner. The Constitutional Documents of the Puritan Revolution. 1628–1660. Selected and Edited by SAMUEL RAWSON GARDINER, M.A. Crown 8vo 9*s*.

Gascoigne's Theological Dictionary ("Liber Veritatum"): Selected Passages, illustrating the Condition of Church and State, 1403–1458. With an Introduction by JAMES E. THOROLD ROGERS, M.A. Small 4to. 10*s*. 6*d*.

London: HENRY FROWDE, Amen Corner, E.C.

III. Political Science.

George. Genealogical Tables illustrative of Modern History. By H. B. GEORGE, M.A. *Third Edition.* Small 4to. 12s.

Greenwell. British Barrows, a Record of the Examination of Sepulchral Mounds in various parts of England. By W. GREENWELL, M.A., F.S.A. Together with Description of Figures of Skulls, General Remarks on Prehistoric Crania, and an Appendix by GEORGE ROLLESTON, M.D., F.R.S. Medium 8vo. 25s.

Greswell's Fasti Temporis Catholici. 4 vols. 8vo. 2l. 10s.

—— Tables to Fasti, 4to., and Introduction to Tables, 8vo. 15s.

—— Origines Kalendariæ Italicæ. 4 vols. 8vo. 2l. 2s.

—— Origines Kalendariæ Hellenicæ. 6 vols. 8vo. 4l. 4s.

Gross. The Gild Merchant: a Contribution to English Municipal History. By CHARLES GROSS, Ph.D. 2 vols. 8vo. *Nearly ready.*

Hodgkin. Italy and her Invaders. With Plates and Maps. By THOMAS HODGKIN, D.C.L. Vols. I–IV, A.D. 376–553. 8vo. 3l. 8s.

—— The Dynasty of Theodosius; or, Seventy Years' Struggle with the Barbarians. By the same Author. Crown 8vo. 6s.

Hume. Letters of David Hume to William Strahan. Edited with Notes, Index, etc., by G. BIRKBECK HILL, D.C.L. 8vo. 12s. 6d.

Jackson. Dalmatia, the Quarnero, and Istria; with Cettigne in Montenegro and the Island of Grado. By T. G. JACKSON, M.A. 3 vols. With many Plates and Illustrations. 8vo. half-bound, 2l. 2s.

Kitchin. A History of France. With numerous Maps, Plans, and Tables. By G. W. KITCHIN, D.D. In three Volumes. *Second Edition.* Crown 8vo. each 10s. 6d.
  Vol. I. to 1453.   Vol. II. 1453–1624.   Vol. III. 1624–1793.

Knight's Life of Dean Colet. 1823. 8vo. 7s. 6d.

Lucas. Introduction to a Historical Geography of the British Colonies. By C. P. LUCAS, B.A. With Eight Maps. Crown 8vo. 4s. 6d.

—— Historical Geography of the Colonies. Vol. I. By the same Author. With Eleven Maps. Crown 8vo. 5s.

Lloyd's Prices of Corn in Oxford, 1583–1830. 8vo. 1s.

Luttrell's (Narcissus) Diary. A Brief Historical Relation of State Affairs, 1678–1714. 6 vols. 8vo. 1l. 4s.

Magna Carta, a careful Reprint. Edited by W. STUBBS, D.D., Lord Bishop of Oxford. 4to. stitched, 1s.

Metcalfe. Passio et Miracula Beati Olani. Edited from a Twelfth-Century MS. by F. METCALFE, M.A. Small 4to. 6s.

History, Biography, Chronology, etc. 47

OXFORD, University of.
  Oxford University Calendar for the Year 1890. Crown 8vo. 6s.
  The Historical Register of the University of Oxford. Being a Supplement to the Oxford University Calendar, with an Alphabetical Record of University Honours and Distinctions, completed to the end of Trinity Term, 1888. Crown 8vo. 5s.
  Student's Handbook to the University and Colleges of Oxford. *Tenth Edition.* Revised to December 1888. Crown 8vo. 2s. 6d.
  The Examination Statutes; together with the present Regulations of the Boards of Studies and Boards of Faculties relating thereto. Revised to the end of Trinity Term, 1889. 8vo., paper covers, 1s.
  Statuta Universitatis Oxoniensis. 1889. 8vo. 5s.
  Statutes made for the University of Oxford, and the Colleges therein, by the University of Oxford Commissioners. 8vo. 12s. 6d.
  Also separately—University Statutes 2s.; College Statutes 1s. each.
  Supplementary Statutes made by the University of Oxford, and by certain of the Colleges therein, in pursuance of the Universities of Oxford and Cambridge Act, 1877; approved by the Queen in Council. 8vo. Paper covers, 2s. 6d.
  Statutes of the University of Oxford, codified in the year 1636 under the Authority of ARCHBISHOP LAUD, Chancellor of the University. Edited by the late JOHN GRIFFITHS, D.D. With an Introduction on the History of the Laudian Code by C. L. SHADWELL, M.A., B.C.L. 4to. 1l. 1s.
  Enactments in Parliament, specially concerning the Universities of Oxford and Cambridge. Collected and arranged by J. GRIFFITHS, D.D. 1869. 8vo. 12s.
  Catalogue of Oxford Graduates from 1659 to 1850. 8vo. 7s. 6d.
  Index to Wills proved in the Court of the Chancellor of the University of Oxford, &c. Compiled by J. GRIFFITHS, D.D. Royal 8vo. 3s. 6d.
  Manuscript Materials relating to the History of Oxford; contained in the Printed Catalogues of the Bodleian and College Libraries. By F. MADAN, M.A. 8vo. 7s. 6d.
Pattison. Essays by the late MARK PATTISON, sometime Rector of Lincoln College. Collected and arranged by HENRY NETTLESHIP, M.A. 2 vols. 8vo. 24s.
Ranke. A History of England, principally in the Seventeenth Century. By L. VON RANKE. Translated under the superintendence of G. W. KITCHIN, D.D., and C. W. BOASE, M.A. 6 vols. 8vo. 3l. 3s.

London: HENRY FROWDE, Amen Corner, E.C.

III. Political Science.

Rawlinson. A Manual of Ancient History. By GEORGE RAWLINSON, M.A. *Second Edition.* Demy 8vo. 14s.

Ricardo. Letters of David Ricardo to T. R. Malthus (1810-1823). Edited by JAMES BONAR, M.A. 8vo. 10s. 6d.

Rogers. History of Agriculture and Prices in England, A.D. 1259-1793. By JAMES E. THOROLD ROGERS, M.A.
  Vols. I and II (1259-1400). 8vo. 2l. 2s.
  Vols. III and IV (1401-1582). 8vo. 2l. 10s.
  Vols. V and VI (1583-1702). 8vo. 2l. 10s.

—— First Nine Years of the Bank of England. 8vo. 8s. 6d.

—— Protests of the Lords, including those which have been expunged, from 1624 to 1874; with Historical Introductions. In three volumes. 8vo. 2l. 2s.

Sprigg's England's Recovery; being the History of the Army under Sir Thomas Fairfax. 8vo. 6s.

Stubbs. Select Charters and other Illustrations of English Constitutional History, from the Earliest Times to the Reign of Edward I. Arranged and edited by W. STUBBS, D.D., Lord Bishop of Oxford. *Fifth Edition.* Crown 8vo. 8s. 6d.

—— The Constitutional History of England, in its Origin and Development. *Library Edition.* 3 vols. Demy 8vo. 2l. 8s.
  Also in 3 vols. crown 8vo. price 12s. each.

—— Seventeen Lectures on the Study of Medieval and Modern History, delivered at Oxford 1867-1884. Crown 8vo. 8s. 6d.

Tozer. The Islands of the Aegean. By H. FANSHAWE TOZER, M.A., F.R.G.S. Crown 8vo. 8s. 6d.

Wellesley. A Selection from the Despatches, Treaties, and other Papers of the MARQUESS WELLESLEY, K.G., during his Government of India. Edited by S. J. OWEN, M.A. 8vo. 1l. 4s.

Wellington. A Selection from the Despatches, Treaties, and other Papers relating to India of Field-Marshal the DUKE OF WELLINGTON, K.G. Edited by S. J. OWEN, M.A. 8vo. 1l. 4s.

Whitelock's Memorials of English Affairs from 1625 to 1660. 4 vols. 8vo. 1l. 10s.

B. ENGLISH AND ROMAN LAW.

Anson. Principles of the English Law of Contract, and of Agency in its Relation to Contract. By SIR W. R. ANSON, D.C.L. *Fifth Edition.* 8vo. 10s. 6d.

—— Law and Custom of the Constitution. Part I. Parliament. 8vo. 10s. 6d.

Bentham. An Introduction to the Principles of Morals and Legislation. By JEREMY BENTHAM. Crown 8vo. 6s. 6d.

Digby. An Introduction to the History of the Law of Real Property. By KENELM E. DIGBY, M.A. *Third Edition.* 8vo. 10s. 6d.

Grueber. Lex Aquilia. The Roman Law of Damage to Property: being a Commentary on the Title of the Digest 'Ad Legem Aquiliam' (ix. 2). With an Introduction to the Study of the Corpus Iuris Civilis. By ERWIN GRUEBER, Dr. Jur., M.A. 8vo. 10s. 6d.

Hall. International Law. By W. E. HALL, M.A. *Third Edition.* 8vo. 22s. 6d.

Holland. Elements of Jurisprudence. By T. E. HOLLAND, D.C.L. *Fourth Edition.* 8vo. 10s. 6d.

—— The European Concert in the Eastern Question, a Collection of Treaties and other Public Acts. Edited, with Introductions and Notes, by T. E. HOLLAND, D.C.L. 8vo. 12s. 6d.

—— Alberici Gentilis, I.C.D., I.C., De Iure Belli Libri Tres. Edidit T. E. HOLLAND, I.C.D. Small 4to. half morocco, 21s.

—— The Institutes of Justinian, edited as a recension of the Institutes of GAIUS, by T. E. HOLLAND, D.C.L. *Second Edition.* Extra fcap. 8vo. 5s.

Holland and Shadwell. Select Titles from the Digest of Justinian. By T. E. HOLLAND, D.C.L., and C. L. SHADWELL, B.C.L. 8vo. 14s.

Also sold in Parts, in paper covers, as follows:—
Part I. Introductory Titles. 2s. 6d.
Part II. Family Law. 1s.
Part III. Property Law. 2s. 6d.
Part IV. Law of Obligations (No. 1). 3s. 6d.
Part IV. Law of Obligations (No. 2). 4s. 6d.

Markby. Elements of Law considered with reference to Principles of General Jurisprudence. By Sir WILLIAM MARKBY, D.C.L. *Fourth Edition.* 8vo. 12s. 6d.

Moyle. Imperatoris Iustiniani Institutionum Libri Quattuor; with Introductions, Commentary, Excursus and Translation. By J. B. MOYLE, D.C.L. *Second Edition.* 2 vols. 8vo. 22s.

Pollock and Wright. An Essay on Possession in the Common Law. By Sir F. POLLOCK, M.A., and R. S. WRIGHT, B.C.L. 8vo. 8s. 6d.

Poste. Gaii Institutionum Juris Civilis Commentarii Quattuor; or, Elements of Roman Law by Gaius. With a Translation and Commentary by EDWARD POSTE, M.A. *Second Edition.* 8vo. 18s.

Raleigh. The English Law of Property. By THOS. RALEIGH, M.A. *Just ready.*

Stokes. The Anglo-Indian Codes. By WHITLEY STOKES, LL.D. Vol. I. Substantive Law. 8vo. 30s. Vol. II. Adjective Law. 8vo. 35s.

—— Supplement to the above, 1887, 1888. 2s. 6d.

Twiss. The Law of Nations considered as Independent Political Communities. By SIR TRAVERS TWISS, D.C.L.
Part I. On the rights and Duties of Nations in time of Peace. New Edition. Revised and Enlarged. 8vo. 15s.
Part II. On the Rights and Duties of Nations in time of War. Second Edition, Revised. 8vo. 21s.

C. POLITICAL ECONOMY, ETC.

Rogers. A Manual of Political Economy, for the use of Schools. By J. E. THOROLD ROGERS, M.A. *Third Edition.* Extra fcap. 8vo. 4s. 6d.

Smith's Wealth of Nations. A new Edition, with Notes, by J. E. THOROLD ROGERS, M.A. 2 vols. 8vo. 21s.

IV. PHILOSOPHY, LOGIC, &c.

Bacon. Novum Organum. Edited, with Introduction, Notes, &c., by T. FOWLER, D.D. *Second Edition.* 8vo. 15s.

—— Novum Organum. Edited, with English Notes, by G. W. KITCHIN, D.D. 8vo. 9s. 6d.

—— Novum Organum. Translated by G. W. KITCHIN, D.D. 8vo. 9s. 6d.

Berkeley. The works of GEORGE BERKELEY, D.D., formerly Bishop of Cloyne; including many of his writings hitherto unpublished. With Prefaces, Annotations, and an Account of his Life and Philosophy, by ALEXANDER CAMPBELL FRASER, LL.D. 4 vols. 8vo. 2l. 18s.

The Life, Letters, &c., separately, 16s.

—— Selections. With Introduction and Notes. For the use of Students in the Universities. By ALEXANDER CAMPBELL FRASER, LL.D. *Third Edition.* Crown 8vo. 7s. 6d.

Bosanquet. Logic; or, the Morphology of Knowledge. By B. BOSANQUET, M.A. 8vo. 21s.

Butler's Works, with Index to the Analogy. 2 vols. 8vo. 11s.

Fowler. The Elements of Deductive Logic, designed mainly for the use of Junior Students in the Universities. By T. FOWLER, D.D. *Ninth Edition,* with a Collection of Examples. Extra fcap. 8vo. 3s. 6d.

Fowler. The Elements of Inductive Logic, designed mainly for the use of Students in the Universities. *Fourth Edition.* Extra fcap. 8vo. 6s.

—— The Principles of Morals (Introductory Chapters). By T. Fowler, D.D., and J. M. Wilson, B.D. 8vo. boards, 3s. 6d.

—— The Principles of Morals. Part II. By T. Fowler, D.D. 8vo. 10s. 6d.

Green. Prolegomena to Ethics. By T. H. Green, M.A. Edited by A. C. Bradley, M.A. 8vo. 12s. 6d.

Hegel. The Logic of Hegel; translated from the Encyclopaedia of the Philosophical Sciences. With Prolegomena by William Wallace, M.A. 8vo. 14s.

Hume's Treatise of Human Nature. Reprinted from the Original Edition in Three Volumes, and Edited by L. A. Selby-Bigge, M.A. Crown 8vo. 9s.

Locke's Conduct of the Understanding. Edited by T. Fowler, D.D. *Second Edition.* Extra fcap. 8vo. 2s.

Lotze's Logic, in Three Books; of Thought, of Investigation, and of Knowledge. English Translation; Edited by B. Bosanquet, M.A. *Second Edition.* 2 vols. Crown 8vo. 12s.

—— Metaphysic, in Three Books; Ontology, Cosmology, and Psychology. English Translation; Edited by B. Bosanquet, M.A. *Second Edition.* 2 vols. Crown 8vo. 12s.

Martineau. Types of Ethical Theory. By James Martineau, D.D. *Second Edition.* 2 vols. Crown 8vo. 15s.

—— A Study of Religion: its Sources and Contents. *A New Edition.* 2 vols. Crown 8vo. 15s.

V. PHYSICAL SCIENCE AND MATHEMATICS.

Acland. Synopsis of the Pathological Series in the Oxford Museum. By Sir H. W. Acland, M.D., F.R.S. 8vo. 2s. 6d.

Aldis. A Text-Book of Algebra: with Answers to the Examples. By W. S. Aldis, M.A. Crown 8vo. 7s. 6d.

Aplin. The Birds of Oxfordshire. By O. V. Aplin. 8vo. with a Map and one coloured Plate. 10s. 6d.

Archimedis quae supersunt omnia cum Eutocii commentariis ex recensione J. Torelli, cum novâ versione Latinâ. 1792. Fol. 1l. 5s.

Baynes. Lessons on Thermodynamics. By R. E. Baynes, M.A. Crown 8vo. 7s. 6d.

V. Physical Science and Mathematics.

BIOLOGICAL SERIES. (Translations of Foreign Memoirs).
I. Memoirs on the Physiology of Nerve, of Muscle, and of the Electrical Organ. Edited by J. BURDON-SANDERSON, M.D., F.R.SS.L. & E. Medium 8vo. 1*l.* 1*s.*
II. The Anatomy of the Frog. By Dr. ALEXANDER ECKER, Professor in the University of Freiburg. Translated, with numerous Annotations and Additions, by GEORGE HASLAM, M.D. Medium 8vo. 21*s.*
IV. Essays upon Heredity and kindred Biological Problems. By Dr. AUGUST WEISMANN, Professor in the University of Freiburg in Breisgau. Authorised Translation. Edited by EDWARD B. POULTON, M.A., F.L.S., F.G.S., SELMAR SCHÖNLAND, PH.D., and ARTHUR E. SHIPLEY, M.A., F.L.S. Medium 8vo. 16*s.*

BOTANICAL SERIES.

History of Botany (1530–1860). By JULIUS VON SACHS. Authorised Translation, by H. E. F. GARNSEY, M.A. Revised by ISAAC BAYLEY BALFOUR, M.A., M.D., F.R.S. Crown 8vo. 10*s.*

Comparative Anatomy of the Vegetative Organs of the Phanerogams and Ferns. By Dr. A. DE BARY. Translated and Annotated by F. O. BOWER, M.A., F.L.S., and D. H. SCOTT, M.A., Ph.D., F.L.S. Royal 8vo., half morocco, 1*l.* 2*s.* 6*d.*

Outlines of Classification and Special Morphology of Plants. A new Edition of SACHS' Text-Book of Botany, Book II. By Dr. K. GOEBEL. Translated by H. E. F. GARNSEY, M.A., and Revised by ISAAC BAYLEY BALFOUR, M.A., M.D., F.R.S. Royal 8vo., half morocco, 1*l.* 1*s.*

Lectures on the Physiology of Plants. By JULIUS VON SACHS. Translated by H. MARSHALL WARD, M.A., F.L.S. Royal 8vo. half morocco, 1*l.* 11*s.* 6*d.*

Comparative Morphology and Biology of Fungi, Mycetozoa and Bacteria. By Dr. A. DE BARY. Translated by H. E. F. GARNSEY, M.A., Revised by ISAAC BAYLEY BALFOUR, M.A., M.D., F.R.S. Royal 8vo., half morocco, 1*l.* 2*s.* 6*d.*

Lectures on Bacteria. By Dr. A. DE BARY. *Second Improved Edition.* Translated by H. E. F. GARNSEY, M.A. Revised by ISAAC BAYLEY BALFOUR, M.A., M.D., F.R.S. Crown 8vo. 6*s.*

Introduction to Fossil Botany. By Count H. VON SOLMS-LAUBACH. Authorised English Translation, by H. E. F. GARNSEY, M.A. Edited by ISAAC BAYLEY BALFOUR, M.A., M.D., F.R.S. *In the Press.*

Annals of Botany. Edited by ISAAC BAYLEY BALFOUR, M.A., M.D., F.R.S., SYDNEY H. VINES, D.Sc., F.R.S., and W. G. FARLOW, M.D. Vol. I. Royal 8vo., half morocco, gilt top, 1*l.* 16*s.*

Bradley's Miscellaneous Works and Correspondence. With an Account of Harriot's Astronomical Papers. 4to. 17*s.*

V. Physical Science and Mathematics. 53

Chambers. A Handbook of Descriptive Astronomy. By G. F. CHAMBERS, F.R.A.S. *Fourth Edition.*
   Vol. I. The Sun, Planets, and Comets. 8vo. 21s.
   Vol. II. Instruments and Practical Astronomy. *Immediately.*

Clarke. Geodesy. By Col. A. R. CLARKE, C.B., R.E. 8vo. 12s. 6d.

Cremona. Elements of Projective Geometry. By LUIGI CREMONA. Translated by C. LEUDESDORF, M.A. 8vo. 12s. 6d.

—— Graphical Statics. Two Treatises on the Graphical Calculus and Reciprocal Figures in Graphical Statics. By the same Author. Translated by T. HUDSON BEARE. Demy 8vo. 8s. 6d.

Daubeny's Introduction to the Atomic Theory. 16mo. 6s.

Donkin. Acoustics. By W. F. DONKIN, M.A., F.R.S. *Second Edition.* Crown 8vo. 7s. 6d.

Etheridge. Fossils of the British Islands, Stratigraphically and Zoologically arranged. Part I. PALAEOZOIC. By R. ETHERIDGE, F.R.SS. L. & E., F.G.S. 4to. 1l. 10s.

EUCLID REVISED. Containing the Essentials of the Elements of Plane Geometry as given by Euclid in his first Six Books. Edited by R. C. J. NIXON, M.A. *Second Edition.* Crown 8vo. 6s.
   Sold separately as follows:—
   Book I. 1s.   Books I, II. 1s. 6d.
   Books I–IV. 3s.   Books V, VI. 3s.

Euclid. Geometry in Space. Containing parts of Euclid's Eleventh and Twelfth Books. By the same Editor. Crown 8vo. 3s. 6d.

Fisher. Class-Book of Chemistry. By W. W. FISHER, M.A., F.C.S. Crown 8vo. 4s. 6d.

Galton. The Construction of Healthy Dwellings. By Sir DOUGLAS GALTON, K.C.B., F.R.S. 8vo. 10s. 6d.

Hamilton and Ball. Book-keeping. New and enlarged Edition. By Sir R. G. C. HAMILTON, and JOHN BALL. Extra fcap. 8vo. limp cloth, 2s.
   Ruled Exercise books adapted to the above may be had, price 1s. 6d.

Harcourt and Madan. Exercises in Practical Chemistry. Vol. I. Elementary Exercises. By A. G. VERNON HARCOURT, M.A., and H. G. MADAN, M.A. *Fourth Edition.* Crown 8vo. 10s. 6d.

   Madan. Tables of Qualitative Analysis. By H. G. MADAN, M.A. Large 4to., paper covers, 4s. 6d.

Hensley. Figures made Easy. A first Arithmetic Book. By LEWIS HENSLEY, M.A. Crown 8vo. 6d.

—— Answers to the Examples in Figures made Easy, together with two thousand additional Examples, with Answers. Crown 8vo. 1s.

London: HENRY FROWDE, Amen Corner, E.C.

V. Physical Science and Mathematics.

Hensley. The Scholar's Arithmetic. Crown 8vo. 2s. 6d.
—— Answers to Examples in Scholar's Arithmetic. 1s. 6d.
—— The Scholar's Algebra. Crown 8vo. 2s. 6d.

Hughes. Geography for Schools. By ALFRED HUGHES, M.A., late Scholar of Corpus Christi College, Oxford. Part I. Practical Geography. With Diagrams. Crown 8vo. 2s. 6d.

Maclaren. A System of Physical Education: Theoretical and Practical. By ARCHIBALD MACLAREN. Extra fcap. 8vo. 7s. 6d.

Maxwell. A Treatise on Electricity and Magnetism. By J. CLERK MAXWELL, M.A. *Second Edition.* 2 vols. 8vo. 1l. 11s. 6d.
—— An Elementary Treatise on Electricity. Edited by WILLIAM GARNETT, M.A. 8vo. 7s. 6d.

Minchin. A Treatise on Statics with Applications to Physics. By G. M. MINCHIN, M.A. *Third Edition.* Vol. I. Equilibrium of Coplanar Forces. 8vo. 9s. Vol. II. Statics. 8vo. 16s.
—— Uniplanar Kinematics of Solids and Fluids. Crown 8vo. 7s. 6d.

Müller. On certain Variations in the Vocal Organs of the Passeres. By J. MÜLLER. Translated by F. J. BELL, B.A., and edited by A. H. GARROD, M.A., F.R.S. With Plates. 4to. 7s. 6d.

Nixon. See EUCLID REVISED.

Phillips. Geology of Oxford and the Valley of the Thames. By JOHN PHILLIPS, M.A., F.R.S. 8vo. 21s.
—— Vesuvius. Crown 8vo. 10s. 6d.

Prestwich. Geology, Chemical, Physical, and Stratigraphical. By JOSEPH PRESTWICH, M.A., F.R.S. In two Volumes.
  Vol. I. Chemical and Physical. Royal 8vo. 1l. 5s.
  Vol. II. Stratigraphical and Physical. With a new Geological Map of Europe. Royal 8vo. 1l. 16s.
  New Geological Map of Europe. In case or on roller. 5s.

Price. Treatise on Infinitesimal Calculus. By BARTHOLOMEW PRICE, M.A., F.R.S.
  Vol. I. Differential Calculus. *Second Edition.* 8vo. 14s. 6d.
  Vol. II. Integral Calculus, Calculus of Variations, and Differential Equations. *Second Edition.* 8vo. 18s.
  Vol. III. Statics, including Attractions; Dynamics of a Material Particle. *Second Edition.* 8vo. 16s.
  Vol. IV. Dynamics of Material Systems. *Second Edition.* 8vo. 18s.

Pritchard. Uranometria Nova Oxoniensis. A Photometric determination of the magnitudes of all Stars visible to the naked eye, from the Pole to ten degrees south of the Equator. By C. PRITCHARD, D.D., F.R.S. Royal 8vo. 8s. 6d.
—— Astronomical Observations made at the University Observatory, Oxford, under the direction of C. PRITCHARD, D.D. No. 1. Royal 8vo. paper covers, 3s. 6d.

Rigaud's Correspondence of Scientific Men of the 17th Century, with Table of Contents by A. de Morgan, and Index by J. Rigaud, M.A. 2 vols. 8vo. 18s. 6d.

Rolleston and Jackson. Forms of Animal Life. A Manual of Comparative Anatomy, with descriptions of selected types. By George Rolleston, M.D., F.R.S. *Second Edition.* Revised and enlarged by W. Hatchett Jackson, M.A. Medium 8vo. 1l. 16s.

Rolleston. Scientific Papers and Addresses. By George Rolleston, M.D., F.R.S. Arranged and edited by William Turner, M.B., F.R.S. With a Biographical Sketch by Edward Tylor, F.R.S. 2 vols. 8vo. 1l. 4s.

Smyth. A Cycle of Celestial Objects. Observed, Reduced, and Discussed by Admiral W. H. Smyth, R.N. Revised, condensed, and greatly enlarged by G. F. Chambers, F.R.A.S. 8vo. 12s.

Stewart. An Elementary Treatise on Heat, with numerous Woodcuts and Diagrams. By Balfour Stewart, LL.D., F.R.S. *Fifth Edition.* Extra fcap. 8vo. 7s. 6d.

Vernon-Harcourt. Treatise on Rivers and Canals, relating to Control and Improvement of Rivers, and Design, Construction, and Development of Canals. By L. F. Vernon-Harcourt, M.A. 2 vols. 8vo. 1l. 1s.

—— Harbours and Docks; their Physical Features, History, Construction, Equipment, and Maintenance; with Statistics as to their Commercial Development. 2 vols. 8vo. 25s.

Walker. The Theory of a Physical Balance. By James Walker, M.A. 8vo. stiff cover, 3s. 6d.

Watson and Burbury.
   I. A Treatise on the Application of Generalised Co-ordinates to the Kinetics of a Material System. By H. W. Watson, D.Sc., and S. H. Burbury, M.A. 8vo. 6s.
   II. The Mathematical Theory of Electricity and Magnetism. Vol. I. Electrostatics. 8vo. 10s. 6d.
     Vol. II. Magnetism and Electrodynamics. 8vo. 10s. 6d.

Williamson. Chemistry for Students. With Solutions. By A. W. Williamson, Phil. Doc., F.R.S. Extra fcap. 8vo. 8s. 6d.

Westwood. Thesaurus Entomologicus Hopeianus, or a Description of the rarest Insects in the Collection given to the University by the Rev. William Hope. By J. O. Westwood, M.A., F.R.S. With 40 Plates. Small folio, half morocco, 7l. 10s.

VI. ART AND ARCHAEOLOGY.

Butler. Ancient Coptic Churches of Egypt. By A. J. Butler, M.A., F.S.A. 2 vols. 8vo. 30s.

Head. Historia Numorum. A Manual of Greek Numismatics. By Barclay V. Head, Assistant-Keeper of the Department of Coins and Medals in the British Museum. Royal 8vo. Half morocco, 42s.

Jackson. Dalmatia, the Quarnero and Istria; with Cettigne in Montenegro and the Island of Grado. By T. G. JACKSON, M.A., Author of 'Modern Gothic Architecture.' In 3 vols. 8vo. With many Plates and Illustrations. Half bound, 42s.

MUSIC.

Hullah. Cultivation of the Speaking Voice. By JOHN HULLAH. *Second Edition.* Extra fcap. 8vo. 2s. 6d.

Ouseley. Treatise on Harmony. By Sir F. A. GORE OUSELEY, Bart. *Third Edition.* 4to. 10s.

—— Treatise on Counterpoint, Canon, and Fugue, based upon that of Cherubini. *Second Edition.* 4to. 16s.

—— Treatise on Musical Form and General Composition. *Second Edition.* 4to. 10s.

Troutbeck and Dale. Music Primer (for Schools). By J. TROUTBECK, D.D., and F. DALE, M.A. *Second Edition.* Crown 8vo. 1s. 6d.

Robinson. A Critical Account of the Drawings by Michel Angelo and Raffaello in the University Galleries, Oxford. By J. C. ROBINSON, F.S.A. Crown 8vo. 4s.

Tyrwhitt. Handbook of Pictorial Art. With coloured Illustrations, Photographs, and a chapter on Perspective by A. Macdonald. By R. St. J. TYRWHITT, M.A. *Second Edition.* 8vo. half morocco, 18s.

Upcott. Introduction to Greek Sculpture. By L. E. UPCOTT, M.A. Crown 8vo. 4s. 6d.

Vaux. Catalogue of the Castellani Collection of Antiquities in the University Galleries, Oxford. By W. S. W. VAUX, M.A. Crown 8vo. 1s.

VII. PALAEOGRAPHY.

Gardthausen. Catalogus Codicum Graecorum Sinaiticorum. Scripsit V. GARDTHAUSEN Lipsiensis. With six pages of Facsimiles. 8vo. *linen*, 25s.

Fragmenta Herculanensia. A Descriptive Catalogue of the Oxford copies of the Herculanean Rolls, together with the texts of several papyri, accompanied by facsimiles. Edited by WALTER SCOTT, M.A., Fellow of Merton College, Oxford. Royal 8vo. 21s.

Herculanensium Voluminum Partes II. 1824. 8vo. 10s.

DATE DUE

GAYLORD   #3523PI   Printed in USA

ImTheStory.com

Personalized Classic Books in many genre's

Unique gift for kids, partners, friends, colleagues

Customize:
- Character Names
- Upload your own front/back cover images (optional)
- Inscribe a personal message/dedication on the inside page (optional)

Customize many titles Including
- Alice in Wonderland
- Romeo and Juliet
- The Wizard of Oz
- A Christmas Carol
- Dracula
- Dr. Jekyll & Mr. Hyde
- And more...

CPSIA information can be obtained at www.ICGtesting.com
Printed in the USA
BVOW08s0351250713

326862BV00007B/13/P